MAKING HERETICS

MAKING HERETICS

MILITANT PROTESTANTISM AND FREE

GRACE IN MASSACHUSETTS, 1636–1641

Michael P. Winship

PRINCETON UNIVERSITY PRESS

PRINCETON AND OXFORD

LIBRARY OF CONGRESS CATALOGING-IN-PUBLICATION DATA

WINSHIP, MICHAEL P. (MICHAEL PAUL).

MAKING HERETICS : MILITANT PROTESTANTISM AND FREE GRACE IN MASSACHU-

SETTS, 1636–1641 / MICHAEL P. WINSHIP

P. CM.

INCLUDES BIBLIOGRAPHICAL REFERENCES AND INDEX.

ISBN 0-691-08943-4 (ALK. PAPER)

1. PURITANS—MASSACHUSETTS—HISTORY—17TH CENTURY.

2. PROTESTANTISM—MASSACHUSETTS—HISTORY—17TH CENTURY.

3. ANTINOMIANISM—MASSACHUSETTS—HISTORY OF DOCTRINES—

17TH CENTURY. 4. MASSACHUSETTS—HISTORY—COLONIAL PERIOD, CA. 1600–1775.

5. MASSACHUSETTS—POLITICS AND GOVERNMENT—TO 1775.

6. MASSACHUSETTS—CHURCH HISTORY—17TH CENTURY. 7. RELIGIOUS

PLURALISM—MASSACHUSETTS—HISTORY—17TH CENTURY. 8. RELIGION AND

POLITICS—MASSACHUSETTS—HISTORY—17TH CENTURY. I. TITLE.

F67.W7 2002

277.44'06—dc21   2001036867

For Eleanor, Nathan, and Anna

CONTENTS

ACKNOWLEDGMENTS

SUCH VIRTUES as *Making Heretics* may possess are due in no small measure to the gifted community of scholars that nurtured it. I was extremely fortunate to embark on this book at a time when Peter Lake and his then student, David Como, were beginning similar projects on English puritanism. The ongoing rounds of discussions, shared panels, and manuscript critiques have been invaluable for the book. Besides Lake and Como, readers of various drafts of *Making Heretics* include Dwight Bozeman, Michael Ditmore, Frank Lambert, Michael McGiffert, John Murrin, Mary Beth Norton, and Eleanor Winship. Peter Hoffer read the manuscript and gave extensive advice about the legal aspects of the controversy. He was also an unfailingly involved and sympathetic sounding board on a topic about which, as my colleague at the University of Georgia, he heard inconceivably far more than any non-specialist should have to endure. Francis Bremer read chapter 7. All remaining factual errors, stylistic infelicities, and questionable interpretations are entirely my responsibility; I shudder to think how much greater their quantity would have been had various drafts not passed under so many vigilant eyes. Merja Kyto provided me with her transcription of the non-sermonic sections of the Robert Keayne Boston sermon notebook. Peter Lake made available his *Boxmaker's Revenge* while still a manuscript. As *Making Heretics* was going into copy editing, Sargent Bush, Jr., sent me galley proofs of his edition of John Cotton's correspondence, allowing me to check and expand citations in the light of his virtuoso paleographic skills and key them to Bush's invaluable book. Patrick Curry provided a home away from home in London, as ever.

Research for the book was generously supported by grants from the University of Georgia History Department and the University of Georgia Research Foundation. A fellowship from the University of Georgia Center for Humanities and Arts provided time for writing. Archivists and librarians at the American Antiquarian Society, Bodelian Library of Oxford University, Boston Public Library, British Library, Connecticut State Archives, Doctor Williams Library, Houghton Library of Harvard University, Lincolnshire Public Record Office, Massachusetts Historical Society, Massachusetts State Archives, National Library of Scotland, New England Historic Genealogical Society, New York Historical Society, New York Public Library, Pennsylvania Historical Society, Philips Academy, Pilgrim Hall Museum, Victoria and Albert Museum, and York Minster Library were unfailingly courteous and helpful during my visits to their institutions. I would also like to thank the numerous other archivists and librarians who responded to my queries. Portions of various chapters have appeared in various guises in "'The Most Glorious Church in the World': The Unity of the Godly in Boston, Massachusetts in the 1630s," *Journal of British Studies* 39 (2000): 71–98 (© 2000 by the North American Conference on British Studies. All rights Reserved); "Were There Any Puritans in New England?" *New England Quarterly* 74 (2001):118–38; and "Weak Christians, Backsliders, and Carnal Gospelers: Assurance of Salvation and the Origins of Puritan Practical Divinity in the 1580s," *Church History* (70 (2001), 462–81).

All quotations have been reproduced as found in their sources, save that contractions have been expanded, and *1*, *u*, and *v v* have been replaced when they stood for *j*, *v*, and *w*. Dates are old style, while the years themselves are new style.

ABBREVIATIONS

AC	David D. Hall, ed. *The Antinomian Controversy, 1636–1638: A Documentary History.* 2d ed. Durham, 1990.
Baillie, *Dissuasive*	Robert Baillie. *A Dissuasive from the Errors of the Times.* London, 1646.
Baillie, *Dissuasive Vindicated*	Robert Baillie. *The Dissuasive from the Errors of the Time, Vindicated from the Exceptions of Mr Cotton and Mr Tombes.* London, 1655.
Battis, *SS*	Emery Battis. *Saints and Sectaries: Anne Hutchinson and the Antinomian Controversy in the Massachusetts Bay Colony.* Chapel Hill, 1962.
BCR	*The Records of the First Church in Boston 1630–1868.* ed. Richard D. Pierce. Colonial Society of Massachusetts *Publications* 31 (1961).
Breen, *Transgressing*	Louis A. Breen. *Transgressing the Bounds: Subversive Enterprises among the Puritan Elite.* New York, 2001.
Cohen, *God's Caress*	Charles Lloyd Cohen. *God's Caress: The Psychology of Puritan Religious Experience.* New York, 1986.
Como, "Puritans"	David D. Como. "Puritans and Heretics: The Emergence of an Antinomian Underground in Early Stuart England." Ph.D. diss., Princeton University, 1999.
Cooper, *Tenacious*	James F. Cooper, Jr. *Tenacious of Their Liberties: The Congregationalists in Colonial Massachusetts.* New York, 1999.
Cotton, *Cotton*	*John Cotton on the Churches of New England.* Ed. Larzer Ziff. Cambridge, 1968.
Cotton, *Treatise*	John Cotton. *A Treatise of the Covenant of Grace.* London, 1659.
Delbanco, *Puritan*	Andrew Delbanco. *The Puritan Ordeal.* Cambridge, 1989.
Firmin, *[Panourgia]*	Giles Firmin. *[Panourgia] A Brief Review of Mr. Davis's Vindication: Giving No Satisfaction.* London, 1693.

Firmin, *Real Christian*

Giles Firmin. *The Real Christian, or A Treatise of Effectual Calling.* London, 1670.

Fiske, *Notebook*

The Notebook of the Reverend John Fiske. Ed. Robert G. Pope. Colonial Society of Massachusetts *Collections* 97 Boston, 1974.

Foster, *Long Argument*

Stephen Foster. *The Long Argument: English Puritanism and the Shaping of New England Culture, 1570–1700.* Chapel Hill, 1991.

Foster, "New England"

Stephen Foster. "New England and the Challenge of Heresy, 1630–1660: The Puritan Crisis in Transatlantic Perspective." *William and Mary Quarterly.* 3d ser., 38 (1981): 624–60.

GH

William Hubbard. *A General History of New England, from the Discovery to MDCLXX.* 1815. Reprint, Boston, 1848.

God's Plot

God's Plot: The Paradoxes of Puritan Piety, Being the Autobiography and Journal of Thomas Shepard. Ed. Michael McGiffert. Amherst, MA, 1972.

Gura, *Glimpse*

Philip F. Gura. *A Glimpse of Sion's Glory: Puritan Radicalism in New England, 1620–1660.* Middletown, CT, 1984.

Hall, *Faithful Shepherd*

David D. Hall. *The Faithful Shepherd: A History of the New England Ministry in the Seventeenth Century.* Chapel Hill, 1972.

Hartlib Papers

J. Crawford, et al., eds., *The Hartlib Papers: A Complete Text and Image Database of the Papers of Samuel Hartlib (c.1600–1662) Held in Sheffield University Library; Prepared by Members of the Hartlib Papers Project.* Ann Arbor, 1995.

HC

Hutchinson Collection. 2 vols. Albany, 1865.

Hutchinson, *History*

Thomas Hutchinson. *The History of the Colony and Province of Massachusetts-Bay.* Ed. Lawrence Shaw Mayo. 3 vols. Cambridge, MA, 1936.

JC

The Correspondence of John Cotton, 1621–1652. Ed. Sargent Bush Jr. Chapel Hill, 2001.

Kamensky, *Governing*

Jane Kamensky. *Governing the Tongue: The Politics of Speech in Early New England.* New York, 1997.

Knight, *Orthodoxies*	Janice Knight. *Orthodoxies in Massachusetts: Rereading American Puritanism.* Cambridge, 1994.
Lake, *Boxmaker's Revenge*	Peter Lake, *The Boxmaker's Revenge: "Orthodoxy," "Heterodoxy," and the Politics of the Parish in Early Stuart London.* Manchester, England, 2001.
Lang, *Prophetic*	Amy Schrager Lang. *Prophetic Woman: Anne Hutchinson and the Problem of Dissent in New England Literature.* Berkeley, 1987.
MCA	Cotton Mather, *Magnalia Christi Americana*, 2 vols. 1702. Reprint, Hartford, 1853.
MA	John Wheelwright or John Wheelwright, Jr. *Mercurius Americanus* (1645). In *John Wheelwright*, ed. Charles H. Bell. Prince Society *Publications* 9 (1876): 188–228.
MHS	Massachusetts Historical Society.
Miller, *Colony*	Perry Miller. *The New England Mind: From Colony to Province.* Cambridge, 1952.
Miller, "Preparation"	Perry Miller. "'Preparation for Salvation' in Seventeenth-Century New England." *Journal of the History of Ideas* 4 (1943): 253–86.
Morgan, *Dilemma*	Edmund Morgan. *The Puritan Dilemma: The Story of John Winthrop.* Boston, 1958.
Morgan, *Visible*	Edmund Morgan. *Visible Saints: The History of a Puritan Idea.* New York, 1963.
Morton, *Memorial*	Nathaniel Morton. *The New-England's Memorial.* 1662. Reprint, Plymouth, 1826.
MR	*Records of the Governor and Company of Massachusetts Bay.* Ed. Nathaniel Shurtleff. 5 vols. Boston, 1854.
NEHGR	*New England Historical and Genealogical Register.*
Norton, *Abel*	John Norton. *Abel Being Dead Yet Speaketh.* London, 1658.
Norton, *Founding*	Mary Beth Norton. *Founding Mothers and Fathers: Gendered Power and the Forming of American Society.* New York, 1996.
Pettit, *Heart*	Norman Pettit. *The Heart Prepared: Grace and Conversion in Puritan Spiritual Life.* 2d ed. Middletown, CT, 1989.

Porterfield, *Female*   Amanda Porterfield. *Female Piety in New England: The Emergence of Religious Humanism.* New York, 1992.

PTV   Thomas Shepard. *The Parable of the Ten Virgins Opened and Applied.* 2 vols. in 1. London, 1695.

Rathband, *Briefe Narration*   William Rathband. *A Briefe Narration of Some Church Courses Generally Held in Opinion and Practice by the Churches Lately Erected in New England.* London, 1644.

Rutman, *Winthrop's Boston*   Darrett B. Rutman, *Winthrop's Boston; Portrait of a Puritan Town, 1630–1649.* Chapel Hill, 1965.

S. G., *Glass*   S. G. *A Glass for the People of New-England.* N.p., 1676.

Scottow, *Narrative*   Joshua Scottow. *A Narrative of the Planting of the Massachusetts Colony, Anno 1628, With the Lords Signal Presence the First Thirty Years* (1693). In Massachusetts Historical Society *Collections*, 4th ser., 4 (1858): 279–321.

Shepard, *Works*   *The Works of Thomas Shepard.* Ed. John A. Albro. 3 vols. Boston, 1853.

Sibbes, *Works*   *The Complete Works of Richard Sibbes.* Ed. Alexander Grossart. 7 vols. Edinburgh, 1862–64.

Staloff, *Making*   Darren Staloff. *The Making of an American Thinking Class: Intellectuals and Intelligentsia in Puritan Massachusetts.* New York, 1998.

Stoever, *Faire*   William K. B. Stoever. *'A Faire and Easie Way to Heaven': Covenant Theology and Antinomianism in Early Massachusetts.* Middletown, CT, 1978.

Vane, *Retired*   Henry Vane. *The Retired Mans Meditations, or the Mysterie and Power of Godliness Shining Forth in the Living Word, to the Unmasking of the Mysterie of Iniquity in the Most Refined and Purest Forms.* London, 1655.

Webster, *Godly*   Tom Webster. *Godly Clergy in Early Stuart England: The Caroline Puritan Movement c. 1620–1643.* Cambridge, 1997.

Wheelwright, *Brief*   John Wheelwright. *A Brief, and Plain Apology.* London, 1658.

Williams, *Complete Writings*	*The Complete Writings of Roger Williams.* Ed. Reuben Aldridge Guild et al., 7 vols. New York, 1963.
WJ	*The Journal of John Winthrop, 1630–1649.* Ed. Richard S. Dunn, James Savage, and Laetitia Yeandle et al. Cambridge, 1996.
WP	*The Winthrop Papers.* Ed. Allyn B. Forbes et al. 5 vols. Boston, 1929–47.
WWP	Edward Johnson. *The Wonder Working Providence of Sion's Saviour in New England.* Ed. J. Franklin Jameson. 1654. Reprint, New York, 1910.
Ziff, *Career*	Lazar Ziff. *The Career of John Cotton: Puritanism and the American Experience.* Princeton, 1962.

MAKING HERETICS

INTRODUCTION

"ANTINOMIAN CONTROVERSY" is the conventional but relatively modern term for the events this book chronicles. The label is a misleading nineteenth-century simplification that marks the fading of the complexities of seventeenth-century English radical religion in cultural memory.[1] The more the research and writing for this book progressed the less satisfactory it seemed. Historians routinely acknowledge that when hostile contemporaries used a general term to describe the radical religious doctrines being dispersed in Boston, they were far more likely to use "familist," referring to the heterodox group, the Family of Love, than "antinomian," meaning to be freed from God's moral law. They did so deliberately, and if one must use a partisan term, then the dispute should be called the familist controversy, which would have the merit of defamiliarizing it while providing a richer contextual framework. Or we could take the vantage point of the losing side, who viewed their opponents as heretically arguing that obedience to God's laws, not faith in Jesus, would save them, and call it the legalism controversy. I deemed the purposes of this book best served by a term that all parties in the conflict claimed for themselves. As Boston's minister John Cotton once preached, the dispute revolved around how to best magnify the free grace of God, and to call it the free grace controversy seems both descriptively accurate and prejudicial to none of the actors.

The free grace controversy, for the stature of the persons involved and its long-term results, was the greatest internal dispute of pre–Civil War puritanism, either in England or New England. The controversy shook the infant Massachusetts Bay colony from 1636 to 1638. Accusations of false doctrine flew back and forth, the government went into tumult, and by the time the crisis had subsided, leading colonists had voluntarily departed or had been banished. It left a permanent stamp on New England, and in terms of its impact in England, it was arguably the single most important event in seventeenth-century American colonial history.[2]

Such an important event has never lacked for scholarly interpretations, and historians have debated a number of perspectives in recent decades. Were Cotton and his admirer Anne Hutchinson defending the mystical heart of the Reformed Christian tradition from a creeping and earthbound humanism?[3] Were their ministerial opponents defending a profound understanding of the human condition from persons who flinched before its tough-minded realism?[4] Was the controversy a graphic display of the danger that a radical lay wing presented to puritanism, or was it chiefly between Cotton and his opponents, who represented two equally valid schools of orthodoxy?[5] Did the dispute represent a revolt of proto–free market merchants against organic agrarians, or a panicked patriarchy clamping down on gender dissidence?[6]

These are very different perspectives, but they share a common element. They all presume the clash of structural opposites. Whatever the given opposites might be—radical/orthodox; conservative/innovative; free market/agrarian; patriarch/proto-feminist—the scholar lines them up and they collide. This heavy emphasis on the explanatory power of structural forces, however varying, gives an inevitability to the conflict and thus encourages the neglect of the narrative itself—if a collision was bound to take place, the details of the crash are of secondary importance.[7] The last book-length narrative on the controversy was published in 1962. While much has been written on its various aspects since then, this literature, for all its variety of approaches, tends to presuppose that the events themselves have already been adequately reconstructed. "The facts [of the controversy] can be recounted quite easily," says one recent account invoking the structural tensions of puritan patriarchy.[8] Even the authors who do pay attention to narrative do not utilize all the printed sources, although these are not extensive and important evidence lies scattered throughout them. The archives, with critical documents, are left undisturbed by virtually everyone.[9]

This historiographical state of affairs is analogous to scholarship on the nearly contemporaneous English Civil War before the revisionism of the 1970s. There, too, the emphasis was on interpretation and structural issues, mostly varieties of "rises of"—the bourgeois, the puritans, the gentry—with the facts of the event being taken for granted. But the revisionists stressed that it was the event itself that needed to be recreated before interpretations were superimposed. Recreation, they argued, required the careful search for and sifting of documents and, above all, a feeling for contingency and the importance of personal actions and short-term causes.[10] As with English revisionism, this project's ambition was to reconstruct the process of the controversy itself, utilizing as full a range of published and manuscript sources as could be located. The book envisions the controversy in the first instance not as fixed and structural, but as political, as personalities, personal agendas, and an ongoing process of judgment calls, stakings of positions, and shifting coalitions, a series of short-term events having short-term effects with cumulative results.

Underlying this conception of the free grace controversy as undetermined is an undetermined conception of puritanism. The term "puritanism" functioned as an almost free-floating insult in seventeenth-century England. It started as a term of abuse in the 1560s aimed at those who found the ceremonies of the newly reestablished Protestant Church of England still excessively Roman Catholic. In England's ongoing religious unsettledness, its use expanded until it could be deployed against anyone whom someone else thought excessively Protestant and/or zealous and strict in his or her religion. "*Rascal people* will call any man that beareth but the face of honesty, a *Puritan*," as a minister complained in 1619. Recipients of the label bitterly resented it; John Cotton claimed that "the righteous hand of the Lord struck him with madnesse who invented the term."[11] Given those amorphous and polemical roots, "puritanism" resists being pinned down into a fixed scholarly label, despite a wide variety of attempts to do so. This book therefore uses "puritanism" roughly and imprecisely, and interchangeably with overtly imprecise terms like "godly" and "hot Protestant."[12] It covers various groups—ministers, magistrates and gentry, and more ordinary lay people—jockeying for respective advantages while seeking salvation and sharing to varying degrees different aspects of the general goal of creating a religiously and morally purified Reformed Christian commonwealth. They also shared overlapping groups of negative reference points—the ungodly, church ceremonies and hierarchy, and Rome, among others—that were perceived as obstacles both to salvation and to a properly reformed England. Neither the goal nor the negative reference points necessarily added up to a harmonious whole, and puritanism points to unstable and dynamic coalitions not only between individuals and between groups, but even within individuals themselves. It has recently been suggested, somewhat hyberbolically, that it is more useful to talk of "puritanisms" rather than "puritanism," for there were almost as many puritanisms as there were puritans.[13]

This irreducible pluralism was not a sought-after situation. A hundred years after the Reformation shattered Western Christendom, the unity of the saints remained a powerful ideal. As Massachusetts magistrate John Endicott put it, "God's people are all marked with one and the same mark . . . and where this is, there can be no discord."[14] In pursuit of that freedom from discord puritans proved among the most zealous heresy hunters in the Elizabethan and early Stuart Church of England. There was a powerful drive among them, as Patrick Collinson puts it, toward a "monolithic, disciplined Christian community."[15] That drive had a basis in reality; if there were no prevalent tendencies and widely shared assumptions in puritanism, there would be nothing we could call puritanism to describe. Yet it is important to be aware that such unity as existed in hot Protestantism was always provisional. There was an ongoing and unresolvable tension between the aspiration to unity and the constant generation of diversity.

Puritans, for example, like all Christians at the time, were confident that the Bible contained a single, saving truth. But extracting that truth was a highly complex and contingent affair. The raw biblical motifs out of which puritans constructed religious knowledge—Adam's Fall, the Law, the Gospel, Christ's Atonement—were rich with a potential abundance of meanings. An interpretive elite of ministers, held together by similar educational backgrounds, similar theo-political goals, and often common kinship networks, attempted to contain that fecundity within what they considered normative channels and direct it to what they considered appropriate ends. Their task was fraught with potential difficulties as the knowledge was hardly timeless and self-evident, but social and provisional. The Bible, with its contradictory texts, was available for all to read, and godly clergy themselves could not always agree on what it meant. The laity's interpretation and evaluation of biblical truth took place across a wide variety of sites—discussion, debate, prayer, meditation, conferences, and reading—over which the clergy had less than absolute control.

On no topic was the social and provisional nature of godly knowledge more evident than the one over which the free grace controversy was fought, assurance of salvation. It was a subject of eternal life and death importance. The godly wanted to experience it; they wanted their brethren and sisters to confirm that they genuinely had it; and they wanted to regulate access to it. What legitimately constituted assurance and how it was legitimately obtained were issues that were thrashed out over a range of venues that stretched from public doctrinal and scriptural debates to the most intimate and private recesses of personal identity formation and experience. Ministers dictated guidelines and proposed scriptural boundaries, guided by a wide variety of concerns, while the laity and the ministers themselves through their own private and public devotional lives evaluated, reaffirmed, and challenged those guidelines and boundaries on this, the most precious of accomplishments.

The ministerial interpretive elite certainly set the dominant tone on debates over assurance and other issues of puritan piety. One does not have to step too far back from that elite to see it blend into a doctrinal and affective unified orthodoxy. But one does not have to step too close to it to see a broad range of unresolved problems, differing doctrinal emphases, various and potentially conflicting affects, and evolving debates and disagreements. It is important to be aware of just how extensive that diversity was.[16] For example, William K. B. Stoever's excellent study of the theology of the free grace controversy describes well most of the important formal differences between John Cotton and the rest of Massachusetts's ministers.[17] But by presenting Cotton's opponents as an ideological monolith, a "New England mind," which they were not, Stoever leaves unexplained the critical questions of how such a well-respected minister as Cotton could wander so far astray and why his fellows did not rise up en masse to condemn him. Cotton was not unique. From Anthony Wotton in the

1610s to Ezekiel Culverwell in the 1620s to Cotton in the 1630s to Richard Baxter in the 1640s, a succession of prominent godly ministers, "puritan" in their training, social networks, and theo-political aspirations, came up with idiosyncratic doctrinal formulations as they pursued a psychologically and socially effective Reformed theology.

Just how much theological variation puritans were prepared to tolerate was an open question. All of the above ministers had their fierce detractors, but they also had brethren who, for a variety of reasons, chose to consider their doctrinal deviations as either not serious or outweighed by other aspects of their godliness, and they also had admirers. Some godly ministers cultivated an "antinomian" style of divinity far removed from the mainstream and self-consciously set up the mainstream puritan divines as their opposition—"contra-puritans" T. D. Bozeman has called these divines.[18] Yet these ministers pitched themselves as in effect doing what their puritan opponents were supposed to do and failed to, and they played their more-puritan-than-the-puritans stance to a godly lay audience who might gad from radical antinomian ministers to their militant puritan foes and see no inconsistency in doing so. Even some very radical ministers passed as "godly" with at least some of their mainstream brethren. Puritans might and did aspire to unity, but developing a consensus that a particular minister or lay person's doctrinal peregrinations had crossed over into heresy and attempting to make that consensus stick was inevitably a political, heavily negotiated, and, in England, usually less than successful process.

The means by which puritans massaged conflict and maintained a rough consensus, the politics of puritanism, is not easily studied, but it is critical for understanding both the dynamism and the limitations of puritanism as a movement. Ministers were reticent up to the 1640s about frankly airing their differences in print while the laity did not publish, and by the 1640s efforts to maintain consensus had largely broken down in the confusion of the Civil War. Much of the raw historicity of English and American puritanism where ministerial and lay consensus maintenance took place is lost to us—the conferences, debates, meditations, manuscripts, conventicles, the vast majority of the sermons, and all the extempore prayer. The free grace controversy has left a relative abundance of unusual documents: sermons that can be tied to specific occasions; records of lay and ministerial conferences; position papers; extended clerical manuscript debates; and trial transcripts. Through these, we can construct a relatively detailed "moving picture" of the godly community engaging in the politics of self-definition in a moment of unusual stress, attempting to draw and enforce the parameters of genuine godliness and determine the acceptable amount of play between diversity and unity.

This book thus analyzes the free grace controversy as a heavily contingent series of events revolving around the maintenance and breakdown of consensus. The approach provides a significantly unfamiliar perspective for assessing the roles of various participants. Studies of the controversy uniformly revolve around John Cotton and/or his lay admirer Anne Hutchinson. These two were certainly the doctrinal anchors of ministerial and lay Boston departure from the puritan mainstream. Cotton, the most renowned minister in Massachusetts, adjusted doctrine to meet manifold challenges and preserve what he deemed a central core of saving truths and as a result ended up himself facing accusations of heresy. Hutchinson, fluent in the language and practices of godliness, successfully for a time traded her spiritual accomplishments and Cotton's approval of her for considerable status and power in the semi-public sphere of puritan lay piety. But she eventually employed standard puritan tropes about the corruption of the ministry and the influence of Antichrist deeply and divisively within the ranks of the godly themselves, and her own spiritual life, personal ambitions, and circle of acquaintances encouraged her to graft on to Cotton's teaching elements from sources most puritans considered heretical.

If conflict was not only structural, however, but a consequence of contingencies and personalities, then Hutchinson, Cotton, and doctrinal differences in themselves are not necessarily enough to account for its appearance. Cotton, a famous and accommodating preacher, whatever his peculiarities, seems to have initially gotten along with his brethren in Massachusetts. Neither he nor they chose to make a point of their differences. To enmesh Cotton in controversy, he needed to be positioned in ways that made it seem important to others to engage in the considerable disruption that confronting him entailed. There is no question that Hutchinson was critical in the free grace controversy—the historians who focus on Cotton can make her little more than an appendage in his struggles, which scarcely reflects the role she played. Nevertheless, the earliest chroniclers of the controversy writing from the late 1630s to the 1650s had political reasons to magnify her importance. They wished to draw attention away from the parts played by leading and still important men. Most interpretations since have been guided by their emphases.

There was one man in particular, besides Cotton, from whom the early chroniclers were anxious to deflect attention—Henry Vane. Vane was perhaps the most important and influential person to come to Massachusetts in the 1630s. Son of one of King Charles I's privy counselors, he arrived in Massachusetts at the end of 1635, was elected governor in May 1636, and after a controversial year in office, returned to England in August 1637. He subsequently pursued important careers first in Charles's government and then in the revolutionary governments that succeeded it.

Vane was always well positioned to harm or benefit Massachusetts, and the first chroniclers had good reason to bury his role.

Although Vane is almost entirely neglected by scholars, he may have been the single most important reason why the controversy reached the pitch that it did. Vane was deeply taken with the radical possibilities in Cotton's theology. He encouraged Hutchinson to set up her own conventicles, and it is possible he encouraged her to begin actively engaging in her own theological speculation. Soon a small number of persons, mostly from Boston, with Hutchinson in the forefront, were melding together doctrinal elements from Cotton's divinity and the English antinomian/familist underground, with Vane's encouragement and participation. Many scholars assume that a dominant group of "antinomians" or "Hutchinsonians" emerged within the Boston congregation, which explains why others reacted so strongly against that church. There is no evidence for such a group; the Boston congregation is instead an invaluable study of the variety of threads that could tie a group of hot Protestants together in the absence of doctrinal uniformity. Through Governor Vane's patronage, however, heterodoxy centered in the Boston congregation obtained a potentially destabilizing visibility in the colony as a whole.

In other words, what energized the free grace controversy was not simply suspect doctrine, but that doctrine's visibility and claims to authority, which raises a number of critical new questions. How visible did heterodoxy have to become before the complicated process of trying to repress it was set in motion, and how heterodox did it have to be in the first place to warrant the disruption that repression inevitably brought about? What means of repression were appropriate, and how and when should they be employed, and to whom? While the opposition to Boston is usually presented as a monolith, clearly there could not be one set answer to any of these questions. Translating widely different perceptions into collective action was inevitably a negotiated, contentious, and political process.

There is a natural tendency among scholars of the free grace controversy to focus on overtly "radical" Boston elements in driving this process. But if puritanism was a set of negotiations, if its stability depended as much on the avoidance or massaging down of conflict as it did on agreement, and if radicalism consisted of the disruption of this stability from any direction, then the adjective "radical" can be bestowed more widely than it usually is. There were individuals who, in their zeal to police and pull in the bounds of orthodoxy, could just as radically disrupt the stability of puritanism as the occasional heterodox experimentalist.

One such individual was the minister Thomas Shepard. Shepard has long been recognized as one of the leading opponents of Boston; he was the only minister honored for his services during the conflict by the Massachusetts General Court. His role in the conflict, however, has generally been considered reactive and straightforward rather than proactive and problematic. He was not simply the mouthpiece of the Massachusetts establishment defending orthodoxy from its besiegers. Shepard was an activist, an angry militant on the lookout for deviancy, a ministerial type especially prone to perceive serious conflict and dangerous heresy where others might not and act so as to realize that perception. He has also left an extraordinarily rich documentary base. Along with a few letters and other documents, sermons of his, some printed and some still in manuscript, exist for virtually the entire span of the controversy, a unique survival. This base allows a close study of the ways in which Shepard, and presumably those of his allies who left no archival traces, propagated and perpetuated a crisis. Not the least reason for Shepard's exemplary importance in understanding the fissiparous dynamic of puritanism is the demonstrable role he played in turning a gifted, independent, spiritual searcher like Hutchinson into a full-blown, all-bridges-burned-behind-her radical.

The clash between destabilizing radical heterodoxy and destabilizing radical orthodoxy was likely to be particularly severe in Massachusetts because the particular circumstances of the colony encouraged both. Released from the shackles of an increasingly hostile English state and church hierarchy, the godly could attempt to purify in ways unimaginable in England—one might deface the English flag to remove it of its dregs of superstition, demand the complete shunning of English brethren whose purity had not kept up with one's own, purify the church to such an extent that one began to develop millenarian fantasies about what had been accomplished, and set off on one's theological wanderings in anticipation of the imminent descent of the Holy Spirit. At the same time, unconventional elements of hot Protestantism that might have escaped official notice in the complex and erratically policed social environment of England played themselves out under the noses of a puritan ministerial and magisterial elite who now had the organs of state power in their control. One could monitor the laity and attempt to prescribe and enforce orthodoxy in ways that had not been possible in England.

This newly empowered drive to conformity was fueled not only by the internal tensions of puritanism but also by the fraught transatlantic framework within which the emigrants functioned. The geopolitical context of these devout Reformed Christians was a supernaturally driven one of an increasingly imperiled Reformation in the Last Days of the world, with God wrathfully ravaging Protestant Germany while Antichrist laid a sinister plot against England of "Spanish monarchy and Roman tyranny." That context encouraged the participants to frame the emergent controversy in Massachusetts in ways that further stoked its flames. On a more mundane level, even before the free grace controversy gathered momentum, English puritan leaders suspected that their New England brethren were too radical, and the English government initiated proceedings to revoke the colony's charter. The free grace controversy and the shifting fortunes of the precarious Massachusetts charter are conventionally treated as separate stories, with the former getting vastly more attention than the latter, but they are inseparably intertwined.

The free grace controversy arose as Boston radicalism in 1636 grew increasingly visible and some of the orthodox grew increasingly militant, anxious, and well armed with the tools of monitoring and repression. Two years of escalating party building and struggle ensued. The struggle climaxed not with Anne Hutchinson's trial in November 1637, although this trial gets the lion's share of scholarly attention, but with the shock waves that followed the trial of her brother-in-law, the bellicose minister John Wheelwright, on heresy and sedition charges the previous March. Wheelwright's was a hard-fought and closely contested trial, and it created bitter resentment in Vane and Cotton and most of Cotton's congregation. Vane and his followers challenged the legitimacy of the decision and even the legitimacy of Massachusetts's government. After Vane was defeated in the election for governor in May 1637, his supporters started talking of checking the power of the local government with the power of the king, while Boston's opponents spun fantasies about a massive satanic plot led by Vane to destroy the deeply insecure liberties and churches of New England. At the same time, Cotton and a large part of his congregation began making serious plans to emigrate. When that plan collapsed, Vane himself departed to England, promising his party that he would return, in all likelihood as a royal governor-general, an event that would have brought a very different ending to the stories of the controversy and the charter—fears and hopes about Vane and his return were very much alive for at least a few more years.

But Charles I was by now preoccupied with the war with the Scots that was to lead to his downfall, and Vane did not return. Cotton made his peace with the Massachusetts establishment. The Massachusetts authorities, taking advantage of Vane's absence, sentenced a few intransigent dissidents, including Hutchinson and Wheelwright, to banishment in November 1637. Some dissidents were cowed into acquiescence, while others were reconciled to the Massachusetts authorities by the increasingly radical stances of their brethren. Hutchinson's opinions grew more extreme and open, extreme and open enough that the Boston church examined her in March 1638 and excommunicated her, immediately prior to her departure from the colony. Although this outcome is conventionally presented as a victory for Shepard, he himself was dissatisfied with it. His coalition's policing action stopped far short of the ideological purging and purifying that he desired, and he continued to agitate conflict at least up to 1641.

The free grace controversy finally wound down just as the ultimate crisis of puritanism erupted, the English Civil War. The leading revisionist English historian, Conrad Russell, has provided his own explanation for that war—a ramshackle monarchical system broke down under the strain of crises in Scotland and Ireland, and issues that had been successfully massaged or sidestepped before rose up to overwhelm it.[19] Puritanism itself was a ramshackle entity, an uneasy set of alliances and pietistic impulses generated by the fraught and unstable relationship of Reformed Protestantism to the Crown and Church of England, and nothing illustrates its ramshackle nature better than the free grace controversy. The strains induced by puritanism's finding itself in power in England in the 1640s doomed the management of now exacerbated tensions between diversity and unity to failure. The free grace controversy is usually portrayed merely as symptomatic of issues in English puritanism. But just as it transpired in a context of transatlantic politics and concerns, its results were transatlantic in scope. In England it played a not inconsiderable part in the 1640s and 1650s in magnifying puritanism's systemic capacity for disorder.

In Massachusetts itself, old instincts of cohesion through compromise and tacit restraint reasserted themselves belatedly in spite of the efforts of ideologues like Shepard, and after much water over the dam. Those instincts, along with even more important good luck and favorable circumstances, enabled New England's godly establishment to weather the free grace controversy. It was a great crisis and a formative episode in the transatlantic transition from a never securely positioned and never well-defined movement to purify England's church and society to relatively stable and relatively coherent colonial American Reformed Christian polities.

Close narrative may be the best way to get at puritanism as a process, but it has its own limitations. Narratives are tentative and reflect the presuppositions and interests of their authors, and the present one is no exception. A narrative of the free grace controversy also faces the unavoidable problem that a very few documents have to do a great deal of explanatory work. One leaps from less than transparent source to less than transparent source, guided by one's accumulating assumptions, and tries not to look down at the dizzying gulfs of archival blankness beneath. This is far from an ideal situation, but there is no dodging it; analysis of an event cannot be separated from trying to determine, however tentatively, what it was that happened that one is trying to analyze. I have recreated what seems to me a plausible story consistent with such surviving documents as I was able to locate and judged relevant. Inasmuch as some elements of the narrative and interpretation are inevitably more speculative and inferential than others, it has been my intention to describe in the text and notes the process of narrative recreation thoroughly enough that readers may decide without difficulty where the word "creation" would be a more appropriate term. The present narrative does not aspire to be interpretively exhaustive. It is intended to make a case that there are vital issues, personalities, and outcomes that have been unduly neglected in previous interpretations of the free grace controversy and to say something useful about how puritanism worked and failed to work.

ONE

ASSURANCE OF SALVATION IN THE

EARLY SEVENTEENTH CENTURY

I N MY mind's eye, I see Thomas Shepard, twenty-five years old, pale
complexioned and lean, mounting the pulpit of the ancient church
in Earles Colne, Essex, in 1629 to give his weekly sermon.[1] Some
listeners sitting on the benches are hostile to this aggressive, strict
preacher, some curious, and others hanging on every word as if their immortal souls depended on it. One of the last has come with bottle of ink,
quill, and quire of paper to take notes. Shepard warns his audience that
they dare not presume they are going to heaven; they might convince
themselves and the "best Christians" that they are saved and "be canon-
ized for a saint in thy funeral sermon." Nonetheless, they will end up in
hell; their hearts are foul sinks of "all atheism, sodomy, blasphemy, murder, whoredom, adultery, witchcraft, buggery." Many English ministers,
he tells them, are "false teachers," through whose offices "whole towns,
parishes, generations of men are burnt up and perish miserably." But even
in parishes lucky enough to have divines like Shepard, only one in ninety-
nine might be saved. Shepard tells his listeners that they are complacent,
unwitting hypocrites and that they will not awaken to their peril until,
through the force of his oratory, "God's fists be about men's ears, and he
is dragging them to the stake."[2] While fierce, denunciatory preaching is
standard puritan fare, Shepard is especially good at it. The listener's notes
will be published thirteen years later as *The Sincere Convert*, a tract exceptional enough at generating terror that it gets republished frequently into
the nineteenth-century.[3]

Shepard in 1629 was a moderate puritan, more concerned about saving
souls than eliminating the dregs of antichristian Roman Catholicism remaining in the ceremonies and organization of the Church of England.
But that church's rising star, Bishop William Laud of London, loathed as
a disruptive troublemaker anyone he considered a puritan, moderate or
not. He would expel Shepard from Essex within a year. Shepard later viv-
idly described his confrontation with Laud in his autobiography, innocent
piety confronting the personification of satanic hostility to godliness. He
omitted the ways he kowtowed to Laud previously to hold on to his position; he would always be better at attack than apology.[4] Shepard of course
could not have known in 1629 that he would shortly be off on the forced
peregrinations that would finally take him to Massachusetts in 1635. Nor

could he have known that once in Massachusetts and embroiled in the free grace controversy he would perceive himself as confronting hypocrites far more sinister than any he dreamed of in England. He certainly would not have imagined that what was to become one of the world's greatest universities, Harvard College, would be sited in his town as a monument to his early, militant leadership against those hypocrites.

The doctrinal "great question" of the free grace controversy was the very issue over which Shepard had been pummeling the parishioners of Earles Colne, assurance of salvation. If God loved you, you loved him in response, and you could therefore be assured that you were one of the fortunate few who were going to heaven. The problem was, did you have to first experience that God loved you before you could trust that the signs of your love—faith and holiness—were genuine? No, said Shepard and most of the ministers of Massachusetts, for God had implanted these signs. Yes, replied John Cotton and various lay people, for a zealous hypocrite, consciously or unconsciously, could create virtually undetectable counterfeits of true faith and holiness; the signs demonstrated nothing until you knew God loved you (if then, added some of the lay people more quietly). But, came the response, how much easier and more likely for hypocrites simply to delude themselves that God loved them than to counterfeit godly sanctity; corrupt humanity was always seeking a "faire and easie way to Heaven."[5] The debate grew increasingly intricate and intemperate; all sides saw themselves as besieged by satanically inspired enemies; and Massachusetts nearly fell apart.

Yet although Shepard was willing to strike as God's fist over the topic, assurance of salvation was a conflict-laden issue, even for him. It lay at the unstable intersection of experience and doctrine, where a broad range of unresolved theological, pastoral, and even geopolitical problems interacted and collided. Shepard and his erratic ally in the free grace controversy, first and frequently reelected Massachusetts governor John Winthrop, left detailed accounts of their searches for assurance. Those accounts with their dramatically different outcomes recreate that unstable intersection; and to understand just how complex and unresolved an issue assurance of salvation was is to begin to understand why Shepard and other interested parties would have to work hard to create a controversy over it in Massachusetts.

By the time of the settling of Massachusetts assurance of salvation had been a century-long Reformation battlefield. Catholics taught that Christians could only hope to go to heaven, but that teaching, the Reformed knew, was just a cunning trick to chain the laity to an endless round of works—masses, pilgrimages, penances, and whatever other superstitions wicked priests could devise; Reformed Christians, by contrast, claimed their salvation with certainty.[6] While God had predestined the over-whelming majority of a sin-drenched humanity to reprobation and eternal hellfire, he elected a tiny group for salvation. Christ on the cross, out of love for the elect, voluntarily endured God's infinite wrath that the elect would have otherwise rightfully suffered for their predestined wickedness. As a result of Christ's sacrifice, God at some point during the lives of the elect pronounced them inalterably justified, or saved, at which time they received true faith. They were now brands miraculously plucked by God's free grace from the burning, and they could be assured that their rescue had taken place.

But how? Elizabeth I made England officially Protestant with the Church Settlement of 1559, and early Elizabethan puritan divines spreading the Reformation gospel expressed a powerfully self-confident conception of assurance.[7] It was not something one strove for; it came along with faith. Indeed the most common definition of faith was that it was assurance—God's declaration of justification produced its own testimony of his love. "If we be in the covenant of his grace," Militant presbyterian Edward Dering said in the early 1570s, "it is impossible wee should not feele the comfort of it." Around the same time, John Moore, the "apostle of Norwich," audaciously claimed that true faith carried an assurance as certain "as if I performed [Christ's sacrifice] in mine owne person." Although these ministers preached a rigorous piety, they did not associate it directly with assurance. The sanctification, or holiness, that followed justification was presumed to spring from assurance of salvation. It served to confirm assurance, not in the first instance to provide it. "Faith groundeth upon Christes passion, faith geveth the sappe of love, love blossometh forth in good workes," the martyrologist John Foxe preached in 1570, and other ministers at the time echoed him.[8]

Yet many of their most earnest and willingly Protestant listeners proved "weak" Christians. They were unable to match their experience with such exalted claims; indeed, those claims only increased their doubts—if assurance was so self-evident, why did they not have it; were they not among the saved? Doubting easily led these Elizabethan puritans to despair. "If they see a knife," Essex minister Richard Rogers said, "all their thoughts are to destroy themselves; if they goe by water, they are vehemently perswaded to drowne themselves . . . if they see any merry, their heavines is the more increased, seeing (say they) we shall never come out of deadly sorrow and dispaire."[9]

In the face of these weak Christians, ministers in the 1580's began wondering if the earlier preachers were correct. As the highly influential late sixteenth-century divine William Perkins complained, earlier puritans linked assurance and faith "at so high a reach, as few can attaine unto it."[10] Perkins and other pioneers like Rogers set about refashioning their practical divinity for those who could not reach so high. Rogers had himself been a "weak Christian." In the early 1580s he began devising a technique for helping both himself and others out of their dilemma. God, according to Reformed theologians, had promised in the Bible that the condition of holiness was a sign, although not a cause, of salvation. 1 John 3:18, 19, for example, promised that those who loved in truth and deed could be assured they were saved. Therefore, Rogers concluded, if assurance did not happen to you, you could find it through hard work; if you practiced strict and ongoing piety and compared it with God's conditional promises, that visible piety proved that you were saved. Through his method, which Rogers wrote up in a book titled *Seven Treatises*, he claimed to have found the settled peace he sought.[11]

The initial reaction among Rogers's listeners was skeptical, but the techniques the frequently reprinted *Seven Treatises* advocated proved influential. *Seven Treatises* started Shepard on his own search for assurance in the early 1620s, and John Winthrop turned to it in his quest for assurance.[12] Rogers dedicated the book to the newly crowned James I, while its preface writers, including Francis Marbury (Anne Hutchinson's father), praised Rogers for having delivered a crushing blow against the Catholics and thereby vindicating the Church of England.[13] The prefatory material neatly summed up the puritan unitary vision for England—one godly ruler, one godly church, and one godly path to heaven, with puritan ministers writing the guidebooks.

Perkins was even more frequently reprinted than Rogers, and like Rogers, he stressed the ability of sanctification to provide assurance. Signs like fervency in prayer, attendance on sermons and sacraments, upright behavior, and heartfelt ongoing repentance for sin all demonstrated justification. Sanctification, he confidently proclaimed, was "an infallible sign of salvation."[14] Where massively reprinted pathbreakers like Rogers and Perkins led, other prominent ministers soon followed, echoing them about the ability, and necessity, of sanctification to generate assurance.[15] It is not surprising that when the free grace controversy broke out, Shepard and most of Massachusetts's ministers vigorously argued against John Cotton and his lay admirers that sanctification could be primary evidence of salvation.

But as the godly tried to put this new advice into practie, things proved not so clear-cut. John Winthrop, for example, discovered that sanctification offered a poor path to assurance. As he recounted it later, Winthrop, born in 1588, heir to Groton Manor in Suffolk, and offspring of a puritan family, had a conventional, outwardly pious youth. His first real awakening to religion came only in 1605, when he married Mary Forth and began attending to the preaching of her minister, Rogers's close friend Ezekiel Culverwell. Winthrop "began to come under strong exercises of conscience," and "not withstanding all my stubbornesse and unkind rejections of mercy, [God] hath left mee not till hee had overcome my heart to give itselfe to him." He then found "peace and comfort" and began to acquire a reputation as an eminent Christian. People came to him for counsel, and he freely provided comfort to persons in despair. If his friends had not dissuaded him, he would have become a minister.[16]

Despite his steady rise in status among the godly, however, Winthrop's comfort proved unsteady. Although he led a strict life, his "zeale and love" decayed. As the evidence of his sanctification faded, so did his assurance. He still occasionally found comfort from sanctification, chiefly in his prayer and in the love he had to the "saints," but Winthrop discovered that he could no longer commune with Christ in a way that provided steady assurance.[17]

With his inability to attain a "sure and settled peace" through the evidence of his sanctification, Winthrop took up the path Richard Rogers recommended in *Seven Treatises*. He pursued sanctification even harder. It did not work. Winthrop "durst not use any recreation, nor meddle with any worldly business, etc. for fear of breaking my peace." But Winthrop's "peace would fayle upon every small occasion . . . yet neither got strength to my sanctification nor betterd my Evidence."[18]

Shepard, like Winthrop, failed to find assurance from sanctification. A portion from his introspective journal of the early 1640s survives, which resonates with his earlier sermons and descriptions of his spiritual life. In that journal, sanctification was little more than a snare. If Shepard's "duties" seemed "full of life," he developed a complacency that made him question his salvation, for he was unconsciously trusting not Christ but his works of holiness to save him. But if he "felt the secret and constant evil in them," he also grew discouraged, because if his sanctification was not genuine, he was not saved. Yet if he did not "walk holily in all things before God," he had no assurance at all.[19] Sanctification could not prove justification for Shepard, in other words, but the lack of it strongly suggested that he was a reprobate and doomed to hell.

Shepard and Winthrop were scarcely alone in their struggles with sanctification. Perkins himself acknowledged that sanctification's assuring evidence was "often feeble and weake." For these struggling Christians, Perkins and other ministers recommended introspection not for evidence of a regenerate nature but for evidence of faith. Faith was the vehicle by which God applied justification to believers, and if one could even find something so tiny as what Perkins called the "mustard grain" of faith—so little a thing as a true desire for Christ, or a true understanding of how desperately one needed a savior—it was a sign that one was already among the saved. "Grace is little at first," the famed preacher Richard Sibbes assured the "bruised reeds" who questioned their salvation. Therefore when the evidence from sanctification failed, Perkins, Sibbes and others recommended recapitulating the process of conversion and searching for the beginnings of faith. As Sibbes put it, despairing Christians "must give a sharp sentence against themselves, and yet cast themselves upon God's mercy in Christ, as at their first conversion." Sibbes recommended this technique not only for persons who had committed major sins but as a general remedy for Christians who could see no evidence in themselves of sanctification.[20]

In the 1620s and 1630s, a few important ministers, discouraged by the inability of many Christians to find peace through their sanctification, claimed that the evidence of faith was far superior to the evidence of sanctification. Ezekiel Culverwell in *A Treatise of Faith*, for example, argued that the reason why so many Christians were suffering from lack of assurance was precisely because they were doing what they had been told to do; they were seeking assurance in their sanctification. But far from being "infallible," sanctification, as Culverwell put it, "oft is deceitfull, and at best variable, and indeed is onely an effect and fruit of Faith." Culverwell advised those who found their assurance weak to build it only on the signs of their faith, for without those signs, no degree of sanctification could give assurance.[21] Shepard carefully read Culverwell's critique, and he agreed with him—sanctification was a poor primary evidence for justification. The evidence of faith had to come first.[22]

Therefore, Shepard frequently searched for evidence of his faith. His journal is filled with his incessant self-scrutinizing for hidden sin and self-love. This very determination to find one's corruption, Shepard hoped, proved, as Perkins had said it did, the presence of faith and thus justification. If he could convince himself that he was truly lost and genuinely desired Christ to deliver him from his lost state, he could conclude that he was truly saved. Winthrop himself had attempted this kind of self-scrutiny when his efforts at assurance through sanctification failed. Like Shepard, he found in himself a hungering and thirsting after Christ and a willingness to love God even if he should not be among the saved, all encouraging signs. But for Shepard, these alleged signs of faith led only to more doubts. How did one truly know that one looked upon Jesus with a divinely inspired faith and not just with one's imagination? Faith, he worried, "might be wrought by my own reason and cleave to Christ by my own will."[23] Given the uncertainty that arose even around the evidence of faith, faith itself might offer as little certainty as sanctification.

By the time of Shepard's struggles, divines had already worked out a variety of ways to bolster Christians so insecure that no amount of introspection for signs of faith or sanctification could give them assurance. They routinely told their listeners that wrestling with fear and doubt was itself a mark of godliness. Perkins noted once that "many deceive themselves,

which thinke they have no faith because they have no feeling." His answer
to that deception was blunt: "[T]he chiefest feeling that we must have in
this life, must be the feeling of our sinnes and the miseries of this life."[24]

Shepard found the Perkinsian approach of finding comfort by the lack
of it to make particular sense. Lack of positive feeling was a benefit in
itself, he wrote in his journal. It was "the greatest mercy" of the Lord to
reveal to Shepard more of Shepard's sinful nature than of God and his
love. If Shepard had the feeling of faith he wanted so badly, "I should
build my faith and assurance upon my feeling and not on God's promise
[of salvation] which the Lord would have me do." God wanted Shepard
"to rest and take hold upon the promise without feeling, and therefore he
did justly deny me feelings, and mercifully also."[25]

Shepard thrashed out the issue of assurance not only on a personal but
a theoretical level. At the beginning of the seventeenth century, ministers
began to conclude that the earlier equation of faith and assurance had to
be wrong, given that so many Christians who certainly seemed to have
faith did not have assurance. Faith was not entirely identical to assurance,
they decided. They found a way to explain this in scholastic terms. Faith
had two gestures—a reaching out to Christ, a direct act, and then a reaching back to oneself with the knowledge of salvation, a reflex act. It was
only the reflex act that provided assurance.[26] One could genuinely have
faith and not have the reflex act that gave assurance. Perhaps because this
distinction was only theoretical acknowledgment of what was daily obvious, it appears not to have engendered extensive conflict. Shepard occasionally rehashed the debate of whether faith was identical to assurance,
working out to his own satisfaction that it was not, which was just as well
for him.[27]

Shepard and Winthrop's inability to find through introspection the settled comfort of which Richard Rogers had spoken scarcely made them
unique. Historians sometimes argue that the godly did generally find a
satisfactory assurance.[28] If puritan ministers on the eve of the Massachusetts migration are to be believed, however—there is no reason not to
believe them, and we have no other basis for making generalizations—
many, perhaps most, of those who sought their guidance would not have
agreed. Shepard himself knew he was scarcely unique. As he said, "Very
few living Christians have any settled comfortable evidence of Gods eternal love to them."[29] Prominent ministers echoed Shepard. Many of the
godly, the well-known nonconformist Arthur Hildersham lamented, continued in a "heavy, pensive and uncomfortable walking" that was far from
expressing the inward joy that the new birth was supposed to convey.
Ezekiel Culverwell reiterated that assessment in *A Treatise of Faith*: "There
be not many even of those who take upon the Christian profession, who
have gotten that certaintie of their salvation, and constancy in holy conver-

sation, which might abundantly comfort themselves, and move others to desire and labour to be like them." John Brinsley noted that "many doe never attaine to any assurance of Gods favour . . . or else come to lose their assurance of it." Robert Bolton felt that he "must, even with some Indignation, expostulate and contest with many of Gods *hidden ones*, about their heavy, pensive, and uncomfortable walking." Even Richard Rogers, almost ten years after the publication of *Seven Treatises*, had to acknowledge again that "many [Christians] are usually heavy and sad: yea so farre, that they cause others to be so, and they make many to thinke, that their religion alloweth no joy: which holdeth some backe from it."[30]

Thus, if a major goal of puritan practical divinity was simply to deliver assurance to earnest seekers, it was less than a smashing success. Perhaps that failure was inevitable.[31] God's wrath was awful, as ministers stressed, and the odds of heaven were slim. One in a thousand might make it, according to Shepard in his most pessimistic mood. John Cotton warned his Boston, Massachusetts, church that "it would be well if at the day of judgment ten men in a Church were saved."[32] It was too much to expect that many serious Christians could easily assure themselves of their salvation, especially since ministers routinely stressed that the first step to salvation was realizing how thoroughly one deserved damnation.

Yet the new practical divinity set itself up for this result. By building itself around weak Christians who had internalized the terror of their plight all too well, it in effect made weak Christians normative. Listeners were told to doubt—indeed, to consider the absence of doubt as in itself suspect.[33] They were told not to expect to feel very much; real faith began weakly and only slowly and intermittently, if at all, grew stronger. The result was supposed to be joy and peace, but too much joy and peace were also suspect; prominent early seventeenth-century ministers like Arthur Hildersham and Robert Bolton warned their listeners that assurance, if genuine, was "often exercised with feares, jealousies, doubts, distrusts, varieties of temptations, Satans firiest darts." Even if you should find in yourself all the conditions ministers laid out for assurance, nothing was necessarily proved thereby. As Shepard warned his Earles Colne audience, you could be approved as godly by the best Christians and still be merely an unconscious hypocrite heading for damnation. The unconscious hypocrite, Perkins asserted, "may deceive himselfe, and the most godly in the world, which have the greatest gifts of discerning."[34] Assurance itself might be the surest sign that one was not saved.

The ministers thereby valorized weak Christians in the process of trying to help them. Those might seem to be conflicting results, as indeed they were. But that conflict was no accident. It may have been due in large measure to the inevitable high stakes and slim odds of contemporary serious Christianity, Catholic or Protestant.[35] But it was also driven by a set of clerical problems that extended beyond comforting weak Christians. Ministers did not simply set out to fashion assured Reformed Christians, they set out to fashion assured Reformed Christians who were zealous, in it for the long haul, and under their tutelage. On the front line of the Reformation, the church pulpits of England, they discovered that their listeners did not always cooperate.

There were, for example, people about whom the ministers increasingly complained from the 1580s onward, the "carnal gospelers." Carnal gospelers took very little convincing to accept that they were among the saved; unlike the weak Christians, they were not weighed down by the frightful and all-too-obvious burden of sin. They had no interest, however, in the life of strenuous piety that the ministers also insisted on. They were happy to hate Catholics and believe that Jesus had died for their sins, but having been freed by the Reformation from a strict, priest-ridden Christianity, many were none too anxious to return to it in puritan guise. "Multitudes in our parts of the land," complained Rogers, assumed they were saved, and they could not "abide" being told otherwise. When Rogers preached on the need for heightened strictness of life, suspicious listeners accused him of "bringing in of Monkery againe."[36]

Even if the ministers' listeners showed enough zeal, there was no guarantee that they would keep it up. As godly communities coalesced, ministers started to complain that persons who, for all intents and purposes, appeared to be saints were falling from grace. They were backsliders. Surely those who backslid could not have been among the elect. Yet they had considered themselves in that company and, for a time, they had appeared that way to others. How could they be accounted for in a way that did not challenge the doctrine of the perseverance of the saints and thus the reliability of assurance? No less seriously, how could this flagging of zeal that threatened the coherence of the godly community be averted? "We cannot perswade our selves of perseverance," complained the "Church" in one of Perkins's dialogues, "seeing men so commonly fal away from Christ among us."[37]

Nor was there any guarantee that listeners would adequately appreciate the importance of their ministerial guides. Catholic priests had been divinely ordained intercessors with the supernatural, whose ongoing importance was obvious. These new Protestant ministers were teachers, and the need for long-term schooling from them was not as clear.[38] Ministers, Perkins had one lay person claiming, "can say nothing, but that every man is a sinner, that we must love our neighbours as well as our selves, that every man must bee saved by Christ: and all this ye can tell as well as he."[39]

For all of these problems, the association of assurance with long-term zeal, pious behavior, and participation in the public and private ordinances of the church represented a solution. It offered tangible signs for beginners and spiritual non-virtuosos, and with its valorization of the weak Christian, it made assurance, almost by definition, attendant upon a long-term commitment to the godly community and its social and ecclesiastical rituals—Perkins once gave as the last of a long list of signs of genuine sanctification "to persevere in these things to the last gasp of life."[40] Terror could be spilled out over the complacent carnal gospelers, which reassured those who did have a long-term commitment to godliness that they had chosen the right path. And if the results ended up sending ambiguous messages to the weak Christians, ministers did not want to let them entirely off the hook of anxiety lest they themselves turn into backsliders. Given the complex, contradictory, and ongoing nature of finding assurance, the new practical divinity ensured the continuing necessity of expert ministerial guidance; ministers were not reluctant to announce their diagnostic expertise.[41] The introspective puritan approach to assurance worked well enough, given the multiple and contradictory purposes for which it was intended. In any case, godly ministers were hardly the last professionals to exacerbate the problems they ostensibly set out to solve.

There remained, however, the nagging problem that the result for Shepard, Winthrop, and many or most of puritanism's serious practitioners in the early seventeenth century was a raging sea of doubt punctuated by glimmers of hope. And even this result was produced only by strict attention to one's inner and outer works. The practice of puritanism may have been an emotionally compelling drama for those caught up in it, ministers and lay people alike; it may have invested their lives with supernatural and urgent purpose; and it may have lifted them out of their parochial perspectives and located them within an international Reformed Christian community. The ministerial stress that absence of assurance was a sign of faith might in time have even given anxiety a reassuring quality.[42] Nonetheless, this state of affairs was not exactly what the original Reformers, with their claims about infallible assurance and liberation from Catholic bondage to works, had promised to deliver.

With the introspective search for signs of sanctification and faith often offering little comfort, some ministers in the decades before the free grace controversy advocated another, drastically different method. Richard Sibbes, for example, acknowledged that introspection provided the most accessible knowledge of justification, but, he claimed, it did not provide "settled knowledge." Settled knowledge came only through what Sibbes called the witness or "extraordinary seal" of the Spirit, a vehicle that was to be a major point of conflict in the free grace controversy.[43]

That the Holy Spirit, third person of the Trinity, conveyed assurance was not in dispute among trained theologians. It was the means by which God communicated all divine qualities and knowledge. If you found genuine evidence of your faith or sanctification, it was because these qualifications had been sealed and witnessed by the Holy Spirit. But, Sibbes argued, the Spirit-witnessed evidences of faith and sanctification were not stable. Guilt often overcame the evidence of faith, and "stirring corruptions" often overwhelmed the evidence of sanctification.[44] Most ministers only wrote about the Spirit's witness to faith and sanctification.[45] Sibbes and a few others, however, spoke of the Spirit having a third and independent witness, separate from its providing assurance through the other two vehicles.[46]

This third witness and extraordinary seal of the Spirit was purely divine and did not have the others' limitations. It witnessed, said Sibbes, "by way of presence; as the sight of a friend comforts without help of discourse," and it brought with it "ravishing joy." Sibbes's friend, John Preston, described the seal of the Spirit as "a thing that we cannot expresse, it is a certain divine expression of light, a certain inexpressible assurance that we are the sons of God, a certain secret manifestation that God hath received us, and put away our sin. I confess it is a wondrous thing, and if there were not some Christians that did feel it, and know it, you might believe there were no such thing." Another moderate puritan, Robert Bolton, spoke of it as "a secret, still, hart-ravishing voice," testifying "as certainly and comfortably, as if that Angell from Heaven should say to thee, as he did to *Daniel, Greatly Beloved.*"[47]

The immediate seal of the Spirit, a charismatic revelation of God's love, was far removed from the relentless discursive, introspective grind that ministers usually offered as a path to assurance. Although Sibbes and Preston were less severe than many puritan ministers, the experience they described cannot be limited to a particular style of divinity. Bolton, the only other minister to describe it at length, was otherwise a harsh moralist, very different from the others in general affective tone—"low and legal," unlike Sibbes and Preston, claimed the mid-century radical William Erbery.[48]

Scholars recreating a generic model of puritan piety can underestimate or overlook entirely the distinctiveness of the seal of the Spirit.[49] Yet Sibbes, Preston, and Bolton knew that what they were talking about was both exceptional and potentially put them in very disreputable company. Protestant history taught that associating sainthood with revelations of the Holy Spirit opened a path to hell, paved with moral anarchy. The Holy Spirit's alleged revelations had driven the murderous anabaptists of Münster and their notorious bloody control of that city in the 1530s. The anabaptists' revelations had in turn inspired a heretical group puritans particularly loathed, Hendrik Niclaes and his Family of Love. Familists believed that an elite group of Christians under the illumination of the Holy Spirit could eventually enjoy perfect union with God and freedom from both sin and the responsibility for it. In England, the Family of Love flourished as a distinctive entity in the Elizabethan and early Jacobean period, and puritan ministers were its earliest and most vocal opponents.[50] Familism encompassed a host of heresies, most immediately antinomianism, or release from the moral Law God gave Moses. Were that not enough, the Family of Love believed that their own revelations superseded the Bible, which they treated as an allegory of the individual's spiritual development, and for conventional Protestants, the Scriptures formed the sole foundation of the church and of salvation.[51]

Sibbes, Preston, and Bolton were not about to disown their experience of the seal of the Spirit, but given the possible unsavory results of the Spirit's revelations, they were firm about hedging that experience in. It was not, they insisted, an "enthusiastical fancy," nor an "Anabaptistical follerie" nor "enthusiasme." This direct encounter with God's love carried its own conviction, said all three. However, those who had experienced it had to be especially careful to see that they had first obtained solid evidence that faith and sanctification had gone before it; if it was not anchored in demonstrable piety and zeal, that witness had been a delusion. And it was not common, a point reiterated by Sibbes's protégé and John Cotton's good friend Thomas Goodwin.[52]

Anabaptist folly though it might appear, word of this immediate seal of the Spirit traveled through respectable godly circles. Winthrop heard of it when in the throes of uncertainty about his salvation, and his failure to experience it only added to his self-doubt. But he did eventually attain it. Somewhat over a decade before he led the large-scale English settlement of Massacusetts in 1630, Winthrop went through a spirtiual crisis. The Lord showed him "the emptines of all my guifts and parts, left me neither power nor will." In this state of extreme abasement, Winthrop let go of all his desires: "I could now no more look at what I had been or what I had done [that is, no more reliance on sanctification] nor bee discontented for want of strength or assurance."[53] Through temperament, perseverance, and whatever other variables were at play, Winthrop at this point experienced the immediate witness of the Spirit in its primordial force:

> The good spirit of the Lord breathed upon my soule, and said that I should live. . . . Now could my soule close with Christ, and rest there with sweet content, so ravished with his Love, as I . . . was filled with joy unspeakable and glorious and with a spirit of Adoption . . . I could now cry my father with more confidence. Mee thought . . . that frame of heart which I had after, was in respect of the former like the reigne of Solomon; free peacable prosperous and glorious, the other more like that of Ahaz, full of troubles, fears and abasements.[54]

Thereafter, although Winthrop continued to wrestle with the flesh and the Devil, his underlying sense of assurance never completely vanished: "In my worst times hee hath been pleased to stirre, when hee would not speak, and would yet support mee that my fayth hath not fayled utterly."[55] As Sibbes had promised, the immediate witness of the Spirit provided Winthrop with settled knowledge—he would nevermore entirely forget that he was infallibly bound for heaven.

Shepard himself had long felt the lure of a charismatic shortcut past the mires of introspection. As an undergraduate at Cambridge in the early 1620s, his despair at his inability to find comfort from sanctification was such that he wondered if his guides had been wrong. Perhaps, as some people told him, Rogers and others were "legal" men who, with their emphasis on sanctification, secretly expected to be saved by their ability to follow God's laws, just like the Catholics—there may have been a direct lineage from the initial skepticism about Rogers's new approach to the critique Shepard heard in the 1620s. Shepard would tell Harvard under-graduates in the 1640s shocking tales of his college past. He had such a hard time finding assurance that "some advised him in this condition to go to *Grindlestone* & to hear [the notorious radical minister] *Mr. Brierley*, and being informed that the people there were wont to finde a mighty possessing, over-powering presence and work of the spirit when they heard him, he resolved upon the journey." Trade the hard work of sanctification, these renegade godly people told him, for the immediate comfort of the Holy Spirit. But before he set off he read in a book by Hendrik Niclaes, as Shepard remembered it, that a Christian could do anything the Spirit willed him to, "even whoredom, and it was no sin." Shepard's "natural conscience" rose up in revolt, and he was saved for orthodoxy.[56] Introspection might be a poor way to find assurance, but there were even worse alternatives.

Yet not all those who knew the Spirit directly could be written off as immoral heretics. Winthrop was Shepard's ally in the free grace contro-versy, and John Preston's preaching at Cambridge had begun his conver-sion process. Shepard was well aware that under certain circumstances the seal of the Spirit fell within the parameters of legitimate "orthodox" experience, and he knew how it could resolve the anguished traps into which introspection led him. No matter how hard he tried to experience it, however, it eluded him.

Perhaps the saddest aspect of Shepard's journal is his unceasing effort to come to terms with the Spirit's absence. Why did "the Lord not give me those feelings I desired and presence of his spirit?" "I did not hear him speak peace to my soul." On one occasion Shepard "mused" on the witness of the Spirit and prayed that he might know the seal. On another occasion he pondered why the Spirit did not act him in the way it had the Apostle Paul, a chain of thought that led him to contemplate how glorious the seal of the Spirit must be. If he only had that seal, he would have all the other graces—it could "heal, help, quicken, humble suddenly and easily," it worked eternally, and, unlike his own emotions, it could not deceive him when it acted. The lack of Jesus' revealing his "electing love" absolutely was one reason Shepard questioned his election. Even when Shepard thought he might have experienced the witness of the Spirit, he could not free himself from the suspicion that he had been deluded.[57]

Anxiety- and doubt-ridden though Shepard was, he was not without his moments of assurance. In meditation his heart was sometimes "filled with lively hope and assurance" and sometimes "sweetly ravished." Applying a conditional promise could give him "some sweet assurance." Sometimes, though, he "found some assurance but mixed with many misgivings and fears" or "with some scruples." Yet even the mixed moments were fleeting and, considering the effort expended, seemingly a poor return for his attempts. Shepard, by this time the composer of several classic treatises of puritan practical divinity, could easily fear that he had no faith and picture himself among those who were to be eternally destroyed.[58]

Thus when Shepard felt impelled to act as God's fist during the free grace controversy, it was not in defense of a clearly defined, reliable orthodox path of assurance, for there was no such thing. Puritan practical divinity as it had developed up to the 1630s was not a unified whole but an assemblage of not entirely consistent techniques, doctrinal emphases, and affects, intended to meet a set of not entirely consistent goals, and its cross-purposes ensured that it continually evolved and generated its own critiques. This variety and tension of what is too easily presumed to be a fixed orthodox position is one reason why the reduction of the free grace controversy to binary orthodox and radical poles is highly misleading.

Another reason is that the radical pole was just as complex as its orthodox counterpart. It is significant that contemporaries in New England used the term "familist" far more than they did "antinomian" to describe their radical opponents, for they were deliberate in their choice of terms. As the early Massachusetts chronicler Edward Johnson put it; "Antinomians . . . deny the Law of God altogether as a rule to walke by in the obedience of Faith, and deny good works to be the Fruit of Faith . . . Familists . . . forsake the revealed Will of God, and make men depend upon strong Revelations, for the knowledge of Gods Electing Love towards them."[59] The distinction is roughly accurate. The most prominent of the English "antinomian" ministers, John Eaton, stressed that those who had been justified did not have to worry about the consequences of breaking God's law; "God sees no sin in his elect," was his rallying cry. But he had no place for strong revelations in his writings—within the casual puritan classificatory systems of the early seventeenth century, familists were assumed to be antinomians, but antinomians were not necessarily familists. Antinomianism was perceived to bring with it soul-damning moral laxity; familism, on top of that, brought revelation-driven Münsterian chaos and the abandonment of the Bible, and it was familism that the winning side in Massachusetts thought they were struggling against, not entirely without reason.

This is not to suggest that there is any need to commence searching for systematic familism behind the free grace controversy. The Family of Love started to fade out as a visible sect in the early 1600s, but a number of its motifs could be adapted to puritan issues, including assurance of salvation, which in its Reformed sense, was not a concern of Niclaes himself. Those motifs, through books, manuscripts, and individuals, circulated freely along with antinomian ideas in what amounted to an eclectic godly soteriological (that is, pertaining to salvation) underground. That underground, centered in London but scattered in pockets across the country, consisted of alienated ministers and dissatisfied or simply eclectic lay people. It was drawn to arguments that God no longer judged the justified by the moral law and consequently they need not obsessively worry about sinning; they would obey God out of love, not anxiety and fear. In place of the usual puritan stress on continued doubt about one's election, the soteriological underground stressed the certainty and joy that the justified enjoyed.[60] Although its members differed among themselves, they were unified in rejecting, sometimes angrily and abusively, the emphasis within mainstream puritan divinity on the linkage of assurance with sustained zeal and long and painful introspection. They articulated the suspicion that mainstream ministers had made assurance so difficult for ulterior purposes, either to magnify their own importance or as a reaction to the carnal gospelers, and they deemed themselves to be the true torchbearers of the Reformation, the real "puritans," in other words.[61]

It is not easy, however, to draw hard and fast lines between this underground and orthodoxy, although various members of both groups tried. The members of the soteriological underground often came from more conventionally puritan backgrounds. That underground's lay and even ministerial members traveled in mainstream puritan circles, and many of its motifs could be found within the capacious folds of mainstream ministerial puritanism. Was the soteriological underground skeptical about the usefulness of sanctification as a way of finding assurance? So were Ezekiel Culverwell, and John Archer, and Shepard, too, when not in the pulpit—Richard Sibbes thought it was not the best way. Did some of them stress instead the importance of an overpowering encounter with the Spirit? That was how Winthrop found assurance, through a technique expounded by eminently respectable ministers. In any event, puritan divines had always invoked the charismatic power of the Holy Spirit in their ministry—"[Y]ou are all of the spirit: you are so full of it, that it runneth out of your nostrils," was one hostile way of putting it. Did the soteriological underground stress the certainty and joy that came with assurance? Here ministers were much more cautious, perhaps because daily evidence confuted it. But Sibbes spoke of those who "do not question their condition."[62] Winthrop never entirely lost his assurance. Ministers themselves never exactly abandoned their commitment to joy and peace, even if the qualifications they set up made it a distant goal. To a certain extent, all of this is to simply repeat the cliche (at least as far as antinomianism goes) that antinomianism/familism was the doppleganger of puritanism.

But the point is more complex and goes to the heart of the dynamic of the free grace controversy. Historians have long debated what meaning to give to the word "puritanism," a debate that is understandable, since in the seventeenth century, it was a free-floating insult rather than a clearly defined term. But such meaning as it has is bound up with the cues by which zealous English Protestants recognized each other. With whom did you pray and fast, with whom did you discuss church matters, the state of your soul, and the most recent sermons you heard? Whom did you encourage your children to marry? Who, in other words, were the "brethren," those who "in Judgement of Charity goe for true Christians," as Winthrop put it.[63] No small question, since your love of the brethren, as ministers constantly reiterated, was a sure sign that you were among the elect.

It was not a question that was easily answered, however. If much of the discursive, experiential, and political orientation of antinomianism/familism could be found in more conventional puritanism; if mainstream ministers themselves were not settled on the issues surrounding assurance; if it were impossible to say with certainty what the origins were of any given doctrinal or affective motif; and if orthodox doctrine could be transmuted into experiences as far apart as Sheppard's and Winthrop's, then not all "puritans" emigrating to New England might regard policing the boundary between antinomianism/familism and puritanism with the same degree of urgency or even agree where the boundary was and by what standards it was constituted in the first place, and who therefore fell on the wrong side of it.

Which is why the boundary-pushing church community being established in Boston, Massachusetts, in the 1630s would present such a complex challenge to its neighbors and itself.

TWO

LIVELY STONES

JOHN COTTON AND ANNE HUTCHINSON

I N THE summer of 1630 in an encampment by the side of the Charles River in Massachusetts, the recently arrived leaders of a small puritan-run joint stock company, the Massachusetts Bay Company, formed a church. They were living in tents and wigwams and their ministers preached under a tree, but the unavoidable lack of material accessories would not have fazed them.[1] Unlike their most bitter opponents in the Church of England, puritans did not worship God through elaborate ceremony or beautiful images; these were the superstitious dregs of popery. Puritans practiced their religion through obeying God's ordinances: prayer, meditation, godly conferences, keeping careful watch over each other, reading, listening to sermons, participating in the sacraments, and carrying out an almost unlimited number of such other duties as close reading of the Bible suggested. Their churches were erected in the first instance not out of rock and mortar but out of the "lively stones" of their participants (1 Pet. 2:5).[2]

Disease and lack of good water soon dispersed the encampment, causing some people to cross the Charles to a narrow, salt-marsh fringed peninsula they named Boston. The governor of the company, John Winthrop, moved there in the fall and the government and church followed. Boston's central location on the coast and its ideal deep-water harbor ensured that it would become the metropolitan town of the company's colony. They also ensured that Boston's church would be of prime importance as the first and last ecclesiastical stop for traffic between Massachusetts and a larger world, "the most publick, where Seamen and all Strangers came."[3] Its lively stones would be set upon a hill for the whole world to admire, and in 1633 and 1634, with the arrival of John Cotton and Anne Hutchinson, the Boston church acquired two highly visible stones shaped into unconventional forms by their quests for assurance.

Cotton's arrival on the *Griffin* on September 4, 1633, must have seemed literally in answer to the Bostonians' prayers. He and his fellow passenger Thomas Hooker were the first two ministers of high English reputation to come to Massachusetts. The Boston church was desperately seeking a minister, even though it already had a very good one, John Wilson. Born

in 1588, Wilson was a grand-nephew of the Elizabethan "puritan" archbishop Edward Grindal and a nonconformist since university days. He
preached as a lecturer at Sudbury, Essex, and then contracted with the
Massachusetts Bay Company to emigrate with the Winthrop fleet. New
England's early historians were fulsome and consistent in their praises of
Wilson, all admiring his extraordinary humility and his great charity
"where there was any sign and hopes of good." The few manuscript sermons of his that survive show a compassionate and certainly not an overly
harsh minister. Wilson's prayers were thought to be especially powerful
and effective, and he was widely considered to have prophetic powers.[4]

Good though Wilson was, Massachusetts puritans thought that a biblically sound church required two ministers. Wilson as the pastor handled
church discipline, and a teacher was needed to handle doctrine. Boston's
previous attempts to secure one had proved abortive, and getting Cotton
was not guaranteed, as other fledgling towns desired his services. On Cotton's arrival, Governor Winthrop met with his Court of Assistants, the
colony's elected magistrates, to decide where to place him. The Court
agreed that Boston, already named in honor of Cotton's town in Lincolnshire, would be the most appropriate location, and so Boston filled
its complement of ministers.[5]

One doubts, though, if in their enthusiasm the Bostonians fully knew
whom they had taken on. Born in 1584 and Cambridge educated, Cotton
was on one level a model puritan/Reformed clergyman, a powerful evangelical preacher with a reputation in the international Reformed world for
his learning, grave piety, and his counseling. As a committed nonconformist, he organized a covenanted group within his English parish to whom
he could minister without using the offensive rites of the Church of England.[6] To his piety and learning Cotton added, by all accounts, a mild,
nonconfrontational personality—as his friend and successor in the Boston
pulpit, John Norton, put it, he enjoyed "a sweet temper of Spirit, whereby
he could placidly bear those that differed from him in their apprehension."
In 1614 visitors for Bishop Neile toured the diocese of Lincoln, hunting
for ministers leaning toward puritanism. Yet even they praised Cotton
extravagantly and claimed that "grave and learned men . . . are willing to
submitt their judgements to his, in any point of controversie as though
he were some extraordinary Paraclete that could not erre."[7]

This "extraordinary paraclete" was also a distinctive preacher.[8] He preferred to entice rather than drive people to Christ and was in general less
harsh and less fascinated with sin than some ministers. Union with Christ
was a major theme for Cotton, and while other ministers might portray
that union in terms of submission and domination, Cotton tended to express it in terms of intimacy and mutual affection.[9] With that emphasis on
union came a pronounced charismatic streak. Cotton, like many ministers,

drew up long lists of signs by which people could take assurance that they had been saved, but it is unlikely that many other ministers included a "spirit of prophecy" as such a sign.[10] Cotton's Presbyterian opponent of the 1640s, Robert Baillie, claimed that Cotton's emphasis on believers' intimacy with the Holy Spirit while he was at Cambridge was extreme enough for him to have been suspected of the ancient heresy of Montanism, which had stressed the final authority not of the Bible but of personal revelations by the Holy Spirit.[11]

Although one can find a distinctive preacher from Cotton's published English sermons, what one cannot find is the critical position that generated so much controversy in Massachusetts, the denial that sanctification could be a first evidence of justification. On the contrary, in those sermons, Cotton preached all the usual means of finding assurance, whether through the evidence of faith or the evidence of sanctification, or the witness of the Spirit, without prioritizing them.[12] Yet Cotton claimed his fundamental shift on assurance happened in England, and there is no reason to doubt him. It is possible to make a tentative reconstruction of the protracted process that led to Cotton's shift, and that reconstruction gives a striking picture of the perilous, slippery dialectic among theology, politics, and religious experience in the seventeenth century. Cotton, an idiosyncratic, gifted minister, adjusted dogma all the better to battle heresy and preserve and nurture the local godly community—the usual imperatives of a puritan divine—but his doctrinal results made him, in some people's minds, one of the prime agents responsible for unleashing "Hell's Cataracts . . . of Errors" on the churches of Massachusetts.[13]

Cotton may have started on his route at the beginning of his English ministry in the port and market town of Boston. When he arrived in 1612, he found that a local physician, Peter Baron, had been forcefully expounding Arminianism, the recently emerged "heresy" from the Dutch Reformed Church that argued that salvation and damnation were not simply dependent on God's arbitrary will, but involved human choice. Baron's questioning of reprobation was particularly effective; why should the vast majority of humanity be sentenced to damnation before they were even created?[14] Puritans were especially vulnerable to this critique because they tended to favor an extreme form of predestination called supralapsarianism. Supralapsarianism argued that God decreed the eternal damnation of sinners before he decreed Adam's Fall that provided the opportunity for sin—in effect, God flunked the damned even before he wrote their test. The doctrine was manifestly indefensible by any standard of human justice, and it was the weakest and least established component in the "Calvinist" theological consensus within the Church of England.[15]

Cotton approved a certain logic in Baron's critique. Not that he was prepared to abandon supralapsarianism, but he was prepared to rethink it, and he did so through the medium of covenant theology. Most puritan ministers by this time conceived that God made two covenants of salvation with humanity, one of works and one of grace. The covenant of works, which God decreed after decreeing the damnation of the reprobates, gave salvation only in exchange for an unfailing perfect obedience impossible to fulfill since Adam's predestined Fall in the Garden of Eden. God reserved the covenant of grace, by contrast, for the fortunate few whom he intended to save. It required only faith for salvation, and God gave the elect that faith.[16]

In order to emphasize that reprobates were condemned by their own deeds, Cotton juggled with the order of God's decrees. God, Cotton decided, decreed that there would be a covenant of works before he decreed that there would be reprobates, not afterward. Cotton could therefore argue in all sincerity that the covenant of works originated as a genuine path to salvation; the test was at least written, in other words, before the failing performances were preassigned. Moreover, reprobates were not damned arbitrarily but because they flunked the test. These may seem like nominal alterations for the dammed still had no real control over their fates, but Cotton claimed that his innovations, along with the rest of his defense of predestination, produced the desired practical effect: "Presently after, our public feasts and neighborly meetings, were silent from all further debates about predestination, or any of the points which depend thereupon."[17] He had repelled the Arminian attack on Boston.

Not all of Cotton's orthodox brethren, however, appreciated what he had done for them. Neile's visitors in 1614 heard Cotton preach on the implications of this theme, and much as they admired him, they thought he preached false doctrine. The eminent puritan theologian William Twisse came across a treatise of Cotton's on reprobation written around 1625, and he was more emphatic. By putting the decree for the covenant of works before the decree of damnation, Cotton, it seemed to Twisse, had argued that salvation and damnation were not based on God's good pleasure but on human activity. He therefore stumbled, according to Twisse, into the very heresy he was trying to combat, Arminianism.[18]

Not the only godly minister whose doctrinal response to Arminianism infuriated some of his brethren, Cotton, unfortunately never justified himself to Twisse.[19] Nonetheless, his foray into covenant theology sheds some light on his later troubles—a minister sensitive to his audiences; willing to experiment with doctrine to defend major truths and to evangelize effectively; and confident enough of his own rectitude to be seemingly indifferent to the possibility that his experiments might be read by other ministers as bordering on heresy. We start to approach the person who was to contribute so much to the confusion in Massachusetts.

We approach even closer when we move down from the level of theological abstraction to that of experience. Cotton's foray into the doctrinal politics of the Reformation had an unexpected result for him: terror. In his 1625 treatise on reprobation, if not earlier, he emphasized that the covenant of works was still in theory sufficient for salvation. Gauging from positions Cotton expressed in the mid-1630s, the more he thought about the necessity that the covenant of works appear to be a genuine offer of salvation, the more deceivingly genuine it became. He eventually concluded that in the covenant of works, God still provided a semblance of justification, adoption, sanctification, and even pardon of sin.[20] For Cotton, the covenant of works had become not so much a useless path to salvation, but a fatal trap for reprobates who vainly sought salvation through their own efforts. It lured them to their eternal destruction by mimicking, chameleon-like, but temporarily, all the conditions of the unbreakable covenant of grace that ministers invoked to give assurance.

With his reconceptualization of the covenant of works, Cotton painted himself into a theoretical corner. Any sign of his salvation could have been generated within the covenant of works. That dilemma accounts for the final stage of Cotton's journey to his drastic conclusions about assurance. He told a fellow minister, Samuel Stone, in 1638 that he grew so filled with "renewed Feares and Agonyes" about his salvation and "of some others Depending on me" that "I could not Rest mine owne Spirit upon every signe [of grace]."[21]

Cotton's agonized inability to rest on the signs of his grace drove him, he told Stone, to the sixteenth-century continental theologian Zanchius. There he learned that God's biblical promises of salvation were absolute and not dependent on any condition in the elect, be it faith or sanctification.[22] Arguments along these lines had been circulating controversially, orally and in manuscript, among English divines for at least two decades. Ezekiel Culverwell's *Treatise of Faith* had passages arguing that God's promises were absolute, but a censor sympathetic to puritanism trimmed them out.[23] "Antinomians" were to take this position in the 1630s, if not sooner, while godly laity in that decade sought advice on how to use absolute promises in their quest for assurance. Cotton's own covenant theology, Twisse noticed with annoyance, already implicitly leaned toward a sharp division between the absolute covenant of grace and the conditional covenant of works.[24]

Wracked by his inability to find peace, terrified by his interpretation of the covenant of works, and drawn to the argument that the covenant of grace was absolute, Cotton took the final step that sundered him from the mainstream of puritan practical divinity. If the covenant of grace was absolute, believers could not initially discover that they belonged to it by any condition in them, all of which the covenant of works mimicked. Even faith itself could not initially give assurance. Faith could not be active in initiating the covenant of grace, for that would make the covenant conditional on faith's activity. It was strictly passive, as antinomians and a few mainstream Reformed divines argued—it received justification, it did not reach out for it.[25] This passivity meant that divines were wrong when they said that you could take assurance from your active "mustard grain" of faith, infinitesimal though it was. You could only know that faith itself was genuine if you knew already that God loved you. Any kind of human effort to discover justification could be equally well done under the covenant of works.

If human effort could not produce assurance, how could it be acquired? Assurance could only come, Cotton concluded, in the first instance through the Holy Spirit's witnessing to a unilateral and absolute divine promise of salvation. If assurance did come through a conditional promise, it was one that had been given by the Spirit absolutely.[26] Cotton once explained to his fellow Massachusetts ministers how he envisioned his conclusion translating into experience, citing a description by the Henrican martyr, Thomas Bilney, taken from Foxe's Book of Martyrs.[27] Bilney wrote:

> I chanced upon this sentence of St. Paul . . . in 1 Tim. 1.15, "It is a true saying, and worthy of all men to be embraced, that Christ Jesus came into the world to save sinners; of whom I am the chief and principal." This one sentence . . . did so exhilarate my heart, being before wounded with the guilt of my sins, and being almost in despair, that even immediately I seemed unto myself inwardly to feel a marvellous comfort and quietness, insomuch that "my bruised bones leaped for joy."[28]

Bilney's experience of assurance clearly differed from the usual ministerial model. He did not reason on 1 Timothy 1:15, conclude that he was a sinner, and deduce that therefore Christ came to save him. Instead the Scripture "exhilarated" Bilney's heart directly, speaking to him immediately with its use of "I" and giving him joy and comfort. This divine communication of a Scripture verse Cotton considered a revelation, a word ministers tended to avoid, with some exceptions, because of its association with familism and anabaptism.[29]

There is only one description of how an ordinary New England lay person translated Cotton's new precepts into practice, given by Olive Farwell when she was admitted to the Wenham, Massachusetts, church in 1660. Farwell described a progression from the depths of darkest preparatory despair, brought on by Cotton's preaching, to a confident resting on an absolute promise, again after hearing one of Cotton's sermons. Her account differs from usual conversion narratives in that she made no mention of introspective searching for the divinely implanted signs of faith or sanctification, nor did she acknowledge continuing doubts and uncertainties. Nor, for that matter, did she mention a charismatic encounter with the Spirit (although this might have been a topic to be discreet about, given that her narrative was not presented in Cotton's congregation).[30]

It is conventional in studies of the free grace controversy to stop the analysis of Cotton's theology at this point. Cotton has decoupled assurance from the evidence of faith and sanctification, which seems incipiently antinomian enough for a dispute called the antinomian controversy. There is, however, another twist to understanding Cotton and the confrontations in which he got involved, and this twist is only obscured by focusing on the issue of antinomianism. Shepard wrote the first surviving document from the free grace controversy, a letter to Cotton probably dating from early 1636.[31] The letter grilled Cotton on various lay opinions in the Boston congregation, but it focused on a recent Thursday lecture sermon of Cotton's. In his letter, Shepard all but accused Cotton not of antinomianism but familism, and both of them knew that Shepard chose his terms deliberately.

One topic from Cotton's sermon especially alarmed Shepard. Cotton had preached, Shepard remembered, that "he that stayes his soule upon the promise is bound to wait for a farther revelation or declaration of gods mind to him." Shepard wanted to know, among other things, "whether this revelation of the spirit, is a thing beyond and above the woord [of the Bible]; and whether tis safe to say so." Shepard returned to this point in his letter's final query. He warned Cotton not to think that familists denied the Bible; instead they professed to find extraordinary revelations in it.[32]

The pattern of Shepard's concern has faded enough over the centuries that modern scholars have missed its precise form. Cotton, however, saw it all too clearly. Familists, he answered, treated the Scriptures as only the beginning of the Holy Spirit's work. They used them "till the Day Starre arise in theire hearts: but then they are free from the word." Cotton, however, did not want familist, Spirit-assisted liberation from the Bible confused with his teaching on the Spirit's work. He warned Shepard not to

> Resemble such a delusion to the faithfull Practise of such christians [as] feeling [their] neede of christ, and finding a Promise [of grace] applyed to them by his word though they close there with [missing words] give god the glory of his trueth, and love, yet doe not rest therein till they have gott this Promise sealed unto them by the further Annoyntment of the spirit.[33]

What Cotton was warning Shepard off from was the experiential face of an elaborate, strange, theological scheme.[34] Until it got swamped under an increasingly extraordinary stream of doctrines coming from Anne

Hutchinson's circle in 1637, this scheme was a significant component in the free grace controversy. Cotton had worked out in highly idiosyncratic detail the different roles that each member of the Trinity played in the process of conversion and assurance. The Father prepared Christians with the full terrors of the Law, showed them there was therefore no salvation except through Jesus, and justified them. Through absolute promises, the Son revealed to Christians, via the Holy Spirit, that the terrors they had gone through were part of the process of salvation. From the Son, Christians received assurance. That assurance, however, was not yet full; it was still mixed with heavy fears and doubts.

What the Son did, besides bestowing the first experience of genuine assurance, was give hope that the Holy Spirit would reveal itself directly, as it did to the apostles at Pentecost after Christ had ascended to heaven. When this Pentecost experience came, believers would no longer experience God speaking in "parables." The Spirit would "so clearly reveal our acceptance through the righteousness of Christ, that from thence springeth peace unto the soul, which groweth until it passeth understanding." With this new "more full assurance," all of the Spirit's gifts, including the gift of revelation, would become far more powerful and bring "strong consolation," although God might sometimes eclipse a believer's joy.[35]

Failure to recognize that Cotton taught a gradualist scheme of assurance can lead to serious scholarly distortion of his theology and the experiences it licensed. A persistent way of interpreting Cotton sees him as articulating a more or less zapped-by-God conception of conversion, a "rape of the surprised will" or "a concentration of all personal history into one transforming moment."[36] But however phrased, that interpretation is incorrect; Cotton taught no such ecstatic instantaneous transformation. As was conventional, he considered the moment of justification and assurance itself to be two separate things. "Christians when the Lord first worketh these gifts in them," Cotton acknowledged in the midst of the free grace controversy, "not one of a thousand but they think they are in a sad and fearful condition."[37] And when a Christian finally did experience assurance for the first time, it was not necessarily an overwhelming experience.

Cotton's distinction between justification and assurance is not a small scholarly detail; it is the key to explaining how he and Wilson could work together. If a justified man who had not found assurance unburdened himself to a minister, said Cotton, that minister could see the effects of conversion and "justly so apply them to him as good Evidences of his justified estate." The person could take comfort, although not assurance, that the minister was correct. No less to the point, that person could then be admitted to a Massachusetts church, according to Cotton, for which prospective members had to give evidence that they were among the saved, even though "he do neither know Christ nor his covenant to be his."[38]

Wilson and Cotton disagreed about whether the experience of the first stirring of faith and sanctification could give assurance itself, but they agreed that this stirring made a person a visible saint and eligible to join the Boston church; they had no practical reasons to quarrel over their theological differences.

There was, however, certainly much in Cotton's new divinity capable of provoking arguments with more conventional ministers. His conception of assurance implied that virtually all of his brethren were wrong in their teachings. Moreover, the immediate witness of the Spirit, which had been for ministers like Sibbes and Preston a rare and special experience and a supplement to the assurance derived from faith and sanctification, was now both the beginning of assurance and the apex and aspiration of the Christian life. As Cotton's pains to distinguish his scheme from familism indicate, interpreters could gloss his doctrine in a dangerously hostile fashion. Yet even at the height of the free grace controversy, when Cotton was most careful to distinguish himself from the ministers attacking him, he remained conventional in many ways. He never denied the reality of sanctification, nor that it was a secondary source of assurance. Genuine converts visibly grew in grace. The Law, Cotton insisted, remained a rule of life for believers, and if justified people lapsed into sinful ways after justification, they would feel God's "fatherly displeasure." Cotton's gradualist conception of assurance, while it had the potential to stir controversy, left a great deal of room for practical finessing. Even if Cotton was a "semi-antinomian" or a "crypto-sectary," as scholars have labeled him, or a semi-familist, as Shepherd would have it, his divinity had enough escape clauses to allow him to work closely with tolerant ministers like Wilson.[39] It was up to him and them, though, whether or not those clauses were invoked.

Cotton's new practical divinity had little time to make an impact in England, for his luck ran out probably not too long after he began to develop it. He had led a charmed life in Lincolnshire, free to ignore the church ceremonies he disapproved of, free to organize an inner church of the committed godly within his parish, free to take his theological musings where he would. His career was a striking example of the Jacobean peace of the English church, during which puritan divines under sympathetic or indifferent bishops had a great deal of latitude in running their parishes as they pleased. But in 1632, William Laud became archbishop of Canterbury. He started pressuring lax bishops like Williams of Lincoln to tighten up on nonconformity in their dioceses. That summer, word came to Cotton that he was about to receive a summons to the Court of High Commission. Facing deprivation from his living and excommunication, Cotton left Boston before the summons could arrive. After a conference with the puritan patriarch John Dod, he decided to emigrate, although it would not be until the following May that he wrote a letter to Bishop Williams formally resigning his living.

The flight of such a prominent minister created reverberations across England. In Dedham, Essex, old John Rogers called down the judgment of God upon Cotton's informer, who shortly thereafter, we are told, died of the plague. The godly from as far away as Herefordshire offered up prayers for him.[40] Around the small market town of Alford, Lincolnshire, close enough to Boston for an occasional twenty-mile trip to hear its famed preacher, a number of people began to wonder if it was time to emigrate.

One of those people would become the most famous English woman in colonial American history. Anne Hutchinson was born in 1591, in Alford, where her father, Francis Marbury, ministered. Marbury was a militant presbyterian, not averse to confrontations with bishops, who thought that the majority of ministers in the Church of England were leading their listeners to hell because of their inadequate preaching and their adherence to rituals. In the 1580s, Marbury's confrontational radicalism and his sharp wit got him suspected of being the author of the bitterly satirical and very rash anti-episcopal Martin Marprelate tracts. He eventually denounced presbyterianism, however, in a sermon that forthrightly and controversially argued that "politique vertues" were sometimes superior to "moral vertues."[41] Some of Hutchinson's future attitudes and behavior perhaps might be explained in part by her having learned from her father that almost all ministers in the Church of England were problematic for one reason or another and that deviousness in the pursuit of higher ends was not always bad. Hutchinson's mother, Bridget Dryden, came from a prominent godly Northamptonshire family, and Bridget's brother, Sir Erasmus Dryden (grandfather to the poet John Dryden), was known for his active protection of the puritan ministers of the Midlands.[42]

Presumably Hutchinson had an exemplary godly upbringing. She knew how to write, as well as read, an accomplishment rare among English women in general although not unusual in the upper strata of society.[43] Family prayers, reading and exposition of the Bible, drill in a catechism, and psalm singing would have been part of the daily rhythm in the Marbury household. Hutchinson's formidable command of the Bible would have started with the memorization of Scripture passages almost as soon as she could speak, and she might have started reading it not long afterward. On Sunday evenings, the family would have gathered for "repetitions" of sermons and Anne was probably probed on what she remembered; some godly girls were taking notes at sermons before they were six. Private fasts and godly gatherings with like-minded friends would have been part of the family routine. Hutchinson would have been encouraged to develop her own regular private habits of prayer and meditation even as she was being trained in the arts of mothering and running a household.[44]

Hutchinson moved from one high achieving godly family to another when she married William Hutchinson, an Alford merchant, in 1612. The Hutchinson males may have had grammar school educations, and they were theological producers as well as consumers. Two of William's brothers, Samuel and Edward, both of whom came to New England, published religious treatises that showed a command of Latin—to be "learned in the Latine" was a mark of prestige among the leading males of Massachusetts.[45] Another brother, Richard, a wealthy London merchant, was an early political militant against Charles I.[46] William respected and admired his wife, and she was certainly not expected to be simply a passive recipient of the religious discourse of her husband's family. William and Anne eventually had fourteen children.

Hutchinson's spiritual life during her forty-three years in England has left few traces. She admired Cotton; how much, if ever, she actually heard him, however, is unknown.[47] The little we do know about this period comes from her testimony during her trial for sedition, slander, and heresy in November 1637, after things had gone very wrong for her in Massachusetts.[48] She told the Massachusetts General Court, the colony's legislative and chief judicial body, of three crucial experiences: how she had found assurance; how she had come to mistrust the evidence of sanctification; and how she had learned to evaluate the spiritual status of the Church of England's ministers. The experiences in all likelihood occurred in the early 1630s.[49]

Hutchinson's assurance came through an absolute promise. From Jeremiah 46: 27, 28, said Hutchinson, "the Lord shewed me what he would do for me and the rest of his servants." This was a promise that Hutchinson was among the elect: "Fear thou not, O Jacob my servant, saith the Lord: for I am with thee." The verse might have been significant to Hutchinson at first only in personal terms, but it carried prophetic significance. It continued, "I will make a full end of all the nations whither I have driven thee: but I will not make a full end of thee."[50] Hutchinson seems to have originally associated God's warning of national destruction with England, but its promise of protection remained with her and eventually helped lure her to her death.[51]

The assurance Hutchinson obtained from her experience did not last, however. In an effort to regain it, Hutchinson looked for signs of her own holiness to reassure her that she had been saved. The result was, she decided, that she actually turned aside from the covenant of grace to a covenant of works. She unconsciously expected God to save her not through his free grace but because of her own good works. As a consequence, Hutchinson experienced a richly deserved spiritual crisis: "[God] did let me see the atheism of my own heart, for which I begged of the Lord that it might not remain in my heart."[52] She had shifted her reliance from Christ to herself, which was tantamount to denying Christ, and God rubbed her face in her practical atheism. Needless to say, Hutchinson never lost the distrust of using sanctification for assurance that her experience taught her.

A year after this crisis, Hutchinson connected her own spiritual experiences to a larger insight about the ministry of the Church of England. She was pondering over the "falseness of the constitution of the church of England" and was so upset over the church's structural impurity that she felt herself "like to have turned separatist." Totally separating from the Church of England, even in the fraught circumstances of the 1630s, was frowned on by puritans—it was the religious equivalent of renouncing King and country—and Hutchinson kept a fast day for the better "pondering of the thing." Hutchinson was not the only future New England woman who felt impelled to fast for this reason, but her results were singular.[53]

On her fast day, Hutchinson set out to learn more of the nature of Antichrist, a biblically derived figure who set up a false Christ for worship and ranked only just below Satan in cosmic wickedness. Up until the 1630s, there was a consensus in the Church of England that the pope was Antichrist; after all, he was an idolater, falsely taught salvation through works, and waged war on the saints. The godly, a great deal more controversially, perceived Antichrist's evil influence penetrating deeply into the Church of England itself via its bishops, ceremonies, and inadequate preachers. The doctrine of Antichrist fed the puritan proclivities for censoriousness and sweeping, sharp divisions between the godly and the ungodly; the most zealous puritan ministers argued that any listeners who failed to respond positively to their message belonged to Antichrist's kingdom.[54] Hutchinson proceeded in her inquiry by practicing a kind of Scripture free association, in which verses that came to mind were assumed to be messages from the Holy Spirit.[55] This technique was neither uncommon nor in itself unorthodox, although the experiencing of Scripture verses as disconnected, living, almost physical presences might have been easier for relatively unsophisticated lay readers than for ministers with highly developed textual training. Hutchinson was exceptionally fluent in the practice, which was cultivated in her circle in Lincolnshire (see chapter 3).[56]

A succession of Scripture verses from both the King James and Geneva translations taught Hutchinson that all ministers who did not preach Cotton's doctrine preached salvation incorrectly, albeit some more evidently in thrall to Antichrist than others.[57] As she gradually worked out the distinctions the experience hinted at, over an unknown period of time, she concluded that some preached with the voice of Antichrist itself (the full implications of which will be discussed in chapter 5), while some preached with the voice of Moses, which meant they preached salvation through works. Some preached with the voice of John the Baptist, the most hopeful of these voices, for he at least was a follower of Christ. However, he did not understand the full meaning of Christianity, since he died before Christ's Resurrection and Ascension. As Calvin explained, he "stood between the law and the gospel. He set forth the sum of the gospel, but what John began the apostles carried forward to fulfillment, with greater freedom, only after Christ was received in heaven." Hutchinson may have extrapolated her ministerial distinctions from Cotton's own preaching, although the difference between pre- and post-Pentecostal Christianity is a fairly overt theme in the New Testament, and she might have come to it on her own.[58]

Hutchinson's fast was a profoundly empowering experience. Driven to it by her need to make sense of the changes that were taking place in the Church of England, she ended up with a divinely bestowed heuristic tool to analyze, mostly unfavorably, the ministers of the Church of England. Charles I's effort to purge the Church of England of puritans, besides leading to the creation of Massachusetts, launched a new prophet. No wonder she grew assured about the divine origins of her scriptural free associating: "[E]ver since that time I have been confident of what he hath revealed unto me." Hutchinson told another prospective Massachusetts emigrant that "she never had any great thing done about her but it was revealed to her before hand."[59] No evidence suggests that she ever had immediate revelations, in the sense of extra-scriptural voices, as contemporaries were, and historians are, sometimes too quick to assert.[60]

One thing the fast had not done for Hutchinson was turn her into a separatist. But the only place left where she could have the ministry of a divine who preached with the voice of her savior was Boston, Massachusetts. In the summer of 1634, with the encouragement of another Scripture revelation and the prophecy of destruction looming over England, Hutchinson, her husband, eight of their children, and an unknown number of servants boarded the *Griffin* in London. Like numerous other Massachusetts-bound passengers in that decade, the Hutchinson family then prepared themselves for "many a week within six inches of Death to see Christ."[61]

The Boston church, meanwhile, was doing very well under Cotton's preaching, whatever his idiosyncracies. Membership in the church grew by more than 50 percent in the first four months of Cotton's stay, from roughly eighty to over a hundred and twenty men and women, in a town of now perhaps five hundred people. Winthrop exulted that "more were converted & added to that Churche, then to all the other Churches in the Baye."[62]

The Hutchinsons arrived in Boston on September 18, 1634, but Anne's admission to the church met with minor turbulence. En route to Massachusetts, she had quarreled with Zechariah Simmes, a minister who had been preaching to the ship passengers that love of the brethren was evidence of justification—Cotton had built a whole lecture cycle on this theme a few years previously. Hearing too much emphasis on sanctification and not enough on Christ, Hutchinson, according to Simmes, told him that "when she came to Boston there would be something more seen than I said." Moreover, she "abused" Christ's speech of John 16:12, "I have many things to say but you cannot bear them now."[63]

Simmes probably heard in Hutchinson's citation of that verse only the ranting of a self-inflated woman, whom he had already rebuked for predicting the time it would take to cross the Atlantic. Hutchinson, however, was probably trying to explain to him his spiritual status, for the verse immediately following continues, "Howbeit, when he, the Spirit of truth is come, he will guide you into all truth." Hutchinson, in other words, was explaining to Simmes, as she would do in a few years to the generality of Massachusetts ministers, what was deficient with his ministry: he was like John the Baptist or the apostles before Pentecost. Simmes made a mental note that Hutchinson was a person of narrow and corrupt opinions, a reasonable enough reaction given the provocation, and one that would be widely shared before too long.

Simmes promptly alerted the Massachusetts authorities about his dubious fellow passenger. Cotton and Wilson questioned Hutchinson closely upon her entrance into the Boston church. She insisted that sanctification could provide assurance only after justification had been known. Cotton told her the church did not stand on any particular order, and Wilson said that she gave "full satisfaction" in her answers. She was admitted to the Boston church on November 2, 1634, a week after her husband.[64]

Despite Anne's initial difficulty with the church, the Hutchinsons quickly settled down in their new community, their way smoothed by a number of Lincolnshire family and neighbors. There would eventually be at least thirty-eight people in Massachusetts to whom they were related by birth or marriage.[65] They built a house across the lane from Winthrop where today the famous eighteenth-century Old Corner Bookstore stands, dwarfed by skyscrapers. As in England, the better-off inhabitants in Boston dominated both church and town. William Hutchinson, a successful merchant and thus a "gentleman" by Boston standards, soon became a deputy to the General Court, representing the people of Boston, and thereafter a town selectman, petty magistrate, and deacon in the church.[66] Anne, as a gentlewoman, cut an impressive figure with her piety, charity, and neighborliness. Winthrop later said that "her ordinary talke was about the things of the Kingdome of God" and "her usuall conversation was in the way of righteousness and kindnesse." She took a prominent role in helping at childbirths, which were protracted, heavily attended, and potentially fatal events, as well as preeminent exclusively female social occasions.[67]

Childbirths, given their life and death nature, afforded ample time and ample incentive for the exercise of lay puritan social religiosity. When godly laity gathered together, they routinely shared with each other their powers of prayer, command of Scripture, spiritual insights, and general religious capacities, all of which would be on call at childbirths.[68] Through those demonstrations and exchanges of piety some of the laity could develop formidable capacities and reputations as spiritual virtuosi and counselors, as had the young John Winthrop. The "illuminated Christians" that lay social piety fostered and trained could make clergy feel, in Cotton Mather's words, "as if their flocks were rather their judges than their disciples."[69]

Hutchinson was adept at making herself a dominant presence in godly company. In her attendance at childbirths, as Cotton recalled, she "readily fell into good discourse with the women about their spiritual estates." She would explain to the women just how easily they could fool themselves that they were in the covenant of grace while they were still in the covenant of works. They might engage in all the practices expected of godly laity: "secret Prayer, Family Exercises, Conscience of Sabbaths, Reverence of Ministers, Frequenting of Sermons, Dilligence in calling, honesty in dealing and the like." They might even find "flashes of spirituall comfort in this estate." And yet, Hutchinson ominously and terrifyingly warned them, they had never been truly, savingly converted—she spread a "false terror," Winthrop later sniffed, when he had soured on Hutchinson.[70]

False or not, it was effective. Women, and through them their husbands, according to Cotton, "were convinced, that they had gone on in a Covenant of Works, and were much shaken and humbled thereby, and brought to enquire more seriously after the Lord Jesus Christ." Men as well as women came to Hutchinson for counsel. Hutchinson would say, according to Winthrop, "that if she had but one halfe houres talke with a man, she would tell whether he were elect or not." Hutchinson was not reluctant to offer her own advanced spiritual state as a model to these now serious inquirers. The result, according to Cotton, was initially entirely positive. Hutchinson "wrought with God, and with the Ministers, the work of the Lord . . . [and] found loving and dear respect from both our Church-Elders and Brethren, and so from my self."[71]

Hutchinson's semi-public religious activism and its easy acceptance by both sexes was not aberrant. English society took for granted that women were a weaker sex, more emotional and less capable of reason than men, although perhaps more religious, and it laid out narrow roles for them. Nonetheless, lay social godliness was a career that, if not gender neutral, was open to the talented of both sexes.[72] A vigorously and visibly pious woman, not averse to displaying her advanced spiritual status and capacities, curious about other people, more than willing to offer them counsel, and admired for her general good judgment, could accrue considerable cultural capital among ministers as well as the laity.[73] Women could acquire enough respect to even get a certain amount of doctrinal leeway from ministers and successfully weather quarrels with them. Carving out an ostensibly private but de facto semi-public role for herself, Hutchinson was following a well-beaten path. It was certainly helpful if a woman as visible as she was kept herself relatively protected from criticism about neglecting her wifely calling, and Hutchinson had an admiring and supportive husband and enough servants to keep the family's domestic ordering above reproach. Ideally in this patriarchal society, the laity deferred to ministers, women deferred to men, and ignorant heterodoxy deferred to learned orthodoxy.[74] But these were ideals that existed alongside a variety of other ideals, and any given ideal's correspondence with reality was rough and subject to continual negotiation.

Evidently those negotiations went smoothly in the first year or so of Hutchinson's stay in Boston. As Cotton recalled, "[A]ll the faithful embraced her conference, and blessed God for her fruitfull discourses." Winthrop painted a similar picture of Hutchinson's successes.[75] It could be, of course, that she was already spreading distinctive teachings among the women of the town as soon as she arrived and Cotton and Winthrop were just unusually slow to hear about them. But that is unlikely. Winthrop claimed that it was not until later that she began to "set forth her own stuffe." John Oliver at Hutchinson's church trial in 1638 recalled that originally "Mrs. Hutchinson did plead for Creature Graces [sanctification] and did acknowlege them and stood for them," in which case there would have been little difference between her teaching and Cotton's.[76] For perhaps her first year Hutchinson basked in general local approval, with good reason, while Cotton preached the method of assurance he had recently worked out in old Boston without, as far as we know, generating any controversy. One possible conclusion to be drawn from this general archival placidity is that neither Hutchinson nor Cotton, for all their distinctiveness and all the attention they receive from scholars, were of themselves sufficient to draw significant sustained hostile attention to Boston. Among other things, the church still lacked some critical lively stones.

THREE

THE MOST GLORIOUS CHURCH

IN THE WORLD

BOSTON, C. 1636

T HERE IS a common scholarly assumption that the free grace controversy occurred in large measure because somewhere around
1635 or 1636 the Boston laity collectively plunged into radicalism. They almost all became "antinomians" or "Hutchinsonians." This
explanation, besides accounting for the Boston church's impressive unity
throughout most of the conflict, renders unproblematic, even uninterest-
ing, the controversy itself—puritans were supposed to be opposed to antinomianism. Two extraordinary members the Boston church acquired in
late 1635 and early 1636, John Wheelwright, an aggressively unconventional minister, and Henry Vane, a voluntary religious exile from King
Charles I's court, would seem to lend the assumption credence. Many of
Wheelwright's fellow clerics soon viewed him as a familist and antinomian
traitor, while Vane promoted, protected, and may have even prompted
Anne Hutchinson's heterodox speculation. These two were critical in en-
suring that when conflict broke out, it would become intractable.

However, even as the controversy reached its peak, the Boston church
functioned as a broad evangelical coalition in which "Hutchinsonians,"
although a real and heterodox presence, were a small minority and in
which pietistic solidarity, for a variety of reasons, overrode details of doctrinal difference. The Boston church was certainly a potential agent of
disorder, yet it was at the same time a striking example of the flexibility
and capacity for containing and avoiding doctrinal conflict that gave puritanism its rough, practical coherence.

Cotton would be a solitary doctrinal figure no longer among Massachusetts's ministers in 1636. That May, Anne Hutchinson's brother-in-law
John Wheelwright arrived and became a Boston church member on June
12.[1] It would be helpful if we knew a great deal more about Wheelwright
than we do. He was to be banished from Massachusetts and excoriated in
a number of books as a heretic, but Cotton always testified to his doctrinal
soundness. His fellow Massachusetts ministers played a large role in his
banishment, yet he himself supported the New England communion of

churches and detested "sectaries." Deeply committed to locating himself in Reformed ecclesiastical and doctrinal traditions, aggressively opposed to those he saw as deviating from them, and admired by at least one eminent figure within those traditions, Wheelwright clearly conceived himself as "orthodox." But a more unorthodox orthodoxy than his would be hard to imagine.

Probably born near Alford in Saleby, Lincolnshire, in the early part of 1592, Wheelwright received his B.A. from Sidney Sussex College, Cambridge, in 1614 and his M.A. in 1618. New England tradition had Oliver Cromwell saying that he had been more afraid of meeting Wheelwright on the football fields of Cambridge than of any army, for Wheelwright would invariably trip him up. Wheelwright was also noted in college for his skill at wrestling. His later bellicosity gives some credence to these stories. He was also intimately connected to Anne Hutchinson's family. The brother of Marie Storre, Wheelwright's first wife, married a sister-in-law of Anne Hutchinson, while Wheelwright's second wife, Mary, was William Hutchinson's sister.[2]

It is possible that Wheelwright was among the people from the Alford area who decided to emigrate when they heard John Cotton was leaving. At the end of 1632 Wheelwright tried to sell his living in Bilsby, a village adjacent to Alford, back to its patron, an effort that led to his conviction for simony, the sale of church offices.[3] Large numbers of his relatives, friends, and neighbors began arriving in Massachusetts six months later, and they supported him in his struggles with the Massachusetts establishment. It would not be at all improbable if they had originally intended to migrate as a group, with Wheelwright as their minister. Had things gone as planned, the group might have arrived in Massachusetts in 1633 and settled in an out-of-the-way location where unconventional impulses did not attract too much attention.[4] In this alternative scenario, Anne Hutchinson would have been spared her violent death, and no one except the most diligent of social historians or determined of genealogists would write of her at all, unless in her middle sixties, like some of her previous Boston associates, she became a Quaker (which would be unlikely, given the importance of the historical Christ in her theology). Then perhaps Wheelwright's break with her would have taken place in the late 1650s instead of 1638, and when he appears in Quaker histories as a persecutor, it would be she whom he was urging on a constable to whip to the town line.[5] Provincial obscurity was indeed to be Wheelwright's fate, but he took a while to achieve it. Instead of going to some dark corner of the land he ended up in the Boston congregation, where his very unusual gifts as a minister could shine in the central church of the colony.

Only one detailed description of those gifts survives, written by the Baptist Hanserd Knollys. The events Knollys described took place in Lincolnshire in the early 1630s while Knollys was still a young Church of England clergyman under the tolerant watch of Bishop John Williams. Williams made no protest when Knollys told him that due to his objections to the church's rituals and its insufficient discipline, he could no longer conform or administer the sacraments. But after two or three more years of preaching without any satisfactory conversions taking place, Knollys questioned whether he was a legitimate minister, and he vowed to stop preaching until he received a "clear Call and Commission from Christ."[6]

After several weeks of praying, Knollys heard a voice telling him to go see Wheelwright, of whom Knollys "had heard by some Christians, that he had been Instrumental to convert many Souls." Wheelwright was living three miles away, having recently moved after losing his living. Wheelwright counseled Knollys that he was still unfamiliar with the covenant of grace, building his comfort instead on a covenant of works; he "had got my peace by performing duties, and rested in them."[7] This was standard advice to give to people troubled about their salvation, but what happened next was anything but standard. He told Knollys to come back in two or three days. In the interval, while in intense prayer, Knollys received an absolute promise making no reference to any condition in him, Hebrews 13:5: "I will never leave thee, nor forsake thee." Two other Scripture promises followed in the same vein. Knollys returned excitedly to Wheelwright the next day and shared his experience. Wheelwright, rather than dismissing him as a raving enthusiast, told him that he "was somewhat prepared to preach Jesus Christ and the Gospel of Free Grace to others, having bin taught it of God, and having heard and learned Jesus Christ myself."[8]

Now Wheelwright told Knollys to wait for a clear divine commission to preach. Knollys prayed earnestly to God, whereupon one day "those words were spoken by his Spirit to my Heart, *Act. 26.16 I have appeared unto thee for this purpose, to make thee a minister, and a Witness both of those things which thou hast seen, and of those things in which I will appear unto thee.*" Divine instruction followed Knollys's commission. In a dream God sent him a Scripture to preach on and taught him the doctrine he should derive from it. Knollys went to Wheelwright the next day, and Wheelwright told him that Christ had indeed given him a commission to preach.[9]

Knollys wrote this anecdote almost a half century after it occurred, which might be reason for caution in taking it at face value. It is more reminiscent of present-day Pentecostal exuberance than the stern and restrained gravity we associate with the black-robed ministers of the early Stuart Church of England. But the charismatic experience of the divine was not limited to the sectarian fringe of puritanism, as the immediate witness of the Spirit demonstrates, and eminently respectable ministers disagreed on whether the Spirit could teach through dreams. Knollys's example of divine sermon preparation through dreams certainly sounds extraordinary and probably was, but to some extent it may also reflect how little we know of early seventeenth-century puritan spiritual practice. There is at any rate a gradual progression from conventional puritan piety to Knollys, and, as with so many other aspects of puritan spirituality, that progression eventually reaches the soteriological underground, some of whose members placed a heavy emphasis on dreams.[10]

Although charismatic and visionary experience might have been more common than we suspect, it certainly was a topic on which ministers practiced a great deal of public reticence. There was, at the minimum, a gap between private practice and public pronouncement. Ministers were most comfortable when the Holy Spirit stayed within institutional bounds and reinforced areas of their expertise—preaching and textual exposition. One received one's commission to preach from properly trained people, not from Christ directly, and sermon preparation involved hard study and learning. Divines habitually emphasized, with solid scriptural support, that conversion came about under preaching, and certainly not through dreams. The extent to which Wheelwright encouraged Knollys suggests that unlike some ministers, he was not overly concerned about confining spiritual experience within channels that fell within ministerial control and specialized competence.

Only one sermon of Wheelwright's on the topic of practical divinity survives. It was preached almost twenty years after Wheelwright arrived in Massachusetts, but it reinforces the plausibility of Knollys's anecdote and gives more insight into Wheelwright's character. In May 1654, Wheelwright's town, Hampton, New Hampshire, requested a certification from the General Court that Wheelwright, angered by repeated attacks on him, was a sound minister. The Court gave him the certificate on August 24.[11] Four days earlier John Norton, Cotton's friend and successor of the Boston church, had handed over his Thursday lecture pulpit to Wheelwright. Thomas Shepard's young protégé, Jonathan Mitchel, was in the audience and recorded the result. Wheelwright had powerful incentive to restrain himself. He had managed to get himself pardoned ten years previously for his conviction on sedition and contempt charges during the free grace controversy; now he was on the verge of getting his name cleared. If ever there was an occasion when Wheelwright had good reason to deliver an innocuous sermon, this was it. So what did he decide to preach on?

"All true believers and Saints have received the Spirit as their inward teacher," was his doctrine. A more provocative topic coming from Wheelwright would be hard to imagine; the Spirit had done a great deal of unconventional inward teaching in Massachusetts's recent history, and many people felt that Wheelwright bore a large amount of responsibility for this. Perhaps Wheelwright made a gesture to these people's concerns when he said that the Spirit taught usually through the word of the ministry. Nonetheless, he added, sometimes it taught immediately, "bearing the word of god to our remembrance" (as it had done for Hanserd Knollys and Anne Hutchinson twenty years previously in England). The result would not be spiritual and moral anarchy, as many in Massachusetts feared, based in part on experience. If this was genuine teaching by the Spirit, it would result in sanctification: "[T]he faith of Gods elect works by love and make them love god and love his comands and love his people and soe for repentance the Lord poures that Spirit . . . you will stay diligent in praier and walking according to gods word." But the condition of sanctification was not the root of assurance, Wheelwright stressed, for "there is nothing Condition-all it is absolute."[12]

It is hard to imagine that Wheelwright's preaching was much more radically free of the usual emphases of puritan practical divinity, doubt, self-scrutiny, and moral exhortations, during the free grace controversy itself; indeed it is hard to imagine how it could have been, if Cotton considered him orthodox. Assurance not through introspection but as a revelation of the Spirit through the Word, working ordinarily through the ministry, but not always; repentance and holiness not conditions over which to labor, but the spontaneous outpouring of Spirit-assisted love—Wheelwright was tacking very close to the usual emphases of the soteriological underground. He did mention, thoughtfully enough in view of the role he had played in encouraging lay attacks on most of Massachusetts's divines, that in speaking of immediate revelations he did not "thereby open a dore to such as slight gods ministers." He added that "those that are truly gracious they love the ministers of Christ."[13]

Mitchel did not take notes for the following week. The note recording Norton's lecture the week after read as if they are recording the fag end of an effort at damage control. The effectual illumination of the hearer, Norton agreed with Wheelwright, came by the revelation of the Spirit, "yet god doth make use of reason in the gospell and there is place for other helps logick Rhetorick and grammar." Moreover, "there is a place for the use of sanctyfyed and inlightened reason the gospell is above reason but it doth not destroy reason."[14]

Norton's response gives a glimpse of how sympathizers dealt with Wheelwright and, more broadly, how puritans accommodated, or failed to accommodate, diversity. Norton, although Cotton's friend and admirer, did not share his doctrinal peculiarities. Nevertheless, he must have been comfortable turning over his pulpit to Wheelwright, whose theological tendencies would have been no mystery to him. Norton and those like him saw in Wheelwright a passionate and devout learned evangelist who hated sectaries, was committed to the congregational communion of churches, and decisively broke with Anne Hutchinson and the other Boston radicals when they became too definitive in their heterodoxies. As

William Hubbard—not prone to sympathize with Boston—described Wheelwright, he was "not so ill grounded in the truth as to be carried away with any dangerous errors of the Antinomian doctrine"—broadly correct, if you chose to keep your definition of antinomianism tight enough. Since Wheelwright provided enough materials for those who wanted to construct him as one of "us," such people engaged in mental translations like Norton's, stepping down the voltage of Wheelwright's preaching, as it were, until they ended up with something less shocking. But others might be less inclined to make that not inconsiderable effort— Wheelwright complained that after his sermon some people wanted to put him on trial again, saying that he "raked up the old matter."[15]

It is reasonable to suppose that upon arrival in Massachusetts Wheelwright settled in the Mount Wollaston part of Boston and preached there informally, as he was to do later officially. It is also reasonable to suppose that he preached the kind of borderline charismatic practical divinity that he had earlier and would later. And this is precisely what made him a dangerous addition to the already escalating tensions in Massachusetts. Like Cotton he taught that assurance could not come in the first instance by introspection. But even more than Cotton (if generalizations are possible from our limited knowledge of his preaching) he stressed charismatic experience over ethical striving. As will be seen in subsequent chapters, he was far more reckless than Cotton in his theological terminology and in one critical doctrinal formation. Very much unlike Cotton, Wheelwright did not attempt to avoid conflict; it is hard to imagine a less diplomatic sermon than the one he preached in Boston in 1654—"I am no stoick," he said later of himself.[16]

Wheelwright had a multivalanced capacity to foster conflict. Once loose theological opinions began circulating, he could serve far more easily than the distinguished and mild Cotton as proof to a hostile observer that there was clerical provocation behind the lay people who were meddling in doctrinal matters over their heads. He took the legitimacy that gave the clerical establishment its authority and used it for a message that seemed threatening to many members of that establishment, and he would not readily back away from any ensuing conflict. Yet attack Wheelwright and, in the eyes of his supporters, you attacked not some ignorant lay person but one of God's anointed servants, who, apart from the respect due his office, was as well qualified to expound Scriptures as any opponent of his and could defend his positions in the scholastic categories and learned tongues of the universities.

Wheelwright's arrival brought to Massachusetts a minister who, if troubles were to develop, would be likely to exacerbate them. And the odds of troubles developing were virtually guaranteed by the arrival on October

6, 1635, of the Boston church's other new addition, Henry Vane, Jr. New England saw some singular immigrants in the 1630s, but none more improbable than Vane. Born in 1613, he was the son of one of the most powerful men in England, a privy counselor to Charles I. A powerful experience of repentance and rebirth when Vane was in his mid-teens left him assured of his salvation and inclined him toward nonconformity. Vane came to New England with Archbishop Laud's blessings; Laud thought it the best place to get puritanism out of his system. He was also acting as an agent for a group of puritans including Lord Saye and Sele and Lord Brooke, who were considering emigrating to the Warwick patent, land they had just acquired in what was to become Connecticut. On the boat over, some of Vane's fellow passengers suspected him to be a spy "to betray their liberties" because of his long hair, aristocratic bearing, and Court associations.[17] Suspicions disappeared, at least for the time being, for Vane was serious about his piety and his discontent with the ceremonies of the Church of England. One of his fellow passengers wrote to him, applauding him for having shortened his fashionably long hair but urging a complete reformation by bringing it to the "primitive length and form" (1 Corinthians 11:14—we do not know how short his hair got).[18]

Vane was only twenty-two years old when he arrived in Massachusetts and took up residence in Boston. The positive impression created by his piety and social rank was reinforced by his personality: "a man of great natural parts . . . of a quick conception, and very ready, sharp, and weighty expression . . . [with] an unusual aspect, which . . . made men think there was somewhat in him extraordinary," as an English enemy later described him. A "noble gentleman," an initially starstruck Winthrop called Vane in his journal. Vane liked Cotton enough to build an addition to Cotton's house for himself—it is probably safe to assume that he was a regular at the Cotton family's meals, and his physical proximity to Cotton for the duration of his stay in New England needs always to be kept in mind. He quickly took on a leadership role both in Boston and the colony, predictably enough in a society in which political and social rank went together. On November 1, 1635, Vane became a member of the Boston church, and he was seated with Winthrop in a place of honor on the magistrate's bench for church services and assemblies. On November 30, the Boston town meeting passed an order requiring that all legal disputes be first submitted to Vane and two elders of the church for arbitration. In January 1636, Vane assumed it upon himself to reconcile Winthrop and Thomas Dudley. In spite of his youth and inexperience, he was elected governor in May 1636. A little over a year later, however, as the rhymester Edward Johnson put it in his history, "With small defeat thou didst retreat to Brittaine ground againe."[19] In England Vane took prominent roles in Charles's government and the subsequent revolutionary parliamentary regime.

Vane also brought with him to Massachusetts a perhaps already nutured formidable apetite for unconventional theological speculation. It was this appetite that profoundly altered the spiritual dynamic in Massachusetts. It caused John Cotton, after a quarter century of flirting with extremism and managing to keep on his feet, to make his first serious stumble; it pushed Anne Hutchinson into the public limelight, thereby initiating a trajectory that was to end with her and most of her immediate family hatcheted by Indians eight years later; it drove the Massachusetts government into the most irreconcilable factionalism that it experienced until the American Revolution; and it led Vane himself to a blend of power politics and millenarian-tinged doctrinal speculation that would result in his beheading as a traitor on Tower Hill in 1662.

Yet Vane is almost entirely overlooked in modern accounts of the free grace controversy, scholarly neglect that is not entirely surprising. His continuing importance as an English political figure meant that it was always far more worthwhile to cultivate him than alienate him. Therefore, contemporary official or quasi-official accounts intended for English audiences deliberately diverted attention from him. He goes unmentioned in *Short Story*, a collection of documents and narratives about the controversy assembled and written by John Winthrop, with an introduction by the minister Thomas Weld. One would not have an inkling from Johnson as to what Vane's retreat was about. Winthrop wrote somewhat more frankly about Vane in his journal, since this semi-official chronicle of the colony was intended for local, not transatlantic, viewing, but even here he kept his guard up, as he worried that what he wrote might get back to the English government. William Hubbard, the first historian to write after Vane's death, was far franker about Vane's role, but since for the most part he was content to copy Winthrop verbatim, his evaluation of Vane needs to be teased out from his asides and interpolations. Cotton Mather at the end of the seventeenth century, anxious to keep a veil of filiopiety over the entire founding generation, threw up his hands when having to deal with Vane in his epic history of New England, the *Magnalia Christi Americana*, as he did over the controversy in general.[20]

Vane's opponents, though, when they were not feeling exposed, were blunt about his importance to the controversy. Doctrinal radicalism received "too much countenance and growth under [Vane's] wing," William Hubbard said. Vane, according to Giles Fermin, a member of the Boston congregation, writing long afterward, "was the great Favourer and Maintainer of these Errors, and did animate that Faction." Vane was probably one of the persons Winthrop referred to in *Short Story*, when he said that "some of eminent place and parts" attracted to Hutchinson's "party" "profited so well, as in a few months they outwent their teacher." It may be no coincidence that we are not able to find traces of peculiar theological doctrines circulating in Boston before Vane arrived. The very first doctrine Shepard queried Cotton on at the beginning of 1636, a recondite point about the nature of Christ's suffering on the Cross, does not show up anywhere else in contemporary documents but resurfaces in a book Vane published in 1655. As Shepard put it a decade later writing for his son, the "opinion of Familists" were "begun by Mistress Hutchinson," "maintained too obscurely by Mr. Cotton," and "raised up to a great height by Mr. Vane." It was the great height to which Vane raised the opinions, the extraordinary circumstance of the governor of the colony advocating and running interference for opinions that others considered deeply heretical, as much as the opinions themselves, that was vital to the creation of such an intense controversy. "The prime craftsman of forging all our late novelties, the Sheba of our distractions," Shepard called Vane after he had been turned out as governor in May 1637.[21]

The "late novelties" Vane sheltered and helped forge were a complex blend of Cotton's theology, original speculation, and, at their core, a concept that almost certainly came from familism via the English soteriological underground. Underground preachers Peter Shaw, active in London in the late 1620s, and John Traske were both accused of familism for, among other things, the way they strongly emphasized the intimacy of the union of Christ with believers—"Christed with Christ and Godded with God" was the notorious familist expression. Shaw, for example, argued that a believer "subsists in Christ, after the same manner, as the humane nature [of Christ] subsists in the divine." They denigrated the evidentiary importance of sanctification because Christ himself became the believer's sanctification. Traske, perhaps the most flamboyant of the early Stuart underground ministers, expressed this conception dramatically, arguing that for a believer sanctification was not a "habit of grace in his flesh; but the Lord *Jesus* dwelling in him."[22] The little that we know of Hutchinson's theology in England does not need antinomianism/familism to account for it, which suggests the possibility of other sources for Boston heterodoxy. The prosperous Boston milliner William Dyer, for example, and his strikingly good-looking wife, Mary, endowed with a "piercing Knowledge in many things," were, according to Winthrop, "of the highest forme of our refined Familists, and very active in maintaining their party." Both were ex-Londoners, and William had been apprenticed to a fishmonger from the London parish of Saint Michaels Crooked Lane at a time when its pulpit was regularly occupied by Shaw.[23]

Hutchinson and her circle speculated in some form no later than the end of 1636 and probably earlier that conversion was not a divinely induced transformation of the "creature," measured by sanctification; it was a flat-out substitution of the divine for the earthly. In conversion the faculties of the soul "in things pertaining to God" were destroyed. Christ was the new creature and he worked in the regenerate "as in those that are dead." "Creature graces" were mortal and fading, and the saved had no "inherent righteousness" (another term for sanctification). Even faith itself was not our faith but Christ's faith.[24] Christ was literally a believer's sanctification, and only Christ, not sanctification in itself, could provide evidence of justification. Wheelwright and Cotton, by contrast, always argued in the orthodox manner that conversion changed human nature; the graces of sanctification were continuously sustained and generated by the activity of Christ and the Holy Spirit, but they were real, personal, and visible through holiness. After you knew you were justified, your sanctification confirmed it.

It has been suggested that Hutchinson's extreme attraction to the triumph of the Spirit over the body represented in part a continuation of her healing work, "an aspect of her ministry to people in pain."[25] If so, that aspect of her ministry eventually developed dramatically. As the winter of 1637 approached, she expressed her already heterodox opinions more forthrightly and openly and elaborated her emphasis on the death of the believer in conversion in newer and even stranger directions. Souls were mortal, she argued; there was no resurrection of the body, Christ's body did not ascend into heaven—all familist doctrines, as well as denials of foundational beliefs of orthodox Christianity—and the Boston church excommunicated her.

Hutchinson's disavowal by her church might seem surprising, for historians regularly conjure up a mass of "antinomians" or "Hutchinsonians" out of the Boston congregation. As the standard scholarly composite version has it, "the Boston church came over to the antinomian persuasion" and "comprised almost entirely Antinomians." These "well-disciplined cadres in the Antinomian movement" and "warm adherents" of Hutchinson followed Hutchinson's "leadership" and "walked the streets of Boston wearing the expressions of devotees." This ideologically coherent, numerically extensive, radical cohort made conflict well-nigh unavoidable, although historians disagree about whether the resulting controversy came from their aggression or the authorities' panicked reaction in the face of such massive ideological and/or gender dissidence.[26]

Clearly much interpretive weight, both in terms of the causes of the free grace controversy and in terms of Hutchinson's role in it, hangs on the existence of this group. But did the group exist, and if so, in what sense? Virtually the only evidence for it are statements by Winthrop and Weld to the effect that, as Winthrop put it, "the whole church of *Boston* (some few excepted) were become [Hutchinson's] new converts. Yet elsewhere Winthrop and Weld made plain that they used words like "converts" and "followers" loosely. Weld, for example, said that a great many of Hutchinson's "followers" for "a great while . . . did not believe that Mistris *Hutchinson* and some others did hold such things as they were taxed for." Or as Winthrop put it, Hutchinson's "opinions and practise have been so grosse in some particulars, as [many wise, sober, and well-grounded Christians'] knowledge and sincerity would not suffer them to approve, yet such interest hath she gotten in their hearts, as they seeke cloakes to cover the nakednesse of such deformities, as in the meane time they are ashamed to behold."[27]

Weld and Winthrop, in their roundabout way, were saying that Hutchinson's "following" was one that picked and chose discriminatingly, to the point where the word "following" becomes debatable, at the least. An abundance of other evidence supports this conclusion. William Hubbard, a teenager at the time, wrote much later in his history of New England that "some" in the Boston congregation had turned to errors; elsewhere he referred to "the strange spirit of error that had begun to leaven several forward professors." He clearly did not picture the mass of the congregation as "Hutchinsonians." According to Winthrop, the main opinion of Hutchinson's that "stuck fast and prevailed" was "a dependence upon an immediate witnesse of the Spirit, without sight of any gift or grace." Well might such an opinion stick since it was not at variance with Cotton's teachings and said nothing about sanctification being inadmissable as a secondary evidence, which Hutchinson, for at least a good portion of her Boston career, appears to have accepted. Hubbard and Wintrop's statements support the claim of Cotton that "many held with those Opinionists (as they were called) when they knew of no other opinions held forth by them, but what was publickly taught in our Church."[28]

Even the circles closest to Hutchinson were not uncritically "Hutchinsonian." Giles Firmin related how Hutchinson asserted in the summer of 1637 at her own dinner table that Cotton had said there was no difference between the graces of saints and hypocrites, only to have members of her household tell her that he had said no such thing. Hutchinson's advertising of her revelations may have impressed some people, but others appreciated her in spite of it. *Mercurius Americanus,* written either by Wheelwright or his son, admired her good judgment in spiritual and secular matters but considered her too susceptible to dictates from her imagination; later evidence from various sources suggests that even some of Hutchinson's closest family were skeptical about "revelations," and if they followed her into "Hutchinsonianism," for which there is no evidence, they did not long remain there. *Mercurius Americanus* said of her in-laws, "The *genius* of that family hath not much inclined to subtilties, scarce any of the *Hutchinsons* have been Sectaries."[29]

Boston's radical fringe itself was pluralistic, not simply "Hutchinsonian." Some radicals seem to have been, or become, more extreme than Hutchinson herself, while others expressed English tenets that did not quite fit into "Hutchinsonianism."[30] Henry Vane, for all the extravagance of his theological speculation, may have always accepted that sanctification demonstrated justification, so there was probably disagreement on this point even within the most radical circles of Boston. The endorsement of Hutchinson's doctrines that Vane was reported to have given in England in the early 1640s was positive but restrained: "[S]he was a most pious woman, and . . . her Tenets, if well understood, were all true, or at least very tolerable."[31]

The conventicles Hutchinson set up at her house, after Vane encouraged her, might seem to be concrete evidence for a large group of Hutchinsonians. They started out on a small scale, after Vane's prompting, with five or six people. According to Winthrop writing in early 1638, they ultimately grew to where sixty or eighty attended her twice-weekly "lectures," at the peak of the controversy, in a town with roughly six hundred adult residents in 1637 plus an unknown number of visitors and newly arrived immigrants. In any case, Hutchinson's house must have been filled to its capacity at these meetings. The meetings at their height of popularity were of two kinds, one for men and women and one for women only; Hutchinson led the latter. Their ostensible purpose, going over notes of Cotton's sermons, was eminently conventional for godly laity. According to Cotton, Hutchinson in the women's meeting led the discussions of his sermons highly selectively, emphasizing the parts of his doctrine that were most attractive to her, and "what shee repeated and confirmed, was accounted sound, what shee omitted, was accounted Apocrypha." According to Winthrop, Hutchinson would "declare his meaning, and correct wherein you think he hath failed." Thomas Weld claimed that Hutchinson would "vent her mischievous opinions as she pleased," her "Scholars" would "propound questions," and Hutchinson "gravely sitting in the chair" (chairs were rare items), would answer.[32] Winthrop and his allies considered the meetings in Hutchinson's house the focal point for theological and political dissidence in the colony, and from their perspective, they were probably correct. Yet we know little about what took place in them, who attended them, or what the attitudes of the bulk of those present were. Cotton claimed that when he sent "Sisters of the Church" to report on her meetings, "no speech fell from her, that could be much excepted against."[33] Attendance at Hutchinson's meetings peaked when Boston was under attack and buzzed with theological and political discussion; the town's future was very much up in the air, and the Boston meetinghouse itself was a highly contentious site—there would have been a variety reasons at that unstable time bringing people to them: news, debate, curiosity, solidarity, sharing of grievances. Radical doctrine was certainly discussed at these meetings, but there is certainly no evidence that all, or even most, of those who attended them thereby committed themselves to "Hutchinsonianism." As will be seen below, one could listen to Hutchinson creatively embroidering Cotton's theology without necessarily worrying that one was encouraging heresy.

Our limited glimpses into the conventicles suggest that even in these Hutchinson was not free from criticism. It may not be surprising that her enemies described her as self-aggrandizing, but the same criticism came from the Boston community itself. *Mercurius Americanus* noted that she was "ambitious of *proselytes.*" *Mercurius* described how Jane Hawkins, Boston midwife, ex-puritan trance prophetess, and rumored witch, played on this desire by being the first to agree with Hutchinson whenever she advanced some new doctrinal notion. As a result, she was frequently fed in the Hutchinson household. Hawkins "followed Christ for *loaves*" was the jaundiced contemporary remark. The reason Hutchinson gave for starting her conventicles was that she had heard resentment expressed that she stayed away from such gatherings—she was "proud and did despise all ordinances."[34]

But if the church as a whole was so sound, as Cotton's Presbyterian critic Robert Baillie asked him, why did Hutchinson's excommunication not take place sooner? Why had the church been so slow to recognize that she and her circle were not godly, not "puritan"? Cotton offered a simple explanation. Hutchinson hid her errors from him and the sounder members of the community. Cotton was not naturally suspicious in the first place, and when he sent trusted people to her conventicles, she would not say anything incriminating. Hutchinson avoided Cotton, in any case, "loathe to resort much to me, or, to conferre long with me, lest she might seeme to learne somewhat from me." Although other ministers complained of her teaching, they were not willing to be witnesses in disciplinary proceedings. Cotton preached against the errors the ministers complained about, but when the ministers then confronted the "erronists" in person, they would reply, "No matter . . . what you heare him say in publick: we know what hee saith to us in private."[35]

Moreover, Cotton wanted Baillie to know that he cautioned Hutchinson about her spiritual status, even at the "times of her greatest acceptance," for three reasons. She would never acknowledge that her faith was "begotten nor . . . scarce at any time strengthened by publick Ministery, but by private Meditations, or Revelations, only"; while she acknowledged that there was such a thing as sanctification, she professed to discern hers "but little or nothing at all," although she could clearly discern her justification; and "She was more sharply censorious of other mens spirituall estates and hearts, then the servants of God are wont to be."[36]

There is some truth to Cotton's account. As will be seen, he did preach against errors; he very well could have cautioned Hutchinson, even while making no secret of his admiration for her evangelical skills, and he was neither suspicious nor particularly vigilant in policing his congregation. A bookish man, he let his ruling elders keep him informed of what was going on among his flock; moreover, he preferred a consensual rather than coercive relationship with his church. Cotton was among the ministers who insisted on being reordained by their New England congregations before taking up ministerial duties again, and he vehemently opposed mandatory lay maintenance of ministers. There is no independent support, however, for his self-serving claims that Hutchinson avoided him, was deliberately deceitful, or asserted that Cotton had private teachings. Baillie, who had a number of New England informants, reiterated that he had been told that Hutchinson visited Cotton more "then any other of his whole flock." Thomas Weld said that Hutchinson and others, if challenged about the difference between their claims and Cotton's teachings, were not overtly duplicitious, but "would winde out with some evasion or other, or else say, I understood him so." In the two documented instances of Hutchinson's being challenged about the contrast between her and Cotton, she refused to believe they differed and said nothing about his having a private and public teaching. Radicals did not shroud their opinions in secrecy; they openly discussed them in the Boston meeting house, while Cotton acknowledged that he debated "erronists" in private.[37] The account Cotton gave Baillie saved his face, but it was at best misleading and certainly incomplete. Hutchinson and the other "several forward professors," as Hubbard called them, went so long without disciplining because the ways in which they fit into the larger community weighed more heavily with their brethren and sisters than the ways in which they stood out.

Those who eventually turned into committed radicals, apart from Hutchinson, left no explanation of what took them to Massachusetts. The only clue comes from *Mercurius Americanus*, which claims those immigrants with erroneous tendencies were attracted, like others, by Massachusetts's reformed church order. They were thus on some levels representative "puritans." Edward Fisher might be taken as a hypothetical model for them. A London barber who wrote the controversial antinomian-tinged *Marrow of Modern Divinity* in 1644, Fisher in the 1630s associated with ministers convicted of antinomianism, yet he credited Thomas Hooker with awakening him to his deluded efforts to save himself through his own righteousness.[38] The more radical immigrants' quest for salvation and a purified Christian community brought them to godly Massachusetts, and discussions being fostered by Hutchinson and Vane brought to the fore perspectives that had previously been pragmatically muffled and might have gone on as such for the rest of their lives.

The radicals, in other words, wanted to be part of the congregations for which they crossed the Atlantic. The free grace crisis is sometimes presented simply as a revolt against ministerial authority or, more broadly, against a repressive patriarchy.[39] But the attitude of lay people to ministers was never simple, and it should not be assumed that heterodox speculation automatically canceled out respect for their authority. For example, when William Pynchon published his highly original and heterodox theology in 1651, he made up a fictitious minister as his mouthpiece and expressed the wish that ministers would take up his arguments.[40] Hutchinson respected Cotton enough to leave England for his ministry.

Radicals can be best seen as adventurous Scripture students excited and empowered by their own discoveries, which they held with varying degrees of conviction, but not therefore automatically prepared to turn their backs on or reject the larger church community to which they belonged. Hutchinson, for example, took some care at least up to her civil trial in November 1637 to present her own distinctive teachings as "inquiries." As Cotton put it, when he debated the meaning of Scripture verses with "erronists," "they would ever excuse themselves from settling upon any such things." A resident of Boston remembered much later that "the Serpents subtilty shew'd it self in a Multitudinarism of Questions, started under pretence of seeking light." While the radicals' claim to unsettledness was undoubtedly deceptive, it was probably self-deceptive, at least in part—a way for Hutchinson and the other "forward professors" to minimize their differences with the congregation's official teachings. A heretic was someone who stoutly asserted soul-damning opinions, not someone who made inquiries.[41]

Moreover, most of the doctrinal differences between Hutchinson and Cotton would not necessarily leap out to a casual bystander. On the face of it, Hutchinson's saying that justification occurred without faith was not strikingly in conflict with Cotton's explaining that justification preceded active faith and that union with Christ came in order of nature even before God's promises. One would need a great deal of elaboration before one reached the difference between the Hutchinsonian position that "it is poverty of spirit, when wee have grace, yet to see wee have no grace in our selves" and Cotton's saying, "This is truly spiritual sanctification, that when the soul in itself is full of the *Holy Ghost*, and *gifts* of the *Holy Ghost* . . . yet is like a man in great penury, as having nothing of himself." Since Cotton emphasized that assurance came through a "revelation" that was "more than the Letter of the Word," someone might not be immediately scandalized by Hutchinson's saying that the "gospel in the letter and words holds forth nothing but a covenant of works." While Cotton in-

sisted that the graces of sanctification were real, he also claimed that their
motive power came continuously from Christ and the Holy Spirit, and
a listener hearing Hutchinson maintain that there was no difference in
themselves between the graces of hypocrites and believers might not hear
a discrepancy. In all cases there was a difference, and a difference that
could be magnified as critical. But one had to look hard to find it and had
to have pressing reasons to do so, which many people probably simply did
not have. Sermon repetition was the primary activity in godly lay meetings, and although Hutchinson may have bent Cotton's meaning into
some fairly strange shapes while discussing his sermons, as long as she
anchored her discourse in Cotton's own words, a lay person might have
participated without concluding that anything outrageously unconventional was taking place.[42]

In any case, doctrine was not the only factor that determined "orthodoxy." Even if Hutchinson and others voiced truly radical doctrinal "inquiries," in other ways they were scrupulously, normatively, and impres-
sively godly. Thomas Weld acknowledged that the radicals "would appeare
very humble, holy, and spirituall Christians, and full of Christ; they would
deny themselves farre, speake excellently, pray with such soule-ravishing
expression and affections."[43] They were performatively orthodox, in other
words, and demonstrably sanctified, whatever their opinions about sanctification: strict in their lives, godly in their conversations, and outstanding
at extemporaneous prayer, the latter a semi-public activity that could make
or break lay reputations (and that certainly featured prominently in
Hutchinson's conventicles).[44] Hutchinson was widely admired as a counselor and someone who could bring about ministerially approved conversions. All this was good reason for others to simply treat her and her circle
as godly sisters and brethren whom one was commanded by the Scriptures
to love and not worry overmuch about the occasional odd statement they
might make. All this was good reason as well for Cotton to assume that
the experimentalists in his congregation were basically sound and would
come round eventually to settle into orthodoxy—people like Vane,
Hutchinson, and the Dyers, after all, were not ministers who had under-
gone a long university training in the rigors of Reformed theology. One
could be patient with their "misexpressions," as Cotton deemed them, in
the meantime. When Hutchinson was being grilled at her church trial in
1638 about her denial that a physical body would be resurrected, for example, the ruling lay elder of the church, Thomas Leverett, in charge with
Wilson of the church's discipline, pointed out that she did not deny that
some kind of body would be resurrected.[45]

There were then a variety of subtle discursive and performative threads
tying the most radical members of the community to the rest. They would
present their deviant opinions, to others and to themselves, at various

times, in various circumstances, and with varying degrees of sincerity, as "inquiries"; they would conspicuously act out their orthodox performative piety; they wanted to be where they were. The actual committed number on the pluralistic lay experimental theological fringe, was, by the bulk of contemporary comments, small; a larger number probably dipped in and out of this fringe, and a still larger number admired the others as godly brethren and sisters, enough so that they were willing to make considerable allowances for them. Cotton himself deeply admired Hutchinson's evangelical skills, and the allowances he was prepared to make for her, as will be seen, were formidable.

Hutchinson, in a sense, did have a large number of "followers," but that was only insofar as most of what people saw in her they deemed worth following. The rest they ignored or filtered out. Cotton, in this sense, was a follower of Hutchinson. Admiration for Hutchinson could easily seem compatible with larger and more critical loyalties. In other words, for many people it required educating before they would perceive Hutchinson and other radicals not as admirable godly "puritans," albeit perhaps with flaws, but as heretical sectaries. That is probably at the root of Weld's complaint that "in Towne-meetings, Military-trainings, and all other societies, yea almost in every family, it was hard if that some or other were not ready to rise up in defence of them [Hutchinson and the other radicals], even as the apple of their owne eye" (and it must always be remembered when reading Weld that he was the pastor of the second most disturbed church during the controversy).[46]

The Boston congregation was able to absorb this fringe more easily because it had strong postive bonds. The congregation was free of an unsympathetic church hierarchy and state that had inhibited hot Protestantism in England, and the result was a vital and vibrant participatory church community, of which the radicals were only one component. It must have been exciting to have been in the Boston church in 1636, with a famous divine as minister, the son of a privy counselor an eager participant, a powerful new minister just arrived, and lay people charged with a sense of scriptural adventure. Hot Protestantism was finally free from the shackles of a hostile state and church hierarchy and was free to get as hot as it wanted. The eminent gifts and piety of Boston's lay members from this period were long remembered, as was the power of its discipline under Wilson and Leverett. The Boston church in its highly visible sanctity and exemplary moral supervision approached the puritan ideal of a Christian community; it is not surprising that some believed it to be "in so flourishing a condition as were scarce any where else to be paralleled."[47]

This atmosphere of spiritual vibrancy probably encouraged radical speculation, but it also encouraged a form of ministerially approved speculation with powerful bonding potential: millenarianism. Millenarianism postulated a "glorious church" before Christ's Second Coming and after the overthrow of Antichrist and final conversion of the Jews.[48] Instead of history simply sliding downhill from bad to worse until Jesus returned and ended it altogether, it would have a brilliant conclusion. The connection between millenarianism and Massachusetts was made many decades ago by Perry Miller, the famous scholar of American puritanism, who argued that the original migration was itself a millenarian errand in the wilderness to create a model church for the end of time. Miller's argument was widely accepted until Theodore Dwight Bozeman pointed out that there was no contemporary evidence that the founders of Massachusetts were influenced by millenarianism, and that milleniarianism was never as widespread in puritanism as some scholars seemed to think. The only original founder whose views about the Millennium have survived, William Pynchon, was hostile to the concept.[49]

It is hard, however, to determine exactly how widespread millenarian expectation was in puritanism before the 1640s, for espousing it in print could land you in jail. It was a phenomenon that left its traces in correspondence and godly conversations, which makes the extent of its diffusion impossible to measure. John Winthrop's friend Simon D'Ewes discussed the Millennium approvingly with a correspondent in 1629. Around the same time, Shepard told his Earles Colne audience that it was "not probable" that Christ's Second Coming would occur before the Jews had been converted and the "glorious church" had continued "many a year." Cotton preached millenarianism to his Boston, Lincolnshire, congregation before he, and many of them, emigrated to New England. Given the respect in which his congregation held him, some of them certainly picked it up. Cotton's Lincolnshire neighbor, Robert Sanderson, forthrightly delivering an anti-puritan sermon in Cotton's church in 1619, associated millenarianism and puritanism.[50] There may be no evidence that millenarian expectations inspired anyone to cross the Atlantic, but should circumstances make millenarianism seem a viable interpretive framework, the ground for that framework had been prepared.

As the New Englanders' early church improvisations grew more confident, and as they became more convinced that their congregationalism had finally restored the New Testament purity of the Christian church, millenarianism could start to make sense. In the summer of 1636, Shepard reiterated his millenarianism and remarked that some colonists believed their perfected church order meant that "the daies we live in now, are not only the daies of the Son of man, but part of the daies of the coming of the Son of man [that is, part of the approach of the Millennium]." John Wheelwright in his fiery fast-day sermon on January 19, 1637, preached at the height of the free grace controversy, cast the crisis as part of the struggle with Antichrist that preceded the conversion of the Jews and the subsequent "glorious Church." English scholars had speculated that God might raise up a prophet to convert the Jews, and sect leaders claimed that role. Hutchinson was a millenarian, and, according to Winthrop in his most extravagant description of her, "many of the most wise and godly" considered her "a Prophetesse, raised up of God for some great worke now at hand, as the calling of the Jewes, &c." Minister Hugh Peters once charged that Hutchinson "thinkes us to be nothinge but a company of Jewes and that now God is converting of Jewes."[51]

The coherence of the Boston congregation thus came from mutual forbearance, common standards of behavioral orthodoxy, a well-functioning, satisfying church, and a shared sense at least among some of them, in this newly established puritan commonwealth, of the impending Kingdom of God and Boston's role therein. These factors were powerful enough to make differences in theology petty and provisional. If a few forward professors went a bit off the deep end in their discovery of God's free grace, it was in a good cause. As Cotton later acknowledged, the forward professors hoped that their beloved brethren and sisters would catch up with them.[52]

The success of the Boston church points to a sometimes overlooked element in puritanism. Tolerance for linguistic idiosyncracies among people perceived as godly could override commitments to doctrinal uniformity. Clearly, reports of doctrinal deviance began coming out of Boston very early in 1636, since Shepard had already heard of them. But the original minister, John Wilson, later to be reviled by most of the congregation, went a long time before he decided that the errors were serious enough to require a response.[53] After the affair had died down he showed himself more tolerant of Boston's theological peculiarities than some of his ministerial brethren, and the same was true of his soon-to-be embattled partner in the Boston church, John Winthrop. Like those London godly in the 1620s, who refused to get involved when minister Stephen Denison prosecuted William Etherington, a layman holding truly odd opinions, many in the Boston church probably felt that their brethren and sisters held "absurd points" but "nothing against the foundation"—which was what separated someone simply in error from a heretic—and how long they continued to feel that way varied from individual to individual.[54]

It is in this context of a broad evangelical united front that we should read the claim, given as evidence of heretical deceitfulness, that Boston radicals always asserted that John Cotton fundamentally agreed with them, even when confronted with statements of his that clashed with their opinions. And perhaps it was in the same spirit that Wheelwright cited Ephesians 4:3 in his fast-day sermon: "Let us have a care, that we do not alienate our harts one from another, because of divers kind of expressions, but let us keepe the unity of the spiritt in the bond of peace." It may have been at least partly in this vein that the opinionists, according to Weld, when they found themselves in disagreement with others would say, "I doe meane even as you doe, you and I are both of one minde in substance, and differ onely in words." Giles Firmin recorded disapprovingly that at the height of the free grace controversy when he pressed a Bostonian to tell him what justification was, the person replied, "Truly, 'tis so great a thing, that I do not know what it is." What to Firmin appeared simply confusion, to the Bostonian might have appeared a circumstantially warranted terminological flexibility.[55] It has been argued that Boston's ministers tolerated Hutchinson because their church was going through a spiritual depression at this time. Hutchinson was the only high point in this depression, which gave her an immunity from close scrutiny. The evidence for this claim, however, is not persuasive.[56] The congregation may have had a "Mud-Wall Meeting House with wooden Chalices," but at least some of its members thought it, according to William Hubbard, in a phrase loaded with millenarian overtones, "the most glorious church in the world." Boston in 1636, with its wildly diverse but functioning assemblage of gifted individuals and doctrinal currents, may have represented the apogee of puritanism at its most successfully eclectic, swaying grandly before, and even in the midst of, its spectacular crash. Hubbard explained that crash as divine chastisement for pride; we need to seek more mundane explanations.[57]

FOUR

PRACTICING PURITANISM IN A STRANGE LAND

MASSACHUSETTS, C. 1636

THE UNITY in diversity of the Boston church might have been an impressive example of puritanism's protean capacity to absorb hot Protestantism's diversity. By 1636, however, the circumstances of Massachusetts were pushing toward the opposite pole of puritanism, toward a monolithic, actively intolerant, exclusive Christian community. Those circumstances—incipient ministerial factionalism, increasing government intervention in church affairs, and the problems attendant upon transporting old world piety to the new world—helped define the contours of the free grace controversy and increase its capacity to cut deeply and divisively, and they were at play in, around, and as a consequence of the controversy's earliest recorded encounter, the Shepard-Cotton exchange of letters of early 1636.

On the surface, Shepard's letter to Cotton was courteous and deferential, as well it might be; Cotton and Hooker's flight to America three years previously had convinced Shepard that God was leaving England. But underneath, a very different tone sounded. After linking Cotton's doctrines to familism, Shepard claimed, surely disingenuously, that he knew of no one holding heretical opinions in Massachusetts. But he warned Cotton that some day such people might appear in his congregation and Cotton's doctrines would allow them to do irreparable harm.[1] Up to this point, Cotton and other ministers may not have been aware that Cotton's preaching was so egregious as to threaten Massachusetts's doctrinal harmony. Shepard announced that it most dangerously was. He grilled him as a preemptive strike, in order to "cut off all seeming differences and jarrs." "You will not thinke," he ended his letter ominously, "I have thus writ to begin or breed a quarrell, but to still and quiet those which are secretly begun."[2]

Whatever his tone, there was no deference in the meaning of Shepard's letter. Shepard was trumping the actual diversity among the godly, which Cotton had managed hitherto with good effect in the Boston church, with the puritan drive to a tightly defined orthodoxy. Moreover, he was informing the most prominent minister in Massachusetts that not only had his sheep strayed, but his own opinions hinted at familism. The clear implication was that Cotton must change or be responsible for the further propagation of quarrels, differences, and jars. Ostensibly, Shepard's letter was a moderate gesture, a way to contain and conceal division rather than expose and aggravate it. Shepard explained that after hearing Cotton preach, he thought he had "no call publickely to respond" on the spot and thereby make conflict overt.[3] But the letter itself was a public gesture. Shepard informed Cotton that it was not only his desire to hear Cotton's response but the desire of "diverse of our members" as well.[4] In other words, Shepard had put his authority on the line with his congregation in his grave accusation of crypto-heresy, and he could not back down without losing face. The only acceptable response would have been Cotton's doctrinal surrender, which was not an auspicious way to start a dialogue.

Cotton responded temperately enough, given that a relatively unknown minister twenty years his junior all but accused him of preaching a heresy that puritan divines had been denouncing for half a century. He had inquired in his congregation, and he was confident that no brethren or sisters held forth Christ any differently than he did—the most radical opinions Shepard mentioned had been offered only as inquiries, and Cotton had warned against accepting them. Shepard had misinterpreted some of the points of his sermon, and Cotton was not only unaware of any quarrel between himself and his ministerial brethren, but he doubted that there was any disagreement "if wee understand each other"—a polite invitation to Shepard to retreat. But he did not miss the undertone of Shepard's letter. He cautioned Shepard not to compare the "faithfull practise" of Christians to familist "delusion" and warned that he was not going to change his preaching in response to Shepard's doctrinal saber rattling.[5]

Cotton's response might have been temperate, but he had not backed down, and Shepard was not about to either. Now what had previously been at most a "secret quarrel" fostered by lay people was an open ministerial collision. Moreover, Shepard's sweeping broadside ensured that Cotton and his supporters would interpret any attack on more radical lay opinions as a coded attack on Cotton himself, an interpretation for which Shepard would continue to provide ample justification. No less important, the relentless insistence of Shepard (and others) that Cotton's doctrines significantly departed from the puritan mainstream would gradually convince Cotton that his critics were correct; the one surviving example of Cotton's preaching from the first half of 1636 blends his theological peculiarities almost inconspicuously into the larger universe of conventional puritan doctrine and rhetoric, whereas a year later and after much sustained attack, Cotton portrayed the difference between him and the mainstream as the difference between salvation and damnation.[6] Peace would not begin to return to Massachusetts until ministers were able to allow that there could be disagreements with Cotton that did not necessarily implicate him in lay heterodoxy, an allowance that Shepard himself never managed.

It might seem straightforward enough, even generic, for Sheppard to challenge Cotton about his theological idiosyncrasies. Religious tolerance was not generally considered a virtue in the early seventeenth century, and for a devout Protestant to imagine the Bible speaking in anything but one doctrinal voice was to imagine nihilism. The prominent theologian William Ames, who himself almost came to New England, put it starkly: if the Scriptures did not have one clear meaning, "there would be no meaning at all—for anything which does not mean one thing surely means nothing." Doctrine helped define God's true visible church, and since puritans to a pronounced degree tended to elide the true visible church with the invisible church of God's elect, correct doctrine helped define the contemporary community of the saints.[7] At the same time, it also defined the enemies of the godly by clarifying the boundaries past which loomed awful heresies—antinomianism, familism, Arminianism, popery, Socinianism—that served as polemical Others against which the godly constructed themselves.

Ministers also had self-interested reasons to be concerned about fraternal doctrinal deviants like Cotton. Reformed divines pictured themselves as the highly trained channels by which God through the Bible explained himself to the laity. Thus a ministerial interpretive united front was critical to their authority. As the prominent London minister Edward Elton put it, "When teachers meete together in one truth . . . it doth free the teachers from the note and blemish of lightnesse and newfangled giddinesse, and that they teach not opinions of private fancie . . . if we follow factions, some hold of one and some of another, we shall be brought to that exigent, that we must either confesse Christ to be divided (a thing impossible) or our selves to be no members of Christ, and that we are carnall." John Cotton's Massachusetts brethren at the end of 1636 beseeched him that "we all may think and speak and preach the very same thing." Otherwise, they warned Cotton, their listeners "will be not a little disheartned and unsetled." Given that evangelical English Protestants not infrequently found themselves bitterly quarreling with each other, ministers might occasionally strike a more realistic note about doctrinal unanimity. Arthur Hildersham cautioned "it is a thing greatly to be wisht & sought after, that all Gods servants might be of one judgement in all points . . . yet it can never be attained in this life." But the acknowledgment of irreducible diversity was inevitably grudging. John Norton, Cotton's successor at the Boston church, had serious theological differences with both Cotton and Thomas Hooker. Yet the only concession he could make to this range of opinions among the obviously godly was that "some difference touching the truth must be endured, because of the weakness of man."[8]

Assurance was a doctrinal topic especially likely to strain the puritan capacity for diversity. Varieties in doctrines of assurance carried varying practical implications that could be seen as reinforcing or subverting the social and religious order, as well as the strong puritan drive to holiness: Could assurance come through reading and meditation or did it come only through ministerial preaching? Was it a once-and-for-all event or did it require ongoing attendance on the ordinances of the church? Should one continue to doubt after assurance, or should one never question one's salvation, even if fallen into a heinous sin?

In England the strain between the diversity of paths to assurance and the commitment to theological unity had mounted over the two decades prior to Shepard's letter. Culverwell's arguments about the priority of absolute promises formed part of sometimes vituperative debates in the early 1620s over absolute and conditional promises. Assurances of salvation was one of the issues in the bitter London clashes between radical antinomian/familist ministers and their mainstream opponents around 1630, and that clash must have taught a significant number of godly ministers and laity at first- or secondhand to be extremely vigilant for any signs of what they deemed familism or antinomianism. Their vigilance generated conflicts in the puritan mainstream itself. In 1630, the London minister Stephen Denison, a fierce opponent of radical ministers, preached extensively against another puritan minister with close connections to Massachusetts, Philip Nye, for arguing that one should never doubt one's election.[9] It was no accident that Sibbes and other ministers who exalted the witness of the Spirit guarded themselves from criticism by insisting that this should not be confused with enthusiasm or "Anabaptist frenzies."

Thus, the increasingly visible doctrinal irregularities in Massachusetts's chief town and port of entry were a provocation. Nonetheless, the nature of any resulting conflict would be determined in no small part by who chose to be provoked and how. Doctrinal conflicts, even when the specters of familism and antinomianism could be invoked, required individuals determined to trump the practical diversity of the godly with the puritan aspiration for theoretical unity. For example, the mutual abuse of mainstream and "antinomian" ministers in the London antinomian dispute foreshadowed and, to a lesser extent, set the stage for the mutual abuse of the free grace controversy. Yet one of those mainstream ministers, Thomas Taylor, complained when he attacked some "antinomian" leaders that "many . . . doe conceive more slightly of their tenents, and more charitably of their persons than there is cause . . . and [say] that the labour might have beene better bestowed against more dangerous persons, and fundamentall errours much more prejudiciall to the truth of the Gospell." Martha Collins, a member of Shepard's Massachusetts congregation, might have been such a person as Taylor complained of. She mentioned the preaching of the antinomian/familist minister Peter Shaw approvingly when she applied for membership in the Newtowne church. Shaw himself, after a very turbulent time in London, returned to Lancaster and joined its puritan collegiate church. The Grindleton congregation in Yorkshire was a byword for Spirit-obsessed fanaticism, and rumors that people from this church were emigrating to Massachusetts in 1637 were used to justify a repressive immigration law. Yet its minister, Robert Brearley, seems to have been accepted among the godly divines of Yorkshire.[10] The task for ministers like Taylor and, eventually, Shepard was to persuade the godly public, lay and even ministerial, that their opponents really were dangerous persons espousing truly fundamental errors in spite of what might appear to be a considerable range of shared values. The heinousness of opponents needed to be magnified in order to get people to perceive them as opponents, and the process aggravated conflict even in the guise of ending it.

In other words, at what point and on what terms doctrinal differences, a longstanding feature of English hot Protestantism, became intolerable was a matter of perception. Cotton's friend and admirer John Norton, for example, cared strongly enough about the maintenance of orthodoxy that he became the General Court's hammer against heretics in the 1650s. In his biography of Cotton, he acknowledged that had Cotton moved more firmly and swiftly against those in his congregation who denied sanctification, "some disorders, disturbances, and irregularities might have been prevented." But Cotton's own doctrinal singularities Norton, unlike Shepard, was prepared to explain away. It was true, Norton conceded, that some of his tenets were singular, but Cotton was someone whom you forgave a great deal. The "fuller discovery of Truth" would not be possible "except men of a larger Acumen and greater industry [that is, Cotton], may be permitted to communicate their notions, especially whilst . . . they use this liberty by way of disquisition, not of position." Cotton did not insist on his opinions: "no man did more placidly bear a Difference."[11] In other words, because of Cotton's lack of rigidity, his wisdom, and his exemplary godliness, differences with him could be borne. Cotton was to Norton roughly what the more radical members of the Boston congregation were to their own brethren and sisters.

Thus, Shepard was thus not simply the mouthpiece of Massachusetts orthodoxy reacting in an obvious way to an obvious threat when he chose to assimilate Cotton's doctrines to the most radical lay "inquiries." It was always Cotton's heartfelt belief that the free grace controversy blew up to the proportions it did not simply because of errors in his congregation but because some people pursued those errors with "more jealousies, and heates, and paroxymes of spirit, then would well stand with brotherly love, or the rule of the Gospel."[12] There is no reason to doubt Cotton's assessment. As subsequent events showed, Shepard played a critical role in sustaining the free grace controversy, and, as his letter to Cotton demonstrates, he was important in setting the volatile terms on which it was conducted. Why then was Shepard not willing to bear a difference placidly with Cotton?

To a large extent the answer to the question is lost in mysteries of personality that are unrecoverable after four hundred years. Certain ministers simply placed a higher priority on aggressive heresy-hunting than others. Shepard once ominously wrote, "A wise shepard had rather let a hunter come in and kill one of his sheep than let a wolf or fox escape." Moreover, Shepard himself had almost succumbed to the lure of unorthodox doctrines while in college, which undoubtedly sharpened his subsequent ability to see patterns of hardened heresy before they necessarily existed—"I have bin with many [familists]," he urgently told Cotton while unsuccessfully trying to waken this minister he had once idolized to the dangers in his preaching.[13]

Quite apart from personality and personal history, however, there is a doctrinal issue that helps explain why Shepard in particular had such trouble bearing a difference with Cotton and, no less important, why Cotton was to get his back up so stiffly as a consequence. Godly ministers agreed that sinners had to face their utter wickedness before they could genuinely yield themselves to Christ and salvation; they required preparation for justification. "If you never found yourself a firebrand of Hell . . . you were never yet in Jesus Christ," as Cotton put it. Perry Miller in 1943 pointed out that preparation was a critical flash point in the free grace controversy. However, overlooking the difference between preparation and seeking assurance that one had already been justified, he argued that Shepard and others bitterly attacked Cotton because Cotton denied the validity of preparation. Historians accepted Miller's argument until William K. B. Stoever demonstrated, easily enough, that Cotton was a preparationist like the other ministers and their debates revolved around other topics.[14] There may have been questioning of preparation on the fringes of Boston, just as there was in London in the 1630s.[15] There is no evidence, however, that Boston antiprepartionism was a major flash point in the controversy.[16]

That is not to say, however, that prepartionism did not enflame the controversy, for it did. But it was not Cotton's peculiar attitude to preparation that was the issue; it was the peculiar attitude that Shepard shared with Thomas Hooker and perhaps a few other ministers in Massachusetts. Most seventeenth-century ministers, whatever their different emphases, agreed with the highly influential William Perkins that prepartion, though necessary, was not exclusive to the elect; anything prior to justification could be experienced by reprobates bound for hell.[17] In the 1620s prominent Essex divine John Rogers reached back to earlier models when he insisted that the preparation of the elect was qualitatively different from the experience of the damned. In its final stage it included a genuine turning away from sin that most puritans placed after faith. A small Essex coterie, including Hooker, who regarded Rogers as "the prince of all the preachers in England," and Shepard, produced variations on Rogers's argument.[18]

Shepard's ties to Hooker were far more than doctrinal. Hooker placed Shepard in his first English preaching post, eventually became his father-in-law, and shared his dark suspicions about Cotton's fundamental soundness. Hooker and Shepard's fascination with preparation and conditions seems to have gone hand in hand with an inability to intuitively experience grace. Cotton's path was wrong to Shepard not only because it was perilously close to the familism with which Shepard had flirted and violently rejected as an undergraduate; it also attacked the one way Shepard could find any assurance at all. Scholars note that Hooker's writings are far more eloquent on the process of preparation than they are in describing the subsequent union with Christ, and Hooker dismissed even the Sibbesian conception of the witness of the Spirit.[19] It is not out of the question that Hooker encouraged Shepard to attack Cotton—he led an emigration to Connecticut in June 1636 in part, it was believed, because he and Cotton did not get along. Shortly before Hooker left Massachusetts, he disputed Cotton's arguments about assurance from the pulpit. A letter to England in 1637 identified the free grace controversy as between Cotton and Hooker and "their parties," and, as will be shown in subsequent chapters, Hooker, like Shepard, had a pronounced dissatisfaction about its resolution.[20] It is perhaps symbolic that Shepard and his congregation literally took over Newtowne as Hooker and his congregation moved out.

Indeed, the scanty documentation of the free grace controversy suggests that it might have been a Hooker-Rogers network of ministers who were in the forefront of opposition to Boston. The pastor of the Roxbury church, Thomas Weld, a friend of Shepard's from England and with him a close member of Hooker's informal clerical network in Essex, England, was considered an especially aggressive enemy by *Mercurius Americanus*. Wheelwright seems to imply that Weld shared Rogers's conception of preparation. The other minister of that congregation, John Eliot, had been the master at a school Hooker maintained in Essex. The free grace controversy was focused on Boston and its immediate environs, with Roxbury, Boston's neighbor, experiencing the most violent conflicts outside of Boston proper.[21] It may be that Weld and Eliot were the first to react with alarm to what they were catching wind of from Boston and passed the word on to Shepard, leading to Shepard's letter. Perhaps not coincidentally, the only other minister besides Shepard remembered in more than one source as being doctrinally in the forefront of the free grace controversy was John Rogers's son Nathaniel, who arrived in November 1636.[22]

Shepard's doctrinal idiosyncrasies and ministerial allegiances thus gave him an extra incentive to write his letter to Cotton; at the same time they made him particularly inappropriate to be the bearer of difficult news. In practical terms, when ministers were dealing with Christians desperate for signs of salvation, the peculiarities of the Rogers group need not have amounted to anything.[23] The group's emphasis on observable, unique conditions to the covenant of grace even before justification, however, was potentially explosive. While the increasing visibility of radical preachers in London in the 1620s heightened puritan sensitivities to antinomianism/familism, the growing visibility of Arminianism heightened sensitivities to any doctrine that appeared to threaten justification's unconditional nature by emphasizing human works, as more than one godly minister discovered to his cost.[24] Thomas Goodwin, a friend sharing Cotton's theological emphases though not his absolutism, bitterly attacked Hooker's distended conception of preparation in the 1630s, and even more moderate ministers expressed skepticism.[25]

In other words, Shepard and his closest associates were themselves out on something of a doctrinal limb, although not nearly as far as Cotton, and thus when Shepard started leaning on Cotton, he invited Cotton to lean back just as hard. "There are no steps to the altar," Cotton preached in 1637, dismissing Hooker and Shepard's preparationism. In preparation, Shepard preached from his pulpit during the free grace controversy, God is "making me a good tree [for the ingrafting into Christ]"—Cotton replied from his pulpit, "Good trees we cannot be, till we be ingrafted into *Christ*." When pushed and angry enough, Cotton could work himself into considering Hooker and Shepard's doctrine as not only wrong but papist—they were really arguing that people were saved by their own work before justification could take place. Therefore, compromise with them meant betraying the Reformation, and if Hooker and Shepard could assimilate Cotton to Hutchinson's "familism," Cotton could assimilate more conventional ministers to Hooker and Shepard's "legalism." No less critically, the vehemence of the attack against Cotton when combined with the doctrinal idiosyncrasies of those leading the attack reinforced Cotton's solidarity with the radicals in his congregation. As a result, he put off serious, sustained concern about their "inquiries" and their misappropriations of his teachings until they had ample time to become settled in them. Cotton later summed up this crucial dynamic when he explained to a correspondent that he had "endeavoured to make the fayrest and best construction of [the radicals'] speaches so farre as their Words would well beare and the rather because I perceyved, others who opposed them did not therein walk with a right foote according to the Trueth of the Gospell."[26]

Just as effective ministerial rapprochement in the controversy would not take place until divines had clearly separated their quarrel with Cotton from their quarrel with his radical lay brethren, it would not take place until Cotton was willing to allow that Hooker and Shepard's idiosyncrasies fell within the category of weaknesses to be tolerated. Ministerial clashes of this vehemence were not unknown in England, but there they had been contained by divines of sufficient stature to restrain the parties involved. The only minister in New England of Cotton's stature, Thomas Hooker, was hardly going to serve as a peacemaker. In any event he removed himself from Massachusetts.

The confrontational possibilities latent in the doctrinal differences between Shepard and Cotton were exacerbated by an environmental problem that affected both men, and indeed all the immigrants, and one that they had not anticipated in their eagerness to cross the ocean—the peculiar problem of practicing puritan piety in the New World. Shepard himself offered valuable insight into this aspect of the rising tension in Massachusetts. He preached a sermon cycle beginning in June 1636 that ran until 1640 on Matthew 25:1–13, the parable of the wise and foolish virgins. The cycle was shadowed by Shepard's fear that New England harbored an especially virulent strain of a disease that had always haunted puritanism and had been one of the impetuses for ministers to link assurance firmly with sanctification in the first place: slackening of zeal.

Shepard saw in New England two new, related threats to zeal. The first was the unexpected challenge of doing puritanism in a land filled with puritans, and the second the exaggerated expectations puritans had for New England. English puritanism constituted itself in situations of ongoing intense opposition, even while it might occasionally enjoy a local political ascendency. The self-designated godly expected to be a fiercely opposed minority because God had predestined the mass of people to hell, and the ungodly inevitably were implacable enemies to the godly. Even if the godly's neighbors were not initially implacable enemies, they could easily become so after hot Protestants started forcing their program of church and social reform down their throats. "Wheresoever Christ cometh, he breedeth division," as Richard Sibbes put it. It has been suggested that the godly's social perception of themselves as an embattled minority even increased as the Reformation took root in England.[27]

In England when the saints were a persecuted minority, it was easy to maintain fervor and easy to picture New England as utopia. "When men are persecuted by enemies," Shepard said, "driven into corners, or to Towns six miles off to find a Sacrament, or hear a Sermon, then the Gospel of peace, and them that brought the glad-tidings of peace, their feet were beautiful, and then men thought if one Sabbath here so sweet where Ordinances are much corrupted, if some of them be so comfortable in the midst of enemies, Oh how sweet to enjoy them all among Saints, among Friends?" But, he continued, the actual effect of getting in New England what one had dreamed of while in England itself was very different: "New-Englands peace and plenty of means breed strange security."[28]

The strange security of New England, with "no enemy to hunt you to heaven," did not take a single form, according to Shepard. It might manifest itself in neglect of the Gospel as people scrambled to get a living together: "Now want makes men hungry and greedy: and now . . . a man . . . casts himself into the world, and also will not forsake Christ utterly, but bring both into the same heart." Or it might take the form of spiritual burn out: "It was a sad speech of a Brother lately, which has oft affected me," Shepard said, "*that a man may pray out, hear out all the Grace of his Heart.* Would to God there were not a generation of those men among us, that having been so oft Sermon-trod and Prayer-beaten, that now their Hearts are hardned." Either way the result was the same: "Men come over hither for Ordinances, and when they have them, neglect them."[29]

Shepard was not the only one to note the abatement of fervor among New England's puritans. Many of the laity's conversion narratives speak of a sense of spiritual disorientation and deadness upon arrival in Massachusetts. Thomas Hooker, shortly before departing for Connecticut, made a blistering attack on the godly's lack of zeal in New England, comparing it unfavorably with their attitudes under persecution in England.[30] Although a later generation of ministers would insist that the 1630s were a golden age for piety in New England, for at least some influential divines in that decade the golden age lay on the other side of the Atlantic.

New Englands's disease of strange security, most dangerously of all, according to Shepard, could take the form of Boston. His opponents might piously intone, "tis not means . . . but Christ, not duties but Christ," but all they were doing was giving a superficially religious gloss to this larger neglect of means: "Is not Prayer neglected," Shepard went on, "wanting place and heart? if not in family, is it not in secret. . . . What is become of meditation? Dost not let Sabbaths, Sermons pass over?"[31] Cotton and his congregation were to themselves the most zealous of Protestants in the most glorious church in the world. But to Shepard, their decoupling of assurance from a constant stream of inward and outward duties only confirmed his larger anxiety about the New England environment: America exacerbated the perennial puritan problem of the passage of zeal into security or indifference.

Shepard's concern superficially resembles an argument advanced by Perry Miller and others to explain why Cotton and Hutchinson seemed so dangerous to their opponents. These scholars have suggested that in New England, as one puts it, "the balance in preaching shifted [from England] to include frequent proclamations on social order, conditional obedience, and corporate mission," and that Hutchinson and Cotton with their emphasis on assurance through free grace alone failed to appreciate the "new emphasis on civil loyalty and public obedience." The argument is necessarily completely speculative given the paucity of New England sermons surviving from this period.[32] Nonetheless, it has been widely disseminated. Perhaps part of its attraction lies in its providing a "reasonable" (that is nonreligious) explanation for an obscure religious dispute. Like the recently resuscitated argument that the free grace controversy was about guilt-ridden capitalists fleeing their moral responsibilities to the haven of antinomianism, it privileges secular motivations over religious ones, and in both cases, congeniality with the proclivities of the twentieth-century academy overrides evidentiary problems—Kuhnian normal science at work.[33]

In any case, the religious security over which Shepard worried was not the same as civil disloyalty, and all parties to the conflict favored good citizenship. John Wheelwright in his notorious fast-day sermon of January 1637 argued that the public welfare of the colony rested on its heeding his and Cotton's doctrines, while those who opposed them were "the greatest enimyes to the state that can be." Given that members of the Boston congregation were serving as governor of Massachusetts and assistants and deputies to the General Court, the Bostonians can hardly be called "opponents of the New Israel," as one scholar does, unless one starts with the assumption that their enemies had exclusive rights to that title.[34] A variant of this Boston-as-socially-irresponsible thesis asserts that Cotton and Wheelwright did not see themselves as preaching for conversion but only to the converted, a claim that would have rightly offended both ministers.[35]

Moreover, it would be inaccurate to associate disorder, either religious or civil, exclusively with Boston or Boston doctrines. When Shepard described the letdown of zeal that he perceived around him, he was also, and perhaps even in the first instance, projecting his struggle to maintain his own zeal in this strange new world. Shepard in England had experienced to the hilt the construction of piety in an unstable and oppositional context. There he had first served as a temporary lecturer until Laud drove him out. From 1630, he moved from place to place in the north of England, never remaining long at any one location. Unlike many of the colony's ministers, Shepard for the first time in his career found himself in a stable and routine situation. If the zeal of Shepard's piety could be sustained only by the creation of a rich array of negative references and crisis points, and if the familiar ones of England were missing, then he would need to devise new ones.

Cotton's unusual church might arguably have been a genuine menace to the peace and stability of the New England churches, especially since those churches had a hard time conceptualizing legitimate disagreement. But it was also useful as a menace. If hell delighted in creating divisions among churches, those who set off divisions were, by definition, as Shepard would later say outright, hell's agents, who might be otherwise in short supply in a colony full of saints. Indians could also serve in a pinch. The colony was gearing up for war in 1635 and 1636 with the Pequot Indians of southern Connecticut for reasons that have eluded both historians and contemporaries—the most recent historian of the war has accounted for it in part in terms of the puritan need for opponents.[36]

The need for new sources of goats from whom the godly sheep could separate themselves helps account for the single most striking feature of the emergent New England church order in the mid-1630s, and the one most baffling to English puritans, the requirement that prospective church members publicly testify to a work of grace within their souls. Previously, members had to only give a confession of faith and lead an outwardly holy life.[37] This new daunting requirement resulted in somewhere around half the adult poopulation being excluded from the sacraments in the late 1630s. Shepard noted unsympathetically the laments of these bewildered immigrants discovering that they were not puritan enough for Massachusetts: "Many complain [they] are not respected, they are no body; they had this and that esteem in their own Country of such Ministers, Christians, and were of this esteem; now the market is fallen . . . and cannot pass for members in many Churches." But he himself extolled the Massachusetts church admissions process as foreshadowing Christ's rejection of the damned at the Last Judgment.[38] Add together Boston, Pequots, the church members whom you could berate for slackening in fervency, and the would-be saints being kept at arms's length, and you had a rough-and-ready New World replacement, suitably dire enough in its own way, for the English social landscape that inspired puritan zeal.

Shepard himself in 1636 recognized that the godly in Massachusetts created enemies out of their brethren for lack of other targets. Not too many months after he wrote his all-or-nothing letter to Cotton, he warned against "decaying in love to those whom Christ loves." Shepard cautioned that "Temptation is strong in this place" to do just that "1. Because we have multitudes of them. . . . 2. Because there wants a common enemy to drive them together." The result of this overcrowding, lack of enemies, and subsequent decaying of love, Shepard said, were "your petty Duels and jars in Churches, surmisings, censurings, &c."[39]

Had Shepard thought longer and harder about the problems inherent in maintaining oppositional piety when large numbers of saints were put in close quarters, the free grace controversy might never have reached the level of virulence it did.

Secular explanation, however, was not Shepard's preferred type. He more frequently understood conflict as stemming from "the delight of Hell to set & see Churches at variance among themselves." His solution did not involve mutual toleration but ideological purity and vigilance for the first signs of deviation: "Love the Truth, receive no opinion differing from the most approved in the Church suddenly, but weep, and pray, and ask counsel, and tremble to entertain a thought of contention."[40] Shepard would continue to tremble at the thought of contention until he had finally driven Hutchinson out of the Boston church and had exhausted his efforts to convince his brethren that Cotton preached familism.

Those whom he was attacking had many positive stimuli to zeal, but they felt the same push toward a disorienting security as the rest of the colonists. Cotton remarked that "when Christians come into this Country, though they have been marvellous eminent in our native Country, yet here they cannot pray fervently, nor heare the word with profit." Like Shepard and Hooker, he worried that people would grow too complacent "in this Countrey of universall Profession." While puritan ministers routinely warned that the practices of piety in themselves did not demonstrate salvation, the extremity of Cotton's warnings might have come in part from an effort to recover a minority-status confrontational edge lost in a land where those practices were officially encourgaged.[41]

Along these lines, if the creation of opponents was an attractive way to deal with the strange security of New England, then perhaps therein lay Hutchinson's single most important contribution to the free grace controversy. She had already worked out a scheme that dismissed the validity of most ministers' preaching; she had shared her viewpoint with Simmes while crossing the Atlantic; and at least after a little while she had no hesitation about sharing her appraisal with others. Whatever else her repetitions of Cotton's sermons did, they magnified the difference between his doctrines and those of the other ministers. It may have been at the same time as Shepard was darkly intimating that Cotton preached familism that Hutchinson and those around her started aggressively disseminating the opinion that all of Massachusetts's ministers except Cotton and Wheelwright taught a covenant of works. Hutchinson claimed at her trial that the minister Nathaniel Ward once said to her that Cotton's way was the "nearest way" but asked her, "will you not acknowledge that which we hold forth to be a way too wherein we may have hope?" Had she been able to bring herself to answer yes, it is highly unlikely that Boston's hottest enemies could have rallied the forces necessary for a major and potentially self-destructive confrontation. "No truly if that be a way it is a way to hell," she replied to Ward.[42]

Hutchinson's effect on the Boston congregation as a whole was thus probably not so much to cause them to embrace any of her distinctive positions as to encourage them to perceive that there was a critical gap between Cotton's way of finding assurance and that taught by most of Massachusetts's ministers. That contrast only heightened their appreciation of how wonderful their own church was. William Hubbard claimed that only a few in the Boston congregation were seriously involved in doctrinal errors; he clearly did not picture the mass of the congregation as "Hutchinsonians." However, he also said that because of these errors "many" were inspired with a "seditious and turbulent spirit" and were "ready to challenge all, that did not run with them, to be legal Christians." Cotton himself indicated as much, after things had calmed down. The resulting controversy created a refreshingly familiar stimulus to piety. As Boston radical John Underhill told an English audience, explaining to it the necessity of conflict, even in pure churches, "Do we not ever find, the greater the afflictions and troubles of God's people be, the more eminent is his grace in the souls of his servants?"[43]

Shepard's aggressive, sweeping letter to Cotton thus had strong personal pietist motivation behind it; perhaps no less of an encouragement to its composition was that Massachusetts brimmed with policing possibilities not available in England, and Shepard was already showing himself adept at using them. Puritan empowerment in Massachusetts heightened the millenarian extravagance of Boston. Yet even as that empowerment fostered speculation and diversity, it held out the possibility of an ideological control unimaginable for puritans in England, where their access to official mechanisms of power had always been problematic. English circumstances compelled puritans to endure differences about doctrine. In Massachusetts, with the government ruled by godly magistrates, "nursing fathers" to the Gospel, perhaps they would not have to.[44] The puritan settlement of Massachusetts started out in 1629, after all, with the expulsion of two members of the company who had wanted to worship with the Book of Common Prayer.

Moreover, Shepard arrived at a time when unity was a burning question for the government, for a variety of interrelated external and internal reasons. The very legal survival of the colony was one of these, and this particular issue would soon become deeply interwoven into the free grace controversy. In 1628, puritan entrepreneurs procured a patent with generous boundaries for the colony from the Council for New England, perhaps through the conniving of sympathetic council member the earl of Warwick. The only problem with these boundaries was that they intruded on lands already granted to Robert Gorges, son of Sir Ferdinando Gorges, prime mover behind the council. Having gone behind Gorges's back to get their patent from the council, the puritans sealed their dubious acquisition in a charter for a new company, the Massachusetts Bay Company, granted by Charles I in 1629. It is unsurprising that thereafter Gorges devoted much of his energy to having the charter revoked. And it is no more surprising that in the increasingly hostile atmosphere of Charles's court he started to meet with success.[45]

The opening salvo in the attack on Massachusetts's charter reached the colony in June 1634 in the form of a letter from ex–Massachusetts Bay Company governor Matthew Craddock transmitting a Privy Council order to return the charter. The General Court chose to ignore the request and instead improved the colony's defenses. News that trouble was likely to continue arrived later in the fall via the same ship that brought Anne Hutchinson. With her came a letter announcing the formation of the Royal Commission for Regulating Plantations, headed by Archbishop Laud. The commission had, in principle, final power over all colonies. Rumor had it that a ship with troops was being fitted out to come over and compel the colony to take a governor-general and accept the discipline of the Church of England and perhaps even a bishop. The colony poured out its prayers before the "Divine throne" while setting up a war council, regularly drilling the train bands, and fortifying Boston harbor. To ensure solidarity, it required that all men over the age of twenty take an oath of allegiance to the government.[46]

Despite the defiant response, the threat to Massachusetts's charter set nerves on edge. When two unidentified ships were sighted at Salem shortly after news of the impending governor-general arrived, the train bands in Boston and adjacent towns mobilized: "[T]he generall and Publick report was that it was to oppose the landing of an Enemie, a Governour sent from England."[47] There was good reason for nervousness to increase. In the summer of 1635, Charles announced his intention to appoint Ferdinando Gorges governor-general and the attorney general initiated quo warranto proceedings against the Massachusetts charter. It is likely that Vane's speedy ascent to the governorship was due at least in part to the desire to have someone so well connected at Charles's court in that crucial position at that crucial time.

Even as external circumstances made unity urgent, internal circumstances threatened it. In the mid-1630s, Massachusetts's leaders were discovering that managing the anarchic streak in hot Protestantism was not necessarily any easier for puritans than it was for Laud. In November 1634 Captain John Endicott cut the Cross of Saint George out of the royal ensign at Salem as a protest against idolatry. His removal of this "badge of the Whore of Babelon" roused a great deal of popular sympathy, but it was easily interpreted as blatant subversion of royal authority. Vane proved the sensibleness of electing him governor when he deftly worked out a compromise between local zealots who had removed the Cross everywhere and English sailors angry at its absence.[48]

Endicott was a minor issue, however, compared to the reemergence of Roger Williams. Williams, a charismatic young minister whose zealotry sublimely transcended any grounding in practical politics, had arrived in 1631 and almost immediately started creating trouble. He demanded that the churches of Massachusetts publicly repent the communion they had with the Church of England, the very last issue with which these puritans desperate to prove to their English brethren that they were not separatists wanted to deal. Moreover, he insisted that the magistrates had control only over secular matters, not religious ones, a proposition that to most European magistrates was little short of blasphemy. He was tucked safely away in Plymouth colony for a few years, but he returned to Salem in 1634. Williams added to his old doctrines the argument that the Massachusetts charter was void; the king had no right to have granted it in the first place, for Massachusetts belonged to the Indians, not him. At the same time, he argued for the spiritual unlawfulness of the General Court's oath of allegiance, and under his influence, "sundry" refused to take it.[49]

Small wonder that by the end of 1634, Massachusetts's leaders increasingly saw the need for a campaign of ideological control running parallel with the colony's defense measures against the enemies of its charter. They accordingly started deploying, as well as fashioning when necessary, the theoretical and practical weapons they would soon use against each other during the free grace controversy. Each church in Massachusetts was, by the colony's congregationalist principles, autonomous, but how far did that autonomy stretch in practice? At the beginning of December, the General Court sent Cotton and Hooker to extract an apology from John Eliot for criticizing the magistrates from the pulpit; if they had failed to get it, Eliot would have faced an appearance before the Court. On March 4, 1635, the General Court asked the elders of the churches to establish a "uniform order of discipline" and requested that they consider how far the magistrates could intervene in church affairs in the interest of order and peace. Probably in response, Cotton and other ministers drew up an elaborate "Model of Church and Civil Power," declaring that magistrates were "nursing fathers" empowered to defend the true worship of God, as determined by the churches meeting in synods. They invited the magistrates to monitor the gathering of churches and to set up a college to provide the churches with officers[50]

Williams and the Salem church goaded Massachusetts's ministerial and magisterial elite to move further in developing both repressive theory and practice. In 1635, Salem, in the face of pressure to conform, defiantly asserted "that a church wholly declining in arianism, papism, familism or in other heresies, being admonished, and convinced thereof by other churches, and not reforming, may not be reformed by the civil magistrate." Cotton and his two ruling elders, Thomas Oliver and Thomas Leverett, sent an admonition to the Salem church confuting its assertion. On the practical side, the Court withheld a grant of land from Salem as punishment for making Williams their teacher. The Salem church responded by sending letters to the other churches accusing the magistrates and deputies of a heinous sin that invited God's vengeance.[51]

The General Court, like all seventeenth-century English governing bodies, did not take kindly to having its decisions impugned. In September, it suspended Salem's deputies until the town disclaimed its letter. John Endicott hastily reconsidered his own defiant defense of the letter when threatened with jail, and when Williams followed up with a belligerent letter to the Salem church, the Court sentenced him to banishment for his letters and his opinions. The authorities planned to send him back to England at the beginning of 1636, but someone, in all likelihood Winthrop, tipped him off, and he went instead to Narragansett Bay. At the meeting of reconciliation that Vane and Hugh Peters arranged between Winthrop and Dudley shortly thereafter, the assembled ministers and magistrates criticized Winthrop for his leniency. They agreed that henceforth the magistrates should rule more sternly and take care to present a united facade to the rest of the colonists, "as the voyce of God." In 1636, newly elected Governor Vane wrote a letter to the Salem constable warning him to suppress separatist conventicles in his town or face government intervention.[52]

It cannot be a coincidence that the requirement for conversion narratives commenced as the move against religious variety got underway in 1634 and 1635. Whatever their other purposes, they allowed doctrinal orthodoxy to be inspected in a way impossible in England, a purpose that Shepard fostered. On February 1, 1636, he gathered his church at Newtowne in an elaborate and carefully observed ceremony attended by magistrates and elders, part of which involved Shepard and six others making confessions of faith and giving conversion narratives, on the advice of the other ministers present. It is hard to imagine it as coincidental that this gathering took place two weeks after ministers and magistrates agreed that henceforth the magistrates would govern with more reserve, strictness, ceremony, and facade of unity. On March 3 the General Court codified the procedure Shepard used in gathering his church by passing an order requiring that churches wishing to gather notify the Court and church elders. The unprecedentedly large immigration of roughly 2,000 people the previous year, swelling the colony's population by half, may have given urgency to this order, as well as to the government's other efforts to assert its authority.[53]

A month after the order was passed, on April 1, Shepard was at the forefront of halting the gathering of Richard Mather's Dorchester church. After questioning the would-be lay founders, he deemed that the conversion narratives of three of them indicated that they might not have had genuine conversions. They had made, according to Shepard, two mistakes. The first was that they relied unconsciously on their own righteousness, which probably means that they had spoken, as two generations of puritan ministers had encouraged them to do, of the evidence of their sanctification as signs of their justification. The other mistake was that they evidenced their justification by "fits and dreams." Having blocked the church, Shepard wrote to Mather, nine years older and a much more experienced minister, reassuring him that Shepard had no doubt that Mather himself was among the saved. Mather wrote back thanking Shepard for his intervention and blamed the affair on the hasty importunities of his congregation. Historians are sometimes prone to see dark intimations of Arminian and antinomian impulses in the narrations.[54] William Hubbard later gave a simpler and more probable explanation of what went wrong. The would-be visible saints failed simply "through unaquaintedness with the nature of the thing desired." Neither Mather nor his congregation realized that what was expected was something other than accounts of the various methods by which they found assurance. Instead they were to produce narratives of their conversions, something that English critics of New England insisted would be a hard thing for many genuine Christians to do ever, let alone when the expectation was not clear to begin with. Five months later when, according to Hubbard, they had been "better informed about the nature of what was expected from them," the church was gathered without any problem. They had pulled themselves in line sufficiently to meet the expectations of Shepard and the Massachusetts authorities, which was much more than could yet be said about Boston.[55]

Shepard wrote his ominous letter to Cotton in a fast-growing, if fragile, colony, and one increasingly well suited to detect and act against ideological deviance, thanks in part to his ability to capture the ears of the magistrates. His personal and theological idiosyncrasies made him disposed to see threats where others may not have noticed them, and the aggressiveness of his attack on Cotton may be partly explained by his being the front man for Hooker's transplanted Essex circle of ministers. Having seen those threats, Shepard framed his dispute with Cotton in a way most suited to realize the dangers he needed to combat. Shepard's congregation was being encouraged to perceive that the Word and ordinances of God were under deadly assault by Cotton and his congregation, and, as will be shown, they learned the lesson well. Even as Shepard accused Cotton and his admirers of propagating familism, lay zealots among the Bostonians were probably already writing off most of the colony's ministers as under a covenant of works, while Shepard's own doctrinal peculiarities gave that charge some force. The charge made it easier for Cotton to overlook that some members of the Boston congregation were participating in heterodox "inquiries" with the new governor's encouragement and participation, and this not in some obscure new settlement, but in "the most publick [church], where Seamen and all Strangers came."[56] It would take little prophetic skill to predict that the "secret quarrels" of which Shepard warned Cotton were not to remain secret for long.

FIVE

SECRET QUARRELS TURN PUBLIC

SUMMER 1636–JANUARY 1637

COTTON MAY have optimistically told Shepard that he and his brethren did not differ, but his assumption was to be sorely tested in the second half of 1636. Doctrinal debates in a wide variety of venues raged among the leaders of the colony and among ordinary laity. Participants in those debates moved uneasily between efforts to restore consensus and stoke contentions, to dampen conflict and amplify it. Some participants genuinely sought common ground. Some, however, had already decided that the differences in Massachusetts were fundamental, and they worked hard to get others to share their conclusion. The debates failed to resolve differences; rather, they confirmed and magnified them. As a consequence, participants increasingly concluded that their brethren were dangerously deluded and perhaps not brethren at all, but heretics. By the beginning of 1637, the debates had deadlocked, the first blows had been exchanged, and broad party lines had formed. Participants put their energy into defining their enemies, in preparation for mobilizing against them.

The documentation for the commencement of this broad process of polarization is both extremely sparse and impressionistic. The layman Edward Johnson returned to the colony in the summer of 1636 after a five-year absence. To his surprise, he found himself in the midst of a heated controversy, which he eventually described over a decade later in his history of New England. Johnson wrote his account as an unabashed partisan. Of all the authors who depicted the free grace controversy, he was the most concerned to portray it, in order to dismiss it, as social rebellion: lay people against ministers; ignorance against learning; women against the authority of men. Johnson went to great pains to keep out any information that might complicate his portrayal: Vane's role was discussed in one line of an otherwise flattering verse, and the line would mean nothing to the uninformed reader; Wheelwright appeared only twice, once as a pun and once in a veiled, brief allusion to his banishment; and the reader was referred to Cotton's massively self-serving reply to Robert Baillie for insight into his involvement.[1] Nevertheless, Johnson's account of his initial exposure to the controversy because of its affective charge has the ring of truth, if not literal accuracy.

Johnson met with some "Erronists" after he landed—the immigrants coming into Massachusetts usually stayed in Boston while getting oriented, a situation that greatly magnified the visibility and destabilizing potential of its doctrinal diversity. The erronists urged Johnson to meet Anne Hutchinson. She surpassed the ministers in spite of all their learning, they told him, and "admit that [the ministers] may speake by the helpe of the spirit, yet the other goes beyond them"—it is unlikely that the erronists made no mention of Wheelwright or Cotton. A "little nimble tongued Woman" told Johnson that Hutchinson would show him a way, "if I could sustain it," that would be "full of such ravishing joy" that he would "never have cause to be sorry for sinne." She had already attained this state, meaning perhaps that she had passed from the work of the Son to the work of the Holy Spirit. But she warned Johnson, "A company of legall Professors . . . lie poring on the Law which Christ hath abolished, and when you breake it then you breake your joy, and now no way will serve your turne but a deepe sorrow."[2] Whether the woman actually said that Christ had abolished the moral law, which would make her literally an antinomian, or whether she meant that he had abolished the covenant of works for the elect, there is no way of knowing. Perhaps it was not an important distinction for her. But her practical meaning was clear enough—do not look to your sanctification for assurance, for it will continually fail you, and then there will be nothing for it except a desperate plea for Christ's mercy.

The woman undoubtedly viewed herself as offering Johnson a release from the ministers' conflicted treadmill of guilt and anxiety. What Johnson heard, however, only made him more anxious, for that treadmill was an essential ingredient of his piety. He could not conceive of the Christian path as anything but an ongoing ethically based struggle: "What is the whole life of a Christian upon this Earth?" he portrayed himself as soliloquizing upon hearing her and others, "But through the power of Christ to die to sinne and live to holinesse and righteousnesse, and for that end to be diligent in the use of means." The "glasse of the Law" daily exposed to him his "sinfull corrupt nature" and by contrast magnified the "free grace of Christ."[3] The ongoing discovery of his own weakness was for Johnson the opportunity to experience the power of Christ in the evidence of his faith and sanctification. If he could not rely on this discovery but instead had to depend on something as ineffable as the Holy Spirit's delivering an absolute promise, he would lose the source of all his comfort.

Confused and contemplating returning to England, Johnson made his way along the narrow Indian path from Charlestown to Newtowne, where the beating of a drum alerted him that the Thursday lecture had begun. He hastened to the meetinghouse to find Thomas Shepard, "a poore weake pale complectioned man," preaching the sermon cycle he had begun in June on the parable of the ten virgins. Shepard was a vivid, urgent preacher, and much of what Johnson might have heard would have been congenial to Boston. Shepard spoke of the reciprocal love and desire of Christ and the saints in lengthy passages whose erotic imagery has long attracted historians slogging through the alien wordscapes of puritan sermons. Assurance sounded not like the product of struggle and self-scrutiny but simply a matter of wanting it badly enough. And yet he outlined in fastidious and frightening detail the many minute and virtually undetectable ways in which would-be Christians could fool themselves that they were married to Christ when they were in fact married to the Law. Hutchinson could not have spread fear better among the women of Boston. It is not surprising that of all the ministerial preaching of false doctrine in Massachusetts, she liked Shepard's the best.[4]

The cycle in its entirety, however, was in oppositional counterpoint to, and not infrequently a polemical attack on, Boston's lay and ministerial opinions. Shepard's frequently reiterated bottom line was that Boston's methods of assurance, inaccessible to him, were the refuge of false Christians. Very early on,[5] he denounced those who thought that "if a man fasts, prayes, watches against his distempers, mourns for want of Christ and Grace, and follows God hard here, he is a legal Christian." That opinion, according to Shepard, could only come from "a servant of corruption." Those who denied evidencing justification by sanctification, he claimed, did so because they had never felt the power of sanctification; they were not among the saints, in other words. Shepard covered this attack with only the slightest of fig leaves: "I know not whether it be thus with any, but if I did, I would pity them."[6]

Shepard aimed his early jabs not only at Boston lay radicals such as Johnson encountered but at Cotton himself. He acknowledged that "very few living Christians have any settled comfortable evidence of Gods eternal love to them in his Son." Nonetheless, Cotton taught a false way of assurance. "Though there is an immediate witness of the Spirit of the love of Christ," said Shepard, repeating the argument of Sibbes and Preston, "yet it doth most usually and firstly witness by means."[7]

If Shepard's message was hardly nonconfrontational, the method by which he disseminated it was hardly discreet. In England, lecture days were a part of puritanism's "festive" culture, with magistrates, ministers, and ordinary godly lay people traveling great distances together to attend the lectures of noted preachers. This tradition continued in New England. Cotton Mather told of how John Wilson would lead large companies of "Christians," including ministers and magistrates, to neighboring lectures, all the while preparing them with his "heavenly discourses." Massachusetts's Christians might have left the lectures in groups, as was the practice in England, singing psalms and going over the sermon. Lectures were popular enough that the General Court made abortive attempts to limit them in 1634 and 1639, claiming that they were burdensome to ministers, audience, and the economy.[8] Expressing an opinion at a lecture was the fastest way a minister could disseminate it throughout the colony.

Thus, it was not simply circumstances but escalating partisan appeals to Massachusetts's godly public that brought Johnson to Newtowne. For Johnson, Shepard's appeal proved the most persuasive. Johnson listened transformed while the hourglass was turned over twice and Shepard cleared Christ's work in the soul from "all those false Doctrines which the erronious party had afrighted him withall." Lest his tears should show, Johnson hung his head, and by the sermon's end, he was ready "to live and die with the Ministers of New England."[9]

The "Ministers of New England" that fall did not confine their engagement to the pulpit. On October 25, at last seven of them met, at their initiative, with Cotton, Wheelwright, and Wilson for a critical conference at Cotton's house, along with Boston lay people including Hutchinson, church elder Thomas Leverett, and deacon John Coggeshall. There are two different versions of the ministers' reasons for the meeting, but Hutchinson figures prominently in both of them. Salem's minister, Hugh Peters, later testified that they came to Cotton's house concerned by charges, in which Hutchinson was allegedly a "chief agent," that their ministry, unlike Cotton's, "was not according to the Gospel." The ministers wished to go on with their grievances directly to the magistrates at the colony's General Court then in session at the Boston meetinghouse. Cotton, however, persuaded them to call for Hutchinson. Winthrop in his journal gave a different, more moderate version of the ministers' intentions, claiming that they wanted to learn more about Hutchinson's and Wheelwright's opinions that they, in proper New Testament manner, might write to the Boston church, if necessary, to warn it of the danger it, along with the other churches, was in.[10]

These two accounts probably reflect a diversity of reasons among the ministers as to why they were there. Peters himself might have been keen for a swift crackdown, since he had the unenviable task of taming Salem, backed by the muscle of the General Court, after its seven years of separatist and semi-separatist ministers. Angry disputes and unfavorable comparisons with Boston preaching may have already begun in Thomas Weld and John Eliot's Roxbury, adjacent to Boston Zechariah Simmes was to have a large contingent of Boston sympathizers in Charlestown, directly across the Charles River from Boston, although he proved a good deal more successful than Weld and Eliot in avoiding irreparable head-on conflict with them. Thomas Shepard had started preaching against lay and clerical Boston errors. Not all the ministers, however, came out of firsthand experience for Cotton recalled that at the meeting's end, some of them told him "they would not so easily believe reports as they had done." One of the ministers, George Philips of Watertown, even said that the other ministers had procured his presence without his "being privy to the ground."[11] It may not be a coincidence that six of the seven ministers were old Essex friends and acquaintances.

The ministers first discussed doctrine, and then Cotton suggested that Hutchinson be called. She came and, after prompting, presented her viewpoint, or as much of it as she was prepared to share with this particular audience. A number of ministers recalled her saying that they preached a covenant of works, which may have been their inference in this instance, but they insisted that she had said they were not able ministers of the New Testament. She told the ministers that they mistakenly preached the seal of the Spirit on a work. They were like the apostles before Christ's Resurrection and Ascension, for they had not yet been properly sealed with the Spirit. Shepard had not been sealed, she informed him, because he preached love as an evidence of justification. Some persons present, including Cotton and ruling elder Thomas Leverett and even perhaps some of the other ministers, did not hear her as saying anything horribly shocking; being compared to Christ's disciples was not on the face of it the worst thing a minister could have said about him. Moreover, some ministers were probably more capable than others of shrugging off what might have seemed simply maladroit, even silly observations by an untrained lay person—Hutchinson at one point told a minister she had never heard that he had not been properly sealed. But Shepard was suspicious enough to shortly thereafter defend the pre-pentecostal apostles from the pulpit: "Why, had the Disciples no spirit now . . . tho' they were not as yet sealed, yet they knew . . . that Christ was their's."[12]

Shepard, in fact, had reason to be suspicious, for Hutchinson's comparison of the the ministers and the apostles came out of a deep, copious, and frequently acidic underground spring of lay theological speculation. The key to that spring lies not with Hutchinson but with Henry Vane and a theological treatise he published in 1655, *The Retired Mans Meditations*. The treatise has been ignored in studies of the free grace controversy, but it is of considerable importance. It is the only surviving document of any length from a Boston lay voice explicating, on its own terms, the themes of the free grace controversy—union with Christ, the nature of assurance, and, most critically in terms of the ministerial conference, why seemingly godly ministers would resist Gospel truth and persecute the saints.[13]

The answer to that last question lies in Vane's elaborate account of the covenants of grace and works, apparently broadly sketched out in Massachusetts.[14] Very freely adapting second-generation Reformed teachings about Christ's active and passive obedience to God, he argued that Christ himself made the covenant of works operative because of his perfect active obedience to God's commands in his earthly life. But Christ transcended his human activity on the Cross and surrendered passively to God's will. Christ's surrender initiated the covenant of grace, which was sealed at Pentecost. Shepard attacked elements of this argument in his 1636 letter to Cotton, as well he might. It had anti-Trinitarian implications—Vane was not a timid theologian—that Vane later openly explored when the consequence of losing a debate over the Trinity was not likely to be a bonfire. Pragmatic reasons may explain why it does not show up again in Massachusetts sources.[15]

Since Christ himself activated the covenant of works, it was a necessary and valuable stage for Christians to go through. From the righteousness of Christ's "natural perfection," partakers of the covenant of works, Vane stated, might through their free will enjoy the "restauration and renewal of mans first nature, given to *Adam* by creation, and corrupted by the fall." God did not impute to them their past sins and forgave them their present ones. Moreover the fruit of this justification was a real sanctification. Christ was in their souls and they enjoyed union with him. The covenant of works was a "birth . . . of holy and righteous operations and actings."[16] No one, not even Cotton, put quite so positive a spin on this covenant.

Yet that positive spin made it potentially all the more lethal. The covenant of works, for believers no less than for Christ, was only a "preparative administration," or a "first step and degree of the new birth" into the covenant of grace, as someone (probably Vane) argued in Massachusetts. People under it would inevitably sin again, and by its terms, their sinning meant that Satan obtained their souls. The most insidious of Satan's lures was to make people in the covenant of works assume, as they looked for marks and signs of salvation within themselves, that they were in fact in the covenant of grace. Puffed up by the holiness of their lives and by their great spiritual achievements, they would become convinced that their preparatory knowledge of Christ was the only true knowledge. They would inevitably then turn to persecuting those who were genuinely in the covenant of grace—just as Shepard and others were starting to do in 1636.[17]

And here is where Vane can clarify a crucial element in Hutchinson's teaching—the nature of the voice of Antichrist that was revealed to her in her English fast. He explained that voice once to Winthrop—or made a gesture at explaining, since the explanation hinged on knowing how Vane was using a critical verse from Hutchinson's fast, 1 John 4:3: "[E]very spirit that testifieth not that Jesus Christ is come in the flesh . . . is that spirit of antichrist." The voice of Antichrist was the voice of those in the covenant of works who had lost sight of the transitory nature of their covenant. Instead of its being a preparation for the coming of Christ in the flesh through the seal of the Holy Spirit, the work of John the Baptist, it became a covenant of damnation, the work of Antichrist, in which those for whom it was terminal would attack those who were in the covenant of grace.[18]

Thus, when Hutchinson told the ministers interrogating her that they were like the apostles before the Resurrection and Ascension, she could be understood in a number of ways, as she very likely intended. She might be understood as articulating Cotton's doctrine. The ministers were Christians under the Son's work who had not yet experienced the Holy Ghost in its full force. We know that people in Boston at the time were measuring their brethren with this yardstick.[19] But Hutchinson herself probably meant a great deal more. She signified that the ministers were still tangled in the covenant of works, which is essentially what the "nimble-tongued woman" told Johnson. Perhaps this was only a passing stage in their spiritual development, but if the ministers persisted in preaching like the apostles before Pentecost and persisted in harassing those like Hutchinson who truly understood the meaning of Christ's coming in the flesh, they preached no longer with the voice of John the Baptist but with the voice of Antichrist.

No need, though, in that October meeting for Hutchinson to go into all the nuances of radical Boston theology to an audience that had not been properly prepared and might not be receptive. Cotton told her that it was regrettable that she made comparisons between the ministers, but, still in his no-disagreements-if-we-understand-each-other mode, he told the assembled ministers that all Hutchinson meant in her speech to them was that "you did hold forth some matter in your preaching that was not pertinent to the seal of the spirit." He certainly heard nothing warranting the negative reactions of some ministers. It was only when Hutchinson was out of Cotton's earshot that she told Nathaniel Ward that the ministers preached a way to hell. One can picture Ward going back to Cotton, Cotton finding himself in an impossible he-said, she-said situation, and, since he himself admired Hutchinson, was under attack by these same ministers, and by now had his own suspicions about the way his brethren preached, giving her the benefit of the doubt, not for the first or last time. It is hard not to agree with a comment Winthrop made later about Hutchinson: she knew very well when to speak and when to be silent. Hutchinson does not seem to have come out with a definitive public negative verdict on the apostles' status until the game for her in Massachusetts was pretty much over, and conceivably she kept a certain amount of socially useful, accordion-like irresolution over the issue in her own mind up to that point.[20]

But slippery though Hutchinson might have been and reluctant to speak in the first place, she had said enough to the ministers to provide damning evidence at her trial a year later: she was contemptuous of their preaching, contemptuous of them, and used an abusive vocabulary that may have brought up unpleasant recollections of the recent London antinomian controversy. Certainly the ministers would have also been disturbed at Cotton's incapacity to hear any serious disagreements in the room. Even if they have not previously been as quick as Shepard to link him with radical lay opinions, his reticence would have raised questions as they shared their impressions of the conference with each other. At the least, the ministers might have easily concluded that they were not going to get much help from the colony's most prestigious divine in dealing with what some of them were starting to see as a serious policing problem.

Hutchinson was not the only person for whom the October conference marked a milestone on the road to a trial. After her exchange with the ministers, the conference moved into a general discussion of the nature of the seal of the Spirit, in which Wheelwright was a major participant. Although overlooked by historians, that exchange mattered enough to the participants to run as an issue through the ministers' written dispute with Cotton in December, and a year later it still mattered enough that they could get into hot quarrels over who said what and in what sequence. The exchange served to solidify an impression forming in the minds of at least some of the ministers that Wheelwright had dangerously heretical tendencies, and it helped shape the first clash in the controversy in which more was directly at stake than words.

Some ministers believed that Wheelwright, in response to some sharp questioning by Shepard about the "earnest" of the Spirit (Ephesians 1:14) and its relationship to the seal, claimed that there were two kinds of seals. Wheelwright allegedly spoke of a little seal common to all believers and a special seal, the broad seal, that only certain Christians enjoyed. "There was a double seal found out that day which never was," Hugh Peters fumed a year later. The ministers "pressed" Wheelwright to prove the difference, and according to them, he appealed to Ephesians 1:17: "That the God of our Lord Jesus Christ, the Father of glory, may give unto you the spirit of wisdom and revelation in the knowledge of him."[21]

The Bostonians disputed virtually every detail of the ministers' account. It is futile to guess what really might have been said, although my suspicion is that Wheelwright was unsuccessfully trying to explain the difference between the Son's work and that of the Holy Spirit. But two points are salient. The first is that the meeting from initial reports seems to have gone well. Hutchinson had confined her most intemperate remarks to private conversations. Winthrop recorded in his journal that Cotton and Wheelwright agreed with the other ministers that sanctification could evidence justification. Cotton remembered that several ministers said at the meeting's end that "they would speak no more of it," a recollection that corresponds to Winthrop's relatively benign journal entry. The next point is that this haze of good feelings, assuming there was one, did not last long, as Cotton also noted, and clearly one of the reasons it evaporated was the exchange with Wheelwright—is it a coincidence that Shepard seemed to have the clearest unfavorable memory of that exchange?[22] I imagine Shepard later ominously contextualizing the discussion for his brethren, and some of them at least coming to agree with him. What then was at stake that caused such different accounts of the exchange?

The answer pivots on the ministers' claim that Wheelwright had insisted on two qualitatively different seals. Even worse, he had defended their existence by asserting that Ephesians 1:17 demonstrated a higher kind of seal, one that communicated distinctive wisdom and revelations; puritans regarded such an exegesis as familist.[23] Wheelwright understandably vehemently denied having made it, or ever even having conceived it.

Unfortunately for Wheelwright, by the time of the October conference, he was already suspected of familism, which helps explain why some ministers interpreted him as broaching it there. Shortly before, he had delivered a sermon concerning the union of Christ and the Holy Spirit with believers and the nature of the believer's "new creature" (2 Corinthians 5:17). Most Reformed theologians when they conceived of that union avoided conceptualizing it in personal terms. Christ dwelt in believers through the Holy Spirit; the Holy Spirit dwelt in believers through his gifts; and the new creature was the body of graces created in a justified believer. Cotton at the October conference held that the Holy Spirit dwelt personally in a believer, as did "some others of the ministers," according to Winthrop. Cotton's argument appears not to have stirred up any controversy, although at least one aggressive English heresy-hunting puritan minister, Stephen Denison, thought that this position already was blasphemy. It may not be a coincidence in view of the lack of Massachusetts controversy on the topic that Shepard's only surviving statement on the topic was ambiguous rather than condemnatory.[24]

Wheelwright, however, went further than Cotton in his sermon. He argued that there was a real, although not personal, union between the Holy Spirit and believers. Moreover, he claimed that the new creature consisted partly of Christ and his righteousness and partly of the believer's new righteousness. This was never a conventional argument, but it might have been passable in calmer times—Shepard himself seems to have accepted something like it a decade earlier. Wheelwright later defended his position by citing the eminently respectable Reformed theologian Zanchius, whom Cotton used to defend his argument about the indwelling of the Holy Spirit. But these were not calm times. Familists and familist-tinged ministers like Peter Shaw and John Traske argued that the new creature was more than a believer—in fact it was Jesus Christ, and the Holy Spirit was personally united with believers. And these arguments, puritans claimed, were the core of familist antinomianism—Christ and the Spirit in them could not sin. It is almost certain that "inquiries" along these lines were already circulating in Hutchinson's circle. A minister alarmed at those inquiries' increasing visibility and the disrespect to most ministers that accompanied them could easily link them to Wheelwright. Not only was his sermon at best only marginally orthodox, he was Anne Hutchinson's brother-in-law and otherwise a largely unknown quantity to the minister. Thus, someone hostile to Wheelwright could, and soon would, argue that Wheelwright meant more than what he was prepared to say openly in the sermon; he meant that the believer was deified and became "God-man, even Jesus Christ"—pure familist doctrine.[25] The October 25 conference may have seemed a success to some; to others, it only confirmed just how perniciously familism was spreading.

That confirmation probably played a large role in a dramatic confrontation that occurred five days later. Someone convinced of Wheelwright's familist tendencies made sure that Deputy-Governor John Winthrop understood the connection (which he did, since he shortly made, or repeated, those key phrases about deification, while acknowledging that he had been told about Wheelwright's heterodoxy only recently). If the absence of comments in Winthrop's journal about the controversy up to this point is any gauge of his attitude, he had been slow to acknowledge its seriousness.[26] Perhaps a variety of factors inclined him to this reluctance. In England, he had sat under the ministry of Ezekiel Culverwell, who, like Cotton, lay stress on absolute promises, and Winthrop, unlike Shepard, had experienced the witness of the Spirit himself, both of which factors might have made him more hesitant than others to hear serious heresy within the Boston congregation. His admiration for Cotton was such that he would run interference for him throughout the controversy. He was also not as severe as some in the magisterial/ministerial Massachusetts elite and thus less inclined to perceive that the usual level of quarreling among brethren had risen to the point where it constituted a crisis. Nonetheless, by the end of October, his level of concern would have certainly been rising and the argument about Wheelwright hit home, perhaps in part because his family had long been friends with the minister John Knewstub, ancient enemy of the Family of Love.[27]

Whoever was trying to get to Winthrop off the fence would have regarded the task as urgent, for the residents of Mount Wollaston had petitioned to have Wheelwright made a co-teacher of the Boston church so that he could serve as their minister.[28] Their request had been publicly announced the previous Sunday, October 23, two days before the ministerial conference, and was to come up on the following Sunday for resolution. On the face of it, the request was reasonable enough. In order to attract Cotton and his Lincolnshire followers to Boston, already straited for land on its narrow peninsula, the governor and Council agreed that Boston settlers could have land in any part of the Bay not claimed by other towns. That arrangement was why a number of settlers acquired land at Mount Wollaston, a cumbersome ten miles and more from the Boston meetinghouse. Those settlers, members of the Boston church, had been trying to get permission to form their own church since the summer but with no success, as the Bostonians worried that the loss of Mount Wollaston would adversely affect Boston's prosperity.[29] Wheelwright probably preached there, but since he had not yet been officially made a minister to the Boston congregation, he could not administer the sacraments. Had he been ordained as teacher, he could have done so while bypassing the necessity of getting approval for forming a separate church.

However, Winthrop regarded the petition, rightly or wrongly, as having been instigated by people who shared Hutchinson's opinions, which he now seems to have been taking seriously as a disruptive menace, with some justification, and he had been successfully persuaded, more problematically, that Wheelwright was a covert familist.[30] On Sunday, October 30, he singlehandedly blocked the request. Winthrop arose from the magistrate's bench with two objections. The church was already well supplied with ministers, he said, and Wheelwright's doctrine was problematic. Winthrop demonstrated the latter by referring to his interpretation of Wheelwright's sermon discussed above. Wheelwright seemed to dissent in judgment from the church, Winthrop concluded—a polite way of saying that he reeked of familism. Winthrop's benchmate, Vane, replied that he marveled at what Winthrop said, since Cotton had lately approved Wheelwright's doctrine. Cotton asked Wheelwright to explain himself, and Wheelwright spoke to Cotton's request. Winthrop refused to be appeased. He said that even though he and Wheelwright perhaps agreed about these doctrines and that Winthrop would be content to live under his ministry, yet seeing that Wheelwright raised doubtful disputations, he could not consent to his appointment. The church "gave way" to Winthrop on the understanding that the gathering of a church at Mount Wollaston would move forward.[31]

Reading between the lines of Winthrop's journal, he seems to have won a pyrrhic victory, at least in the short term. He had preserved the purity of the Boston church, but in the course of the debate, Boston's residents had given way to the earlier demand of Mount Wollaston for its own church. Nonetheless, even if the meeting perhaps spun out of Winthrop's control, his role in it offended "divers of the brethren." They were angry, Winthrop recorded, because church members were not supposed to make grave public accusations against fellow church members before conferring with them privately, because Winthrop had spoken with "bitterness," and because his accusations were untrue. Winthrop's attack on Wheelwright was certainly a serious breach of procedure that would have invited an official rebuke coming from a less-privileged member.[32]

The next day Winthrop defended himself in another speech before the congregation, perhaps in a special meeting called to discuss his actions. He explained that he previously thought that Wheelwright spoke in a metaphorical manner when he used such terminology about union, "but, hearing, very lately, that he was suspected to hold such opinions, it caused him to think, he spake as he meant." He had since spoken with Wheelwright privately. Though Wheelwright denied holding the views he was accused of, he nevertheless held them by necessary consequence, Winthrop insisted—it probably did not help Wheelwright that familists were notorious for their willingness to dissimulate about their doctrines when expedient. Given that contentions and estrangements were growing, Winthrop said, Wheelwright should refrain from using terms of human invention. There was no room to challenge Winthrop's judgment on Wheelwright; it pivoted on "necessary consequences" and not directly on what Wheelwright said, and Winthrop was too prominent to take disciplinary action against. When Winthrop finished, "no man spake to it."[33]

That silence was not the same as consent, for Winthrop, like Shepard before him, had now thrown the net of heresy counterproductively widely. "The *Bostoners in N.E.* . . . would have chosen Mr *Wheelwright* (the notorious Familist) to have been co-teacher with Mr C. there, had not some few withstood it," is how this incident was explained to an English minister. But where Winthrop and his allies may have seen a notorious familist, Cotton saw an orthodox minister, and there is no reason to think that most of his congregation would not have agreed with him. Winthrop's heavy-handed intervention, instead of waking the congregation up to the dangerous nature of the inquiries in Hutchinson's circle, provided the radicals with cover and made more plausible the Hutchinsonian depiction of persecutory antichristian ministers and magistrates. The long-term outcome of the episode might have only reinforced that depiction: it is perhaps not a coincidence that although Mount Wollaston's residents moved ahead with their efforts to gather a church by granting land to Wheelwright and building a meetinghouse for him, the General Court did not start the process of determining the boundaries of their future town until immediately after Wheelwright was exiled, and they did not get their church until the end of 1639.[34]

Winthrop, unlike many of the participants in the controversy, made a serious effort to be conciliatory as well as repressive, however, although the results only aggravated the controversy further. He offered a concrete theological proposal to the congregation in his speech justifying his blocking of Wheelwright's appointment. He suggested that terms like "person of the Holy Ghost" and "real union" be forborne, since they were not in the Scriptures and were generating disputes and "estrangements." A day or two later, he wrote out his argument at length and sent it to John Cotton. A dispute on the issue broke out, carried on mostly in writing, "for the peace sake of the church," according to Winthrop. Wilson, Winthrop, and "divers others" argued that the Holy Spirit dwelt in a believer by "his gifts and powers only." Cotton, Wheelwright, and many in the congregation (as well as some other ministers) held that the Holy Spirit dwelled personally in a believer. Vane, now openly espousing the "Hutchinsonian" position, wrote that this dwelling amounted to a personal union—given that Winthrop had blackballed Wheelwright because of his alleged tendency to this position, it must have been wrenching for him and others to have the governor of the colony, untouchable because of his status, advocate it openly. The Holy Spirit as third member of the Trinity was a relatively late development in Christian doctrine, and Winthrop recorded that the congregation, after due search, "could not find the person of the Holy Ghost in scripture, nor in the primitive churches three hundred years after Christ."[35] Winthrop's November attempt to dampen down confusion and differences through discussion only succeeded in amplifying them.

One measure of the increasingly public and quasi-official status of the free grace controversy as the fall of 1636 progressed is the increasingly pointed and individualized barbs against Boston Shepard delivered in his Thursday lectures. Around this time, he told his audience that "not many days since" someone had closed with Christ and "rejoyced in him." But the person had done so not because of "the beauty they saw in holiness, nor bitterness of sin," the marks of a true conversion, but because the person saw that "Christ has undertaken all." Presumably, the identity of this self-deluded and spiritually lazy person was no secret to some in the audience. Perhaps Shepard's account stemmed from a conversation in which someone from the Boston congregation tried to impress upon Shepard his or her experience of the all-sufficient power of Christ's saving work. If so the conversation failed, for, according to Shepard, the person only rejoiced in Christ "because they would be eased of the work." Shepard equated that position with people he had known who had lived in some sin while promising that the Lord would be blessed if he saved them. One need not work over hard to imagine the ill feeling that this highly insulting dismissal of a lay person's spiritual experiences generated, especially when broadcast from the privileged position of the pulpit. Moreover, Shepard connected this deluded would-be Christian with Cotton and Wheelwright's tiered conception of the Christian life and the seal of the Spirit: "The soul of man desires

rest and peace, seeks for it . . . not in the Grace, but in the joy of Christ
. . . seeking the utmost perfection of a Christian in the seal of the Spirit,
not in the mighty actings of the Spirit for God. Hence he is deluded, and
fancies he has Christ."[36]

Shortly thereafter, perhaps a week or two later, Shepard went even more
forcefully after Cotton himself. There was "no word [in the Bible] giving
assurance, but that which is made to some work." If you sought assurance
any other way (such as Cotton's), it was a "delusion." For Shepard, finding
personal assurance in a biblical absolute promise of salvation was finding
a meaning God did not intend—if you assumed that biblical verses like "I
will never leave thee" referred to you personally, "you may as well bring in
immediate Revelations, and from thence come to forsake the Scripture."
Cotton and Wheelwright, in other words, were destroying the Bible and
inviting in familism, by irrefutable "necessary consequence." Returning
to the debate he had with Wheelwright at their recent conference, Shepard
argued that "the Apostle makes the earnest of the Spirit [sanctification]
to be the Seal. . . . He that sees not the Lord is his by that, sees no God
his at all." Cotton and Wheelwright, having had their positions called
delusions and being told that they very possibly saw no God at all, are
unlikely to have been mollified, or convinced, by Shepard's announcement
that "I do but pity those who think otherwise."[37]

The swelling controversy made its first divisive recorded appearance in the
secular power structure of the colony in December. Vane called a special
Court session for December 7 and announced to the assembled assistants—the colony's magistrates and its most prestigious men—and the
deputies elected by each of the towns that he had received disturbing letters from England. Their contents are unknown, but Vane claimed that
they made his return urgent. The Court requested leave to consider until
the next morning. The next day one of the assistants, perhaps William
Coddington or Richard Dummer, broke into "pathetical passages" about
how badly the colony needed his leadership. Vane thereupon burst into
tears, according to Winthrop, and revealed his underlying reasons for
going. Although the business at home concerned the ruin of his estate,
that in itself would not have been enough to induce him to leave. He
feared God's judgments would descend on the colony for its dissensions,
and he resented "the scandalous imputations brought upon himself, as if
he should be the cause of all." Therefore, he thought it best that he step
down for a time.[38]

Vane's disclosure of his deepest motivation provoked deep concern. To
have the governor of Massachusetts, very well connected both among the
godly and within Charles's court, leave on these grounds would be a disaster. To the godly it would signal that Massachusetts, riven with conflict,

was not a desirable place to which to emigrate; at Charles's court it would strengthen the opponents of the charter, one of whose arguments was that the colony was unable to govern itself. The General Court refused to dismiss him on that basis. Vane then insisted that his first reasons were pressing enough. The Court records state that Vane assured the Court of his serious resolution to return as soon as his affairs in England had been settled, and only with that assurance did the Court agree to let him go in the first place—does it mean anything that Winthrop, increasingly dubious about Vane, left this exchange out of his journal? The Court, fearing that the government would be vacant if the deputy governor died in Vane's absence, decided to move up the annual election from May to December 15, and in an innovation due to the inclement season, it allowed distant voters to send in their votes by proxy. It then adjourned until December 13.[39]

After the Court adjourned, members of the Boston congregation met and agreed that Vane's reasons for leaving did not seem sufficient. A delegation informed the Court of this when it reconvened, and Vane, pronouncing himself an obedient child of the church, said he did not dare go away. According to Winthrop a "great part of the court and country" expressed their desire that he remain as governor. It was decided to cancel the upcoming election, presumably because the date was irregular to start with and because those who voted by proxy would not have learned that Vane was still available.[40] The reluctance of the Court and country to let Vane go was in stark contrast to its attitude toward him only six months later. It probably should be taken to mean that Shepard and other militants had not convinced Massachusetts's godly public that there was such a major controversy in the first place or, if there was, that Vane and Boston were responsible for it.

Nonetheless, the controversy was serious enough that the Court one day called the ministers for advice. Governor Vane, according to Winthrop, was in something of a huff because some ministers had assembled to write a set of questions to Cotton without informing Vane. Hugh Peters took the invitation of frank speech to say that it "saddened the ministers' spirits" that Vane was jealous of their meetings or wanted to restrain their liberty. Vane apologized, but Peters bore in, claiming that the churches had been in peace before he arrived. Vane lashed back that "the light of the gospel brings a sword, and the children of the bondwoman would persecute those of the freewoman." Peters, in turn, did not take kindly to hearing that he was a persecutor of the saints and under a covenant of works. He informed Vane that Vane was young, inexperienced, and given to preemptory conclusions. In both in the Netherlands and Massachusetts, Peters went on, linking Vane to the notorious Amsterdam English anabaptists, the three principal causes of new opinions and divisions over them were pride, idleness, and ungrounded knowledge. If Vane, the future English revolutionary government's naval secretary, replied to this sharp and condescending insult from one of its future leading army chaplains, Winthrop did not record it.[41]

The clash between Vane and Peters had not created the best possible atmosphere for a free exchange of opinions, and partisan wrangling continued. Wilson made a speech denouncing the practice of charging that people were under a covenant of works. He linked this practice to theological delusion, to holding forth a "false Covenant and a fancy-Christ," and warned of a possible separation if the differences were not healed, perhaps a reference to the Mount Wollaston situation. All the magistrates except for Vane, Dummer, and Coddington, and all the ministers but Wheelwright and Cotton seconded him. Cotton had preached a relatively conciliatory sermon in the morning, outlining the different ways in which people could draw comfort from their sanctification. The sermon came up for discussion, and the issue was raised whether sanctification could be evidence without a concurrent sign of justification. Cotton and Vane denied it. At some point near the end of its session, the Court passed a motion calling for the churches to beseech God for aid in a day of humiliation on January 19.[42]

With the failure of the December Court session, the free grace controversy approached a watershed. The ministers and magistrates had tried, more or less, to work out their differences in a public forum and failed. Vane and Peters's heated exchange gave a glimpse of what lay beyond that failure. "God's people are all marked with one and the same mark . . . and where this is, there can be no discord," John Endicott had once declared.[43] But the flip side of that observation was that if you were no longer willing to see your opponents' marks as roughly the same as yours, it was but a short step to the conclusion that they were not God's people at all; they were familists, antinomians, carnal gospelers, legalists, antichristian, Arminians, crypto-papists, false deceiving brethren, in Israel but not of Israel, and discord followed inevitably.

Cotton and his brother ministers soon found themselves experimenting with that short step. Already before the Court met, they had numerous private conversations in which the ministers expressed concern that various heterodox opinions were circulating under Cotton's name and that Cotton himself had preached "darkly and doubtfully." The conferences failed, and around the beginning of the December Court session, an unknown number of ministers gathered to draft sixteen questions to Cotton concerning his views on assurance. They wanted "short and plain" answers, also in writing. They seem to have conceived of this as a semi-public exchange, since they wrote that they knew his opinions on some of the questions, but included these "for others sake."[44] It must be remembered how little we know of the composition of this document: we do not know how many ministers were involved in writing it; we do not know the degree to which they each cared about each of the questions; and we do not know who did the actual drafting. The appearance of ministerial unity in this and the subsequent follow-up composition is, to an unknown extent, an effect of authorial anonymity.

Cotton started his reply somewhat testily, as if not sure of the point of the exercise. He might just refer the ministers to what he had always openly taught, as Christ did to the High Priest (not a flattering analogy, even if he added that they were more dear to him than the High Priest was to Christ). But he answered their questions straightforwardly, save that in one place he erroneously gave the impression that he had made a dramatic concession and allowed that the Spirit might seal sanctification as a first evidence of justification for a "weake believer." Cotton's answers, introduction aside, were relatively devoid of posturing. According to Winthrop, many copies were circulated.[45]

The ministers responded with a longer answer, presumably while the December Court was still in session and they could meet as a group. Cotton came back with an even longer reply that must have taken considerable time to compose. Neither of these documents sheds any new theological light; their considerable interest lies in the collapse of the moderation of the previous exchange. In their preface, the ministers bristled over Cotton's comparison of them with high priests. They let Cotton know that they had been bending over backward to accommodate him. "Diverse" (of the laity) were taking "offense" at their silence, interpreting it as indicating "our consent to all you said." But in fact they had restrained themselves because they were "tender of your honour." Now they wanted the substance, not a facade, of ministerial doctrinal solidarity. They told Cotton forthrightly that "sundry things" he had preached were "darkly and doubtfully delivered," and they wanted "your Consent with us in the truth." Believing that Cotton had agreed that sanctification could be a first evidence of justification for a "weake believer," they forcefully asked Cotton's "seasonable reproof of those that dissent."[46]

The ministers did not accompany their effort to recruit Cotton by conciliatory gestures toward him. They nitpicked over some of his more technical answers: his explanation of how believers were active after regeneration, but how that activity was in Christ; his distinction between a justified person's losing the comfort of assurance and losing the knowledge of it; and his claim that sanctification involved more than the restoration of Adam's image of God. It is hard to believe that in calmer times any of these points would have been noticed, and when Cotton and the other ministers seriously attempted reconciliation the next summer, they were gone. The ministers described the dangers they saw in Cotton's preaching with a bluntness only slightly less restrained than Shepard's pulpit attacks. His method of assurance by revelation "may train up people to a plain forsaking of the Scriptures indeed, while they cleave to them in shew." By denying the evidence of sanctification, it threatened to destroy the only source of comfort that weak Christians enjoyed. Cotton's preaching that people should never doubt their assurance opened a door to sin. His constant denigration of the evidence of sanctification and use of phrases like "going aside to Hagar" and "works" encouraged people to neglect the duties and ordinances of Christianity.[47]

Cotton, in reply, acknowledged the ministers' concerns. They needed not fear that his preaching would encourage people to sin, as he made it clear that the witness of the Spirit was not genuine if it did not lead to sanctification. In fact, one could not truly repent without first having assurance, for true repentance required an awareness of how grievously you injured Christ by returning sin for his love. Cotton advocated the "frequent and diligent use of good duties," as long as one sought the face of God in them. The danger was that persons might regard doing the duties as entitling them to salvation or, more subtly, find "comforts and enlargements" in doing the duties themselves and confuse this with true assurance.[48]

Having established to his own satisfaction that he did not encourage sin or the neglect of duties, Cotton turned unashamedly, if discreetly, confrontational. He carefully informed his brethren that they were mistaken if they read any concessions in his answer, and he explained at length the difference between the Son's work and that of the Holy Spirit. The elders had claimed that Cotton's method of assurance was a pastoral disaster for weak Christians; he replied that on the contrary, it was their reliance on sanctification that could afford no true comfort. They themselves acknowledged that Christians who deployed their technique were often given to "sad doubts of their own estates."[49]

The pastoral failure of the elders' approach, according to Cotton, was matched by their betrayal of the Reformation. Their arguments duplicated Arminian and even Catholic ones. Their claim that sanctification could be a first evidence meant, for all that they denied it, that they really believed that good works were the ground of justification: they "clothe[d] unwholsome and Popish doctrin with Protestant and wholsome words." In reference to what must have been a recent sermon, he warned, "Let not therfore any man professing the fear of God, profess in solemn Assemblies that the gathering of our Evidence and first assurance of Justification from Sanctification or from the promises made thereto, is a doctrin sealed by the blood of Martyrs." Cotton would not reprove the people the ministers wished him to, for he agreed with them.[50]

Only two months previously, Cotton had rebuked Hutchinson for emphasizing the differences between him and the other ministers, and previously he had claimed that there was no difference between them if they understood each other. Now they had more or less tried to reach an understanding in a written public dialogue. But the more they discussed their differences, the more areas of disagreement they discovered and/or created, and they concluded by hurling polemics at each other: Cotton was destroying the Bible, while his opponents were crypto-papists. Shepard might have been describing the ministerial exchange as he warned in a very different context that "when Brethren, otherwise deare to each other, differ in their judgments, and breake out to open contention about the same, they are very apt to make the opinions of the contrary party as unpleasing and absurd to the judgment of others, as may bee, whence griefe, offence, and alienations of affections . . . are ready to follow."[51]

Ministers were not the only ones making their opponents' opinions as unpleasing and absurd as they could by the end of December. Around this time, some of the Boston laity held a conference with some Newtowne laity. All that we know of it comes from a paper the Boston laity wrote in response to a now vanished Newtowne account of the meeting. The Boston laity began the meeting by giving the Newtowne brethren five propositions. The substance of these propositions might be termed confrontational Cottonianism. They presented Cotton's positions on justification, assurance, and sanctification, while making it plain that any alternatives were wrong.[52]

That in itself, one would think, would have been enough to generate stiff debate. But the Newtowne brethren assumed a much more sinister agenda. They refused to write down the Bostonians' propositions during the conference. When the conference was over, however, they summarized them in fifteen propositions of their own, using the Boston members' words in some instances but always distorting their meaning. What is striking about the Newtowne rearrangement of the Boston propositions, as the Bostonians recorded them, is that they changed the Boston propositions from Cottonianism to "Hutchinsonianism" by consistently minimizing the activity of faith and sanctification far beyond what the Bostonians had intended. Some of the Newtownian distortions were so extreme that the Boston brethren professed not to know how they had been derived from their positions. The Newtowne brethren then circulated these propositions to the "Magistrates and Committees [of the General Court]." In self-defense, the Boston brethren wrote their surviving document, explaining what they had meant to say in each of these fifteen propositions fabricated by Newtowne.[53]

It is clear from the Bostonians' surviving paper that both sides in this conference were theologically well versed. The Bostonians knew how Cottonianism differed both from the puritan mainstream and from more radical positions. The Newtowne brethren knew how to demonstrate that the Bostonians were the radicals they denied being. When Boston argued Cottonianism, Newtowne heard antinomianism and familism. Clearly the Newtowne laity, like their minister, had no interest in finding common ground with the Boston laity. They chose instead to magnify differences in order to better separate sheep from goats. It is understandable that the Boston brethren circulated their rebuttal widely (the surviving copy has an endorsement in an eighteenth-century hand, "Propositions of the Churches of Boston to those of Connecticut").[54]

Yet one need not sympathize too quickly with the Bostonians. The Newtowne brethren did not pull their distortions out of thin air; they assumed that Cottonian doctrine was a mask for the most radical opinions being voiced in Boston. It is not entirely mysterious that they would feel frustrated that their Boston brethren refused to take any responsibility for these—after all, the Newtowne brethren may have twisted Cottonianism, but one did not have to twist it too far before one ended up with Hutchinsonianism.

The Newtowne brethren may have been especially concerned around this time because radicals in Boston seem to have become more vocal. Winthrop in his December 1636, journal entry (written at least three months later and probably a good deal later[55]) noted that radical opinions "brake out publicly in the church of Boston," including ones that the Newtowne brethren laid on the Boston brethren—justification occurred before belief and faith was no cause of justification. Winthrop did acknowledge that in these debates the church eventually returned to a Cottonian consensus: "After it was granted, that faith was before justification, but it was only passive, an empty vessel."[56] Yet if male radicals were prepared in public to back off from their positions (women were not expected to speak on doctrinal matters in church meetings[57]), they seem to have been expressing themselves more freely and openly than they had before, and there is certainly no evidence that this freedom provoked the Boston elders to punitive action. The Newtowne brethren had increasingly valid reasons to be alarmed at Boston, even if the way they responded helped ensure that mainstream Cottonians continued to focus more on their opponents than on their own straying sheep.

This accelerating collapse of a middle ground, with Cotton increasingly dubious about his brethren, Boston laymen furious over their exchange with Newtowne, and he and they still smarting from Winthrop's smear of Wheelwright, helps explain one of the oddest events of December, the informal church disciplining of Wilson. Wilson in his Court speech apparently had not specified the new opinions he found dangerous, but afterward he told the church that he did not mean doctrines delivered by Cotton and Wheelwright. Nonetheless, the church called him to defend himself publicly on December 31. Cotton, Vane, and most of the congregation, including "such as had known [Wilson] so long, and what good he had done for that church," pressed their attack, according to Winthrop. Cotton explained to the congregation that he could not censure Wilson, since one or two other members opposed the admonition (the Boston church attempted to make decisions by consensus), but instead he gave him a grave exhortation.[58]

It is obvious enough why persons in Hutchinson's circle would have felt threatened by Wilson's Court speech, but Cotton's vehemence against him, as Winthrop described this incident, is, at first glance, hard to understand. Winthrop wrote to Cotton and the ruling elders explaining again that Wilson had not meant any opinions delivered from the pulpit by either Cotton or Wheelwright. Cotton replied to Winthrop in a "very loving and gentle answer." But he gave a variety of reasons for condemning Wilson, none of which Winthrop recorded. Conceivably Cotton felt that Wilson's analysis was excessively one-sided, given that attacks on fringe opinions always seemed to end up as attacks on him or Wheelwright. Perhaps, too, Cotton was unwilling to concede that errors presented as "inquiries" by untrained laity were worse than crypto-Catholic ones aggressively asserted by his professional opponents. If this incident is puzzling enough in itself in Winthrop's sketchy account, even more so is its coda. Wilson preached the next day to the general satisfaction of the congregation: Vane himself publicly approved. Would that we knew what the contents of this sermon were; its reception indicates that lines within the Boston church were not yet entirely hardened, despite the mutual provocation.[59]

Winthrop responded to the debates swirling around his church in two ways. First, he found his being the promoter of a minority and oppositional religiosity in his own church spiritually invigorating. He wrote in December that after some self-doubt, "the Lord wrought marveylosly upon my heart, reviving my former peace & consolation with much increase & better assurance than formerly." Second, he continued his efforts to reach a theological common ground with his opponents, which is more than many in Massachusetts seem to have been doing by this time. A few weeks after getting his assurance renewed, on his fiftieth birthday, he wrote an account of his protracted English conversion. The account demonstrated his reservations about using sanctification for assurance, and its climax in the immediate witness of the Spirit more than met the Boston standards of proof of salvation. He may have circulated this document to demonstrate his saintly status by any standard being used in Massachusetts. Winthrop also wrote two theological position papers, probably to send to Vane. In one paper he argued against his heterodox brethren that faith was a condition of justification. In the other, as a conciliatory gesture, he argued that justification itself was not in time, the standard argument, but from eternity, and that faith simply declared the existence of this pre-existing state. He gave the papers to Wilson to pass on to Shepard for review, and all we know of them is from Shepard's horrified written response: "If yow shold thinke it fit in your wisdom to forbeare wrighting for a while, I perceive it would be most safe for yow," was his conclusion after a page of deferentially beating around the bush.[60]

Shepard was not interested in seeking accommodation in the first place, and he also had strategic concerns about Winthrop's papers. Winthrop argued that before justification a person needed an "honest and good heart," which was Shepard and Hooker's preparationism. Shepard assured Winthrop that he agreed with the substance of Winthrop's argument. But he also knew that he and Winthrop were in a minority on this point: "many of your freinds that would stand by yow in other controversies, will be agaynst yow in this." Raising this issue would only weaken, not help, the coalition needed to drive down Cotton and the opinionists: "[W]hile yow are about to convince them of errours, they will proclayme you selfe to hold foorth worse."[61]

Shepard's main concern, however, was with Winthrop's doctrines, not his tactics. Justification from eternity was an argument associated with antinomianism, and Shepard took great pains to show Winthrop that he was wrong on this. Shepard of course agreed with Winthrop that faith was a condition of justification, but some of Winthrop's arguments in defense of that position struck him as incorrect, one of them even running danger-ously close to Arminianism, "which I beleeve your soule abhors," he thoughtfully added.[62]

The few historians who comment on Winthrop's efforts take Shepard's criticisms at face value—Winthrop was a lay person's in over his head. He was, but in more complex ways than have been appreciated. Shepard certainly believed that Winthrop was doing bad theology, and in a few places Winthrop might indeed have simply bumbled, but we do not know enough of what he wrote to say one way or the other. In many places his arguments might have been perfectly cogent. Winthrop's "Arminian" argument about faith was repeated by the great high Calvinist mid-cen-tury divine, John Owen, for example, and he may have picked up his de-claratory conception of faith from a number of respectable divines.[63]

What was really at stake with Winthrop's papers was more interesting and complex than a lay person's doing or not doing bad theology. Massa-chusetts's second highest magistrate, who read Latin, had a good library, and once aspired to be a minister himself, had creatively thrown himself into the escalating struggle to keep Christ undivided, and the result, to Shepard's horror, was more doctrinal pluralism, even heresy. Winthrop's ingenuity in defense of the single truth of the Bible, foundation and guarantor of Massachusetts's orthodoxy, indeed, of the colony's entire religious culture, raised the specter that the godly might ultimately find in the Bible a limitless variety of readings—doctrinal debate on its own, as the experience of the last months had abundantly shown, could only worsen, not resolve, the free grace controversy.[64]

Fortunately for Shepard, and perhaps for Massachusetts, Winthrop was an amateur theologian without any professional investment in his achievements. Once rebuked, there is no evidence that he made any further efforts on his own to find a doctrinal via media. Instead, we have a very relieved note by Shepard in January 1637, delighted by Winthrop's "kind acceptance" of his blunt letter. He was delighted, too, that Winthrop was taking sides: "It hath gladded many of our harts to see your hart and the truth embracing each other, even tho errour for peace sake hath pleaded for entertaynment." He told Winthrop that there were "hidden misteries" at the bottom of the Boston ferment, "something aliquid incognitionis, which will in time appear."[65]

Shepard also thanked Winthrop for a radical lay theological tract Winthrop passed on "to us to burne to death: the heretick is yet kept prisoner but we intend to see justice executed on him according to your desire."[66] The humor of Shepard's remark, revealing his underlying attitude toward doctrinal differences, might have understandably been lost on many people in Boston, but that would have not disturbed him. Shortly after writing this note, his party ratcheted up the level of confrontation in Massachusetts still higher by commencing an attempt to execute justice on what it considered a flesh-and-blood heretic instead of a paper one. The ensuing political tumult would convince Shepard that he had finally found his long sought-after hidden mysteries.

SIX

CONVICTING JOHN WHEELWRIGHT

JANUARY–MARCH 1637

THE STORY of the free grace controversy, as it is usually told, runs straightforwardly from the doctrinal clashes of late 1636 to John Wheelwright's notorious fast-day sermon of January 19, 1637, to his conviction two months later for sedition and contempt as a result of that sermon. Wheelwright in his sermon denounced, or certainly seemed to denounce, the greater part of the ministers and magistrates of Massachusetts as being under a covenant of works and called for spiritual warfare against them. His performance fits in well with the dominant scholarly picture of an aggressive group of "Hutchinsonians" stirring up trouble in Massachusetts. It is easy to see the sermon as a clear provocation that ended inevitably in his trial and conviction, so easy that historians uniformly pay little attention to the trial or the machinations that went into it. They focus instead on the much more fully documented pyrotechnics of Anne Hutchinson's trial seven months later.

But even as Hutchinson's trial was the defining event for retrospective accounts of the free grace controversy, Wheelwright's trial was the defining event of the controversy itself. It occupied that position because there was in fact no open path to his conviction but a tangled, dense thicket of multidirectional abuse, religious paranoia, and covert and overt machinations. The route to Wheelwright's conviction, although long and vigorously sought after by some, did not become clear until the end of his trial neared. When the trial was over, those who had hacked their trail successfully to their desired destination would have to deal with the formidable amount of debris they had left in their wake.

Scholars have paid little attention to Satan's agency in the free grace controversy. As the pulpit rhetoric heated up in the winter of 1637, however, he loomed large in the participants' analyses. Zealous English Protestants had a specific supernaturally driven historical framework within which to understand religious conflict. The true church had never had an easy time. Persecuted by Satan as soon as it first emerged in the apostolic age, it had barely become institutionalized under Constantine, the first Christian Roman emperor, before the usurping bishops of Rome began their assaults. In the Middle Ages it had almost vanished altogether under the fury of Antichrist, Satan's chief earthly ally, who had completely taken over the throne of Peter. It survived only as little scattered bands of true believers until the coming of the Reformation, and even that revival was heralded in England by the burning of the Marian martyrs.[1]

Elizabeth I more or less institutionalized the Reformation in England, but these were the Last Days of the world, and it was only to be expected that Satan's fury would increase as his time neared its end. Spain spearheaded a relentless Catholic effort to overturn the true church. God had delivered England from the Spanish armada in 1588 and saved it from the Catholic attempt to blow up the Houses of Parliament in 1605. Mortally threatened from without, English Protestantism began to rot from within in the 1620s as English kings started their infatuation with Catholic brides. Charles I and his evil favorite, the courtier Buckingham, invigorated a twin assault on English religion and English liberties in the late 1620s. They promoted divines who were sympathetic to ceremonialism and Arminianism (a Reformed "heresy" but many suspected that the Catholic Church was behind it) and hostile to puritans. Parliament was the bulwark of true religion in England, but Charles made financial end runs around it of dubious legality. England rejoiced as an assassin did away with Buckingham in 1628, but other evil counselors soon persuaded Charles that he could continue down this sinister road by effectively doing away with parliament altogether, which he ceased to call from 1629. By that year hot Protestants were weaving together a sinister, conspiratorial story in which the Court's innovations in religion and assaults on English liberties concealed the yoked disasters of "Romish tyranny and Spanish monarchy."[2]

The godly's Reformed Christian brethren throughout Europe likewise saw themselves as engaged in a cosmic struggle against Antichrist, and by the 1630s, the Reformed Church abroad was doing no better than the English branch. English Protestants knew this well, as they watched religious warfare lay Germany waste. The Protestant "Lion of the North," Swedish king Gustavus Adolfus, temporarily turned the Catholic tide in Germany, but his death in battle in 1632 dashed the apocalyptic hopes his victories had raised.[3]

Thus when intractable conflicts broke out among the Protestants of Massachusetts, they could easily see these conflicts in the context of Satan's perpetual and currently upwardly spiraling assault on the true church, an assault that had driven them to Massachusetts in the first place. It was no coincidence that the reasons for the January 19 fast included the "miserable estate of the churches in Germany," and "the bishops [in England] making havock in the churches, putting down the faithful ministers, and advancing popish ceremonies and doctrines," along with the "dissension in our churches."[4] Given the current world climate, zealous

Massachusetts Protestants had encouragement enough to interpret local religious conflicts in the framework of Satan's broad international attack. This framework was not a recipe for the peaceful resolution of conflicts—especially when persons on both sides had decided that peaceful resolution was impossible.

In 1645 Shepard wrote that after the ministerial conferences with Cotton failed to produce an understanding, ministers began publicly denouncing Boston doctrines, lay and ministerial, for the first time. Shepard's chronology was disingenuous—he had been denouncing Boston doctrines from the pulpit for at least half a year before the failure of those conferences. But his statement acknowledges a rise in the heat of pulpit rhetoric. Winthrop noted at the end of January, that "the ministers of both sides . . . did publicly declare their judgments . . . so as all men's mouths were full of them," although his bland "declaring judgments" scarcely communicates the inflammatory virulence of at least some ministers' rhetoric.[5]

By the winter of 1637, for example, Shepard's lectures had reached the second verse of his parable, "And five of them were Wise, and five were Foolish." This was a perfect opportunity to explain to Massachusetts exactly who the foolish virgins were and whom they worked for, and with the half-hearted efforts at reconciliation over with, Shepard seized it. Satan "will follow Christ into the wilderness," he told his listeners, for "he seeks to make his party within the Church." If Satan could not pollute the ordinances of the church in Massachusetts, he would "seek to defile it with unclean persons." Shepard's audience had to realize that Satan's delusions in a puritan colony would not come out of the "Popish pack," but that was not to say that Catholicism might not be ultimately behind them. The Jesuits, sinister agents of the Catholic counter-reformation, he told his audience, had a rule when they wished to "conquer Religion by subtilty." They would "never oppose Religion with a cross Religion, but set it against it self." This was not the first time that charges of Jesuit manipulation had been hurled against puritans, although it was perhaps the first time that puritans themselves had made the accusation.[6]

Who was this satanic, perhaps Jesuitical party that set puritanism against itself, and why had most people in Massachusetts been so slow in recognizing it? Shepard explained that they were "secret and subtil enemies, yet seeming friends." They acted the way the godly were supposed to act. They had "gravity and seeming piety." They "cry down their own righteousness, and cry up Christ, and see nothing in themselves." They were in fact the worst embodiment of what Shepard had preached against in England, unconscious hypocrites. Unconscious hypocrites genuinely but incorrectly thought they were godly. A structural necessity in Reformed theology to explain how seeming saints could fall from grace, they were the nightmare of weak Christians, since by definition they could not know who they were. But the hypocrites of Massachusetts were so awful, so deceptive in their godliness, that Shepard needed new terminology to describe them: "[T]heir external operations are chiefly Evangelical, hence, I call them Evangelical Hypocrites."[7]

Evangelical hypocrites, according to Shepard, were an inevitable consequence of "the purest Churches." The fierce preparatory preaching of the Law in these churches generated such terror that when the Gospel's glad tidings followed it, they filled hypocrites with "joy and peace." Thereafter, "You will find them disclaim all Works, and cry up Grace only." However, they do not rejoice "because they feel the power of [the Gospel], but because they are free from the power of it. . . . The safest place to sleep is in Christ's Lap." The delusion of the evangelical hypocrites that they were saved made them the perfect tools of Satan, and they would wake from their delusion only in hell.[8] It is hard to imagine that anyone in Shepard's audience failed to guess who had prompted his new terminology.

Satan, however, was not the ultimate supernatural agent prodding Massachusetts's evangelical hypocrites into action; it was God himself. Look at Germany, Shepard reminded his audience, "what great profession was there." But "the Lord . . . sends a sword," and now it was reverting to Catholicism. Look at England. They received the "Word with joy." But "the Lord sends Persecution, and . . . they fall." Some in England "stand it out there, and suffer and venture hither." Then in Massachusetts "the Lord lets error loose, and they fall." Thus God was the ultimate source of Protestantism's recent travails, for the Lord "delights to manifest that openly which was hid secretly." "God is trying all his Friends through all the christian world," Shepard explained, and most of those friends were proving false.[9]

Shepard therefore was not only defending God's truths when he attacked Boston, and he was not only defending the Massachusetts front in a pan-European religious war, he was participating in God's geographically sweeping, violent exposure of the foolish virgins. With that divine authority behind him, Shepard launched his most sustained and overt attack on Boston to date. He claimed, just as he had done when writing to Cotton to accuse him of heresy many months previously, that he spoke only in the interest of peace: "I will only speak . . . not to begin, but if possible to still division."[10]

Shepard's way of stilling divisions remained exactly as it had been when he wrote his letter to Cotton the previous spring. The entire Boston church, from the most zealous lay speculator to Cotton, had to concede they were wrong. They had to take heed of "making Graces in a Christian the weaknesses of a christian," of denying any difference between the "Graces of Hypocrites & Saints," and of claiming that "a man must not evidence his Justification by his Sanctification." Moving from attacking the general talk of the Boston congregation to a position defended by Cotton in the recent ministerial exchange, Shepard warned against holding "[t]hat a man must see no saving work, nor take comfort from any promise until he is sealed." All those prepositions were dangerous. He warned his audience to make sure that "your closing with Christ do not cause you to make a light matter of sin."[11]

More serious yet were "Doctrines which in shew lift up Grace, but indeed pull it down." Some of these doctrines were ones that probably were floating around at the fringes of the Boston congregation but that Cotton himself condemned, such as "we are not justified by faith," "that the Law ought not to be our rule of life." Others sound likely enough to have emerged in Boston discussions, such as "the Ordinances are not means, but only occasions of conversion," variations on Cotton's own teachings in the interest of magnifying grace; another was Hutchinson's alleged teaching about the whole Scripture in the letter of it holding out no more than a covenant of works. Into this marginal, not to say heretical, mixture, Shepard inserted one grace-destroying doctrine, whose striking resemblance to Cotton's teachings it is unlikely anyone in the audience would have missed: "That a Christian is to gather no assurance from particular conditional Promises under colour of receiving all from Christ and Grace." To make that argument was to "trample under-foot Christs blood."[12]

Shepard closed his discussion of doctrines that pulled down grace by drawing the supernatural party lines emphatically:

> You that are sincere . . . tho' accounted under a covenant of Works with men, yet rejoyce, you know it is better with you in his sight. And you that are weak, beware, and take heed, and do not consider what I, but the Holy Ghost has cleared this day: and as for them that do turn Grace into Laciviousness, not intentionally, but practically; not in all things, but some things: consider this Scripture, *Jude* 4. Men *ordained to this condemnation*; they thrive, and have no hurt, and they joy, Oh but they have condemnation enough upon them. Do but consider *ver.* 12, 13. *Twice dead* . . . for whom is reserved the very blackness of darkness forever.[13]

Change your views, Shepard warned Boston, from Cotton onward, or for you is reserved the very blackness of darkness forever. Had the balance of power in Massachusetts been different, perhaps Shepard might have found himself on trial for his slander of Boston's allegedly "Christ trampling" clergy and magistrates. It is hard to imagine that most ministers were as unrestrained as Shepard in attacking Boston, but it is easy to imagine that Bostonians did not take kindly to hearing that they were "the worms that grow in this wood, in this building, in these churches."[14] Perhaps some of the audience sang imprecatory psalms as they departed from Shepard's lectures into the darkening winter afternoons.

There would have been persons leaving the Boston meetinghouse that winter no less indignant after hearing sermons by Wheelwright and Cotton; salvos in the pulpit warfare were not only coming from the direction of Newtowne. More's the pity that Shepard's sermons cannot be dated more precisely in order to hazard a guess as to who started the shooting. Shepard had never been one to shy away from pulpit aggression, whereas Cotton was known for his mild style, and Wheelwright before his fast-day sermon, according to Winthrop (who might have been exaggerating for polemical purposes), "was wont to teach in a plaine and gentle stile."[15] Perhaps it was the provocation afforded by Shepard and other ministers that led Wheelwright to abandon his previous alleged plain and gentle style and Cotton to make his affinities unmistakable.

Wheelwright's fast-day sermon is the most notorious Boston contribution to the escalation of pulpit rhetoric. Fasting for the purposes of knowing God's intentions behind some calamity and averting his continued anger was one of the institutional practices of the Church of England. The godly, however, pursued it with such zeal that fasts unauthorized by a bishop were banned in 1604. The ban hardly stopped puritans from fasting. Fasting was a chance for them to mark off a special sacred time for reinvigorating their communal relationship with their deity, while demonstrating their importance to the nation and their spiritual superiority to most of the nation's inhabitants. One of Winthrop's English correspondents wrote him in 1636 that fasts were now looked upon "as hateful as conventicles," yet had it not been for "the private prayers and fastes of many of Gods deere Servants," famine would have stalked England that year as divine punishment for Laudianism. Fasting was also a weapon in the arsenal of the saints: God struck the persecuting archbishop of York, Samuel Harsnett, dead in 1630 on the very day when a group of godly ministers gathered to fast against him.[16]

On the Court's fast day of January 19, 1637, those Bostonians who were rigorously following puritan prescriptions for fasting would have stinted on food and sleep the night before and abstained from sex, "forbidden even to them that are newly married." On the fast day itself, dressed in their plainest and cheapest apparel, they would be feeling the pinch of lack of nourishment, and they would have come to the day-long exercises at the church of sermons, psalm-singing, and prayer well loaded with coins to give for alms. Cotton preached in the morning on the need for pacification and reconciliation, according to Winthrop.[17]

Wheelwright was asked to speak in the afternoon. He extemporized, he later claimed, although *Mercurius Americanus* seems to deny this, and others wrote down his words.[18] But though the sermon may have been extempore, it was polished enough to indicate that its motifs had clearly been on his mind for a while. Wheelwright saw the occasion, like the godly fasts of England, as an opportunity to reinvigorate his party's relationship to God while asserting its importance to the colony and its superiority over most of the colony's inhabitants. For Wheelwright, it was no less an opportunity to sketch out the cosmic significance of the struggle in Massachusetts just as dramatically as Shepard.

Why fast, was Wheelwright's first question to his hungry and tired audience. Not in the first instance for temporal blessings nor to avert evils (as the General Court had requested); that was why heathens and hypocrites fasted, "not that I condemne fasting by any means." Genuine Christians, however, fasted only because of the absence of Christ; have Christ and all blessings followed. Thus, in order to accomplish the Court's goals in a truly Christian way, Wheelwright's audience "must desire now that Jesus Christ may be received in other Nations and other places, and may be more receaved amongst our selves . . . he will turne all into a right frame."[19]

As throughout Christendom in general, it was Antichrist who was obstructing Massachusetts's reception of Christ. "The practice of all Antichristian spiritts," pronounced Wheelwright, was to remove Christ wherever they could. They would promulgate a covenant of works and introduce a false Christ by teaching that sanctification could be a first evidence of justification (Wheelwright, like Shepard, named no names), and they would invariably persecute the saints. If the saints did not fight back, he warned, "those under a covenant of works will prevaile." Wheelwright therefore told his audience that in order to keep Christ in Massachusetts, "we must all prepare for a spirituall combate, we must put on the whole armour of God . . . all the children of God, they ought to shew themselves valient, they shold have their swords redy, they must fight and fight with spirituall weapons." "We must kill them with the word of the Lord." If necessary, Wheelwright's listeners had to be prepared to join the long list of Christian martyrs. They must "be willing to be killed like sheepe." But even their projected deaths had an aggressive purpose: "Sampson slew more at his death, then in his life, and so we may prevaile more by our deaths, then by our lives." Christ wanted this combat: "Christ will purge the church. . . . It is impossible to hold out the truth of God with externall peace and quietnes."[20]

Wheelwright himself raised the objection that he was encouraging this militancy against people who for all intents and purposes seemed to be among the godly: "They are wonderous holy people, therefore it should seeme to be a very uncharitable thing in the servants of God to condemne such." But the visible holiness of legalists no more moved Wheelwright than the visible piety of evangelical hypocrites swayed Shepard—Paul, he replied, was wonderfully holy before his conversion while he was under a covenant of works and persecuted Christians.[21]

Most notoriously militant was Wheelwright's reply to the objection, "This will cause a combustion in the Church and Commonwealth." Wheelwright replied, "I confess and acknowledge it will do so, but what then?" And here Wheelwright laid out the extraordinarily high eschatological stakes of the Massachusetts struggle, invoking Malachi and the spiritual burning of Antichrist, meaning the overthrow of the teaching of a false Christ, that had to take place before the Jews were called and the millenarian church could come into existence. Those who opposed this grand cause could only be acting with the spirit of Antichrist.[22]

Having applied his doctrine to Massachusetts's circumstances, Wheelwright exhorted "we that are under a Covenant of grace" on how to behave. His listeners should not compromise Gospel truth. "Whether brethren or sisters," they must "all have a care to hold forth Christ, and not to runne into generalityes, lest Christ vanish away." They must all love each other and maintain their own unity, in spite of their diversity. Most important, they must be sure to act scrupulously holy: "Let us deale uprightly with those with whom we have occasion to deale, and have a care to guide our familyes, and to peforme duties that belong to us." This was partially "that we not give occasion to others to say we are libertines or Antinomians." It was also to bring Christ further to Massachusetts, with all the blessings that accompanied him, for "he will crowne his owne worke with his presence."[23]

Wheelwright ended this bitterly uncharitable sermon with an affirmation of the saints' corporate benevolence. They were "the greatest friends unto the Church and Commonwealth, they intend and labor and indeavour to bring the Lord Jesus Christ, and if Christ be present, there will be no cause of fasting and mourning." Wheelwright's opponents, on the other hand, since they deludedly fasted in the first instance to seek blessings and remove evils, went in opposition to the ways of Christ and were "the greatest enimyes to the state that can be." Foreshadowing his own fate, Wheelwright closed by saying that if every blessing should be taken away from the saints, including the greatest of all, the ordinances of the church, the saints could never lose Christ; therefore they should not fear even banishment.[24]

It might seem a straightforward downhill roll for Wheelwright from this incendiary sermon to a trial. Shepard may have been inflammatory and divisive, but he did not talk about torching the colony. Yet there is no record of a strong immediate adverse reaction to the sermon. Winthrop, who had already demonstrated his deep distrust of Wheelwright, neither mentioned it in his journal when noting the fast day nor left a blank space for afterthoughts. He did immediately thereafter write that the ministers were now disputing the doctrinal issues in their pulpits "so as all men's mouths were full of them." But he also added "there being only Mr. Cotton of one party," which suggests that Wheelwright was far from his mind as he composed the entry.[25]

Why Winthrop's silence about Wheelwright's sermon? Perhaps it was not a particularly rousing sermon as heard; perhaps Wheelwright, speaking slowly and carefully as he searched for the right expressions, said nothing that had not been common talk in the congregation for months and nothing that surprised Winthrop at the time. After all, Vane recently in the General Court had spoken of the Gospel's bringing a sword and of the persecution of the godly by the children of the bondwoman, while Cotton had accused his fellow ministers of popery. Wheelwright's sermon had no discussion of the "new creature," a topic wherein Winthrop was especially prone to suspect Wheelwright of familism. Sanctification and creature graces were real, Wheelwright stressed; God wrote his Law on believers' hearts. He called for holiness and warned his audience not to behave like antinomians.[26]

Perhaps it took conference and reflection before hostile observers realized that they had the materials with which they could finally construct Wheelwright as far enough out on a limb that he could be lopped off. As we will see even from the scanty evidence that survives, setting up the trial against Wheelwright involved backdoor maneuvering, slander, and, in addition to the charge of sedition, a charge of heresy overlooked by historians. The fast-day sermon hardly stood on its own as the basis for Wheelwright's trial.

And Wheelwright was hardly on his own in Boston in his stark portrayal of a sharply bifurcated colony. Cotton is depicted in only one anecdote from the winter of 1637, of which two strikingly different accounts survive. He and Wilson preached on February 3 to a group of persons about to return to England. Winthrop described the sermons in his journal, and he gave a very opaque account of Cotton's performance:

> Mr. Cotton took occasion to speak to them about the differences, etc., and willed them to tell our countrymen, that all the strife amongst us was about magnifying the grace of God; one party seeking to advance the grace of God within us, and the other to advance the grace of God toward us, (meaning by the one justification, and by the other sanctification;) and so bade them tell them that, if there were any among them that would strive for grace, they should come hither; and so declared some particulars.[27]

It is easy to read this sermon, from Winthrop's account, as pacific—both parties, Cotton claimed, were talking about grace, only in different manners, and that is how some historians interpret it.[28] Winthrop's account, however, is difficult to reconcile with the other surviving depiction of this sermon. Ex–Boston church member William Coddington, one of the original assistants of the Massachusetts Bay Company and one of the richest men in the colony, thirty-five years later published a letter to his former brethren in Massachusetts, and therein he recollected Cotton's speech with none of Winthrop's blandness:

> *John Cotton*, on *Acts. 4.13*, on his Lecture Day, the Ships ready to depart for England . . . stated the Difference, it was about *Grace*; he magnified Grace within us, the Priests Grace without or upon them: So all the Difference in the Country was about Grace, notwithstanding the Difference was as great (saith he) as between Light and Darkness, Heaven and Hell, Life and Death: For as in the Text, when they saw the Boldness of *Peter* and *John*, they perceived they had been with *Jesus*; and from the Spirit of Jesus did he then declare.[29]

Coddington's memory was of an angry polarizing sermon but one that nonetheless bore a family resemblance to Winthrop's description; the dispute was about grace, with one party magnifying grace within and the other party grace without. Coddington, of course, may have been remembering the sermon he wanted to remember, a sermon that justified his becoming the most prominent of the original Rhode Island exiles, but I am inclined to believe that he got closer to the tone of what Cotton delivered than did Winthrop. Nothing he described contradicted Winthrop's account; it filled out Winthrop's "etc.s" and "particulars." If Coddington's version has any validity, Winthrop gave the best possible slant to an angry performance, describing it in a way that left room for reclaiming Cotton, while reporting nothing inaccurately.

Coddington's version, moreover, makes the rest of Winthrop's own account of that day intelligible. Wilson followed Cotton, and, according to Winthrop, gave what appears to have been an angry sermon of his own. Wilson told the departing travelers that he knew of no ministers in Massachusetts who did not did not preach justification by free grace "so far as the word of God required." He elaborated on the use and necessity of sanctification. Winthrop was relieved that the sermon cleared the colony's ministers "who otherwise should have been reputed to have opposed free grace." One can imagine Wilson sitting beneath Cotton, listening to his small, stout colleague, who was perhaps waving his right hand with more than his usual vehemence as he preached; growing increasingly indignant at what he was hearing; and then hurriedly climbing the stairs to the raw pine pulpit, determined to clear his brethren from their association with death and hell.[30]

Winthrop claimed that when Wilson ended "no man could tell (except some few, who knew the bottom of the matter) where any difference was." Somewhat contradictorily, he also noted that Wilson's sermon "offended those of Mr. Cotton's party." That offense is understandable enough, given that Wilson had just defended what Cotton, according to Coddington, had denounced as darkness, hell and death. It may not be a coincidence that Winthrop followed his account of the two sermons by describing for the first time acts of cultural aggression by the Bostonians: "The members of Boston (frequenting the lectures of other ministers) did make much disturbance by public questions, and objections to their doctrines, which did any way disagree from their opinions: and it began to be as common here to distinguish between men, by being under a covenant of grace or a covenant of works, as in other countries between Protestants and papists." In view of the prevalent historigraphical tendency to speak of Boston in terms of "antinomians" and "Hutchinsonians," it is important to note that Winthrop spoke of "Mr. Cotton's party." Cotton himself later acknowledged to Wheelwright that it was not only opinionists but persons "that were affected to our Judgments" who participated in the aggressive questioning.[31]

Thomas Weld, in his preface to *Short Story*, provided his own well-known, semi-hysterical list of cultural assaults against Massachusetts's faithful ministers. That list presumably dates back to the same period, since Weld described in more detail the same behavior as Winthrop, including the first reference to anyone snubbing Wilson:

> Now the faithfull Ministers of Christ must have dung cast on their faces, and be no better then Legall Preachers, Baals Priests, Popish Factors, Scribes, Pharisees, and Opposers of Christ himselfe. . . . Such a Church officer is an ignorant man, and knowes not Christ; such an one is under a Covenant of workes; such a Pastor is a proud man, and would make a good persecutor; such a Teacher is grossely Popish. . . . Now, after our Sermons were ended at our publike Lectures, you might have seene halfe a dozen Pistols discharged at the face of the Preacher, (I meane) so many objections made by the opinionists in the open Assembly against our doctrine delivered, if it suited not their new fancies. . . . Now, you might have seene many of the Opinionists rising up, and contemptuously turning their backs upon the faithfull Pastor of that Church, and going forth from the Assembly when he began to pray or preach.[32]

Certainly this is a vivid portrait of one-sided Bostonian aggression, and there are certainly Bostonian roots to that aggression. Both Cotton and *Mercurius Americanus* later acknowledged that Wheelwright's fast-day rhetoric gave license to the extremists in the Boston congregation. According to Giles Firmin, Henry Vane was particularly active in challenging ministers' doctrine. He "was the man that did embolden them, when ministers had done preaching, he would find questions to put to them, though they were strangers."[33]

But there was another side to the story. Weld inadvertently hinted as much when he acknowledged that the "opinionists" came to challenge sermons especially when "they heard a Minister was upon such a point as was like to strike at their opinions, with a purpose to oppose him to his face." We know now that the Massachusetts establishment itself was not averse to discharging pistols in the face of its opponents, and where the aggression lay was often probably in the eye of the beholder. *Mercurius Americanus* claimed that Weld himself made strikingly violent attacks on Boston, and his church appears to have been the most conflicted church outside Boston. Wilson may have been shunned by "Mr. Cotton's party," but he was also forbidding anyone in his household to attend conventicles at Hutchinson's house, warning that "whatsoever they may pretend, they will rob you of ordinances, rob you of your souls, rob you of your God."[34] Moreover, an important set of sermons Cotton preached around this time demonstrates that "Mr. Cotton's party" could easily conclude that they had ongoing encouragement from him to keep up their struggles.

Cotton was on the attack for a great deal of these sermons, posthumously published as *A Treatise of the Covenant of Grace*. Indeed, much of the cycle can be interpreted and in at least one place was clearly consciously meant to be interpreted as a response to the lectures Shepard was delivering in Newtowne. In various ways, some more convoluted than others, Shepard tried to link Boston with Arminianism and popery. Cotton suggested that, on the contrary, his own emphasis on the absolute nature of the covenant of grace was the ultimate antidote to Arminianism and popery, since these both held forth a covenant of works and he clearly did not. Shepard, prior to launching into a long passage on the discernable difference between the grace of hypocrites and that of the saints, acknowledged that " 'tis difficult for men, Ministers, or Angels to reveal it." Cotton commented that Shepard's statement had the "weight of truth" and added sardonically that it was fitter for angels to attempt to perceive genuine sanctification than ministers.[35]

Cotton left no doubt about how dangerous his opponents were, although he did not use Wheelwright or Shepard's inflammatory language. He consistently stressed that conditional promises could not offer assurance. Cotton attacked Hooker and Shepard's conception of preparation, even while noting that it was held by "precious Saints." The ministers who disagreed with him might be gracious saints, but they were nonetheless dangerous deceivers of their audiences: persons who looked for assurance in conditional promises were probably either in a covenant of works or had turned aside to one. Such Christians could be "misled into dangerous ways" even unto damnation. And where did the responsibility for their possibly soul-damning ignorance lie? It was because they had "not been clearly taught the distinct differences between these two Covenants"—

Cotton did not need to say who had failed to teach these Christians properly. As an olive branch, he added that the Lord would eventually clarify the truth to them.[36]

Cotton's reproaches were directed not only at his opponents. He rebuked the censoriousness and loose expressions of his own congregation.[37] More important, *Treatise* criticized Boston's doctrinal errors. It backs up his later claim that he did indeed preach against mistakes in his own camp. However, it problematizes his later projection of himself as in a kind of fog during the controversy: his fellow ministers would come to him and tell him of these errors, he claimed, yet whenever he made inquiries among his congregation, no one admitted to them. He preached against errors more as a gesture of good will to his brethren than as the result of first-hand knowledge. But the Cotton of *Treatise* knew very well what was going on in his church and was not overly concerned.

Cotton rebuked errors both mildly and with qualifications. He cautioned that people knowing they were saved would experience God's chastisements when they sinned and would pray for pardon—he did not sanction the unconditional joy that some of his congregation were trumpeting. Nonetheless, no matter how heinous the sins into which believers fell, he insisted that they need never doubt their salvation, in spite of the fact that his opponents found this doctrine "scandalous." Cotton acknowledged that the Devil might delude people who found assurance through a revelation.[38] But he acknowledged this only once, whereas the endless possibilities for self-deception through relying on conditional promises was a running theme of the sermons.

Most important, in the course of his discussion of sanctification, Cotton criticized the central assumption of "Hutchinsonianism." To the limited extent that sanctification witnessed justification, he said, it did so not because it was evidence in itself, but because it was a very murky glass through which believers might perceive sanctification's roots in union with Christ and the indwelling of the Holy Spirit. Cotton could not have presented sanctification more inoffensively to those in his audience suspicious of the concept, which was probably not unintentional. Cotton then acknowledged that there was a question that "springeth naturally from the Doctrine." "If the Lord give himselfe to be my righteousnes and holines," Cotton phrased this question, "what need we the gift to work any thing, which God is much more able to perform than we can be?" That question sprang from the core of "Hutchinsonianism": there were no "creature graces" in believers; sanctification remained entirely in Christ, who activated the believer through the Holy Spirit. As *Mercurius Americanus* said, "Hutchinsonianism" exalted the covenant of grace while denying the grace of the covenant.[39] Hutchinson herself may have very well asked Cotton this question as an "inquiry."

Both Cotton and Wheelwright agreed that believers had "the gift to work," and Cotton explained at length in this sermon cycle why gifts and graces were both real and necessary. However, he showed strikingly less concern for this central "Hutchinsonian" error than for those stemming from his opponents' position. He gave no hint that people who held it, unlike those who held the errors of his opponents, had turned aside from the covenant of grace. He certainly did not suggest that they were guilty of "haereticall Pravity," as he would later when he had turned against them.[40]

Clearly in the first half of 1637 Cotton still regarded "Hutchinsonian" reasoning, whose proponents always appear to have presented it publicly as speculative rather than dogmatic, to be a wayward byproduct of Christians discovering the miracle of the covenant of grace. Very likely too, anyone listening to his sermons, friendly or hostile, would have concluded that such was his attitude. Cotton considered the radicals in his congregation and his ministerial opponents as mistaken; it was not hard to figure out whom he regarded as more dangerously mistaken. A year previously he had told Shepard that he doubted that he and his brethren truly differed. Now those brethren had become the defining opposition against which Cotton gently but firmly constructed his stairway to heaven.

Shepard militantly made it clear that his opponents were pied pipers heading to hell, as had Cotton, albeit with considerably more tact. Wheelwright's fast-day sermon starts to seem like more of the same. It was arguably elevated above the general level of rhetoric by its encouragement of combustion in the commonwealth, but if so, the elevation was only a matter of degree. Partisans on both sides of this controversy had higher priorities than civic tranquility; Shepard repeatedly warned against tolerating his opponents' "errors" for the sake of peace. Had Shepard and Cotton's rhetoric been the only context within which to put Wheelwright's sermon, perhaps he would have never ended up on trial. Sedition in this context, with ministers and General Court divided and mutually abusive, was as much an emergent, political category as it was a fixed, legal one.

But unfortunately for himself, Wheelwright provided ample additional context. His preaching at Mount Wollaston was being listened to carefully by unfriendly ears, which did not cause him to moderate it. In one sermon, he announced that faith and repentance were no parts of the covenant of grace. Believing belonged to the covenant of works, he was said to have claimed. He meant by this no more than faith and repentance could in some circumstances be works like any other human activity, and that they could therefore not be a first evidence for justification, although faith was the instrument by which that evidence came.[41] That is how he explained what he meant later, and had he been a more temperate or pragmatic man, he would have eschewed such antinomian-tilting rhetoric and carefully distinguished legal faith and repentance from their evangelical counterparts. But he chose not to. He had his eye more on the sins of his enemies than on the common ground he shared with them, and he was indifferent to the fact that he was making it very tempting for them to portray him as a heretic.

He thereby dug a pit for himself. The semi-improvised legal structures of puritan Massachusetts were not set up to deal with godly ministers heaping abuse on each other from their pulpits—the idea was a oxymoron. A heretic attacking those ministers, however, and urging his listeners to band together and struggle against them was another matter altogether. Since heresy was illicit, that minister, by definition, was trying to form an illicit party, and when he encouraged his party to cause a combustion in the commonwealth, the minister was clearly a menace to the public good. His pulpit rhetoric, in other words, was clearly seditious, and, as such, fell within the jurisdiction of the General Court.[42]

Ministers in the colony soon began forging this chain of logic against Wheelwright. The following story comes from Wheelwright and he wrote it much later, but an anonymous document surviving in the Samuel Hartlib papers corroborates it in its broad outline. In the winter of 1637, some ministers presented a list of doctrinal charges against Wheelwright secretly to the General Court. They wrote, they said, not to aggravate Wheelwright's fault in the eye of authority, but to convince him in his conscience and bring him to repent (but why did they not come to me first, Wheelwright complained, failing to add that it would have made no impact on him had they done so). They introduced their solicitude for Wheelwright, he claimed, with "many bitter invectives, ranking me amongst the instruments of Satan, acted by him, to pull down the Kingdom of Christ upon earth, because I could not do it in heaven, &c."[43]

The ministers made four doctrinal charges against Wheelwright, drawn from his Mount Wollaston and fast-day sermons: faith and repentance were no parts of the doctrine of the Gospel; to evidence justification by sanctification was a covenant of works; they who saw in themselves any sanctification, and thence concluded a good estate, should never be saved; and they who disagreed with this doctrine were Antichrists, enemies to Christ, and under a covenant of works.[44] These were extremely serious charges, and they were mostly unfair to Wheelwright's teaching, not that he went out of his way to dispel them.[45] Unfair or not, they provided the wedge by which the lay and ministerial opponents of Boston began the process of attempting to create through legal means the unity they had not been able to effect by debate.

The General Court, twelve magistrates and thirty-three town deputies, gathered in the Boston meetinghouse on March 9, ready to assume the judicial role it shared with its legislative and executive duties. As a judicial body, the Court's members interchangeably acted as prosecutors, judges, jury, and, to a much lesser extent, defense advocates, a flexibility that broadly reflected contemporary English jurisprudence. Coddington later claimed that a majority among the magistrates were not predisposed to punishing Wheelwright, which is entirely possible. Three of them, Governor Vane and assistants Coddington and Drummer, were Wheelwright's partisans, while four other assistants, John Humphrey, Simon Bradstreet, Richard Bellingham, and John Winthrop, Jr., in the years to come on occasion showed more tolerance of religious diversity than many of their fellow magistrates. It was deputies who asked that Wheelwright be sent for because of his fast-day sermon—in the fragment of the trial transcript printed by S. G., deputies William Spencer from Newtowne and Richard Collicot of Dorchester are Wheelwright's most aggressive pursuers. Winthrop later claimed in an "Apology" he wrote for the Court's action that the move to examine Wheelwright came simply because Wheelwright's fast-day sermon tended to "sedition, and disturbance of the publicke peace." His claim, however, was a covering-of-tracks maneuver, done deftly enough that it has escaped subsequent notice. The actual accusation charged Wheelwright with "preaching on the Fast Day a *Heretical* [my italics] and Seditious Sermon, tending to Mutiny and Disturbance."[46] The exact wording of the charge was important; the anti-Boston party on the Court, as will be shown, was preparing the groundwork to make heresy a major component of the sedition charge; if it was not a component, then Wheelwright's opponents were left with the delicate task of demonstrating on other grounds that a sermon approved by the colony's governor was seditious. The Court assented to the deputies' request, and Wheelwright was notified to be ready to appear in the next two or three days.

This was a promising beginning for the anti-Boston party, and its next maneuver also went smoothly. The Court fined Stephen Greensmith, a Boston lumber dealer, for saying with more recklessness than theological acuity that all the ministers in the colony except Wheelwright, Cotton, and, "hee thought," Thomas Hooker, the minister most antithetical to them, were under a covenant of works. It ordered Greensmith, for good measure, to apologize in every church.[47] Overtly slander the ministers, and this Court would punish you.

But into murkier water than that a majority on the Court was still unprepared to go. According to Winthrop, the Court, meaning the self-appointed prosecutors, next "questioned the proceeding against Mr. Wilson" in the Boston church, in order to "fasten upon such as had prejudiced him." The prosecutors did not get all that they wanted. They had to be content that "by the vote of the greater party, [Wilson's] speech was approved, and declared to have been a seasonable advice."[48] The Court as a whole, although willing to voice support for Wilson, was not willing to chase after his opponents. Wheelwright's conviction was not a sure thing.

Winthrop and his allies, however, had not finished strengthening their hand for Wheelwright's trial. They called in the ministers, Winthrop recorded, to "give advice about the authority of the court in things concerning the churches." All the ministers agreed on two things. (But what did they not agree on? What were the debates that led up to this agreement? Does the pronoun "all" really cover Cotton? Winthrop does not tell us.) First, Court members could not be questioned in their churches for their speeches in the Court, and second, the state could discipline before the individual churches had acted "in all such heresies or errors of any church member as are manifest and dangerous to the state." That agreement provided Winthrop cover in his home church and gave ministerial sanction to Wheelwright's prosecution for heresy and sedition. Both assertions conceded authority to the magistrates that the ministers had denied them two years previously in their "Model."[49]

The groundwork having been laid for Wheelwright's conviction, the Court summoned him. Our knowledge of Wheelwright's trial comes mostly from Winthrop's "Apology," which was scarcely a disinterested document. Winthrop, however, wrote for a local audience, fully aware that transcripts of the trial were circulating. Thus, he probably did not present anything overtly incorrect, but, as will be seen, he was careful about what he chose to record. Wheelwright presented the Court a copy of his sermon that he owned was accurate as to the substance of it, and he was dismissed until the next day. The move to question Wheelwright provoked strong opposition in Boston. A petition came in signed by more than forty people challenging the right of the Court to try a case of conscience before the church had heard it and requesting that the proceedings be open. The petition was denied—the Court was not hearing a trial but conducting an investigation, and the issue was public, not a case of conscience.[50] Wheelwright was called in the next morning in private.

At this private morning session the mutual distrust was thick. Wheelwright wanted to know who his accusers were. Someone answered that his sermon was, and since he had acknowledged it the Court might proceed ex officio. An interesting choice of words, since it could be taken to mean, and perhaps was intended to mean, that Wheelwright, through his sermon, would testify against himself. Not a few nonconforming ministers had been ensnared in the ecclesiastical Court of High Commission by being forced to testify through an ex officio oath, and the ministerial "Model" had denied that magistrates could use it. According to Winthrop "great exception was taken, as if the Court intended the course of the High Commission." Someone nimbly stepped in and claimed that all the term meant was that the Court acted by authority. Wheelwright calmed down "through perswasion of some of his friends," but the next question set the room in an uproar again: Did Wheelwright know when he preached his sermon that most ministers in the country taught what he called a covenant of works? Saying yes would have been an acknowledgment that Wheelwright had tried to incite his listeners to form a party. He sensibly refused to answer. Other members of the Court cried out that the Court was trying to ensnare Wheelwright and that the question had nothing to do with the matter of the sermon. Since Wheelwright refused to convict himself, the closed morning session ended in stalemate.[51]

In the afternoon, the Court requested that the ministers be present, and, having opened its doors to the ministers, it decided to let in the general public as well, which resulted in a "great Assembly." The session began with the prosecution giving a summary of Wheelwright's fast sermon. Wheelwright was again asked if he had meant that any of the ministers or Christians in the churches of Massachusetts "walked" under a covenant of works. Wheelwright made the careful reply that if any walked in such a fashion, them he meant.[52] Wheelwright's enemies had gotten nowhere in attempting to force him to incriminate himself.

At this point, the prosecution brought up the Mount Wollaston sermon in order to prove the heresy charge. The deputies raised the issue of Wheelwright's statements about faith and repentance. Wheelwright reported later that their accounts were confused and contradictory, which was entirely possible, given the intricacy of what he had preached. Wheelwright, in response, vehemently denied that he had meant what his accusers claimed he had meant. He was asked if faith was a condition of the Gospel. Yes, he replied, but it was a condition consequent to Christ's giving of himself in a free promise, not antecedent. By that he meant, like Cotton, that faith came into existence in the process of justification and was only active afterward. He was asked if sanctification could evidence one's salvation. Yes, he replied, as a secondary evidence. At any rate, as Wheelwright pointed out later, and may have pointed out to the Court, his fast-day sermon, for which he was ostensibly being tried, said nothing on the topics of faith and repentance.[53]

If you were a professional theologian, you might find much in the convolutions of Wheelwright's answers to provoke you.[54] Winthrop noted various ministers' "griefe to see such opinions risen in the Country of so dangerous consequence, and so directly crossing the scope of the Gospell." However, if you were not a professional theologian and sitting on the General Court, you might be inclined to give Wheelwright the benefit of the doubt over the Mount Wollaston sermon. He insisted that he did not deny the importance of sanctification, or faith, or repentance; was Wheelwright's doctrine really the blatant heresy that was dangerous to states? Winthrop, putting a brave face on a prosecutorial retreat, wrote in his "Apology" that "this being matter of Doctrine, the Court passed it by for the present."[55] On sensible polemical grounds he omitted altogether what happened next.

Recognizing that the nuances of what Wheelwright might or might not have said in Mount Wollaston were proving too confusing to produce a heresy conviction, deputy Spencer took another doctrinal tack. He turned to the basic issue that split Cotton and Wheelwright from the rest of the ministers: "*Wheelwright* teaches, that the Knowledge of our Sanctification, as well as our Justification, is only by Faith in Christ; and that in the Covenant of Grace nothing is revealed but Jesus Christ, and his Righteousness freely given to the Soul, and the Knowledge of it comes by Faith: And this . . . is contrary to the Doctrine preached in New-England; for . . . it is commonly taught in New-England, That a man may prove his justification by his Sanctification." John Endicott seconded Spencer: Wheelwright's doctrine, he said, "is concluded a False Doctrine, because it is a Doctrine against all the Ministers of the Country."[56]

This line of attack failed to produce a heresy conviction, but that failure was not due to any reluctance to prosecute doctrine. It came about because the attack no longer focused on Wheelwright alone and his tendency to make incautious statements; it went to the heart of Cotton's differences with his brethren. And at this moment, Cotton interposed himself, an intervention that Winthrop conspicuously omitted in both his journal and his "Apology": "Brother *Wheelwright's* Doctrine was according to God," Cotton announced, "in the Points Controverted, and wholely, and altogether; and nothing did I hear alledged against the Doctrine proved by the Word of God." Go after Wheelwright and you go after me, Cotton warned in effect.[57]

Cotton's intervention effectively closed off the prosecution's doctrinal line of pursuit—no one was prepared to argue (at least in public) that Cotton preached heresies dangerous to the state. Cotton spoke "much more" to "allay the Heat of their Raging Spirits," claimed a sympathizer summarizing the transcript, but it was to no avail. Spencer retreated back to the issue of Wheelwright's sedition, only now stripped of its doctrinal element: "The Matter in hand is not the Doctrine, whether it be true or false: but the Question is, Whether or not Mr. *Wheelwright* hath stirred up Mutiny in the Country, and cast Aspersions upon the Ministers?"[58] Wheelwright still refused to acknowledge that he had meant the ministers in his sermon, and the trial continued to spin in circles.

It was at this point that Wheelwright's prosecutors finally successfully found their way to a conviction. Someone hit upon the clever expedient of asking the ministers if they regarded themselves as Wheelwright's target. The ministers, without Cotton, met overnight and the next day announced to the Court that they did indeed "walk in" and teach what

Wheelwright had termed a covenant of works. Cotton dissented. The other ministers then asked permission to speak individually, which was granted. According to Winthrop, they told of the great dangers to church and state the present religious divisions presented and claimed they would do everything in their power to effect a reconciliation between them and Wheelwright. They presented Wheelwright with a way to gracefully back down, charitably concluding that his being newly arrived in the colony might have been the occasion of their differences of opinion. Winthrop professed to be struck by the "humanity and respect" with which the ministers addressed Wheelwright and expressed disapproval that Wheelwright showed no willingness to reciprocate.[59] Perhaps this is the place to insert one of Winthrop's anecdotes from the trial. Wheelwright was being reproached for not having consulted with the ministers about his doctrines before preaching his sermon, since he knew that most of them disagreed with him; "hee answered that he ought not to consult with flesh and bloud, about the publishing of that truth which he had received from God." Given Wheelwright's approval of Knollys's divinely communicated doctrines, he may have meant this statement more literally than anyone in the Court suspected.[60]

Collectively laying ministerial authority on the line proved effective. The ministers, save one, had said what Wheelwright himself refused to admit—his sermon had been intended to incite his listeners against them. When they gave Wheelwright a face-saving way to express repentence, a standard route to clemency in early modern English courts and one even more accented in Massachusetts, Wheelwright neither apologized nor expressed any interest in reconciliation. For those on the Court who had been wavering, to refuse to confict Wheelwright now would be to repudiate Massachusetts's clerical establishment for the sake of a minister who was not only theologically marginal, divisive, and largely unknown, but also recklessly inflexible. "The priests got two of the magistrats on their side," was how Coddington remembered the conclusion of the trial, "and so got the major part with them." How the deputies reached their own majority to convict, if it had ever been in doubt, is unknown. Boston's opponents could now move for a verdict, with the heresy charge dropped but with a charge of contempt thrown in to sweeten the pot: "It was concluded by the Court that Mr. Wheelwright was guilty of contempt and sedition" say the colony records as their only mention of the three-day proceeding.[61] The anti-Boston party had gotten a significant victory—one that would almost wreck the colony.

SEVEN

ABIMELECH'S FACTION

MARCH–AUGUST 1637

WHEELWRIGHT'S conviction was the single most critical event in shaping the course of the free grace controversy. The anti-Boston party, in its own eyes, had successfully transformed a complex theological dispute into an issue of state authority versus sedition, and any objection to the issue's being framed that way would only be further evidence of sedition. But their prosecution had not gone smoothly. The charge of heresy, intended to render more plausible the charges of contempt and sedition, had vanished and what was left was the effort to argue that sedition existed when the author of the seditious statements denied meaning what he was accused of and the colony's governor perceived neither sedition nor contempt. Since Wheelwright's doctrine had not been condemned, it was easy enough to interpret his conviction simply as persecution of a minister for preaching the Gospel, easy enough to conclude that the result, instead of giving state legitimacy to the anti-Boston party, drained the legitimacy of the state and gave further credibility to the claim of the most militant Bostonians that their opponents were under an antichristian covenant of works. What had been a polarized theological dispute was now a polarized political dispute, and the debates moved from points of doctrine to the nature and extent of the power of the Massachusetts government.

This dispute would not allow an easy resolution, due in large measure to Henry Vane. He provided Boston with the authority and protection of his own high status, and with his connections he encouraged his side to consider countering the local government's power with that of the king. While Vane's stature stiffened Boston's resistance to compromise, that same stature, combined with the general inability in the seventeenth century to conceive of dissent as legitimate, encouraged Boston's opponents to think of themselves as besieged. They pictured Boston's dissent as the product of a sinister faction led by a conspiratorial Vane, who aimed at the destruction of Massachusetts. The result was a spiraling dance of paranoia, accusations, political maneuvers, scribal "publications," and governmental edicts that continued until Cotton and a sizable number of his congregation made serious efforts to depart the colony in the summer of 1637, and Winthrop's city on a hill ran the risk of coming to an abrupt and inglorious end.

Having convicted Wheelwright, the March Court deferred sentence on him until its next sitting. Perhaps that action was a compassionate gesture to give errant brother Wheelwright a chance to repent, or perhaps it was a pragmatic recognition that the new majority on the Court had pushed its luck in convicting him after half its case had vanished. In lieu of his immediate sentencing, the Court asked the ministers if "they might enjoin his silence." A truly tender moment, as the ministers, many of them themselves silenced in England, juggled this hot potato in front of a divided General Court and a large crowd of less-than-unanimously-sympathetic laity. The ministers passed the buck: "They answered, that they were not clear in that point, but desired rather, that he might be commended to the church of Boston to take care of him."[1] It is not clear how they anticipated Boston would take care of Wheelwright, but at any rate he was dismissed and the Court proceeded to other business.

Boston, however, was hardly ready to move on, and thus the controversy passed on to the stage of political confrontation. Some of the dissenting deputies and magistrates, including Vane, asked that their dissent be recorded. The request was refused, but it was offered to them that they could copy the court record verbatim and subscribe their dissent. (Vane, ostensibly the presiding officer, had presumably long ago lost all control of the session, perhaps an indication of his inexperience at political hardball.) In response, Vane and some other Court members handed in a now disappeared Protestation, which Winthrop said justified Wheelwright as a faithful minister of Christ. That much might have been expected, but more seriously, the Protestation challenged not only the correctness but the legitimacy of the Court's decision. The Court's proceedings were null, it argued, because a minority on the Court dissented; presumably the Protestation's reasoning was that if the Court functioned as a jury in convicting Wheelwright then its lack of unanimity voided the conviction.[2] In other words, the Massachusetts government in convicting Wheelwright had made a decision that it had no authority to make, or so pronounced the governor of Massachusetts and son of one of the king's privy counselors.

Other disappointed and angry Wheelwright supporters, as they spilled into the lane outside the Boston meetinghouse, decided on a similar course against the Court's action. They drew up a "remonstrance and Petition." Petitioning rulers for redress of grievances was a time-honored but tricky custom in England's hierarchical, authoritarian culture. While petitioning in itself was legitimate, petitioners risked a punitive response should they imply that their rulers' conduct might be responsible for those grievances. To use an analogy, it was a commonplace that rulers stood in the place of God to those they governed, and while people routinely petitioned God with prayer about their troubles, a prayer that even hinted at rebuking God for these troubles would be a blasphemous invitation to divine retribution.[3]

Remaining within the amorphous bounds of the acceptably deferential proved a severe challenge to the Wheelwright petitioners. Winthrop claimed that William Aspinwall, the Boston church's deacon and a future radical English Fifth Monarchist, wrote the first draft of the petition in language so "foule" that he had to tone it down. Even so, the finished "remonstrance and Petition" careened dangerously in tone between deference and belligerent defiance. The purpose of the fast was to promote peace and that Wheelwright preached the true Gospel path to peace, the petition stated, hence there had been no contempt of the Court. Nor had there been sedition: Wheelwright had committed no seditious act; his doctrine could not have been seditious because it came from the Holy Ghost; and the application of the doctrine hardly had an insurrectionary effect on its listeners. "It hath not stirred up sedition in us," the petitioners assured the Court and cited biblical examples where the godly had rescued their "innocent" brethren by force without it being seditious. Arguing that Wheelwright was innocent and that there would have been solid biblical precedents for rescuing him by force without that action constituting sedition was perhaps not the best way to persuade the Court that Wheelwright had not fostered a tumultuous party. The petition then untactfully suggested that the Court reflect if Satan were behind its action, since he, "the ancient enemy of Free Grace," always "raised up such calumnies against the faithfull Prophets of God." No more judicious was its warning to the Court to "consider the danger of meddling against the Prophets of God." The petitioners closed by appealing to the Court as "nursing Fathers," which was deferential enough, but added that "if wee should receive repulse from you, with the Lord wee shall find grace."[4] The petition was not an appeal for clemency; it was an offer to the Court to make amends for passing an illegitimate sentence under the influence of Satan, one that invited the Lord's retribution.

That over sixty men were prepared to sign this bellicose document, one that would itself be eventually deemed seditious for its defiance of the Court, suggests the intensity of resentment Wheelwright's conviction stirred up.[5] Most of the signers came from Boston, but at least eleven came from adjacent Charleston. Most of them were freemen, and among them were a disproportionate number of officeholders and the better-off. The great majority had been in Massachusetts for over three years, with 1630 the most represented year of immigration. In general these were not militant newcomers radicalized perhaps by increasing repression in England, but respectable, well-settled members of the commonwealth outraged that the Gospel should be persecuted in a puritan colony. Cotton himself fully shared in that resentment. He thought that Wheelwright "might have some Reason for the vehemency of [his] Expressions," since "the great opposition to arise against the Doctrine of the Covenants delivered by us" meant that "many in the country" "confounded" the covenant of works and grace. In other words, Wheelwright's cry to spiritual warfare against Antichrist in Massachusetts had some basis in fact. Cotton was accordingly furious with the Court verdict. Winthrop later said critics ranged from those who thought the Court had been unjust to those who thought it had been "(at best) over hasty." There is nothing in the petition that demonstrates the existence of a large contingent of "Hutchinsonians," as historians frequently assume, unless one wishes to argue that Cotton was a Hutchinsonian.[6]

Near the end of the Court's session, someone moved from the floor to hold the next Court at Newtowne, which was sensible enough, given the defiance of Boston. Winthrop recorded that Vane refused to put the motion to a vote, the only glimpse we catch of him as presiding officer during this whole fraught session. Deputy Governor Winthrop also refused to put it voluntarily, since he resided in Boston, so John Endicott moved the motion and it carried.[7]

After the Court concluded, the debate over Wheelwright's trial continued with the distribution of manuscripts. A magistrate secretly and hastily transcribed the ministers' attack on Wheelwright and passed it along to him. In response, Wheelwright wrote a small treatise defending his conception of the covenant of grace from the interpretation they had given it. He denounced the "wicked Errours" the ministers had accused him of, "shewing that they were your groundless inferences." However, he was no milder to his brethren than they had been to him. He appears to have told them that his was the doctrine of eternal life, theirs a doctrine of eternal damnation. The treatise has not survived. Winthrop read it and grumbled in his journal that it was doctrinally "differing from his sermon," but he made no mention of the attack that provoked it. The ministers replied to Wheelwright, in another disappeared manuscript, confuting him, according to Winthrop, with "many strong arguments." Cotton replied to the ministers both orally and in writing (see below)[8]

The level of dissatisfaction with the Court decision was high enough that Winthrop wrote a surviving "Apology." The "Apology," announcing itself as a "publick Declaration," circulated widely enough that he could claim that Wheelwright "certainly" saw it—Wheelwright replied that he "did not much inquire after" it because he "knew very well that the cause was incapable of any just defense." Winthrop's "Apology" forthrightly took on the challenge of demonstrating that Wheelwright's sermon was both seditious and contemptuous. Making a party constituted sedition, argued Winthrop, citing biblical and classical sources, and that was what

Wheelwright attempted in his sermon. There had been no disputes about these issues, in public anyway, Winthrop argued, before Wheelwright arrived. To preach a sermon advocating contention on a day the authorities had intended for reconciliation amply warranted the contempt conviction; the sedition conviction was justified because Wheelwright encouraged the formation of parties, and if nothing overtly seditious had happened yet, it might in the future.[9]

Unapologetic about attacking Wheelwright, Winthrop had no patience for efforts to defend him. He dismissed the claim that Wheelwright was prosecuted for preaching the Gospel; Wheelwright's covenant of grace, wrote Winthrop, was "not in our Bibles." The Court had not managed to get a conviction on Wheelwright's doctrine and Wheelwright's church had not censured him for it, but those technicalities were never to matter much to Winthrop. Nonetheless, Winthrop was discreet enough to argue that even if Wheelwright preached the truth, not all truths were appropriate at all times. The trial itself was legal, said Winthrop, because "Courts as have power to make and abrogate Laws [parliament, for example], are tyed to no other Orders, but their own, and to no other rule but Truth and Justice." In any event, the Court was just as impartial as any jury would be. Winthrop did not mention the need for a jury to be unanimous, although in a now lost writing he dealt with Vane's argument that a minority on the Court could nullify the Court's sentence. Perhaps he pointed out that parliaments, unlike juries, did not need unanimous votes to convict. In any case, the freemen of Massachusetts seemed to have already accepted that the General Court, voting by majority, was the functional equivalent of a jury, and jury trials in general were rare in Massachusetts.[10]

Wheelwright's supporters, according to Winthrop, raised an objection not mentioned in the petition. The ministers claimed that Wheelwright had singled them out, but in fact Wheelwright had not intended to target particular people—Wheelwright himself also asserted as much; he said that since the motions of the Spirit were known only to God, "I did not so much as in my thoughts, conclude the Magistrates, and Elders, or any one of them, or any other person, absolutely to be under that covenant." Winthrop professed himself staggered that anyone could seriously advance this argument. Did not Wheelwright himself say all those who used sanctification as a first evidence were under a covenant of works. Whom could he mean but most of the ministers and magistrates of the Bay? "It is beyond reason, how farre prejudice hath prevailed to captivate some judgements, otherwise godly and wise," he exclaimed in disbelief. Most historians' sympathies have been with Winthrop on this point.[11] Presumably people defending Wheelwright with this argument were using their words very carefully. Wheelwright's deployment of the term "absolutely" might have been all that stood between him and an acknowledgment that the charge of sedition was not entirely unjustified; it was not a defense he attempted to make at the trial itself.

Winthrop's "Apology" might seem stiff and unyielding. It was strikingly mild, however, in comparison to the severe Court response to the Salem letter a year and a half previously protesting the refusal to grant Salem land. As will be seen, Winthrop's restraint was not due to lack of comparable outrage at the Court's being challenged. Rather, it reflected hard realities: Boston was a more important town than Salem, Cotton and Vane were themselves considerably more influential and better connected than Williams and his supporters, and Boston was still well represented in the upper echelons of the colony's government. Wheelwright and his supporters would not suffer the Salemites' fates of expulsions from the Court, jail, and banishments until these factors started to change.

Not all interactions between opponents were confrontational or political, but even fraternal exchanges showed how tightly sides had been drawn up. The minister Peter Bulkeley wrote a letter to Cotton on March 25 after his return to Concord from listening to Cotton's Thursday lecture and talking with him. Bulkeley, on slender evidence, is sometimes taken to be one of the leaders of the opposition to Cotton.[12] But relative to Shepard at least, he appears to have been a doctrinal and political moderate. Like some other ministers, he allowed that absolute promises delivered through the witness of the Spirit could provide comfort, but their comfort, he argued, was more ephemeral than that provided by evidence of believers' graces (which was the exact experiential opposite of Cotton's position).[13] Bulkeley's letter is particularly valuable in that it shows a minister trying hard to understand and communicate with Cotton, unlike Shepard, but failing completely.

Cotton had complained to Bulkeley about the "want of Brotherly love" Cotton was experiencing. Bulkeley, too, lamented the hostilities the crisis engendered, although he included himself among the casualties; people who would previously have traveled great distances to see him "yett here will passe by my dore, as if I were the man that they had not knowen." That Bulkeley and his fellow ministers might have had some responsibility for this cold shouldering does not seem to have occurred to him. In any case, he reminded Cotton that lack of love did not change God's truth.[14]

Bulkeley devoted the rest of the letter to theological matters. Assuring Cotton of his unfeigned love toward him, he did not see why love and the other marks of sanctification could not be a first evidence of justification. How was sanctification different before one knew one was justified than after? He had discussed with Cotton Wheelwright's claim that to believe was not part of the covenant of grace, a claim that had featured in Wheelwright's trial, and Wheelwright's argument still made no sense to him.

Cotton had recently given a sermon in which he had said that both our justification and the faith of our justification must be built only on Christ's righteousness. Bulkeley agreed that justification was built only on Christ's righteousness. But he could not see how assurance could be built on Christ's righteousness alone. Believers could not directly perceive Christ's righteousness belonging to them; they could not directly apprehend God's love. They needed some intermediary sign that demonstrated that love, such as sanctification. As Bulkeley and others argued elsewhere, absolute promises might give comfort, but the only way that you could know for certain that they genuinely belonged to you was if you manifested evidence of the transformation justification brought about.[15]

Bulkeley's queries were reasonable, as well as a dramatic indication of the gulf in sensibility that lay between Cotton and Wheelwright and some of their fellow ministers. For Bulkeley, Cotton and Wheelwright threatened the peace of the colony for nothing more than erroneous word spinning—"There must be some difference betwixt Christs righteousness and that which doth manifest it unto me as mine, but those two yow seeme to confound," he told Cotton. "I doe assure you," Bulkeley closed his letter, "it troubles my spirit that I cannot goe along with yow in these lesser things." He requested in a postscript that Cotton take notice that the gathering of his Concord church would take place the following Wednesday night in Newtowne.[16]

Cotton may have noticed that the gathering would soon take place, but he did not attend. Nor did Wheelwright, Vane, or the ruling elders of the Boston church. Winthrop recorded in his journal that they stayed away, it was widely assumed, because they thought Bulkeley a legal preacher.[17] That Wheelwright and his supporters may well have been in no mood to celebrate with people who had just successfully culminated a not entirely aboveboard campaign to convict him was not a possibility that Winthrop would consider.

Cotton, unlike Wheelwright, at least went through the motions of seeking common ground with his opponents. According to Winthrop, around the beginning of May Cotton and the other ministers searched for consensus through written and oral exchanges that followed the ministers' reply to Wheelwright. They were able to agree that justification and sanctification occurred together in time (that is, if not in order of nature), that one had to know oneself justified before one could know oneself sanctified, and that the Spirit never witnessed justification without a Word and a work (the work being faith and sanctification). Winthrop wrote in his journal that had people not previously staked out their differences as fundamental, they could have easily come to a reconciliation. But it is doubtful that there had ever been disagreement on these points. Cotton wrote a final summary of the differences on May 13, to which Winthrop gave a very favorable gloss: "Mr. Cotton also replied to [the ministers'] answer very largely, and stated the differences in a very narrow scantling."[18]

The differences in fact were not at all narrow, nor did Cotton state them as such. Winthrop acknowledged that the ministers still disagreed on the fundamental issue of whether first assurance had to be by an absolute promise and whether true assurance could only be by some work such as no hypocrite could come by (that is, a revelation by the Holy Spirit). This disagreement was serious enough; Shepard in 1645 still thought that Cotton's "familist" position on this issue had been the font of all the other errors that emanated from Boston.[19] But Winthrop left out another subject of disagreement that Cotton saw as major: the Hooker-Shepard conception of preparation. God, Cotton reiterated in his reply to the ministers, made no gracious promises to any condition before justification. Recall that it was this position to which Cotton and Wheelwright assimilated the more widely held argument that one could gain first assurance from sanctification, and that the position itself they saw as papist; recall, too, that Cotton around this time was preaching that the ministers' positions were potentially soul damning—one gains a sense of how far off reconciliation actually was. Moreover, it is entirely possible that even getting as far as these discussions did took a great deal of arm-twisting by moderate ministers of their more entrenched brethren. As will be seen, when Cotton consulted with his fellow ministers in August, items absent in May were on the table.

Certainly the spirit of reconciliation was not obvious at the critical election for the assistants, deputy governor, and governor on May 17, four days after Cotton replied to the other ministers. This election, held at the General Court in Newtowne, was to decide if the shifting political balance of power brought about by Wheelwright's conviction was to be permanent (town deputies were elected in their own towns). Thomas Hutchinson claimed that Winthrop, Dudley, Wilson, and other magistrates and ministers worked furiously to ensure that Vane would not be reelected. Samuel Sewall's father told him "many a time" how he and others traveled thirty miles from Newbury to Newtowne, spurred on by their minister, Thomas Parker, in order to be made freemen, vote in the election, "and help to strengthen Govr Winthrop's Party." Parker was militant enough that Wilson invited him twice to preach against antinomianism in Boston (and thus brave Vane's grilling after his sermons).[20]

Thomas Shepard preached the election-day sermon and, according to Winthrop, minimized the differences between the parties such that only "men of good understanding" and (more ominously) "such as knew the bottom of the tenets of those of the other party" understood what the dispute was about.[21] Since the tenets of the "other party," whatever their protestations to the contrary might be, were antinomianism and familism, that was a significant qualification, and as will be seen below, Shepard still had no interest in assuming the mantle of peacemaker.

In the colony at large, "Mr. Cotton's party" had been at most tolerated, rather than actively supported, and now with the rest of the Massachusetts establishment actively campaigning against them, they could foresee in this election the demise of their already limited political power. Accordingly, they engaged in a desperate last-ditch maneuver on the day of the election. Freemen did not need to actually be present at the election but could vote by proxy. While people from outlying towns may have stayed away, the Bostonians turned out in force in the field in front of the Newtowne meetinghouse for the Court meeting that started in the afternoon. The Bostonians asserted that the election assembly was a proper meeting of the General Court, not just a Court of Elections, with the freemen represented in person rather than by their deputies. They tried to present a petition to revoke Wheelwright's conviction. Since many persons from outlying towns were absent, they were probably hoping that there were enough of them present to overturn the conviction. Winthrop claimed that the entire day was in danger of being spent in debate. The general assumption of historians from the contemporary Edward Johnson onward has been that the Bostonians' motive was to stall the election until the day had ended, since they saw themselves heading toward defeat. One participant thought that Vane was prepared to frustrate the entire election rather than see himself be cast out. It is hard to imagine what would have happened had the Bostonians succeeded in postponing the election, and as to the immediate end of overturning Wheelwright's conviction, Winthrop wrote that if the petition had been allowed to come forward, the Bostonians could have only been represented by their deputies anyway. Whatever the Bostonians' intentions, if persons were predisposed to regard them as seditious, they would have seen nothing that day to cause them to change their minds. They were either trying to block the election or they were trying to overturn Wheelwright's conviction. Perhaps they were trying to do both. In any event, they were using means that were patently in disregard of the regular procedures of the Court. Governor Vane, though, saw no problem with their motion and wished to read the petition.[22]

Deputy Governor Winthrop, on both principled and pragmatic grounds, disagreed and successfully struggled with his benchmate for control of the meeting. He called for the assembled freemen to decide if they wished to move to the election. The "greater number by many" did so. Vane and his allies still refused to proceed, whereupon Winthrop told him the election would take place without him. John Wilson climbed a tree and exhorted the crowd to remember their charter and the business of the

day. He was answered by cries of "Election, election." Winthrop and his
supporters went off to vote, and in that vote the Bostonians went down
in defeat. Winthrop became governor, while Wheelwright's supporters,
Vane, Coddington, and Dummer, were not reelected as magistrates. It is
not clear from Winthrop's account to what extent the size of this victory
came about because the Bostonians boycotted the voting itself. Vane's
side uttered "fierce speeches" and resorted to physical manhandling, according to Winthrop. But they saw they were outnumbered and "grew
quiet." Once the election was over, Boston deputy John Coggeshall complained that the petition should have been read first. Winthrop offered to
hear it, an empty gesture, as he knew well. Coggeshall angrily and disre-
spectfully turned his back to him and made "menacing speeches" to the
effect that "since they could not be heard then, they would take another
course."[23]

Now that the anti-Boston party had firm control of the Court, efforts
to arbitrarily manipulate governmental process were not limited to the
Bostonian side. The Bostonians had prepared themselves for a colony-
wide defeat by putting off their selection of deputies until they saw how
the election for magistrates turned out. Thereafter, they returned home
and elected Vane, Coddington, and Atherton Hough, once the mayor
of Boston, Lincolnshire. The Court, "being grieved at it," annulled the
election on a technicality, whereupon they elected them again. "The court
not finding how they might reject them," in Winthrop's words, "they
were admitted." According to the Court records, the initiative for rejecting the Boston deputies came from their fellow deputies, not the magistrates, which suggests how widespread disapproval of Boston was among
the ordinary laity by this time.[24]

The new General Court, eleven magistrates with thirty-two deputies
representing fourteen towns, quickly got down to business in the Newtowne meetinghouse. It called for a day of humiliation and a synod of the
churches to settle the colony's theological disputes, although since these
were Congregational churches, the synod could only advise, not dictate.
Summoning Wheelwright, the Court (presumably Governor Winthrop)
announced it was putting off sentencing him and informed him that it
might show him clemency if he in turn showed repentance. Wheelwright
replied that if he had really committed sedition the Court should simply
put him to death, and in any event he meant to appeal to the king's court,
"for he could retract nothing." The Court was no less defiant, responding
that it would judge him the same way if it held the trial again, but if as a
result of the planned synod, "the Lord should discover any further light
to them than as yet they had seen, they should gladly embrace it"—given
that Winthrop had already made clear that Wheelwright's doctrine was

not in the Bible, the odds of any further discovery of light in his favor were fairly remote.[25]

Clearly, Winthrop's irenic protestations in his journal aside, the parties were at a stalemate. Boston's opponents had control of the local government. But everyone in the colony knew that with Vane well connected in Charles's court, that local control did not necessarily amount to much. Talk of appeals to the king were only the first signs of much wider talk in Boston about royal authority and Vane's access to it. Vane, busy undermining the authority of the General Court, certainly did not discourage this sort of talk.

Vane's connections may have bolstered Boston; those same connections caused its opponents to weave extraordinary, fearful fantasies around him. Just how extraordinary is shown by a letter Shepard wrote to Winthrop a few days after the election. The letter critiqued a now lost response by Winthrop to the Remonstrance that Vane and other members of the Court had written. Winthrop had not put enough twigs on his lash against the remonstrants, said Shepard. He had treated Vane with a courtesy Vane did not deserve. Vane was "the prime craftsman of forging all our late novelties, the Sheba of our distractions." His principles had "sown the seed of confusion of this and all states in the world," and "it may be he is now hatching evil agaynst this place."[26] Vane's high status had made him seem literally a godsend when he first arrived in Massachusetts. Now that he was in opposition to the Court, that very same status made it easy to picture him as a sinister presence whose principles destroyed states and who was at that very moment conspiring evil.

With the well-connected Vane hatching evils against Massachusetts, the wide and empty expanses of the Atlantic Ocean began to hint at awful terrors, akin to the nightmares about papist invasion that periodically swept regions of England. Winthrop repeated rumors that "many" Grindletonians were about to arrive to reinforce the ranks of the "erronists." Edward Johnson reported that the election petition had been intended to delay the elections because the erronists' numbers were swelling so quickly that delay would enable them to gain control of the Court.[27] It would have required considerable boatloads of heretics to reach that point. When the General Court in November finally identified males whom it perceived as seriously dissident, its total came to perhaps one in twenty-five in the colony as a whole.[28]

This combination of the Bostonians' very real contempt for the Court's authority and Court's culturally normative paranoia in the face of determined dissent drove Shepard to make an open political intervention. He preached to the General Court, the "Fathers of the Country," as he called them, after Wheelwright made his show of defiance at the Court. In a series of rhetorical questions, Shepard invoked all of the turmoil of the past months—the ignoring of Court sentences and talk of appeals to the king, the Bostonians' maneuvers on the day of election, the insults to the ministers, the stubborn refusal on some people's parts to acknowledge that they were in a crisis—and warned that behind them lay nothing less than a plot by "craft and subtilty" to reduce the colony to tyranny:

> If you would have the walls of Magistracy be broken down . . . if they execute Laws appeal from them. Would you have confusion the mother of discord among the people? Let every man then once one day in the year turn Magistrate, and out-face Authority, and profess 'tis his liberty. Would you have Gods Ordinances in the purity of them removed? . . . for peace sake suffer a few seeds [of error] to be sown amongst you. Would you have all the Messengers of the Gospel at first reviled, at last massacred? Profess they are no better than Scribes and Pharisees, persecuting Egyptians, enemies to the Lord Jesus, and the more devout the worse. Would you ruin the Gospel? Set not Popery against it, but Gospel against Gospel. Would you have oppressors set over you, to remove ordinances, to encrease your burdens? Maintain this Principle then, that they will not assult us first by craft and subtilty, but openly and violently. Would you have this state in time to degenerate into Tyranny? . . . Be gentle and open the door to all comers that may cut our throats in time.[29]

Shepard's anti-immigration warning might have helped prompt the Court that May to pass a law forbidding any town to take in strangers for more than three weeks without the permission of the magistrates.[30] Yet it is hard to read his polemic and his letter to Winthrop and not assume that he wanted more than that—stiffer and immediate action against Wheelwright and Greensmith, a firmer crackdown on deviant opinions, probably some kind of action against Vane, and more of an effort on Winthrop's part to convince people that enemies of the state would move by craft and subtlety before they moved openly. The gap between what Shepard wanted and what the Court actually produced suggests Winthrop's moderating role, relatively speaking, in the controversy.

That suggestion is no accident. We know, for example, next to nothing about the machinations of Winthrop's deputy governor, ex-soldier Thomas Dudley, who in general was a harsher man and disapproved of Winthrop's leniency. Both before and after the free grace controversy, Dudley and Winthrop clashed over the amount of patience to be shown to religious dissenters. If the verses found in Dudley's pocket at his death and his personal testimony at the beginning of his will are a fair indication of his religious interests, then hating heresy was the largest component of his piety. Dudley had moved from Newtowne to remote Ipswitch after Hooker left in 1636, but in 1637, due to the "necessity of the Government and importunity of friends," he moved to Roxbury, adjacent to Boston. Contemporaries remembered Dudley admiringly for his critical role in the controversy. William Hubbard recalled him as being at the time "the most resolved champion of the truth, above all the gentlemen in the country." A memorial verse, probably by Nathaniel Rogers, son of John Rogers of Dedham, gives him much the same credit. According to a manuscript account of his life, it was due to "Mr. Dudley's courage and constancy to the truth [that] things issued well."[31] Thus, it was Dudley, not Winthrop, who was the magisterial hard-liner against Boston, although his machinations have left almost no traces. If we had a fuller account of the politics of the controversy, Winthrop even more clearly would appear a moderate, restraining the Court's most aggressive members and frustrating the most aggressive ministers. Shepard's harangue to the Court was, in all likelihood, one side of a debate among the opponents of Boston. Winthrop presented the other, winning side when he explained in his journal why the Court did not move immediately against Wheelwright and what Winthrop called his "insolent" supporters: "The intent of the court in deferring the sentence was, that . . . having now power enough to have crushed them, their moderation and desire of reconciliation might appear to all."[32]

Winthrop's moderation was based on a genuine, if limited, interest in reconciliation; it was almost certainly also based on a realistic assessment of what the General Court was up against. He might write in his journal that his side now had the power to "crush" its opponents; Vane and his supporters had no inhibitions about showing that they were not impressed. Winthrop, gentry-by-the-fingernails, had wrested the governorship back from Vane, who was by breeding and connections as aristocratic as one could get without being titled. No matter how many elections Winthrop and his side won in their tiny colony of about eight thousand English people, in an English context they remained relatively low on the scale of status and power, and should Winthrop forget this fact, the Bostonians would be happy to remind him of it.

Winthrop carefully noted the snubs his fellow church members gave him after he was elected governor. Vane refused to sit on the magistrate's bench with Winthrop in the Boston meetinghouse, placing himself with deacons Aspinwall and Coggeshall. A young English lord on vacation showed up in June. Winthrop invited him to dinner together with Vane. Vane wrote back that his conscience did not allow it, and he took the lord off to dinner with Boston's original settler, Samuel Maverick, on Noddles Island. One church member addressed Winthrop in a church debate as "Brother Governour," a gesture of disrespect so shocking to Giles Firmin that he remembered it a half century later.[33]

Halberds provided the opportunity for the most notorious of the petty incidents. Four sergeants from Boston bearing these combination spears and battle axes marched as an honor guard before Vane to the May General Court, just as they marched before him whenever he went to any public event, including church services. When Winthrop wrested the governorship back on election day, the Boston sergeants laid down their halberds and went home. There were no sergeants wanting to attend him when he returned to Boston. The sergeants later explained to Winthrop that they had waited on Vane not because of his office but because of his eminence. Winthrop felt the affront to his honor keenly. He argued back that, regardless of Vane's superior social rank, they had to do the like for him, "because the place drowns the person, be he honorable or base." Moreover, having once bestowed the honor on Vane in office, they could not take it away "without contempt or injury." Cotton urged moderation on Boston, and other towns offered to send halberd bearers. Boston thereupon offered to provide men, but the sergeants themselves still refused. Winthrop elected to use two of his own servants, "whereas," as he noted in his journal, "the former governor never had less than four."[34]

The best known of the snubs the Bostonians delivered Winthrop and his government came in connection with the war against the Pequots. In April, while Vane was still governor, the General Court organized an expedition against them, assigning each town a quota of men to provide. Everything went smoothly in an expedition that climaxed in the massacre of six to seven hundred Pequot men, women, and children on May 24. This "divine slaughter," as Shepard later called it, made the English participants, or the less squeamish of them, feel that they were back in the glory days of the Old Testament. In June the General Court organized another expedition. But now, Winthrop wrote to an English audience, the town of Boston proved remarkably reluctant to provide men: "not a [church] member, but one or two whom they cared not to be rid of, and but a few others, and those of the most refuse sort, and that in such a careless manner, as gave great discouragement to the service." Wilson had been the minister chosen by lot to accompany the expedition, and no one even bade him farewell.[35]

According to Winthrop, Boston's action was intended as commentary on the recent government turnover: "The former Governour and some of the Magistrates then were friends of Christ and Free-grace, but the present were enemies, &c. Antichrists, persecutors." *Mercurius Americanus* agreed with Winthrop's explanation and accounted for this and the incident of the halberds in highly personal terms. "Inequality of observance" came from "the affection which some designed to those offices, bore to the then Governor Sr. *He: Vane,* who by his noble, affable and discreet carriage, ingaged their utmost attention." Both Winthrop and the present government of Massachusetts, according to *Mercurius Americanus,* were characterized by "despicableness." It is vivid testimony to the invisibility of Vane's agency to scholars that while historians routinely repeat Winthrop's anecdote about the quota, they ignore his explanation about its "Vanist" intentions and see the snub as directed primarily at Wilson.[36]

These increasingly aggressive gestures toward Winthrop appear to have been part of an increasingly intolerant atmosphere in the Boston church. The earlier ecumenical church, which could contain in peaceful coexistence ministers and laypeople as various as Wilson and Cotton, Winthrop and Hutchinson, had broken down. Some members, in effect, institutionalized conflict by amplifying Wheelwright's argument that struggle was normative for pure churches. Winthrop claimed that now none could be admitted who did not renounce their sanctification and "waite for an immediate revelation of the Spirit." Those already in the church who would not "do the same, and acknowledge this new light, and say as they say," would be "presently noted, and under-esteemed." Young Giles Firmin, who returned to Boston in June or July after a four-year absence, described much the same kind of pressure to conform: "divers have lain looking for, and listning after such a word, set home by an impulse of the Spirit, and all other wayes of evidencing are neglected." Evidencing assurance by conditional promises, said Firmin, was "cryed down, as being no sure or sound way of evidencing: Hence, many poor, but sincere Christians, were afraid and dare not go this way to work." For an unknown number of Bostonians, the new regnant soteriological paradigm only substituted one set of anxieties for another. The Boston woman in spiritual despair that summer, for example, who threw her infant in a well to settle in her own mind that she was damned perhaps would not have come to such a crisis in another congregation. Firmin may have felt this narrowing of options as particularly threatening, since he wrestled with severe doubts about his salvation for all of a very long life. Another recently arrived immigrant, listening to the Bostonians' arguments, decided, as had others, that they were motivated by "envy" of the ministers and chose to go to Salem, which was "more free." What to a preacher like Wheelwright and perhaps to many of the Boston laity had been an effort to free Christians from "servile fear" resulted for Firmin and Winthrop in a narrow, intolerant, superficial, and self-deluded community whose conception of assurance bypassed most of the transformative work entailed in the genuine process of conversion and was more inaccessible to sincere Christians than to hypocrites.[37]

Presumably Hutchinson played a large role in the growing intolerance, for all that she is absent from contemporary documents. Winthrop told a few stories that may be from this period and, if hardly unbiased and sparing in their details, they at least give some sense of her engagement. Once some opponent said something mistakenly that touched on her reputation, and when "she could not get the party upon that advantage which she expected, she vented her impatience with . . . fierce speech and countenance." On another occasion, she was so angry that she was not able to "have her will" against Wilson for opposing her that "neither reason, nor Scripture, nor the judgement and example of such as she reverenced could appease her displeasure."[38] The conventicles at her house must have reached their peak of popularity, perhaps in part because Hutchinson's large house was one place where the Boston congregation could meet without having to contend with Winthrop, Wilson, or Wilson's guest preachers—Winthrop could watch the crowds coming and going from his window. It would not have been too difficult for Hutchinson to put a radical spin on the sermons Cotton was preaching at the time, and she and others were probably getting bolder with their "inquiries." Nor would it have been difficult for her to persuade her fellow Bostonians that the ministers and magistrates of Massachusetts were antichristian, given that they were clearly upholding justification through works and persecuting the saints. Hutchinson undoubtedly encouraged Boston women to walk out of the meetinghouse every time Wilson preached. And yet Firmin's anecdote about members of her family disputing her interpretation of Cotton's doctrines dates from these months—Boston may have been increasingly radicalized, but it was still no monolith.

Meanwhile the Court's order against immigrants lay waiting to be put in operation and bring the struggle to its climax. Grindletonians never showed up as far as anyone knows. But a boatload of Lincolnshire immigrants, including Anne Hutchinson's brother-in-law, Samuel Hutchinson, did arrive in on July 12, and there is some evidence that the New England controversies were debated on boat. The magistrates greeted the newcomers with a grilling on whether they knew Wheelwright and demanded that they disavow his doctrine. When the immigrants would not, they gave them four months to remain in the colony. The magistrates' treatment of the immigrants might have been defensible had the General Court condemned Wheelwright's teachings at his trial. But not only had Wheelwright's opponents failed in that, they subsequently made a point that Wheelwright's conviction was not based on his doctrine. The Boston party was understandably furious. The magistrates had no problem in admitting blasphemers and profane persons to Massachusetts, their angry talk went, but they drew the line at true Christians. And in denying true Christians, they denied Christ himself.[39]

The level of protest was serious enough that Winthrop wrote "A Defence of an Order of Court" in response. On one level, Winthrop's defense was a straightforward justification of the Court's action in terms of contractual political theory. All commonwealths were founded by free consent and since all of a commonwealth's members were obliged to entertain the good of the whole, the commonwealth could keep out those who might threaten that good. Churches and towns in Massachusetts accepted and rejected strangers at their discretion, and so might the duly appointed officers of the entire commonwealth.[40]

On another level, Winthrop's apology was a brute assertion of Massachusetts realpolitik. He and others had failed to convict Wheelwright for his doctrines and, when advantageous, would righteously proclaim that they never had any such intention. But in practice, they regarded his conviction as a de facto condemnation of his doctrine and acted accordingly, and Winthrop did not make much effort to pretend otherwise. To the complaints that the immigrants were being denied admission because they refused to disavow Wheelwright's teachings, Winthrop replied that John 2:10 said that such as brought not true doctrine should not be admitted into a house. "It is sayd that this law was made of purpose to keepe away such as are of Mr. Wheelwright his judgment (admitt it were so which yet I cannot confesse) where is the evill of it?" If Wheelwright's opinions were the cause of the colony's troubles, why could the colony not keep out "such as would strengthen him and infect others with such dangerous tenets?" Moreover, those people making such a fuss now about the magistrates' behavior joined in expelling Roger Williams, and his doctrines were less dangerous than Wheelwright's (perhaps not all the magistrates would have agreed, even for polemical purposes).[41]

Vane responded to Winthrop with "A Brief Answer to a Certain Declaration." On one level, "Brief Answer" was a stirring call for the people's rights and a protest against the magistrates' assumption of unbounded powers with this poorly defined law—Vane, the apostle of liberty, as nineteenth-century whig historians of the English Revolution presented him. But it was a fanatical Protestant, no-king-but-King-Jesus liberty with which Vane countered the pretensions of the Massachusetts magistracy.[42] By leaving the judgment of who should come into the commonwealth to the magistrates' discretion and not binding it to God's will, the Court, according to Vane, "made a ground worke of grosse popery [that is, it substituted human judgment for the will of God, as revealed in the Bible]." But what else, he asked, could one expect from such magistrates? Winthrop had nowhere mentioned Christ in his description of a commonwealth, Vane pointed out. Thus, his arguments, besides revealing his true colors, must fail him. As for Winthrop's claim that churches admitted people at their discretion, did he not know that it was not the churches that admitted and rejected them but Christ? The commonwealth itself only had ministerial authority from Christ. Therefore, "there is no libertye to be taken neither in church nor commonwealth but that which Christ gives and is according unto him."[43]

Vane also bore in on Winthrop's attacks on Wheelwright and his immigrant supporters. Putting his finger precisely on the weakest point in Winthrop's treatise, he pointed out that Wheelwright had not been "confuted, only condemned"—the heresy charge had failed. If Wheelwright's doctrines were more dangerous than those of Williams, as Winthrop charged, then so too were the Gospel's doctrines. Vane speculated, presciently enough, that those who felt free to keep out prospective members of the Boston party would soon enough feel free to banish those who were already there. He also pointed out that wicked Ahab had no right to keep out the prophet Elijah, nor could the natives keep out the English simply "because we do not suite with the disposition of theire Sechem"; after all they were getting the true Gospel in return.[44] The implications of these less-than-flattering comparisons were undoubtedly not lost on Vane's audience.

Massachusetts's antichristian government had passed an illegitimate act, and Vane warned that the Bostonians were not going to take it lying down. The most ominous of his attacks on the Court's order came with his invocation of the authority of Charles I. The planters had their charter from him; their power was bounded by him; the law did injury to the king's rights. Vane warned menacingly, "The king will looke for some right, nor may we blame him, if he doe." Given Vane's connections at Court and the fact that Massachusetts's charter had been legally revoked on May 3, this was no light threat.[45] Wheelwright had already invoked the authority of the king at his sentencing hearing, and there is no reason to think that countering the power of the General Court with the power of the king was not discussed elsewhere.

While the opponents of Boston saw Vane and his party as engaged in a conspiracy to secretly undermine the colony, Boston saw its liberty, Christian and otherwise, being squashed by an illegitimate government. It is not surprising that for many in Boston, the order against the immigrants, mild though it was, was the last straw. Winthrop recorded in his journal that the decision "was taken very ill by those of the other party, and many hot speeches given forth about it, and about their removal, etc."[46] Characteristically, he did not record that one of those speaking openly about removal was John Cotton.

Cotton would have ultimately been pleased by Winthrop's omission, since when he returned to respectability he did his best to cover the traces of his intentions that summer. But as he acknowledged to John Wheelwright in 1640, he, along with many in his church, was furious about the Wheelwright trial and the denied entrance of Samuel Hutchinson. Cotton was no less angry about Winthrop's role, and possibly Wilson's (his phrase is only "a considerable part of our Church") therein. Yet his hands were tied, as he recognized; those who were attacking what Cotton considered his party within the Boston church were too prominent to "Proceede against them according to Rule" within the church. Nor could outside churches be called in to settle the dispute, because they too had prominent members hostile to Cotton's party. Blocked from applying the punitive discipline that the situation richly called for, Cotton "verily purposed openly to have protested against all such proceedings as I took to be injurious and offensive and to have departed into some other parts of this Country." His intention was reinforced by a petition with about sixty signatures encouraging him and expressing a willingness to move with him.[47]

At this point the story gets murkier. Robert Baillie claimed (and reiterated in the face of Cotton's denial) that Vane and Cotton employed Roger Williams to buy land for them from the Narragansett Indians. Williams himself seemed to corroborate Baillie's account.[48] Cotton insisted to Baillie that he and his followers had been planning to move not to Narragansett Bay with Vane but to New Haven with John Davenport. His claim cannot be independently corroborated, and it was made in the process of feeding Baillie a number of demonstrable half-truths, at best, about the incident.[49] Davenport and his party sent out an expedition to explore the New Haven area only on August 31, 1637, although they had been seeking other sites all summer, and they did not make up their minds finally to move there until the following spring.[50] Vane, Narragansett Bay, and 1637 were not elements of Cotton's biography that he would be in a rush to acknowledge when trying to defend himself to a conservative Scottish Presbyterian in the late 1640s.

This was perhaps the single most dangerous time for the colony of Massachusetts. The tactics of the opponents of the Boston church had brought the colony to the verge of self-destruction. "The Churches are on fire," fishermen warned the immigrant ships sailing into Boston harbor. Winthrop in his journal penned his fears at the start of July that a church separation seemed imminent.[51] Wheelwright might be expendable, but the departure of Cotton and his prominent supporters would have shattered the morale of the colony and wrecked its standing among English puritans. Having the son of a privy counselor setting up a rival and hostile colony at a time when Massachusetts's charter was officially dead would make the colony's precarious standing no easier with the English government. But Cotton did not leave. For reasons Roger Williams explained to Baillie, but Baillie did not record, the effort to purchase land in Narragansett Bay failed.

Very possibly one fallout of that failure to establish an alternative millenarian city on a hill was the departure of Vane for England on August 3. He promised his supporters he would return, and he almost certainly talked of returning as governor-general. News of the revocation of the charter could easily have reached Massachusetts by this time.[52] Winthrop recorded that "Mr. Vane's party" gathered to see him off at Boston harbor, firing guns and cannon in his honor. Vane's English admirers later saw him as driven out of the colony because of his defense of free grace, "ripened into more knowledge and experience of Christ, than the Churches [in New England] could bear the testimony of," as one later said. To his opponents, however, still reeling from four months of political struggle, he was no heroic martyr for religion. A letter to England summarized his rule by saying that he promoted Boston doctrines "with such violence, as if they had been matters of that consequence that the peace and welfare of New-England must be sacrificed, rather than they should not take place. . . . He hath kindled those sparks among us, which many ages will not be able to undo." Vane's "misguidings and bad conduct," lamented William Hubbard, "much eclipsed" Massachusetts's "beauty, place, and splendor."[53] Just how large a role Vane played in stoking the flames of the free grace controversy, both because of his actions and because of what he could be seen as representing is shown by two blunt documents, one by Winthrop, one by Shepard. It is certainly not coincidental that both were written after Vane had left the country and were intended for transient, limited, local consumption.

Winthrop wrote a reply to Vane's immigration treatise in September while the synod was meeting. In his "Reply to an Answer," Winthrop let down his guard as he did in no other surviving document and did not pretend to treat Vane with anything but disdain and anger. Winthrop responded to Vane's accusations that he was insufficiently Christocentric as a rational man would to a scriptural fanatic, a John Whitgift to a Thomas Cartwright, an "Anglican" to a "Puritan." A Christian commonwealth, Winthrop explained, was included in the general species of commonwealth; it did not have to be mentioned explicitly. But, Winthrop added, he expected Vane's holier-than-thou cant from the Boston party. Vane's argument "suits well with a practise now in use, to speak nothing but what they bring scripture for; so scripture be alledged it matters not how impertinent they be." As for Vane's argument that it was not churches but Christ who chose church members, Winthrop's response was, to paraphrase, get real. Had Vane not seen the New England churches' admission policies in practice, where a few brethren could block the admission of candidates over the wishes of a majority? Christ's authority could not be dispensed except through imperfect human beings; to think otherwise was "meer idea or fantasye."[54]

Winthrop had no more respect for Vane's defense of Wheelwright or his immigrant followers. He maintained a discreet silence on Vane's charge that the authorities were preparing to banish Wheelwright's supporters, but he did say that he regarded the Wheelwright petition as a ground for banishment. He sidestepped Vane's accusation that Wheelwright had been convicted for his doctrines, noting only that the synod then assembled was deciding whether those opinions were the doctrines of the Gospel.[55] Winthrop did not overlook Vane's comparison of the Massachusetts authorities with pagans: "If his charity can hope no better of us, but that we will deale worse with Gods people than the Pagans . . . it is no marvaile if he favour such as have ranked us with the same before; onely herein he deales fairely with us, in giving us tymely warneing what to expect from the imbittered mynd of such a brother."[56] Just what Winthrop expected from Vane's imbittered mind, he did not say, but it surely had something to do with what Vane might be up to on the other side of the Atlantic.

Vane's invocations of Charles I incited Winthrop's harshest response. Winthrop denied that the order infringed on the king's power. More to the point, given how discreet Winthrop usually was about Vane, was what those invocations told him about Vane: "[Vane] discovers how little he regardeth what jealousyes he put us under, so he may shelter his own parties. The Lord give him to see his secret underminings, that it may be forgiven him."[57]

To Winthrop, once Vane was out of hearing distance, he was a religious fanatic with an embittered mind, whose use of Scripture was nothing but cant, whose arguments were fantasies, and who sought to secretly undermine Massachusetts. Shepard was even harsher in his appraisal, unsurprisingly, when he preached the election-day sermon in 1638. Shepard devoted the sermon to Vane, thinly disguised as Abimelech, the "young courtier," as Shepard called him, the bloody son of Gideon, who made himself king on Gideon's death. Shepard gave a close analysis of how an Abimelech, the "bramble," goes about to rise in power, and the remarkable way recent Massachusetts history mirrored Scripture was not likely to be lost on any of his audience.[58]

An Abimelech climbs to power by making a faction for himself. He knows that he must cunningly adapt his creation of a faction to his environment, and in a religious country, "people will be made into a faction but by shewes of religion." Abimelech therefore "advanceth another religion then what they had under Gideon . . . a god of a new covenant." Having advanced the new religion, he "disgraces and rayseth slanders of all Gideons sons." He will "scratch and rent and disfigure all magistrates and ministers . . . fight against them kill them they are worse then Pilate and Scribes and Pharisees, oh but they be holy they be the worse." Abimelech draws his faction to him not only by religion but by "there own private benefit . . . tho it be with publick losse." He might demand that the country "nullify such lawes and deliver up such and such men into its hands"— Wheelwright, for example—but should the country refuse, "looke for none from me, but the sword." All in all, a histronic but not ungrounded description of the talk about the king's rights and Vane's return as governor-general. Abimelech's crowning action in faction formation, said Shepard, is to sow the "seeds of undermining principles of government." He will ask, precisely as Vane and his "faction" had done the previous year, "Is it not fit to make appeales is not the sentence of a major part of court without consent of minor a nullity?"[59]

While Abimelech is assembling his faction, "you will see him so humble and for publicke good." But he "intends publicke ruin." His goal is to "take away magistrate and minister . . . and then looke for fire." Vane had assembled his religious faction as the Spanish had done in Holland, Shepard told his audience, for Arminius and the Arminians were nothing but a front for Spanish power.[60] Vane's faction had laid siege to the religion, laws, and government of Massachusetts as dupes to advance Vane's power, and by only a hair's breadth had Massachusetts escaped bloody tyranny.

Public ruin, fire, faction, another religion—add to the dire list Shepard's earlier intimations about Jesuit conspiracies and the original suspicions that Vane was a spy from Charles's court to betray Massachusetts, and the sum of the menaces suggests what the wildest suspicions were that drove the opposition to Vane in the spring of 1637. Vane was an agent of Catholicism and Spain aiming at the defeat of the Reformation like Laud and Charles's other evil counselors. The leap of logic involved in inferring a Catholic plot from Protestant radicalism might seem formidable, but it was not so daunting to seventeenth-century minds given to analyzing current events in dualistic and conspiratorial terms. Massachusetts ministers saw "Jesuited agents" behind the Child Petition of 1646; in the 1640s in England, Presbyterians saw the Jesuits at work behind both the rise of the Congregationalists and the execution of Charles I; while in the 1650s, puritans on both sides of the Atlantic often suspected that Catholic plotting lay behind the Quakers. In 1659, the conservative puritan minister Richard Baxter accused Vane himself of being a tool of the Jesuits for his defense of English sectaries. Vane thought it worth his while in his execution speech to deny that he had anything to do with "Jesuitism or Popery."[61]

Shepard's analysis of Vane was not that much different from that of Winthrop, who saw Vane as secretly undermining the colony in order to shelter his party; neither analysis invited compromise. Winthrop, however, was a far wiser politician than Shepard. Shepard drew a very harsh conclusion from his analysis. When dealing with a bramble like Abimelech, "call for hatchets do not deale gently it will prick you; but let severity in this case, be used." But when Vane's ship pulled out of Boston harbor, signaling an end to the worst domestic political crisis Massachusetts's government faced until the American Revolution, Winthrop had the fort on Castle Island fire five volleys in his honor. The General Court, in what might have been its own way of celebrating, finally threw Stephen Greensmith in prison for his continued refusal to pay his fine, in spite of his threats to appeal his sentence to the king. Vane, "the great Favourer and Maintainer of these Errors" and the man who "did animate that Faction," was gone, if only perhaps for the time being, and the Massachusetts establishment could get on with some long postponed housecleaning.[62]

EIGHT

RECLAIMING COTTON

AUGUST–SEPTEMBER 1637

A S VANE'S ship sailed into the Atlantic no one in Massachusetts knew that two Sundays earlier in St. Giles Church in Edinburgh, Scotland, Jenny Geddes had thrown a stool at a minister as he tried to introduce the Laudian prayer book. That Sunday marked the beginning of twelve years of war across the British Isles. Laud and Charles I's ultimate reward for their ill-conceived meddling with Scottish institutions would be the executioner's ax, and in the meantime they had far more pressing concerns than New England. "God then rocked three nations," as Cotton later solipsistically put it, "with shaking dispensations, that he might procure some rest unto his people in this wilderness."[1] Winthrop and his party's power, unknown to them, was secure from external threats, including Vane, and if it could reclaim Cotton, it would reestablish its spiritual authority as well.

Efforts to reclaim Cotton were part of the general bustle in August around the synod that would convene on August 30. On August 5, Hooker and Samuel Stone arrived from Connecticut along with John Wilson. They brought news of the end of Pequot resistance, and with their arrival, preparations for the synod commenced. These preparations included a general effort at reconciliation. At the end of the month Boston radical John Underhill wrote to John Winthrop reminding him "how powerfully our Lord Jesus hath lately appeared in the ministrye exhorting us to passe by personall wrongs."[2]

Cotton himself made a serious effort to mend fences, whatever sacrifice of consistency might be involved. Perhaps it was easier for him to be flexible with Vane no longer resident in his house. He decided that he would not leave Massachusetts, later citing as the most important element in his decision a meeting he held with Winthrop and Dudley. The magistrates assured Cotton that they could live with his theology; that Wheelwright had not been punished for heresy but for sedition; and that Samuel Hutchinson and other Lincolnshire immigrants were denied residency in Massachusetts because they denied inherent righteousness in the saints altogether. Why Cotton found the magistrates' assurances on the last two points plausible is far from clear. They had all along been claiming that

Wheelwright had not been punished for his opinions, and that had not stopped Cotton from regarding Wheelwright's conviction as unjustified. Wheelwright always insisted, and reminded Cotton in correspondence from 1640, that Samuel Hutchinson believed nothing more radical than Wheelwright. Hutchinson was in Boston for Cotton to talk to, and he may have been accepted as a member of the church. Cotton also finally accepted Wilson's longstanding explanation that his speech of the previous December in the General Court had not been directed at Cotton or Wheelwright, and he announced as much to his congregation—"This sudden change was much observed by some," Winthrop drily noted.[3]

Cotton had a variety of incentives to see the spirit of Antichrist recede from his Massachusetts brethren. With Vane gone, he had lost the last of his magisterial supporters. Events might be pushing him to a split with his brethren and to the literal role of prophet in the wilderness, but playing that kind of dissident, a role Roger Williams throve in, had never been Cotton's forte. He had made his peace with bishops as long as they were willing to make peace with him, and surely he should be able to make his peace with his brethren in Massachusetts. The failure of the land purchase in Narragansett Bay meant that there would be no move that year anyway. Perhaps too, when faced with the serious prospect of departing, Cotton discovered the depths of his commitment to the church order he had played a large role in shaping. And even as remaining began to appear more attractive, an important new addition to the colony made it more feasible. On June 26, while Cotton was on the verge of leaving, John Davenport arrived. Davenport was a friend and admirer of Cotton and as prominent a minister as Hooker and Cotton. According to Cotton Mather, Cotton welcomed Davenport, as Moses did Jethro, hoping that he would be "as eyes unto them in the wilderness." Davenport had the clout to act as a peacemaker, and according to Cotton Mather, this is what he proceeded to do, even as both of them considered leaving.[4]

There may have been a variety of reasons that drove Cotton to reconciliation. But what brought the magistrates to the table? Winthrop from the beginning clearly had been concerned to distinguish between Cotton and the more radical members of his congregation, even to the point of willfully toning down his descriptions of Cotton's behavior and attitudes. But Dudley is another matter. It is unfortunate that such an important person shows up rarely in the surviving documents, but when he does, his attitude toward Cotton is strikingly different from Winthrop's: sarcastic, hostile, impatient. He seems to have interpreted Cotton much as Shepard did, and it seems that a too vigorous defense of Cotton's theology could get one excommunicated in Dudley's church.[5] And yet he was prepared to say that he could live with Cotton's doctrine.

I imagine, and it is certainly nothing more than speculation, Winthrop pointing out some hard truths to Dudley. The colony had lost Thomas Hooker the year before, which already raised eyebrows in England. Davenport and his wealthy Londoners were making noises about finding another colony. Key English puritan magnates were actively encouraging Connecticut's development. Massachusetts was already close enough to the brink because of the revocation of its charter and the broadcasting in England of its squabbles. The last thing the authorities needed was to have to explain to the immigrants streaming into the port of Boston and perhaps wondering if Massachusetts would be their final destination why the town was half-empty or more and the most famous minister in the colony gone. Not only would Cotton's departure be a blow to the colony's credibility, he would take with him some of its wealthiest and most important merchants. I picture Dudley, who thought that Cotton's doctrine was at best simple illogic, fuming, swallowing his inquisitorial instincts, then with a great deal of effort telling Cotton that his teaching was acceptable.[6] And thereafter, as various trial transcripts show, striking out at him whenever the opportunity afforded.

Cotton and the other ministers held extensive private conferences before the synod. The elders discussed with Cotton all of his opinions "as were perceived by some to be erroneous" in an effort to heal "any anguish, distemper, or disaffection grown in any of our spirits amongst our selves . . . in a private brotherly way." It was probably at this time that Cotton decided that the theological differences between him and the extreme preparationists were, as he put it in a conciliatory statement, "logicall, not theologicall." The conclusion that Hooker and Shepard were not crypto-papists would allow him much more gracefully to make peace with his brethren.[7]

When the ministerial conferences finished, five issues remained outstanding between Cotton and the other ministers: whether union with Christ was complete before and without faith; whether faith was an instrumental cause in applying Christ's righteousness to our justification; whether the Spirit of God in evidencing justification bore witness in an absolute promise of free grace, without qualification or condition; whether some saving qualification could be a first evidence of justification; and whether Christ and his benefits were dispensed in a covenant of works. These issues reflected major disagreements, but at least those disagreements were now bounded and their number had diminished significantly from December. They were to be debated at the synod itself.[8]

Meanwhile the ministers busied themselves collecting the erroneous lay opinions they planned to refute at the synod. These eventually amounted to eighty-two, along with nine "unsavoury speeches" that were little different in tone from the errors. The list of eighty-two errors has been something of a puzzle to historians. They have not been entirely sure what to make of it—it has even been suggested that it represented for the most part enemies left behind in England.[9] But although the compilers of the list were scarcely disinterested reporters, they did not make it up. While obviously not every single error can be independently confirmed, the main propositions and assumptions underlying the list are amply documented elsewhere in Massachusetts sources. The list does present serious problems to would-be interpreters, but literal accuracy is not one of them.

The list itself is most easily untangled if it is approached not as one list but as what it actually is, a compilation of a variety of lists assembled by a variety of persons. It still betrays those origins. In a number of places the errors occur in clear sequences, and it is safe to assume that each sequence indicates the concerted work of a single compiler; in other places the errors occur in no particular order, which probably reflects ministers bringing in at random opinions they had encountered. Pulled apart in this way, it has a great deal to say about the dynamics of the free grace controversy.

The longest list, for example, is at the beginning, errors 1 to 19. This list is a systematic presentation of "Hutchinsonianism." It describes at length how believers die in conversion and Christ becomes their sanctification; it warns at length of the perils of legalism and the sinister, if necessary, pervasiveness of the covenant of works. It is a striking demonstration of how articulate and coherent, even plausible, the lay theologians of Boston were.[10]

The second longest sequence occurs at the end of the list, errors 79 to 82. These almost certainly record the arguments in one congregation between supporters of Boston and opponents. Could a church member leave a church if he were unsatisfied with anything in it and could not convince the church; could he regularly attend another church he preferred, "notwithstanding the offence of the Church, often manifested to him for so doing"; was there not "sufficient bread" in a church where the minister claimed faith was a condition of the covenant of grace and that sanctification evidenced justification; could a minister not denounce errors through prayer or preaching, without stating, when asked, the names of those who held these errors? They are surely a description of the Roxbury church, which had the unhappy combination of a militant group of Boston sympathizers, some of whom had actually moved to Boston, and at least one minister, Weld, who saw eye to eye with Shepard and his confrontational attitude toward controversy.

Between these two long sequences are a few shorter ones and a great many miscellaneous errors, presumably the contributions of a number of ministers. The two errors claiming that ministers could usually convey no more of Christ than they had experienced, (errors 53 and 54) are paired—a single minister recording an argument with a single lay person? Two errors (35 and 61) argue that absolute, not conditional, promises should form the basis of church membership. Winthrop indicated that this was the direction in which the Boston church was moving on admissions in 1637. Only one error (actually two errors, 4 and 5, rolled into one in the list) is literally "antinomian," stating that "those that bee in Christ are not under the Law, and commands of the word, as the rule of life."

Since the list is a compilation of lists, it is unsurprising that it is extremely repetitive, with the same motifs repeating themselves again and again in different forms. This repetition in itself is revealing, as it provides a kind of topographical map of the distribution of opinions in Boston. Unsurprisingly, the most frequent motifs could be found in both Cotton and Wheelwright's preaching and the speculation of the radical fringe. The denigration of sanctification as a means of finding assurance appears implicitly or explicitly in at least twenty-two of the errors.[11] Six of the errors emphasize the passivity of the believer.[12] The distinctive doctrinal motifs of Hutchinson's own divinity also show up repeatedly. There are at least five different errors that boil down to her assertion that believers effectively die in conversion, thereafter to have Christ act in them,[13] six different ways of saying that justifying faith is in Christ, not in the believer;[14] and five different ways of saying that there is no difference between the graces of hypocrites and saints.[15] The assertion that full and/or genuine assurance is completely free of doubt, which may or may not have been Hutchinson's own claim, appears three different times.[16] The complex argument that one has to be born into the covenant of works and then born out of it again for salvation appears only once, which suggests both that it was indeed Vane's conception and not Hutchinson's and that it was too remote from most people's concerns to circulate widely.[17]

The emphases within certain motifs change from error to error, which almost certainly reflects the range of doctrinal diversity in the Boston community from its ministerial orthodoxy to its lay improvisations. The errors about sanctification, for example, minimize to strikingly different degrees its evidentiary value. Error 50, "A man must not prove his election by his vocation, but his vocation by his election," is Cotton and Wheelwright's doctrine, stated without nuances. But Cotton and Wheelwright might have hesitated before error 77, "[A] man may more clearly see Christ, when he seeth no sanctification then when he doth." And they would have regarded error 72 as heterodox: "It is a fundamentall and soule-damning errour to make sanctification an evidence of justification." Error 36 is straightforward Hutchinsonianism: "All the activity of a believer is to act to sinne." But error 34 probably represents an opportunistic take on her doctrine: "We are not to pray against all sinne, because the old man is in us, and must be, and why should we pray against that which cannot be avoided?" Error 59, "A man must not be exhorted to any duty, because hee hath no power to do it," is very much like the sort of thing Wheelwright preached, taken out of context, but it is very unlikely that Wheelwright ever said anything like error 49, "We are not bound to keepe a constant course of Prayer in our Families, or privately, unlesse the Spirit stirre us up thereunto."[18]

But I could be wrong. For the trickiest thing about trying to make sense of these statements is that they are all lifted out of context, and if we knew the original contexts, some of them might not appear as radical as they do in isolation. Error 33, for example, "To act by vertue of, or in obedience to a command, is legall," sounds antinomian—all the ministers agreed that the Gospel contained commands, but in fact it is an example of Wheelwright's usual foot-in-mouth hairsplitting.[19] Error 74 sounds like a radical assault on Massachusetts's church order: "All verball Covenants, or Covenants expressed in words, as Church Covenants, vowes, &c., are Covenants of workes, and such as strike men off from Christ." *Mercurius Americanus* suggests that the sentiment it expresses may have been in reaction to a heavily moralistic covenant Weld wrote.[20]

Although interpretive uncertainties inevitably surround the list, certain conclusions can be drawn from it. Hutchinson's circle had developed a well-articulated theology, clearly based on Cotton's but moving well beyond it. That theology emphasized revelations and the swallowing up of the creature in God. It minimized the conceptual and evidential role of sanctification, and it was at least beginning to question the conventional practices of piety like regular family prayer. Familism, heavily diluted, and antinomianism are understandable descriptive and, to an unknown extent, causal labels for this theological tendency. The list offers no clue at all as to how large the circle might have been. Cotton Mather said that the errors "had been uttered by several men at several times."[21] His statement is the closest we can get to a quantitative underpinning, and, however Mather came up with it, it agrees with other evidence suggesting that the number of lay radicals was small. On the fringe of this small group, some people were fulfilling Shepard's nightmare and translating the reaction against compulsive and anxiety-driven zeal and moral rigorism to a reaction against zeal and moral rigorism altogether.

There is only one person on that fringe whose pietistic development at this time we know of in any detail, Captain John Underhill. Underhill, a professional soldier and a "lusty big man," seems to have been uncertain for a long time where to stand in the colony's theological disputes.[22] However, a nexus of concerns and events tipped the scale for him. He wanted very badly to sleep with the wife of the cooper Joseph Febar. It may have been that going to fight the Pequots represented an escape for him from this temptation. If so, absence only made the heart fonder. He confided in his fellow Boston soldier, Richard Wayte, during the campaign that he had a revelation that his wife and the cooper would die and that Underhill would then marry the cooper's wife.[23] One might suspect that this indeed was an extra-scriptural revelation. At some point, the Holy Spirit brought him an absolute promise of free grace "with such assurance and joy, as he never since doubted of his good estate, neither should he, though he should fall into sin." This happened not while Underhill was at church or even in private prayer and meditation, but while he was smoking a pipe.[24] It was just as well that Underhill found his assurance, since after six months of persuasion, the cooper's wife made love with him, and, he claimed, came totally under his will—he could enjoy her three or four times a day, he boasted to a fellow ship passenger, Jane Holmes, while returning to Massachusetts in 1638. When trying to seduce Holmes, he told her that Febar's wife had told him that she could only be driven off from her righteousness "but by a gross act." Holmes rebuked him, but he replied that "he knew how it was between him and God." He may have eventually argued in Boston that he committed adultery to exalt free grace. Foreshadowing English music-hall humor, presumably inadvertently, Underhill told Holmes that he "held nothing but what Mr. Cotton held."[25]

Underhill's adultery did not become public, or at least general, knowledge until September 1638, but it is easy to imagine that he shared his theological opinions before then and that they might have ended up at the synod in various errors about immediate revelations, the unavoidability of sin, or the unimportance of ordinances. He probably made the serious biblical exegetes in the Boston community uncomfortable and defensive. *Mercurius Americanus* asked, "Shall every little errour touching *Divinity* in militarie men, whose stirred humours may easily attenuate the spirits, when they so apply themselves, and refine them into a *nicety*, be heighten'd into heresie?"[26]

The synod opened on August 30 at the Newtowne meetinghouse with about twenty-five ministers in attendance. Winthrop said they consisted of all the "teaching elders through the country" and some ministers newly arrived from England. In addition, the churches of Connecticut, Plymouth, and Massachusetts sent an unknown number of ruling lay elders, along with "messengers" or representatives of the ordinary laity. Connecticut and Massachusetts magistrates also attended. It seems safe to imagine well over a hundred men as participants, with an unknown number of men and women as spectators. The proceedings commenced with a prayer by Shepard. Then the eighty-two erroneous opinions were read, along with the nine "unsavoury speeches" and a list, which has not survived, of abused places of Scripture.[27]

Starting the synod by reading this extensive list of errors must have had a certain dramatic rhetorical effect, intentionally or not. The combination of repetition and variety served to conjure up a focused and clearly massive cloud of deviancy, surely disproportionate to the actual numbers of fringe lay theologians in Massachusetts; *Mercurius Americanus* suggested the purpose of such a long list was to cast a "*Numerary Spell.*" If so, not everyone was equally enchanted. Hubbard indicated that the ministers had different attitudes toward the errors, "being apprehended, by some, more dangerous in their tendency and consequences than in the notions themselves." Hubbard's division of attitudes corresponds to what Cotton said about the division of ministerial attitudes toward himself at the synod. Some of his brethren at the synod were "scandalized" with him, he admitted, but "sundry godly brethren" were "otherwise affected." Since it is impossible to attach names to the debates of the synod, it is impossible to know who fell into which of Hubbard's and Cotton's categories. The assembly chose Hooker and Bulkeley as moderators; in view of their respective writings and what is recorded of their attitudes toward Cotton during the controversy, it is not inconceivable that the choice gave representation to both the hard-liners and the moderates.[28]

The synod spent the first week debating, or, rather, preparing to condemn, the errors. Although surely no one seriously thought that the synod would approve "errors," anyone was invited to defend them. According to Edward Johnson, those running the synod extended the offer "like as Jehu when he was to execute the judgements of the Lord upon Ahabs bloudy household, would have had his servants defend their Masters Children if they could." No one was to be accused of the opinion that they defended, unless they declared themselves in favor of it, another offer that meant very little in practice.[29]

The messengers from the Boston church included William Aspinwall and John Coggeshall. According to Cotton, these two took the synod's invitation to defend errors at face value, to the surprise of Cotton, and proceeded to argue for some of the points "especially such as concerned union with Christ before Faith, Justification without Faith, inherent righteousness, and evidencing a good estate by it at all, first or last." Cotton took them aside and told them that their defense would make the whole Boston church guilty by association. Aspinwall and Coggeshall replied that they did not necessarily agree with those opinions, yet considering "the tendernesse of some Consciences," they were not clear for condemning them. Whether Coggeshall was being disingenuous in his answer to Cotton is not certain; Cotton later placed him beside Hutchinson as one of the two ringleaders of the opinionists. Aspinwall, on the other hand, might have very well meant exactly what he said. He was to stay only briefly in Narragansett Bay, moving thereeafter to New Haven, and then back to Boston. Aspinwall ended up in England in the 1650s, where he continued to express deep admiration for Cotton while actively seeking to usher in the Millennium. This trajectory suggests that he was among the Rhode Island exiles who were themselves orthodox within Cotton and Wheelwright's parameters but regarded their more radical brethren as among the godly and the Massachusetts establishment as persecutors.[30]

Cotton later claimed that this was the first time he realized that there was a "real and broad difference" between the most radical members of his congregation and himself. Yet at least one of the opinions that Cotton singled out, justification preceding faith, had been openly raised in the Boston church. Cotton himself had preached against the doctrine that there were no graces in the saints. Presumably Cotton had chosen to take seriously the claim that these were only inquiries among persons who were basically sound, which is how they were probably presented—"misexpressions," as he later put it—and he had certainly assumed that such persons would have better sense than try to defend them in an environment less sympathetic than the Boston church. Cotton claimed that after his rebuke the messengers left the synod, and their absence "did much what forbear any prosecution of arguments in such causes."[31]

Winthrop told a different, but not incompatible, story about the messengers' departure. Some of Boston and elsewhere were understandably enough offended by this massive undifferentiated smorgasbord of a list, "as if it were a reproach laid upon the country without cause."[32] They insisted that the persons who held those errors be named. Perhaps there were specific errors that had been presented in inaccurate wording; perhaps they wished to disassociate themselves (and Hutchinson) from the most radical claims about assurance and revelations without any Scripture basis; or, perhaps they wished to disassociate the Boston church and its quarrel with most of the Bay's ministers from the positions of their most radical or biblically inept brethren. Perhaps they were trying to bog the assembly down with procedural issues.

In any event, the persons running the synod refused their request to name sources, claiming that the synod was examining doctrine, not persons, and that it had no disciplinary power. The Boston messengers still protested and, in Winthrop's words, "refused to forbear speech unseasonably, though the moderators desired them." The magistrates stepped in, warning the messengers that they were creating a "civil disturbance." They objected that a civil magistrate had no power at a church assembly. Winthrop replied, in so many words, make my day. And they left, Christian liberty again crushed by the government of Massachusetts, which they probably expected by this time, and abandoned by Cotton, which they might not have anticipated. On September 3, four days after the start of the synod, Edward Hutchinson had his son baptized in the Boston meetinghouse with the name of Ichabod. Presumably everyone in the congregation knew the translation from the Hebrew: the glory has departed.[33]

Various elders, including Cotton, were assigned the task of writing confutations of each of the errors.[34] The confutations usually consist of explanations backed by Scripture verses. With one exception that invoked the danger of "enthusiasm," the ministers avoided polemics.[35] A number of the confutations suggest that their authors were aware that they were answering single sentences that might have been taken out of context; presumably these were written by Hubbard's less alarmed ministers.[36] One minister was content to refute two particularly striking errors by simply listing a few relevant biblical texts.[37] The confutations by and large avoided direct conflict with Cotton's teachings, and only a few of the "errors" concerned him directly.[38] One of the errors, speaking of the "distinct seasons of the workings of the severall Persons [of the Trinity]," was Cotton's teaching, but he would not have necessarily disagreed with the confutation, since it missed the point of his conception. A few confutations strongly indicated that sanctification could be a first evidence of justification.[39] Another made it plain that it could not be; I assume that Cotton wrote this one, although there is no doctrinal reason that he could not have written most of them.[40]

At the end of this first week the synod unanimously condemned the list of errors, according to Winthrop. As usual, he did not present Cotton's position accurately. Cotton declared to the synod more ambiguously that "I esteemed some of the Opinions to bee blasphemous: some of them, hereticall: many of them, Erroneous: and almost all of them incommodiously expressed: as intending to except those chiefly, wherein I had declared mine own opinion, as before." If this is the proper place to insert an anecdote from Cotton Mather, John Wilson prefaced the show of hands condemning the errors by exclaiming, "You that are against these things, and that are for the spirit and the Word together, hold up your hands!" Presumably everyone agreed that they were for the spirit and the Word together. This condemnation was reinforced by a signed document, but here some delegates, including Cotton, backed off. They refused to sign, saying, or so Winthrop claimed, that they did so only because they did not like subscription. A now lost manuscript account of the synod records that those who did not sign included "diverse of Boston, one or two at Charleston, one at Salem, one at Plymouth, one at Duxbury, two at Watertown."[41] Perhaps some of this handful of delegates who did not sign had objections similar to Cotton's about the blanket nature of the condemnation. Others might have been concerned about possible encroachments on congregational autonomy.

With lay errors out of the way, the synod moved on to ministerial disputes. Cotton brought the five outstanding issues left over from the ministerial conferences to the synod, while Wheelwright brought four theses. If the elders had managed to formally separate their disagreement with

Cotton from their disputes with the laity, for at least some of them the separation was artificial. Thomas Weld, for example, writing in *Short Story*, described Wheelwright's and Cotton's positions as "nine of the chiefest points (on which the rest depended)" produced by the "Adversary."[42] He did not inform his English audience with which adversaries the elders were now arguing. The ministers would meet in the morning, drafting their arguments in writing, and in the afternoon read them. The next day the "adversary," Wheelwright and Cotton, gave their written answers and argued for them, and the ministers would reply the following day.[43] This procedure "spent much time without any effect."[44] Thereafter, they moved to open debate, conducted in English rather than Latin as much as possible, and, according to Winthrop, "the questions were soon determined."[45]

The questions may have been soon determined, but, from the limited glimpses we have into the process, they were not determined easily. At one point, the assembly debated the question of the nature of the new creature, an issue that involved Wheelwright, not Cotton. The radicals in Cotton's congregation argued that Christ himself was the new creature, as part of their denial of sanctification and "creature graces," and it was Wheelwright's perceived unsoundness on this topic that caused Winthrop to block his nomination as co-teacher at the Boston church. At the synod Wheelwright asserted, with the authority of Zanchius behind him, that it was partially Christ and his righteousness and partially newly created graces in us. In a calmer season, Wheelwright's point perhaps would not have been very controversial. But in the context of Massachusetts in 1637, this was a loaded topic. Moreover, Wheelwright phrased his answer in such a way that caused some other ministers to assume that he was arguing that there were no inherent graces in the saints. Cotton later called his expressions "unsafe," and Wheelwright himself termed them "unsafe and obscure." Given that this is the only surviving criticism from either Cotton or Wheelwright of Wheelwright's doctrines, he must have used very rash language. Cotton himself agreed with the other divines that the new creature was the body of created graces in a believer, clearly differentiating himself from Wheelwright on this point.[46]

Cotton, however, did not leave Wheelwright to fend for himself entirely. The debate raised again the whole thorny issue of the precedence of faith and union in the process of justification, an issue on which Wheelwright's opponents had tried to convict him for heresy at his trial. And as they proceeded to thrash the issue out, with Wheelwright presumably very much on the defensive, Cotton interposed himself, as he had at Wheelwright's trial. He did so in a way that upped the ante considerably. Cotton had always argued that faith participated in justification, but that participation, he claimed, was passive, and not in part active, as most divines insisted. Now he pushed a step further. Citing a few highly respectable

Reformed divines, William Twisse, William Pemble, and Daniel Chamier, he advanced the proposition that "God may bee said to justifie me before the habit, or act of Faith."[47] Faith had nothing to do with justification itself; it only perceived an event that had previously transpired. As Cotton knew well, this was a doctrine usually associated with antinomianism, and it was close to radical opinions being voiced in his own congregation.

What inspired Cotton to raise this query at such a tense time is a mystery. He later claimed that he did so because "the Discrepance of all these Divines from the received expressions of the most, gave just occasion, why in such an Assembly, the judgment of sundry acute and judicious Elders, might be enquired." Taken as stated, Cotton seems to have been saying that he brought the proposition up at this extremely fraught moment simply out of academic curiosity. His explanation would be convincing only if we assume that the otherworldliness that Cotton and his contemporary and scholarly apologists invoke to defend him had reached a stage of almost complete disincarnation. Or was this a deliberate act of aggression by an angered minister, toying with doctrine more radical than what he was prepared to defend in his own name and cloaking that doctrine under the mantles of some very respectable divines, perhaps as a reaction to arguments from the other side that seemed equally extreme? Wheelwright later said that someone at the synod advanced the argument that there were only conditional promises in the Gospel.[48]

An entire day was spent in debate on Cotton's new proposition. According to Cotton Mather, who was working from a detailed manuscript account, this debate was the most intense of the proceedings, with "much sorrowful discourse" and "solemn speeches . . . made with tears" where the gap between Cotton and his fellow ministers seemed unbridgeable. Perhaps now was the time when those ministers who were "scandalized" with Cotton were most vocal. It takes little imagination to conceive the synod's breaking up in failure. John Norton, remembering years later, was impressed with Cotton's "singular patience" and said he was "a Mirror for the temperament, mildness, and government of his spirit"—one wonders what the provocations were that allowed him to display these virtues so conspicuously. This may be the place to insert an anecdote related by Robert Baillie, who heard it from Frances Higginson, in Scotland, who was present at the synod. Cotton one day "was so far cast down from what he met with from his brethren at the Synod, that one day coming out of the Assembly, he sate down alone on a Cartwheel in the way, in more grief and perplexity of heart, then for any cause with men had ever befaln him."[49]

The discourse, sorrowful though it might have been, was not unproductive. It led to Cotton's having a change of mind, not much of one, in fact so slight that it has escaped the attention of scholars, but it was real to

Cotton. He realized, as he later told Samuel Stone, that "the want of cleare discerning of the Difference betweene the Imputation of Christs Righteousnesse, and our Justification did (in the Conference) putt me upon some incongruous Apprehensions, and Disorderly Expression of the Order and Place of Fayth unto them both, which as God helped me by the Endeavours of some of you better to discerne, I thought it my duety then more clearly to Expresse, and acknowledge."[50] What this means is that Cotton's opponents had argued emphatically, according to Mather, that Romans 4:3–5, the key text for the Reformed conception of justification, demonstrated a sequence of unbelief, faith, union with Christ, and then justification, and Cotton decided that they were right.[51] Why Cotton should have found sudden enlightenment by standard exegeses of a foundational Reformed scriptural text is unclear. Perhaps he himself had been shaken into flexibility by the displays of feeling on the previous day. The next morning Cotton stood up in the assembly and announced his consent with them on this point in "an excellent speech tending to accommodation," as Cotton Mather summarized it.[52]

How Cotton's expressions tended to accommodation, we do not know. What I suspect happened was that it was here that he announced his most important doctrinal concession of the synod: faith was "more than habitual" in union with Christ. This concession would seem to allow that an active faith could be a visible faith for purposes of assurance. Introspection could give assurance, and therefore his opponents were not as seriously in error as he had previously thought. As he wrote to a still dubious Wheelwright three years later, "May not the sight of Faith be some cause of the sight of Justification without straine of Heresy." Whatever he did left some in his congregation who had not already stormed off feeling left in the lurch—the "sectaries," Mather noted, "tried by all the obstreperous ways imaginable to hinder the reconciliation."[53]

The Boston congregation's dismay at this turn of events probably only heightened the appreciation of the other ministers, and a final compromise set of statements was soon hammered out on the four issues outstanding between Cotton and the other ministers. (Cotton seems to have already abandoned his fifth query about Christ and his benefits being offered in the covenant of works.)[54] Union with Christ did not happen without an actual consent of the soul through faith; justification occurred in order of nature after the soul apprehended Christ's righteousness; sanctification must always be coexistent and at least possibly co-apparent with the witness of the Spirit, or else that witness must be considered either a "delusion or doubtful." There were concessions on both sides here. Cotton had, to all appearances, conceded on the first two of the five questions he brought to the synod: union required the act of faith, and faith was more than passive in the activity of justification. The final statement about the witness of the Spirit and sanctification, resolving his third and fourth queries, however, was a masterpiece of equivocation that could be read in any number of ways. It certainly held out the possibility that the Spirit could witness to an absolute promise before it did so to a conditional one; it even could be read as meaning that sanctification, although "possibly" visible, in practice never was, which is what Cotton had always argued. Yet at the start of the synod, the ministers jointly replying to Cotton had claimed that the Spirit only bore witness in a conditional promise (although their wording was ambiguous enough to allow a variety of positions on their side). But on the other side, the compromise more or less committed Cotton to agree at least that his brethren were not so wide off the mark. It was in effect a truce that allowed him to come out relatively unscathed— but not a great many other people in the Boston party.[55]

Cotton's teaching on the witness of the Spirit had been but the starting point for the radical lay Bible exegetes of Boston, and now his concessions in the synod made it firmly terminal. By acknowledging that faith was more than passive in union with Christ, Cotton had cut the link between his doctrine and that of lay radicals. His teachings could no longer be stretched to cover their speculations about justification without faith, and faith and sanctification always having their actual being in Christ and not in us, and believers being dead to graces. Cotton had never meant for such conclusions to be drawn from his teachings. Now he made that doctrinally even plainer, and he had done so in public.

Just as Cotton cut the ground out from theological radicals by what he was no longer willing to defend, he cut the ground out from his more militant supporters by what he was no longer willing to attack. He signaled clearly that the doctrinal enemies who had argued that sanctification could be a first evidence, or even worse, who argued that preparation was in itself saving, were not in fact enemies anymore. Although those ministers' doctrines had not changed; although they may have undercut Wheelwright's bid for a ministerial position in Boston and undertaken a covert effort to get him convicted; although they may have savaged Boston doctrine and individuals from the pulpit; and although they may have pushed to get supporters of Wheelwright excluded from the colony, Cotton's distance from them was no longer equivalent to the gulf between heaven and hell. We know that Wheelwright at least came to the synod prepared to argue against these positions, and he always insisted that it was extreme preparationism that explained the animus with which some of his opponents pursued him.[56] But unlike in May, Cotton was not prepared to pursue this charge against his opponents, and Wheelwright was left isolated. The "sectaries" were understandably upset.

Before breaking up on September 22 the synod made some other nonbinding resolutions, chiefly concerned with restoring ecclesiastical order and respect for ministers. It was concluded that there was no scriptural justification for sixty or more people to attend to one woman every week in a private house and listen to her resolve questions of doctrine and expound Scripture. The resolution is sometimes taken as a general assault on women's freedom, but given its precision, it is unlikely that anyone took it as applying to anyone other than Hutchinson. Similarly the synod condemned the practice of asking questions after a sermon, not for information but for reproving doctrine and reproaching the ministers, "and that with bitterness." This condemnation has been seen as a stifling of lay empowerment, but bitterly asking questions intended to reprove doctrine and reproach ministers had probably never been approved practice in Massachusetts. The assembly concluded that the magistrates should compel persons to attend processes of church discipline against them, and that churches should not permit, and other churches should not admit, persons departing a church because of opinions that were not fundamental. Winthrop's proposal that the assembly meet yearly was well-liked but left unresolved. A motion about ministerial pay was passed by on the grounds that the ministers did not want to be accused of organizing the synod for their own ends.[57]

Scholars considering the Synod of 1637 as performance art have suggested that in it the ministers made a theatrical display of professional unity in which the combination of highly technical learning and piety decisively identified and rejected the left-hand and illiterate path of scriptural error. They thus reinstated their badly bruised collective interpretive authority over the Bible, which was part of the point of the whole exercise; Christ was no longer divided.[58] Perhaps considered strictly as theater, the synod achieved this effect for some of its lay audience. Edward Johnson was clearly impressed by the sight of so many "ministers of Christ (who were so experienced in the Scripture, that some of them could tell you the place, both Chapter and Verse, of most sentences of Scripture could be named unto them)." He waxed eloquent over the memory of them "with scriptures light, cleering up the truths of Christ clouded by any of these Errors and Heresies, as had not been done for many Ages past." Johnson rejoiced that Christ caused "his servants in this Synod, mutually to agree" and thereby broke in pieces the "contrived plot of some" to draw away Cotton (but without mentioning him by name). Weld claimed that the synod "strengthened" over the "indifferent" and "settled" the "wavering." The Scituate church was surely not expressing isolated sentiments when it held a day of thanksgiving for the "Reconcilliation betwixt Mr Cotton and the other ministers."[59]

But the success of the synod, either as theater or in terms of content, should not be exaggerated. Weld made it clear that the results made no impression on a great many partisans. Wheelwright presumably went down fighting all the way, syllogizing, making fine scholastic distinctions, using Greek and Latin terms, and citing Reformed authorities—there was no reason for Boston partisans to think that the learning of the universities had unanimously condemned their reading of Scripture. Moreover, the ministerial united front, such as it was, was attained after some very tense debate and only by an extremely vague final statement. Even that inclusive final statement represented a papering over of differences, not a resolving of them, which was recognized at the time. The ministers in effect simply stated that they were all among the godly, whatever their differences, and that, to quote a contemporary manuscript, "no difference in opinion shall alienate their affections any more"—roughly how the Boston church itself had managed to hold together as long as it did. The synod requested Davenport to preach the final sermon; he called upon all assembled to endeavor to live in Christian unity, even in the absence of unanimity of opinion. Cotton later told an English audience that one of the glories of a New England synod was that if not all the participants could come to an agreement, all the parties could nonetheless agree "without dissunion of affection, or disturbance of the Churches peace . . . in this *one*, not to *condemn*, nor to *despise one another in differences of weaknesse.*"[60]

This outcome, unity of a sort through diversity, appears to have been the achievement of a moderate party, probably spearheaded by Davenport and Winthrop. According to one observer, Winthrop played the major role in allowing the assembly to reach as amicable a conclusion as it did. He silenced "passionate and impertinent speeches," regularly called for scriptural references, and would adjourn the assembly when he saw "heat and passion." As a result, "jarring and dissonant opinions, if not reconciled, yet are covered."[61] Winthrop saved the ministers from themselves, and he finally managed to work out on the level of practical politics what he had been unable to accomplish with his theological forays. That was no small achievement. Clearly, a failed synod would have had grave consequences in Massachusetts, and there is no telling how it would have played into the debates between English Congregationalists and Presbyterians in the 1640s, as the synod's outcome was the only evidence the Congregationalists had to counter the widespread assumption that their system could not police itself.

But since the final agreement amounted to little more than an agreement not to condemn and despise each other, it was a fragile one. Cotton's most determined opponents had not had their way at the synod, and they were not happy either with the outcome or with Cotton. As is well known, Shepard continued to articulate his mistrust of Cotton's theology and of Cotton himself. But Hooker, the moderator, was no less dissatisfied. He scarcely waited until he returned to Connecticut before he started attacking the compromise theological statement.[62] Weld, when recounting the exchange with the "Adversary" in *Short Story,* could not bring himself to mention that it ended with a theological accommodation. Winthrop, in his usual irenic vein, wrote in his journal that the synod had "concluded so comfortably in all love, etc."[63] There is enough evidence, however, to suggest that "Mr. Cotton's party" were not the only persons who departed the synod feeling that heaven had excessively accommodated hell—an inauspicious omen for the return of New England's peace.

NINE

THE NOVEMBER TRIALS

OCTOBER–NOVEMBER 1637

COTTON WAS now reunited with the orthodox party, even if the orthodox party was not entirely reunited with him. In light of his later actions, he probably regarded the controversy as over. He had made his doctrinal peace with his enemies and decided to stay in the colony, and he was willing to acknowledge that the straying sheep in his congregation needed more attention than he had previously given them. It was time for everyone to live and let live. But perceptions about a larger peace in Massachusetts were decidedly mixed. Winthrop, writing for an English audience soon thereafter, claimed that the synod had made little impact on Boston. Wheelwright in Mount Wollaston, he said, continued to preach "after his former manner"—but Cotton argued that he preached against errors there. Hutchinson continued to hold her meetings, Winthrop complained, in spite of the synod's pronouncements—we never caught her saying anything heretical, Cotton answered. She and others continued to walk out whenever Wilson preached—they would make excuses about female necessities requiring their departure, said Cotton. According to Winthrop, the Bostonians, far from being subdued by the synod, "boasted" of how a "fitter opportunity" would come their way "upon the return of some of their chiefe supporters," which was certainly a reference to Vane. How widespread talk of Vane's return was we have no way of knowing, and what Winthrop's allies like Shepard were doing to keep controversy stirred up has left no documentary trace. We do know that Hooker in Connecticut, writing a note to Winthrop after the synod, urged a "secret and suddayne" and "resolute and uncontrolable" attack on the "adversary." The synod had dramatized the authority of Massachusetts's ministers to Vane's party, evidently with little effect. Now at the beginning of November the General Court, following Hooker's suggestion, "took courage," as Shepard later put it, and asserted the authority of its magistrates in a manner harder to ignore.[1] The legal and political struggle that had been initiated with Wheelwright's trial in the spring was about to come to an end.

The Court was arguably not the first to strike against the adversary. On the night of October 17, Mary Dyer, like her husband, one of the leading "familists," delivered a deformed fetus that had died in her womb two hours previously. Only Anne Hutchinson, Jane Hawkins, the midwife, and another woman were present at the time. The other women had left earlier, overcome by the stench of the process. Those who witnessed the birth asked Cotton's advice as to what they should do in the face of what seemed like an awful message from God. Cotton said he would want it kept private if it had happened to him and he judged that God also wanted it concealed, since he had removed the other witnesses; the Lord may have intended it only for the private instruction of the parents.[2] The birth remained largely unknown, at least to Massachusetts males, until the following spring. Cotton's sympathetic and pacific restraint differed strikingly from his handling of the monstrous birth Anne Hutchinson had the next summer; he had a distance still to travel in his attitudes.

The Court held an unexpected by-election in October, for reasons now lost. Perhaps Winthrop and other leading magistrates felt that after the synod and the turmoil of the summer, they would get a body of legislators even less sympathetic to Boston than the one that had been elected in May. Almost half the Court's members were new. With the new Court in place, Governor Winthrop and his allies were ready to take a decisive move. Winthrop wrote in his journal that since "Mr. Wheelwright and those of his party" were still "busy in nourishing contentions . . . the case was now desparate, and the last remedy was to be applied," meaning trials that could result in banishment. It was a "speciall providence" that the "chiefe supporters" of Mr. Wheelwright's party were absent, Winthrop said, again a reference to Vane.[3] Winthrop and whoever else was planning the trials decided to use the Wheelwright petition, which Winthrop had already pronounced seditious, as the basis for their cases. As will be seen, they had a Court strongly sympathetic to their intentions, but one that was by no means a rubber stamp.

The Court convened in the Newtowne meetinghouse on November 2 and wasted no time in getting down to the business. It is unfortunate that for accounts of the Court's proceedings up to Hutchinson's trial we have only Winthrop's journal and a narrative he wrote that winter to send to England. His depictions are surely one-sided and downplay disagreements among the Court, but the descriptions of Bostonian defiance and mutual hostility ring true, and since the polemical stakes were relatively low up to Hutchinson's trial, I have taken him as roughly reliable. Deputy Aspinwall from Boston had signed the petition, and the Court asked him about it. Aspinwall maintained the petition was lawful, and for both signing and defending it the Court dismissed him. Deputy Coggeshall may not have been originally intended as a victim, but as the Court dismissed Aspinwall, Coggeshall stood up and said they might as well dismiss him, since he agreed with the petition even if he had not signed it. The Court did so. As Coggeshall left, he said, according to Winthrop, that the Court "had censured the truth of Christ, and that it was the greatest stroke that ever was given to Free-grace." After Aspinwall and Coggeshall had been dismissed, William Coddington, the third Boston deputy and ex-magistrate, proposed, by order from Boston, that the censure against Wheelwright and the immigration law be revoked. His request provoked Winthrop the next day to read his exchange with Vane on the immigration law, "and some that were of the adverse party, and had taken offence at the Law," Winthrop claimed, "did openly acknowledge themselves fully satisfied."[4]

The Court turned its attention to other business—regulating alcohol, deregulating tobacco, and giving out land (a thousand acres each to Dudley and Winthrop), among other items. Meanwhile, Boston was left to decide what to do about its now vacant seats. The town meeting would have returned Aspinwall and Coggeshall had not Cotton dissuaded it. Instead it chose deacon William Colburn and sergeant John Oliver. Oliver had also signed the Wheelwright petition and the Court dismissed him when he defended it. Colburn had been a deputy during Wheelwright's trial. He was among the Court members who signed Vane's Remonstrance against the sentence, but he had not signed the petition. The Bostonians did not send a replacement for Oliver, but, said Winthrop, "that contempt the Court let passe."[5]

With its membership settled, the Court began its judicial action against the Bostonians. Many historians discuss only Hutchinson's trial, which is understandable enough. Her trial survives in far more detail than any of the others; it was clearly more dramatic in its outcome; and Hutchinson, for the first time, comes across in a way that communicates something of her sharp mind and considerable force of personality. Moreover, if one has already assumed that Hutchinson was the central actor in the free grace controversy, there is no reason not to go straight to it. But in fact Hutchinson was the fourth person to come before the Court, and the actions against the first three set the tone for her trial and the subsequent hearings.

Wheelwright's hearing, the first and the longest of any, including Hutchinson's, consisted of three days of little more than mutual head banging, gauging from Winthrop's account. The Court, portrayed by Winthrop as virtually monolithic, blamed all the public turmoil in the colony on Wheelwright's preaching. Wheelwright in response was defiant. He continued to deny that he had intended to condemn specific people in his sermon, and he claimed that any troubles that resulted were the responsibility of Christ, not him. The Court tried to persuade him to leave the colony voluntarily, as did Cotton privately. Wheelwright refused, however, looking upon departure as tantamount to a confession of guilt.[6] At the end of the second day, after "many speeches," the Court sentenced Wheelwright to disenfranchisement and banishment, to depart before the end of March. Winthrop claimed that before pronouncing sentence, the

Court (Winthrop?) declared him guilty of "troubling the civill peace" for a variety of reasons—his seditious sermon, his "corrupt and dangerous opinions" (finally!), his contemptuous behavior in this and previous courts, his refusal to acknowledge his guilt, and his refusal to depart voluntarily. Court secretary Increase Nowell, however, wrote in the record simply that Wheelwright was banished because of his previous conviction for contempt and sedition and for his subsequent justification thereof. Wheelwright announced he would appeal to the king, but the Court said he could not do that. The following morning, Wheelwright showed up in a more accommodating mood and said he would accept the sentence of banishment. The Court ordered him not to preach before he departed. Wheelwright refused, and the Court gave him fourteen days to leave the colony, on penalty of imprisonment.[7]

The Court next tried in sequence the two dismissed deputies, Coggeshall and Aspinwall. Like Wheelwright they were defiant, defending both Wheelwright's doctrine and the Wheelwright petition. Coggeshall, in answer to an accusation that he had claimed that half of New England's church members were under a covenant of works, cited the parable of the ten virgins, a nice touch that the Court probably did not appreciate. They both denied on scriptural grounds that the Court had the right to banish them. Aspinwall was sentenced to banishment and ordered to depart by the end of March. Although "a great part" of the Court wanted to banish Coggeshall, Winthrop claimed that he made some gestures of repentance. His speech and behavior, Winthrop claimed, were more "modest and submisse" than they had been, and he said something about being distracted by work and public affairs. The sentence was reduced to disenfranchisement—this may be another example of Winthrop's moderating influence; it may also be the result of some sharp, edited-out debates among the Court members about how heavy a sentence his crimes deserved, given that he did not actually sign the petition. The Court warned Coggeshall that if he disturbed the public peace "either by speech or otherwise" he too would be banished.[8]

Hutchinson's trial was the next. For its details we are fortunate to be able to rely on anonymous notes as well as Winthrop. The notes read like a stenographic record, but they are not. They are short to begin with, and they leave out plausible material that Winthrop's tendentiously edited, still briefer version includes—he was said to have a very good memory.[9] They are thus the product of a gifted note taker making judgment calls on what the main threads and who the main speakers of the courtroom debates were and probably omitting a great deal in the process. Nonetheless, they provide a much fuller, much more conflicted picture of the Court's proceedings than does Winthrop. Hutchinson's trial is usually analyzed and interpreted in isolation, which is heavily misleading, but it differed from the previous trials in one crucial way: by the time it was over, Hutchinson had provided her interlocutors with the raw materials for a highly convenient rewriting of the entire controversy, one that has shaped much of the subsequent historiography.

Winthrop laid out the prosecution's case to Hutchinson at the beginning of the session. She had been "one of those who hath troubled the peace of the commonwealth and churches"; she had a "great share" of responsibility for "promoting and divulging" the opinions that had caused the recent troubles; she was joined in "affinity and affection" with those the Court had already censured; she had slandered the ministers of Massachusetts; and she had continued to hold her meetings, even after the synod had condemned them. The Court had called her to either convince her of her errors or, failing that, "take such course that you may trouble us no further." Winthrop rounded his address off by asking Hutchinson "whether you do not justify Mr. Wheelwright's sermon and the petition."[10]

Winthrop's question was an invitation to self-incrimination, one that the previous defendants had belligerently taken up. Hutchinson chose a different tack, as she would for most of the trial: she stonewalled. "I hear no things laid to my charge," she replied. In fact she was on stronger ground than those already convicted. Their convictions had stemmed from public acts: preaching, statements in the General Court, the signing of a "seditious" petition. Hutchinson had done none of these, as she pointed out to Winthrop. Winthrop argued back that though she may not have committed overt acts, she had "harboured" and "countenanced" those who had and was therefore in effect a co-conspirator: "[I]f you countenance those that are transgresors of the law you are in the same fact." Hutchinson replied that all she had done was entertain them, not conspire with them. Winthrop, arguing from the Fifth Commandment, said that by entertaining persons who had dishonored the magistrates she had dishonored them herself. Hutchinson responded that Winthrop's argument only applied "if I entertain them, as they have dishonoured their parents." In other words, she had not entertained them in connection with their quarrels with the magistrates. Winthrop replied that she put honor upon them by "countenancing them above all others." Hutchinson replied, "I may put honor upon them as the children of God and as they do honor the Lord."[11]

The drift of the trial notes indicates that Hutchinson had effectively pushed Winthrop into a corner. He was on the verge of having to argue that anyone who "entertained" John Wheelwright and the petition signers, a list that would include most of the Boston congregation and at least one of its ministers, deserved trial—love of the brethren was now an indictable offense. To extricate himself, he attempted for the only time during Hutchinson's court session to invoke patriarchal control: "We do not mean to discourse with those of your sex but only this: you do adhere unto them and do endeavour to set forward this faction and so you do dishonour us." Hutchinson ignored his patriarchal authority and again denied his chain of logic: "I do acknowledge no such thing neither do I think that I ever put any dishonour upon you."[12]

Winthrop, stymied, dropped the charge and moved on to her conventicles, where her alleged entertainment had taken place. He and Hutchinson engaged in much back-and-forth about the legitimacy of these and about her right as a woman to lead them. In *Short Story*'s version, Winthrop finally claimed that Hutchinson, with her regular and well-attended conventicles, had in effect had set up a public ministry, which she as a woman should not have done. Hutchinson acknowledged that if she had been teaching in public it would have been wrong, just as she agreed that it would have been wrong had she honored the "faction" in any dishonoring of the magistrates, but she denied that her conventicles constituted a public ministry. Although Winthrop could see no validity in Hutchinson's denial, recent historians have explored the ways in which her conventicles, like her nursing and attendance at childbirths, were a logical extension, at least to Hutchinson, of "the conventional Puritan pattern of diffused mothering" and behavior appropriate to a woman of her age and social status.[13] Behavior that Winthrop, as a male, identified in masculine terms as public, Hutchinson, as a woman, identified in feminine terms as private.

With Hutchinson refusing to acknowledge that she had done anything wrong with her meetings, Winthrop found himself again making dangerously general assertions: "[W]e see not that any should have authority to set up any other exercises besides what authority hath already set up." He was on the verge of declaring conventicles illegal, an uncomfortable corner for a puritan to find himself stuck in, the more so since they were common practice in Massachusetts. Was Hutchinson being sincere or extremely clever when she then invited him, in a roomful of veterans of Laudian purges, to put down her meetings "by authority"? Another magistrate, Simon Bradstreet, spoke up and tried to stop both of them from making a football of the women's meetings. Did Hutchinson make her offer because the law required her to do so? Hutchinson replied it was a "free will offering." Bradstreet said, in a rebuttal to the thrust of Winthrop's argument, that he did not regard women's meetings as unlawful.[14] Winthrop left this exchange out of *Short Story*, which, if a deliberate omission, showed good judgment—godly magistrates did not suppress the gatherings of the saints.

Winthrop was having a hard time moving from common knowledge— Hutchinson was clearly a central member of the "faction" that the Court had already determined was seditious—to a convictable offense. Hutchinson parried his first charge; she and Bradstreet had shut off his clumsy attempt to get at her via her conventicles. How the trial would have turned out had he continued to direct it, we will never know, for at this point Deputy Governor Dudley stepped in. He had a solid legal background and, as the earl of Lincoln's highly successful estate steward, perhaps a ruthless one.[15]

Dudley stayed on the theme of Hutchinson's conventicles for a few questions. He tried to establish if women ever taught at men's conventicles. Presumably this was an effort to make a direct link between Hutchinson and the men who had already been convicted. Hutchinson denied it, whereupon Dudley harangued her, a not uncommon judicial procedure at the time. The colony had been peaceful before Hutchinson arrived, Dudley told her. He had been suspicious of her upon her arrival, and he himself had no doubt where the source of the colony's troubles lay: "Mrs. Hutchinson hath so forestalled the minds of many by their resort to her meeting that now she hath a potent party in the country."[16]

Having rhetorically convicted Hutchinson for her conventicles, Dudley sensibly dropped the charge and moved to the next one, slandering the ministers. From here to the end of the trial, most of the Court members and Hutchinson went at cross-purposes as to what established her guilt or innocence of the charge. The prosecution's main concern was to demonstrate that she had indeed said disparaging things about the ministers, using as their evidence her comments in the ministerial meeting the previous October. The prosecution came prepared. Six ministers, professing reluctance to testify, presented their version of the conference, with Hugh Peters being particularly forward. They trashed the delicacy of her theological distinctions between sealed and unsealed Christians; for them, her saying that they preached a covenant of works meant that they were under a covenant of works. She freely acknowledged that she had said that their way of witnessing justification, if it was a way at all, was a "way to hell."[17]

Hutchinson had only one significant objection to the substance of the ministers' account. Whatever she said at the meeting came out reluctantly and in private contexts; this had been a discussion between godly shepherds and a devout lay person, "who must either speak false or true in my answers." The ministers had no business making it public. All parties agreed that she had been reluctant at first. They also agreed that she had cited Proverbs 29:25, "The fear of man bringeth a snare: but whoso putteth his trust in the Lord shall be safe," and then decided to speak freely. Hutchinson remembered speaking more reluctantly than the ministers suggested and regarded her speech as remaining private throughout the whole conversation. Moreover, her most incriminating statements occurred, she claimed, only in one-on-one, obviously private situations. She said that Wilson had a record of the meeting that would show that "many things are not so as is reported." Most of the Court, however, seemed not to regard her public/private distinction as very important; it was the substance of what she said that concerned them. Winthrop concluded this day's work by noting that they had labored to bring Hutchinson to acknowledge the error of her ways, and that she should consider it overnight and attend the Court in the morning.[18]

Winthrop began the next morning by announcing that it had been plainly proven that Hutchinson had indeed said what she had been accused of saying about the ministers and "this was spoken not as was pretended out of private conference." Perhaps because his first accusations had gotten nowhere, he reiterated a doctrinal charge that Dudley had brought up the previous day: that she had said the letter of the Scripture held forth a covenant of works was "offered to be proven by probable grounds."[19] He allowed anyone to speak, if anyone had anything to say, but he clearly regarded the case as settled.

Hutchinson must have had legal counsel the previous evening for she had a great deal to say. She remained insistent that the ministers had violated their roles as godly shepherds. Not only had they turned informants, they had deceived the Court about how reluctant she had been to share her mind with them. She had perused some notes of the conference with the ministers, she told the Court, and claimed that these notes contradicted their testimony. The ministers had to testify under oath, Hutchinson argued, on both legal and scriptural grounds, since they, in effect, had not been witnesses but prosecutors in their own cause. The question of her reluctance to speak was the issue she wanted them sworn for, not for the substance of what she may have said to them.[20]

Hutchinson's argument that she had not been as willing to talk as the ministers suggested does not seem to have registered significantly with the Court. But the related due-process issue struck a nerve. The ministers throughout the controversy had tried to avoid involving themselves directly in adversarial proceedings. They preferred to present themselves as disinterested protectors of God's truth and conciliators. They had not been willing to bring formal charges against Hutchinson to the Boston church; they had worked behind the scenes at Wheelwright's trial, and when they did finally accuse him openly, they accompanied their accusations with expressions of fraternal solicitude; on the first day of Hutchinson's trial they stressed that they testified only reluctantly. Now Hutchinson wanted to drag them down from their pedestals to the level of your-sworn-word-against-mine mortals. Winthrop, understanding the larger issue being raised, immediately objected that the ministers had been unwilling to speak, except that it was "the cause of the whole country" and required by the "glory and honour of God." Bradstreet told her that her issues were but "circumstances and adjuncts," and for these trivial matters she would make the ministers sin if they said something mistaken under oath. Hutchinson was not daunted. If the ministers were going to accuse her, "I desire it may be upon oath."[21]

Indeed, not all Court members were prepared like Winthrop to protect the ministers' self-image. Court secretary Nowell warned that there was discontent abroad that the ministers had broadcast things spoken in private. "Many" members of the Court said that they were not satisfied that the ministers testified without an oath, although the notes do not give their reasons. The only individual the note taker recorded explaining himself was assistant Israel Stoughton, who had previously clashed with Winthrop about Winthrop's arbitrariness. He said he was satisfied that the ministers spoke the truth, but that the "way of justice" required an oath "in this as in all other things"—felony convictions required two properly sworn witnesses. The prosecution was caught off guard by this flurry of concern over due process, but Winthrop reluctantly agreed to swear the ministers "that all may be satisfied."[22]

There was some opposition to his decision. Deputy Richard Brown of Watertown feared that requiring the ministers to take something as solemn as an oath was to take God's name in vain. Asssistant Roger Harlakenden, from Shepard's congregation, said that an oath was unnecessary because Hutchinson herself said that the elders were not able ministers of the New Testament—he needed no more testimony to vote to convict her. Hutchinson stated that they did not have to swear to that. She neither denied nor affirmed it, she told them, and would explain herself later on that topic—in fact, she would do that with a vengeance in the best-known passage of her trial.[23]

Hutchinson repeated her claim about her reluctance to speak while Harlakenden and Winthrop told her they saw no significant distinction between her testimony and that of Peters. Nonetheless, the ministers began to acquiesce to Hutchinson's demand. Peters, hearing Hutchinson reiterate that she had spoken only reluctantly, agreed that an oath was the end of strife, but he reminded her that the "main thing against her" was what she had said about the ministers. Eliot agreed that he would testify under oath, but only after he had heard witnesses Hutchinson said she wanted to call. He added, "I know nothing we have spoken of but we may swear to." Simmes interjected, "Ey, and more than we have spoken to." Stoughton reiterated that an oath was necessary for him to vote to censure. John Coggeshall, just disenfranchised, said the ministers should confer with Cotton before they swore, a gentle hint that they could use some memory refreshing. Endicott lashed out at his "carriage," and Harlakenden, keen to get on with convicting, objected to Hutchinson's demand for an oath when she did not dispute the ministers' testimony in its essentials. Hutchinson reiterated her demand for oaths, and William Colburn, a Boston deputy, asked that Cotton come forward that he might be able to hear what was being said, a request that suggests he expected that the prosecution witnesses would testify first, as was the usual English procedure. Cotton came down and sat by Hutchinson—Mr. Cotton's party was about to present its last public united front.[24]

Perhaps the prospect of testifying about the meeting and then being contradicted by Cotton gave some ministers cold feet about their oaths. In any case, Eliot wavered and was joined by Shepard. Stoughton impatiently told them that they ought to swear and "put an end to the matter." Peters said that the ministers' oath was to satisfy the Court, not Hutchinson. Dudley bluntly told those ministers still wavering that "if the country will not be satisfied you must swear."[25] But probably to relax them, he decided to do as Eliot had previously requested and call the defense witnesses first: Coggeshall, Leverett, and Cotton (defense witnesses were not allowed to swear in English trials until 1702).[26]

At this point, the proceedings were moving very close to Hutchinson's famous disclosure of her prophetic capacities, the dramatic high point of the most analyzed event of the free grace controversy. And given the interpretive controversy that surrounds this disclosure, we need to track what was going on precisely. Coggeshall started off by saying that Hutchinson did not say all that the ministers said she did. Hugh Peters snapped at him, "How dare you look into the court to say such a word?" Coggeshall, perhaps remembering that the threat of banishment hung over his head, announced, "Mr. Peters takes it upon him to forbid me. I shall be silent." Stoughton dismissed Coggeshall's testimony by saying that the ministers had gotten the gist of what she said correctly. Ruling elder Leverett spoke next in defense of Hutchinson. He stressed that Hutchinson had only spoken after Peters "did with much vehemency and intreaty urge her to tell what difference there was between Mr. Cotton and them." Leverett corroborated Hutchinson's proverb citation and said that she had told the ministers that they did not preach a covenant of grace as clearly as Cotton because like the apostles before the Ascension they had not received the witness of the Spirit. Winthrop asked him if he remembered her saying that they were not able ministers of the New Testament. Hutchinson interjected and again raised the issue of private conference. If she had stated that, she had done so only with Weld alone by the window. Weld claimed she did it before all the elders, she denied it, and Winthrop called upon Cotton to testify.[27]

Cotton did not have a clear memory of the meeting. Of Hutchinson's exchange with the ministers, he did not remember all that much, he said, since it did not concern him. Nonetheless, he did his best to take the sting out of Hutchinson's comments. He did not remember her directly saying that the ministers could not preach a covenant of grace or that they preached a covenant of works, but he did remember her saying that they did not preach the covenant of grace as clearly as he because they preached the seal of the Spirit upon a work and because they themselves had not been sealed with the Spirit. He explained that Hutchinson did not mean by that that the ministers were unregenerate, only that they had not yet experienced full assurance, which is to say that he took her to mean that they were under the Son's work and not the Holy Spirit's. He also stressed that his brethren did not seem at the end of the meeting to be as upset as they professed to be later.[28]

The conversation then veered off into a discussion between Cotton and some ministers whose full sense is unrecoverable, due to the note taker's leaving out one of Peters's remarks. But whatever was said does not seem to have made any great impact on the Court. Nowell said bluntly to Hutchinson that "the witnesses do not answer that which you require." Winthrop chimed in, "We do not need their testimony any further," explaining that Cotton and the others were not in conflict but simply remembering what struck them the most at the time. Weld and Winthrop expressed further skepticism about Hutchinson's testimony. Cotton, trying to salvage a bad situation with a generous interpretation of Hutchinson, explained that he had told Weld and Shepard that all she meant was that some matter in their preaching "was not pertinent to the seal of the spirit." Two lines are missing at this point and the notes resume with Dudley repeating that the ministers affirmed that Hutchinson had said that they were not able ministers of the New Testament, and Cotton replying he did not remember that.[29]

Analyses of the trial at this point can be divided into two dominant groups. One group, drawing on Winthrop's statements in *Short Story* that the Court was determined to convict its opponents, treats the trial simply as a political event, with the legalities irrelevant: "Hutchinson was not proved wrong by any standard or any law that can be applied by judicial process." This group is given to emphatic assertions of its position rather than demonstration that the prosecution did not try to make a case against Hutchinson.[30] A second group of scholars correctly acknowledges that the prosecutors did try to establish a legal basis for convicting Hutchinson. The group argues, however, that the centerpiece of the prosecution's case, Hutchinson's alleged slander of the ministers, collapsed at this point in the trial. Cotton's cautious minimizing of the seriousness of what Hutchinson said to the ministers and his careful addition that he had not paid attention to everything that was said wrecked the charge.[31]

I find this argument unpersuasive. Hutchinson had all but admitted that she said the clerics were not able ministers of the New Testament, arguing only that she had not said this to the group but privately to an individual. Her privacy defense, though, cut no ice with the Court. Her witnesses had testified and made absolutely no impression. The notes do not suggest that Cotton's fuzzy memory had helped her. Winthrop, Dudley, and Nowell indicated that they had heard nothing from him that would make them change their opinion about her guilt. In Cotton's final exchange with Dudley, all he said was that he did not remember her saying that the ministers were not able ministers of the New Testament, and this after acknowledging that he had not paid attention to everything that was said. There is no reason to think that the Court would have been swayed by Cotton's final memory lapse any more than it had been by his previous fuzziness, which is the pivotal point of the "collapsing prosecution" argument. Moreover, Dudley made clear that ministers were going to testify under oath, will they, nil they, which would end the due-process issue that concerned some Court members.[32]

The charge, Winthrop later wrote in his journal, had been "clearly proved against her, though she sought to shift it off."[33] The only weakness in the prosecution's case was that, unlike Wheelwright, she had not traduced the ministers from a pulpit and wrapped her claim in inflammatory rhetoric. Stephen Greensmith had gotten only a forty-shilling fine in March for saying more or less what Hutchinson was accused of saying, and the prosecution wanted cause to banish her—they had a smoking gun, in other words, but they would have preferred a smoking cannon. Perhaps in order to get one they would have moved on the heresy charge. They never needed to, however, for Hutchinson was about to provide them with a smoking cannon of her own volition.

She now shared her revelation-driven English spiritual experiences with the Court. Historians have produced a rich mine of speculation as to her motivation and mood at this pivotal point in the trial. Was it "an unheeding and exultant impulse to affirm her own being," the product of "hysteria," or a sign that she was "cracking under the strain of the inquest"? Was it a "rhapsody," or was she a "deviant," "compelled by some inner urgings to make a 'profession' of feelings"? Was she "speaking as though possessed of the Spirit"?[34] I am dubious of all these portrayals of Dionysian release or overloaded collapse. Hutchinson was a puritan biblical exegete, not a Quaker prophetess, and given to arguing, it was said, not in raptures but in syllogisms. Mary Beth Norton's suggestion that what followed was not histrionics but pedagogy, an attempt to teach the Court, seems in keeping with her character.[35] Moreover, this was not an unpremeditated outburst but a conscious decision by Hutchinson to do exactly what she had said she would do earlier in the day's proceedings: explain why she knew that the elders of the Bay were not able ministers of the New Testament. Now was as good a time as any in the trial for it, given that her privacy argument had persuaded no one. It was "an act at once politically defiant and religiously satisfying."[36]

She explained to the Court about her fast day in England and how the Lord, by his "prophetic office," had shown her how to discern among the voices of Christ, Moses, John the Baptist, and Antichrist in ministers. She closed her explanation with the absolutism of the prophet: she knew in her conscience what she said was true, and if the Court condemned her for it, she committed herself to the Lord.[37]

Unfortunately for the historian wanting to better understand Hutchinson's theology, the Court did not proceed to grill her on the distinctions among what must have been to them a baffling array of biblical "voices." Secretary Nowell, probing the source of her confidence, asked her how she knew that it was the Spirit who revealed this to her, whereupon Hutchinson asked him how Abraham knew that it was God who commanded him to sacrifice his son, and she revealed that she had access to what she termed immediate revelations.[38]

Perhaps Hutchinson sensed that her audience would not leave her center stage for long, and she proceeded to play her last card. She immediately plunged into explaining how she herself had once been led aside into a covenant of works, how she had become confident of her revelations, and how they had brought her to New England. She then informed the Court that she had been foretold, via Daniel 6, that she would experience her own lion's den and emerge from it unharmed by God's power. On the other hand, she warned her persecutors, "You do as much as in you lies to put the Lord Jesus Christ from you, and if you go in this course you begin you will bring a curse upon you and your posterity, and the mouth of the Lord hath spoken it."[39]

Hutchinson was not being original in invoking divine vengeance on the magistrates; Roger Williams had done so, and the Wheelwright petitioners had implied as much (and her father threatened divine judgment on the bishop who interrogated him in 1578).[40] But neither Williams nor the Wheelwright petitioners made the threat openly before the Court and claimed a revelation as their authority. Hutchinson's disclosure must have been an extraordinary bravura performance—Dudley and Stoughton, caught up in the details, discussed what verse she was referring to. As the members of the Court tried to follow her scriptural texts, she closed by paraphrasing Hebrews 11:27: "But now having seen him which is invisible I fear not what man can do unto me."[41]

Hutchinson, for all her boldness, had just given her opponents a massive twofold gift. The first part was that she had immensely simplified the task of a not very surefooted prosecution. She had voluntarily all but acknowledged in an unquestionably public forum that she thought that all the ministers except Cotton and Wheelwright preached a covenant of works and explained why. She then willingly topped it with a threatening speech both seditious and supremely in contempt of court.

The second part of her gift was that she had shared with representatives from all over the colony her predilection for revelations, as dramatically and menacingly as possible. It is not that the supernatural gift of fore-knowledge was universally frowned upon among puritans—John Wilson, after all, was renowned for his "prophetical *afflatus*."[42] The legitimacy of temporal revelations, however, was contested in puritan circles, with their acceptability at best being dependent on who had them, what context they had them in, and whose interests they served.[43] Thomas Hooker, for exam-ple, in his final sermon in England before fleeing to Holland, had dramati-cally announced that "God told" him the previous day that God would destroy England. He can be pictured embitteredly poring over the Bible before the sermon and having a denunciatory verse hit him with enough force that he couched the experience in this revelatory way, very rare for him. Hooker hardly imagined that his words would resurface on the other side of the Atlantic, cited approvingly by Hutchinson a little further on in her trial. Hooker's friend Eliot made a hasty intervention in the Court, worded in such a way that he might have been trying to give the impres-sion that Hooker had never said any such thing without literally stating as much, which, as Eliot perhaps knew, would have been untrue.[44] But it was one thing for a distinguished minister to invoke the authority of a threatening revelation in a dramatic moment in the pulpit, one whose logic would resonate with many godly ministers and magistrates; it was another thing altogether for a lay person on trial to share revelations that most of the ministers of Massachusetts and England preached a covenant of works and that the General Court would soon be destroyed.

If revelations were problematic to begin with, Hutchinson made her case even worse by claiming hers were immediate. The word "immediate" was a slippery one in this context. Cotton and Wheelwright both consid-ered that when the Holy Spirit communicated a meaningful Scripture text to a person's mind, the result could be called an immediate revelation.[45] It was through the medium of illuminating Scripture verses that Hutchinson seems to have experienced her revelations. But immediate could also be taken to mean without the medium of the Scriptures altogether, as the anabaptists of Münster, their familist offspring, and perhaps a few people in Massachusetts already meant it. It could signal the end of the Bible as the foundational source of religious truth, a result that Shepard had been arguing from the pulpit for months was the logical destination of Cotton's teachings. It could also signal the end of the authority of the Bible's official interpreters, the ministers, as well as the end of all external moral re-straints. By giving as her analogy God's voice to Abraham, Hutchinson may have simply wanted to communicate the certainty of her scriptural experience. Her terminology, however, offered her opponents a barn-door sized opening that they were all too happy to exploit to portray her as a promulgator of extra-scriptural revelations. In any case, even a revelation that came through Scripture, if it fell outside any possible meaning of the text, was clearly illegitimate. Ministers always cited Scripture verses while warning their audiences of God's impending judgments, but Hutchinson's judges took for granted that Scripture verses could not possibly demonstrate that she was under divine protection and that God would destroy them—"bottomlesse revelations, as either came without any word [of Scripture], or without the sense of the word," summed up Winthrop when explaining Hutchinson to his English audience.[46]

While Dudley and Stoughton fumbled with the fine points of Hutchinson's speech, Winthrop caught on right away about the potential use of what had just happened. Hutchinson had been relentlessly stonewalling the Court every step of the way in the trial, as he wrote later to his English brethren, "putting matters on proof and then quarelling with the evidence." And now she had just "freely and fully discovered herself."[47] Now that he no longer had to fumble his way through nitpicking legal details, Winthrop began to effectively recast the story of the free grace controversy. He asked Hutchinson if she expected like Daniel to be delivered by a miracle. Hutchinson replied that she would be delivered by the Lord's providence. (Presumably the providence involved the return of Vane—six months later she still expressed the hope he would be appointed governorgeneral.) When writing to England Winthrop ignored her careful distinction, which separated a zealous providentialist from an anabaptist enthusiast, and claimed that she said she expected to be delivered by miracle. William Batholomew, a deputy from Ipswich, following Winthrop's lead, told of revelations Hutchinson had shared with him in England, including the one of Hooker's. Reverend Simmes and Endicott spoke of her vanity and lack of humility. Endicott wanted to see if Cotton would still run interference for her and asked him what he thought of her revelations.[48]

Cotton was indeed still prepared to run interference. He explained that revelations by the Word and according to the Word were possible and if Hutchinson did not expect to be delivered by a miracle but only by a wonderful providence, he could not bear witness against it. Dudley expressed incredulity at Cotton's defending a prophecy of the destruction of the Massachusetts Court—it does seem extraordinary for Cotton to do, even though technically speaking he was within the bounds of orthodoxy. It might reflect Cotton's continuing anger, which he articulated even a decade later, at the excess of zeal with which certain persons pursued the dissidents in his congregation, as might his willingness, along with Leverett's, to appear as a defense witness in the first place—perhaps he was not totally averse to the idea of Vane's returning as governor-general.[49]

While the others were trying to flush out Cotton, Winthrop continued to press his central insight. Not only had Hutchinson given a massive boost to a not very well-prepared prosecution, she had provided an important new way to understand the free grace controversy. She had been teaching the godly to look to immediate revelations and not to the ministry of the Word, and this, Winthrop announced to the Court, was the "root of all the mischief." To be fair to Winthrop's sweeping conclusion, he may have had a flash of déja vu when he heard Hutchinson cite 1 John 4:3 in explaining how she knew what voices ministers spoke with. He had been completely baffled when Vane cited this verse against him in the summer, and he had read their exchange at the beginning of the Court. Now he knew that Hutchinson was Vane's source. The Court spoke its consent, and Winthrop warming to his task, announced that it was "the most desparate enthusiasm in the world."[50]

The Court, however, continued to wander from the path Winthrop had laid out for it. Endicott again questioned Cotton as to whether he agreed with Hutchinson. Cotton repeated that if the "revelation be in a word or according to a word, that I cannot deny." Endicott expressed satisfaction, although it is hard to see from nearly four hundred years' distance what was satisfactory in Cotton's reply; perhaps the note taker was nodding here. Dudley more understandably announced that Cotton wearied him. Winthrop, growing increasingly worked up with what he had just heard from Hutchinson, claimed he had never read of anything so extraordinary, either among anabaptists or enthusiasts. Cotton reminded him that those revelations concerned new matter of faith or doctrine—the bottom line for puritans was that there could be no more revelations of doctrine. Winthrop replied, with some justice, given the medley of biblical voices Hutchinson had shared with the Court, that Hutchinson's did too. There were revelations that accorded with the Word, Winthrop said, but Hutchinson's certainly did not. Dudley continued to fume at Cotton, and Peters challenged Cotton's defense of Hutchinson's revelations.[51]

Dudley finally picked up on Winthrop's explanatory lead and drew a comparison between Hutchinson and Münster. Winthrop announced he was persuaded that Hutchinson's revelations were delusions, and all the Court, the notes record, "but some two or three ministers," cried out, "We all believe it—we all believe it." Endicott proclaimed that "all the world may see where the foundation of all these troubles among us lies."[52]

The Court was now moving steadily in Winthrop's direction, and he kept it on track. Winthrop restrained John Eliot when he tried to limit the possibility of prophetic revelations more than Winthrop liked. Deputy Richard Collicott, who had been active in attacking Wheelwright at his March trial, threatened the highly convenient closure of the controversy around Hutchinson alone by raising again the question of Cotton's attitude toward her revelations—Winthrop cut him off. Richard Brown then made a long speech in which he called Hutchinson's revelations the "cursed fountain" of the colony's troubles and called for a greater censure than anyone had received so far. Moving to ratify this convenient, consensually developed, monocausal explanation of Massachusetts's recent disruptions, Winthrop asked "if therefore it be the mind of the court, looking at [Hutchinson] as the principal cause of all our trouble, that they would now consider what is to be done with her."[53]

At the start of the trial, Hutchinson had been, according to Winthrop, one of those who had troubled the peace of the commonwealth and churches; now she had escalated in status to the principal agent. The ascent was rapid but unsurprising. When Hutchinson shared her revelations, she saw herself as acting out a Daniel-in-the-lion's-den scenario, but she inadvertently provided the final piece for an all but completed tableau of a very different sort. It had been bruited about for at least a year that a sinister conspiracy of heretics had been plotting the ruin of Massachusetts, and fear that revelations and familism, the products of Münster, were at the bottom of Massachusetts's troubles had been one of the elements that constituted those troubles in the first place. All that was missing from the picture was a destructive prophetic figure like Münster's King John, and this Hutchinson, all the more convincing as a figure of hierarchical disorder for being a woman, had just provided. Given Protestant history, Hutchinson the prophet and conventicle leader provided at least as compelling a monocausal explanation for what Massachusetts had been through as Vane the Machiavellian politician. As will be shown, she was also a much more useful one.

The Boston party made a last ditch effort to slow the proceedings down. Coddington and Colburn raised objections over Hutchinson's alleged slander of the ministers, while other members of the Court grew restless. Stoughton announced that Hutchinson deserved banishment, but since she wanted the standard legal procedure of sworn witnesses, he could not formally condemn her without them. Coddington agreed, adding that the ministers had "broken the rules of God's word" in making their private conversation with Hutchinson public. Winthrop, in order to satisfy Stoughton, agreed to swear two ministers.[54]

Weld and Eliot volunteered, and Peters joined in. They ignored the question of how much effort it took for them to make her talk; for them, as for most of the Court, substance, not process, was the issue. They reiterated her unflattering comparison of them with Cotton and her likening of them to the apostles before the Ascension. Coddington kept interjecting that such a comparison was no disparagement, and Winthrop reminded him that Hutchinson had just predicted she would be delivered from this calamity. Cotton came to Hutchinson's defense, to Peters's indignation, stating again that she had only said she would be rescued by God's providence.[55]

Stoughton claimed he was now satisfied by the ministers' testimony—Hutchinson's privacy defense made no impression on him. Winthrop moved for a vote for banishment for "these things that appear before us." All but the Boston deputies and one abstainer voted for conviction. Winthrop pronounced the sentence of banishment. Hutchinson, like the three sentenced before her, challenged the legitimacy of the sentence. "I desire to know wherefore I am banished," she asked, a reasonable enough question, given the vagueness of Winthrop's summary, at least as the note taker took it down. The trial notes end with Winthrop in response to Hutchinson apparently giving the proceedings a dramatic, arrogant closure: "The court knows wherefore and is satisfied."[56]

Winthrop's sweeping refusal to be specific about her crimes has encouraged historians to fill in the charges for him in a no-less-sweeping manner: "The purpose of the trial was . . . to find a name for that nameless offense which Mrs. Hutchinson had committed." Or "to feel intimacy rather than obeisance toward Him [God] had become an offence." But the hearing hardly stopped with Winthrop's final statement in the notes, which may or may not have been intended at the time to bring closure to anything. There was still the sentencing to deal with—the Court, unsurprisingly, ordered Hutchinson banished. She had to leave by the end of March, and until that time she was ordered confined to the house of Joseph Weld, merchant and brother of Thomas Weld, in Roxbury. Perhaps a number of ministers and magistrates took the opportunity to lecture Hutchinson, as they did Wheelwright after he had been convicted. We know that Wilson at least addressed her, for five months later at her church trial, Hutchinson "grew into a passion against him" for what he said now.[57]

Someone might have even attempted to explain to Hutchinson the legal basis for her conviction, for despite Winthrop's vagueness, she had been found guilty of neither a nameless nor mystical offense. Nowell summarized the proceedings tersely in the Court records before moving on to the next agenda items. Hutchinson had been summoned, he wrote, for "traduceing [slandering] the ministers and their ministry in this country" (Nowell discretely omitted the first, failed charges). The reason she was convicted was that she willingly confessed to that accusation and, and to top it off, engaged in a speech that comprised both seditious libel and blatant contempt of court. Or, as he phrased it, "she declared voluntarily her revelations for her ground, & that shee should be delivered & the Court ruined, with their posterity, & thereupon was banished."[58] There is a common tendency to argue that Hutchinson's conviction was somehow arbitrary and extra-legal.[59] Hutchinson had a real trial, however, by the rough and tumble, disorderly standards of seventeenth-century English jurisprudence, in which cases were decided through a mixture of "prejudice, legal rules, and common sense."[60] The magistrates' charges that were poorly supported were dropped and the remaining charges were amply substantiated; they would have potentially been offenses in England. One sets up a dichotomy with little relevance to how legal systems actually function to state that Hutchinson's trial "was not a trial of justice to solve the problem of guilt or innocence, but a trial of power to solve the political problem of maintaining order." The trial was both, and as various members of the Court made clear to the prosecuting magistrates, it had to succeed as the first in order to succeed as the second.[61] Whether a defunct corporation carrying on in defiance of the king had any legal standing to run trials, especially trials for sedition, a crime always ultimately against the Crown, is another question altogether.

For all the attention it gets from scholars, Hutchinson's trial was not nearly as important as Wheelwright's to the free grace controversy itself. With Wheelwright, the opponents of Boston had to scramble to get a conviction. By the time Hutchinson came to trial, there was a consensus that the behavior and opinions of Wheelwright and his supporters constituted actionable offenses. The banishments had already started; Hutchinson's prosecutors did not have to work to make the Court unsympathetic to her. The result of Wheelwright's trial was months of protracted political clashes, plans to trump the local government's authority with that of the king's, a flurry of scribal pamphleteering, and the serious contemplation of the mass emigration of the Boston church. Hutchinson's conviction produced no threat to appeal to the king; no major shifts in the makeup of the General Court; and no barrage of pamphleteering. A rump of the Boston congregation was already planning to leave. The men of Boston did not petition the General Court on behalf of Hutchinson (or anyone else convicted in November), nor did the women, as they would twelve years later for the midwife Alice Tilly.[62] As a political struggle, the free grace controversy, with the exception of some mopping up, was effectively over by the time of Hutchinson's trial, even if the Court declared ex post facto that her newly discovered revelations carried the sole responsibility for that struggle.

But the outcome of Hutchinson's trial provided one very important new opportunity. It allowed formidable spin control on the entire controversy. Just how useful Hutchinson was in the rewriting of history Winthrop demonstrated in the account of the November trials he sent to England shortly thereafter, "to the end that all our godly friends might not be discouraged from coming to us."[63] There he claimed that the free grace controversy was entirely Hutchinson's fault. It stemmed from her intention to "disclose and advance her master-piece of immediate revelations," which he elaborated at length, and it would have resulted in "the utter subversion both of Churches and civill state" had not so many elders and magistrates stayed "free from the infection." Winthrop had already explained to his readers that Wheelwright's fast-day sermon was the source of all the colony's troubles. Now he informed them that Wheelwright got the courage to give this sermon from Hutchinson. Thanks to Hutchinson, there was no need to explore the extended string of mutual provocations that resulted in Wheelwright's conviction; no need to even raise the delicate issues of Vane and Cotton, thank heaven; and certainly no need to mention incendiary preachers like Shepard—no need, in short, to disturb anyone in his projected audience or suggest anything problematic about the Massachusetts establishment: cherchez la femme.[64] How calculating Winthrop was in what he wrote is beyond recovery, but at a minimum his sincerity moved in highly advantageous channels.

One would have no hint from Winthrop, or from the many historians who have derived their interpretations from his account, that seven months later, the election-day preacher, no less simplistically, would be offering a very different figure to account for the confusion of the free grace controversy. For Shepard, that figure was not Hutchinson, the American Jezebel, as Winthrop would shortly call her, but Vane, the American Abimelech, in whose hands Hutchinson was but one of a number of pawns. Hutchinson would be dead within six years on the American frontier, while Vane's star in the English government was steadily rising— Winthrop, deliberately or not, made a sensible authorial decision. It has recently been argued that historians who do not make gender the central issue in the free grace controversy "figuratively reenact in twentieth-century historical reconstructions of antinomianism the seventeenth-century disavowal of Hutchinson." That argument, however, while reflecting a common sentiment, has it precisely backward. It is a monocausal focus on Hutchinson in the first place that reenacts the seventeenth-century disavowal of her, and to then focus on Hutchinson's gender, if at the expense of neglecting her considerable skills as a creative and polemical biblical exegete, takes the disavowal of her far past what Winthrop and his brethren attempted.[65] Boston's opponents certainly regarded Hutchinson as a major player in the disruptions that had climaxed in the "sedition" of the previous spring, rightfully so, and they did not manufacture their horror at her revelations simply for polemical purposes. But it is safe to assume that most, and probably all, of them regarded Vane as a greater and more dangerous agent of disruption while he was in Massachusetts, no less rightfully so; Wheelwright, for large swaths of the controversy, was probably out in front of Hutchinson as someone whom at least the clerics hated—a professional traitor, as well as a heretic—and it was the hatred of the clerics for Wheelwright that unleashed the political strife that brought Hutchinson to trial. Where Cotton fit in this scheme of things presumably varied wildly from person to person.

The final action of the Court, before adjourning for a week, was to allow Samuel Hutchinson to remain in the colony until after the winter. When the Court reconvened, it continued with its disciplining of Boston. It called in more of what Winthrop called the "principall stirring men" in the controversy. The first two to come in were the Boston sergeants William Balston and Edward Hutchinson. Balston said he knew of no other place in the world where fault would have been found with the petition. Hutchinson told the Court that if they took away his estate they must keep his wife and child. Balston and Hutchinson were disenfranchised, fined twenty and forty pounds respectively, and removed from their offices. Hutchinson was also imprisoned for his comments to the Court, although he was released upon his apology the next morning. Winthrop may have been settling personal scores with these two, since they had refused to escort him with their halberds. He mentioned that the severity of their punishment was in part because they were "such as had offered contempt to the Magistrates."[66]

The Court's severity appears to have started to make an impression on the other petition signers. The next day the Court called Thomas Marshall, William Dinely, William Dyer, and Richard Gridley. They defended the petition, but "more modestly" than the others, and they were only disenfranchised and removed from any public office they might hold, as was John Underhill shortly thereafter. There must have been hasty consultations in Charlestown, for eleven Charlestown petition signers voluntarily came in, either because they read the writing on the wall or because, as Winthrop said, they "soon found their error" and asked that their names be removed from the petition. Their request was "easily granted, and their offence with a loving admonition remitted." The Court adjourned until the twentieth, but not before giving official recognition to the tireless labors of Shepard, the only ministerial foe of Boston so honored.[67] It decided that Harvard College would be located in Newtowne, shortly to be renamed Cambridge, in recognition of "the vigilancy of Mr. Shepard . . . for the deliverance of all the flocks which our Lord had in the wilderness."[68]

There may have been a rough consensus in the colony that the Court proceeded with justice in its trials, but that consensus did not penetrate very far into Boston itself. Margaret Winthrop wrote her husband a remarkable letter around November 15: "Sad thougts posses my sperits, and I cannot repulce them which makes me unfit for any thinge wondrine what the lord meanes by all these troubles amounge us . . . I finde in my selfe an aferce spiret, and a tremblinge hart, not so willinge to submit to the will of god as I desyre. Thear is a time to plant and a time to pul up that which is planted, which I could desyre mite not be yet. . . . The lord knoweth what is best, an his wilbe done," Margaret dutifully closed her letter.[69]

Margaret Winthrop might be prepared as a dutiful wife to ultimately defer to her husband, but others in Boston had no reason to swallow their indignation. Many members argued Boston church that Winthrop should be disciplined, finally. Winthrop, in order to prevent "a public disorder," himself addressed the congregation after the Court had finished its business. He made it clear they had no power over him for his behavior in the General Court. Had they attempted to challenge him, he told them, he would have first checked with the General Court and the elders if he should cooperate. In any event he knew that the church could not inquire into Court proceedings. Nonetheless, he would willingly explain why he had spearheaded the prosecution of his fellow church members. It was obvious that his opponents were at odds with the rest of the country and that their remaining in Massachusetts was incompatible with public peace, so "they must be sent away." This was a man feeling no need for concessions or apologies when he spoke to a room full of the friends and relatives of the three persons banished—he had won and they had lost. "God is with us," Winthrop wrote back to his wife. "It is the Lords work, and it is marvellous in our eyes," he wrote to his brethren in England.[70] But the Lord's work included some rough patches in the road ahead.

TEN

AN AMERICAN JEZEBEL

NOVEMBER 1637–MARCH 1638

S NOW BLANKETED Massachusetts from early November to late March during the "tedious winter" of 1637–38, while the unexpected twist that the free grace controversy now took deepened the gloom. The trials of November, rather than silencing dissent, managed to finally create the openly militant doctrinal radicals that the Massachusetts authorities had long been hunting, and ministers and magistrates watched with horror as they defiantly aired progressively more shocking heresies. In the process, the consensual mechanisms that had more or less held the Boston church together in its wide diversity broke down. That breakdown led, among other things, to Hutchinson's church trial for heresy in March 1638. Her extraordinary performance at the trial ensured both her excommunication and her subsequent inversionary apotheosis as, in Winthrop's words, an "*American Jesabel.*"[1]

The most dramatic and surprising fracture in the Boston church community took place at Mount Wollaston in November, as Wheelwright was preaching his farewell sermon. Wheelwright had always preached against what he took to be the errors within his congregation, and apparently he had not generated any open friction in doing so until now. One of his listeners, a recent convert who, according to *Mercurius Americanus*, had "ever before assented" to Wheelwright's doctrine, rose and denounced him as vehemently as he had denounced his own opponents, using the same rhetoric. Wheelwright preached "Antichristianisme, and had set up a Christ against a Christ." The listener went on to expound a very harsh version of Hutchinsonianism—there was no inherent righteousness; believers were as dead lumps, except as they were acted by Christ; a man might be adopted by God and still damned; the Commandments were a dead letter. But Wheelwright's listener went further, well past the sacraments of the church and the Bible itself. He argued for assurance through immediate revelations without any word of Scripture at all, saying that even the absolute promises of the Bible were for those still under the Law. The New Testament held no signs for believers; baptism itself was of no use to those who had been baptized by the Holy Spirit. Cotton said this listener later became a follower of the familist-inspired sect-master Samuel

Gorton, recently arrived in New England. His familist-styled denial of baptism by water and devaluing of Scripture may indicate Gorton's influence or it may be the articulation of familist ideas already circulating in Boston. In any case, dramatic though it was, it was only the prelude for an even more extensive open appropriation of familist doctrines, as will be seen below.[2]

Wheelwright's listener vented the most radical theology yet recorded in Massachusetts and Winthrop understandably included it when justifying the November trials to an English audience shortly thereafter. He blamed Wheelwright for his auditor's opinions, to the eventual outrage of *Mercurious Americanus* and Wheelwright himself. Wheelwright corrected his listener, explained Winthrop, but not sternly enough. His mildness demonstrated to Winthrop his "neere agreement in the points, though his wisdome served him to bee more reserved till a fitter season." Wheelwright might be truly godly in spite of his "Familisticall opinions," Winthrop conceded, "yet the next generation, which shall be trained up under such doctrines, will bee in great danger to prove plain Familist."[3]

The Mount Wollaston incident pointed to an important transformation in the Boston congregation. Prior to the November trials the bulk of the Boston church had gotten by with mutual forbearance and a sense of larger common purpose. Theological radicals within the community muted their opinions, either opportunistically or in the interest of greater harmony and the larger struggle against the legalists. The banishments and trials appear to have snapped some people's tenuous connections, personal and doctrinal, to mainstream and clerical puritanism, even of the Cottonian variety. Besides publically asserting radical doctrine and defying ministers whom they had previously supported, these people now vigorously espoused immediate revelations, and, according to Winthrop, "professedly maintained these Enthusiasmes as the Oracles of God. And that such revelations as *Abraham* had to kill his Son, and as *Paul* had in the Ship, and when hee was caught up into the third heaven, &c. were ordinary." "Had this sect gone on awhile," said Edward Johnson, commenting on these latest developments, "they would have made a new Bible."[4]

The authorities saw their worst dreams come true. Their efforts to impose doctrinal unity on Massachusetts had ended up creating highly visible heretics. "This discovery of a new rule of practise by immediate revelations," said Winthrop, generated a strong reaction when the General Court reconvened on November 20. The Court ordered all the colony's powder and ammunition removed from Boston to Newtowne and Roxbury, a logical, if hysterical, preface to the proclamation it then made. "The opinions & revelations of Mr Wheelwright & Mrs Hutchinson," the Court claimed, "have seduced & led into dangerous errors many of the people heare in Newe England." As a result, there was a "just cause of suspition" that "some revelation" might produce a repetition of Münster with "some sudden irruption upon those that differ from them in judgment." Therefore the Court announced that any petition signers who would not recant, as well as some others "who had been chief stirrers in these contentions," had to hand in their weapons and ammunition.[5]

The seventy-five men the Court named were not a group of outsiders or recent arrivals. All but eight were freemen; two-thirds had immigrated more than three years previously, with 1630 the most represented year, they included former deputies and assistants to the General Court; and they were perhaps somewhat more prosperous than average. Lincolnshire was their most common place of origin, unsurprisingly. All but seven were either from Boston or adjacent towns.[6] Taking the English population in Massachusetts to be close to eight thousand, the order indicates that the magistrates perceived roughly one in twenty-five adult males as dangerous (or as requiring a symbolic chastising). This total hardly validates the perception of a colony-wide threat. On the other hand, fifty-eight of the seventy-five men came from Boston itself. Thus the magistrates and ministers with the most active and fearful imaginative lives might have pictured up to one-sixth of the adult males of the colony's chief town as ready to reenact in Boston the bloody apocalyptic reign of King John of Münster under the guidance of Wheelwright and Hutchinson (and perhaps in the event of Vane's return).[7]

Whatever its objective validity, the order provided an excuse to compel wide acknowledgment of the Court's authority. Winthrop noted that the order "troubled some of them very much, especially because they were to bring [their weapons] in themselves; but at last, when they saw no remedy, they obeyed." As was not infrequent with Winthrop, his journal recorded a neater closure than reality afforded; stragglers were still submitting over three years later, and some may never have.[8]

With the possibility for another Münster receding and/or the Vanist fifth column humbled, the Court turned to post-crisis business. It decreed that anyone who openly defamed the Court's judicial decisions was liable to fine, imprisonment, disenfranchisement, or banishment, and it legalized the punishment of Court members who used "reproachful or unbeseeming speeches" to their fellow magistrates. Having retroactively sanctioned the punishments of the last months, the Court added that none of the above was intended to infringe on the liberty of petition or other "lawfull publike meanes" to correct "failings in any Court, or member of the same." A tricky clause for any dissatisfied lay person to interpret in view of the Court's recent actions; the Wheelwright Petition was not the last to provoke the furty of the Court. The Court formed a committee to begin the realization of Harvard College in Newtowne. With Wheel-wright safely off into exile, it commenced with the process of transforming Mount Wollaston into a town by determining its future boundaries.[9]

Despite, or perhaps because of, the Court's continued flexing of its mus-cles, both the visibility and contents of theological radicalism grew even more dramatic. Hutchinson was in the forefront, drastically extending a hitherto underground doctrinal tendency of the past few years. Cotton and the other ministers in their December 1636 exchange had gotten into a dispute about the relationship of believers' sanctification to Adam's original righteousness, the image of God in him. Sanctification repre-sented the restoration of that righteousness, they all agreed; the issue was, was Cotton excessive in the degree to which he argued that it represented something more. The quarrel in itself seems nit-picking, which is probably why it had disappeared by the time of the August synod. Driving it, how-ever, were strange and mostly undocumented transformations that Adam was undergoing out on the Boston fringe. If believers had no sanctifica-tion of their own, radicals speculated, why then would they have Adam's sanctification restored at all? Adam was not made in the image of God, claimed William Dyer. He was supposed to pass over to the covenant of grace on the seventh day of creation by experiencing the seal of the Spirit, claimed Henry Vane in *The Retired Mans Meditations*, and failed by rely-ing on the "work" of eating the apple—subsequent history was a restora-tionist attempt to make up for Adam's failure, not reinscribe it.[10]

In this anti-Adamic speculative environment, it was not too big a step for Hutchinson while under house arrest to wipe out Adam altogether. God had warned him of the forbidden fruit in Genesis 2:17: "In the day thou eatest thereof, thou shalt surely die." He could not really die, Hutch-inson decided, unless both his soul and body died, permanently. That death, however, meant that neither the soul nor body of anyone could be immortal, since they were both the "seed of Adam." If the soul was mortal, then what went to heaven or hell had to be something else. Hutchinson decided that this something else was the spirit, as Ecclesiastes 3:21 seemed to suggest, infused in humanity not through nature but through "Christ's purchase." If the physical body was mortal, it could not be resurrected. There was a resurrection to union with Christ and there was a bodily resurrection at the end of time, but, due to Adam's Fall, the latter did not involve the physical body. All of this, save the division of soul and spirit, bore a more than passing resemblence to familist doctrine.[11]

These conclusions were radical enough; denial of the resurrection of the body, for example, had been a heresy in orthodox Christianity since the end of the second century A.D. Hutchinson, however, was not through with

Adam. Unlike Cotton and the rest of the ministers, she "could see no Scripture to warrant that [God's image in Adam] consisted in holiness." What was that image then, and how was it restored in believers? It was, Hutchinson concluded, "Christs manhood," and it was restored to believers because, as familists claimed, not only did the physical bodies of believers not ascend to heaven, neither did Christ's manhood. The church was now literally the body of Christ, just as Adam's body had been Christ's manhood, and the believers who made up the church were "united to Christ with the same union, that his humanity on earth was with the Deity," just as Peter Shaw had argued in William Dyer's London parish. The union of the divine and the ideal human that had taken place first in the Garden of Eden, if abortively, and then in Christ's incarnation happened again in the justification of the elect.[12] With this conclusion, Hutchinson finished a new interpretive grid that covered virtually the entire Bible. She also ended up so vastly far away from even Cotton's version of orthodoxy that he would now finally see her opinions blurring with dangerous heresies.

Hutchinson's theology is a striking example of puritan lay intellectual activity. It is no less a striking example of the diversity of theological resources available within the godly community by the 1630s for a gifted, ambitious lay person, as well as a stark demonstration of the incompatibility of some of those resources. Hutchinson knew her Bible thoroughly, and she had learned from the ministers to read it with all the right emphases of systematic Reformed theology: double predestination, the totality of Christ's salvific work, forensic justification, and the reality of assurance. Hutchinson had also learned, from personal experience, from Cotton, and perhaps from acquaintances from the soteriological underground, that most ministers dangerously, even diabolically, mishandled the place of duties and holiness in the lives of Christians. That ministerial mishandling interfered with what might be seen as her mystical quest for unity with the divine; like Mary, mother of Jesus, in one of Hutchinson's key Scripture verses, she wished to be found with the child of the Holy Spirit.[13] The availability of familist doctrinal motifs within her circles encouraged her to shape both her anti-legal and mystical inclinations in ways that took her far beyond Cotton's theology. Had Hutchinson been male, she easily could have become a minister, and it is more than likely that the professional socialization of her training would have taught her what she so spectacularly failed to learn, the tacit limits on godly biblical exegesis, as it did even Wheelwright to a certain extent. Nor had she learned to keep a proper distance between herself and the miracle of Pentecost, although determining just what that proper distance is has been a perennial issue for Christianity. Nor, for that matter, had she learned how to keep standard puritan tropes about the penetration of Antichrist throughout the English church and its ministry within politically pragmatic boundaries.

Hutchinson was inadequately socialized as a theologian, and that, combined with personal and intellectual ambitions difficult for a woman or any ordinary lay person of that time to realize, as well as the wrong patron and bad political sense, led to her house arrest in Roxbury. But it did not lead to her silence. Winthrop claimed that "all of her Family and divers others, resorted to her at their pleasure." Hutchinson's visitors discovered that her experience of the Court's authority had scarcely intimidated her. She told them that her "Revelations about futire Events are to be beleeved as well as Scripture because the same Holy Ghost did indite both." Her new opinions began to spread in Boston and elsewhere, opinions that included forthright antinomianism. "Sanctification can be no Evidence of a good Estate in no wise," witnesses reported her saying, as well as "We are not bound to the Law, not as a Rule of Life." Hutchinson ceased her ambiguity about the spiritual status of Christ's disciples, announcing that they "wear not converted at Christs death"—so much for the ministers of Massachusetts.[14] The doctrine began circulating, whether from Hutchinson or someone else, that the lynchpin of puritan piety, the Sabbath, had no moral basis.[15]

Moreover, Hutchinson's "old disciples," like Hutchinson herself, grew more vocal. As Winthrop wrote in January, "foul errors were discovered, which had been secretly carried by way of inquiry." The authorities were taken aback by this new freedom of expression and registered what seems like genuine surprise even at doctrines that had been already condemned at the synod. It was only now that Winthrop expressed alarm in his journal at the doctrine that graces were mortal and fading.[16]

With escalating heresy expressing itself defiantly in a few churches, Vane, for all anyone knew, plotting his return, and people on both sides aggressively confrontational, it is not surprising that the mood in Massachusetts was grim that bleak winter. "It cuts a mans hart to thinke what is intended against us," Shepard told his congregation at the end of December, "Judases to betraye us, Enemyes to assault us." The Scituate church, probably not uniquely, held a fast day for "the removeall of the Spreading opinions in the churches at the Bey, as alsoe for the preventing of any intended evill against the churches here." For two days in January the magistrates and elders met in Boston to discuss ways to combat the "growing evils," as Winthrop called them.[17] Radicals may have been small in number and politically neutralized, but they more than made up for it by their demoralizing visibility in the environs of the central town of the colony.

Emigration was the most straightforward way to deal with the increasingly obvious fracturing of "Mr. Cotton's party." Twenty-seven of the seventy-five men ordered disarmed by the Court decided to leave the colony, and roughly a hundred considerably more politically and socially marginal men, many recent arrivals, joined them over the next year; only around thirty were to eventually return.[18] When Wheelwright left in November, the physician and future Baptist John Clarke and a group of people went with him. Clarke, a very recent immigrant, was Cottonian in his theology, and he decided to leave for the sake of peace. The group chose to go north because the previous summer had been so hot. But the cold of the winter made more of an adverse impression on some of them, including Clarke but not Wheelwright, than had the heat of the previous summer, and they turned their attention southward.[19]

It cannot be determined how this story relates to that of William Coddington. Coddington in the 1670s claimed that he reread the early justifications for Massachusetts by John Humphey and John Cotton and decided that the reasons that prompted the puritan removal from England now applied to Massachusetts itself.[20] Although Coddington may indeed have been mulling over leaving, there were people in the Boston church keen to encourage him to go. He wrote once to Winthrop reminding him how another church member approached him and John Coggeshall. Speaking, Coddington assumed, in the name of the rest of the church, he suggested that Coddington, Coggeshall, and some others he named leave the colony for the peace of the church. It seems likely that the incident occurred after Hutchinson's civil trial, when the rash overt statements of radicals began to alienate large numbers of their brethren. Coddington asked how they could depart without offense, as Massachusetts church theory required that church members could only leave to other churches. The unnamed brother said he would organize a church meeting to arrange it. At the meeting at Sergeant Balston's house, the church agreed "with the general advice and consent of all" that the brethren could depart. Cotton ratified the process by preaching a sermon the next Sunday saying that where there was no church that brethren could be commended to, they could be commended to the grace of God.[21] Whether what had transpired constituted a proper church dismissal would later be a bone of contention between the exiles and the Boston church.

Winthrop tried in vain to persuade Coddington to stay; the two men had once been so close that Winthrop hoped Coddington would marry into his family. When that failed, Winthrop wrote the other magistrates to get their assent to the departure of persons under suspicion by the Court. Dudley, as one would expect, was harsher than Winthrop. He ungraciously answered Winthrop on February 19 that he would give them a month to leave.[22]

Coddington and the others acted quickly. They arranged with Roger Williams to purchase an island from the Narragansett Indians near his settlement of Providence, a purchase made possible because of the high regard the Narragansett sachem Miantonomi had for Henry Vane. Their splendid idea of naming the island Patmos, after the exiled apostle John and his revelations, was "hindered" by some people, for reasons unknown, and the island kept its Indian name of Aquidneck until it was changed to Rhode Island in 1644. Coddington and eighteen other men, with the Hutchinson family well represented, met in his house on March 7, 1638, and drew up and signed a brief civil compact whereby they submitted themselves to Christ and bound themselves to be "guided and judged" by "those perfect and most absolute lawes of his given us in his holy word of truth." They chose Coddington, by far the most prestigious man among them, as their "judge," or governor.

While Boston nudged its recalcitrant members out, Roxbury shoved. At the end of 1637, it had many meetings to deal with members who signed the Wheelwright petition (not an issue in Boston) and who held "corrupt opinions." Weld in his preface to *Short Story* described efforts at reconciliation with dissatisfied laity, and he was certainly describing Roxbury when he did so. The ministers, according to Weld, engaged in lengthy private conferences with "opinionists" and held church meetings that lasted up to a half day. In those public meetings, the ministers gave dissenters "free leave" to defend any opinion they wanted, which opinions the ministers (and presumably other lay people) would refute by "cleare arguments from evident Scripture." The "opinionists," according to Weld, were driven in response into silence, or illogicality, but instead of conceding, they would say they needed "time to consider of our arguments." They used that time to confer "with some of their abetters." The next time the congregation gathered "we found them further off then before."[23]

The tension must have been high and the verbal dueling fierce at these meetings. Weld elsewhere noted that dissenters, presumably defending everything from Hutchinsonianism to Wheelwright and Cotton's theology to the Wheelwright petition, were attacked not only for their doctrinal opinions but for "manifest Pride, contempt of authority, neglecting to feare the Church, and lying, &c."[24] He said of one dissenter that

> falling into a lie, God smote him in the very act, that he sunke downe into a deep swoune, and being by hot waters recovered, and coming to himselfe, said, Oh God thou mightst have strucke me dead, as *Ananias* and *Saphira*, for I have maintained a lie.[25]

If it is legitimate to extrapolate from errors condemned at the synod, dissenting members at these meetings may have wanted out of the Roxbury church altogether. They pressed hard for their right to hear the preaching in Boston, which they found more satisfying. Failing that concession, they requested dismissals to the Boston church, rights the ministers refused to concede. As late as 1642 Weld, Eliot, and Roxbury's ruling lay elders refused to dismiss a member to Boston because they suspected that he still held to Wheelwright's opinions. At least three Roxbury members seem to have already voted with their feet, moving to Boston without, however, getting a not-to-be-obtained dismissal.[26]

Discussions at Roxbury having failed, the church admonished a few members. When that did not have the desired effect, five or six were excommunicated. One of those whom Roxbury excommunicated, Thomas Wilson, was probably from the Alford vicinity, and he removed with Wheelwright to Exeter, as did John Compton. Another, Philip Sherman, followed his father-in-law, John Porter, into familism and schism, according to Eliot. Sherman went to Aquidneck. Dudley's "brother," William Denison (their children had married) seems to have been excommunicated for defending the Wheelwright Petition and Cotton's theology too adamantly.[27]

Weld and Eliot wrote a short note justifying the excommunication of the fifth Roxbury member, Henry Bull. The note gives a vivid picture of the dialectical process that created militant heretics out of straying puritans. Bull, ordered disarmed by the Court, was a young and writing-illiterate servant, but he was not prepared to defer to the church's leadership. At one of the church meetings, he argued that faith was not a condition of the covenant of grace, that Christians should never take assurance through a syllogism, and that the letter of the Gospel kills. With a certain expansiveness, all of these doctrines could have been picked up from Wheelwright. He also argued that there was no inherent righteousness in believers, the defining "Hutchinsonian" position, and that it was a "part of poverty of spirit for one in Christ to say that he hath no Grace in himself." But reading between the lines of the ministers' reports, he seems to have been hesitant about these last two positions. The argument about inherent righteousness Bull would "Publiquely Expresse, but shifted and was loath to argue or Defend it, but would not unsay it againe." The last point about poverty of spirit he refused to dispute. One senses that in the Boston church Bull, with his diffidence about defending positions more radical than those associated with ministers, would have passed unnoticed, which may explain why he moved there.[28]

From a distance, Bull does not seem like a particularly threatening layperson. In Weld, however, he faced a particularly combative pastor who ended his days battling Quakers and Baptists in England.[29] Not being averse to a fight, Weld got one. The ministers, and perhaps others in the congregation, tried to change Bull's mind, and Bull refused to back down. According to the ministers, Bull acted impudent and contemptuous in the public meetings, "unseemly in any especially in a young youth." Bull fostered schism, they complained, which is very likely true, given that he himself had moved to Boston. When the church finally threatened him with excommunication, Bull said he would welcome it. Moreover, claimed the ministers, Bull was guilty of "Grate lying, and that in the Publique face of the Church."[30] The church excommunicated Bull, after which he left the colony and eventually became a Quaker. The tale of this young servant's defying the elders of his church might seem a striking example of theological dissent as revolt against patriarchy. In Boston, however, Bull's revolt perhaps would have never taken place. It cannot be coincidental that whereas two-thirds of the Roxbury church members disarmed by the Court left the colony, only one-third of the Boston church members did so; Boston measured godliness by different standards.

This is not to suggest that the new radical militancy did not alarm the Boston church. Cotton himself worked hard, both publicly and privately, to bring back to the orthodox fold those who had wandered too far astray.[31] He must have been horrified and humiliated to discover that when he finally came down heavily on the radicals' "misexpressions" and "inquiries," they often refused to give them up; he probably would have gotten more accommodating responses had he done so eighteen months previously. The only benefit of the defiant, vocal heterodoxy was that it allowed Cotton to create and share the story that he used ever after to explain his role in the free grace controversy. He had been "abused" and made the "stalking horse" of a few heretics, Winthrop recorded him explaining in January 1638, who had cloaked their heresies under the mantle of pretending to "hold nothing but what Mr. Cotton held."[32] Just how willingly and why Cotton had made himself the stalking horse of people he now considered heretics he preferred not to discuss.

Heterodox dissonance reached a point where the Boston elders stopped running interference for Hutchinson. They agreed with the ministers and magistrates that they would try her if they had sufficient evidence from outsiders; according to Winthrop, they thought it would be "not so orderly" if they themselves were witnesses. A number of divines helped them out by meeting with Hutchinson in Roxbury. Shepard himself visited her three times. On his second visit, he assured Hutchinson that he did not come to entrap her, and Hutchinson, a slow learner in the ways of ministers, vigorously debated her new opinions with him. Having drawn her out, Shepard concluded that Hutchinson's "Willingness to open herselfe and to divulge her Opinions and to sowe her seed in us that are but Highway side and Strayngers to her" made her a "verye dayngerous Woman." He returned a third time to "reduce her from her Errors and to bare witness against them." For good measure, he turned a list of her opinions over to the Boston church elders. Weld and Eliot also talked with Hutchinson and drew up another list of her errors. Presented with that evidence, the Boston church decided that she should stand trial.[33]

That trial commenced on March 15, part of a combined church and state disciplinary mopping up action. Three days previously, the General Court had convened. It gave Coddington's group permission to depart "to avoyde the censure of the Court" and ordered some Salem supporters of Roger Williams out at the same time. The Court called a number of military officers whose crime, as Winthrop put it, was that they had "declared themselves favorers of the familistical persons and opinions"—this may mean nothing more than that they had expressed sympathy for Wheelwright and others who had been punished. Most offered satisfactory apologies, saying, according to Winthrop, that "they had been deceived and misled by the pretence, which was held forth, of advancing Christ, and debasing the creature." The events of the recent months had persuaded the officers that "their opinions and practices tended to disturbance and delusion." As will be seen in the next chapter, there is reason to think that these recantations, while obviously opportune, reflect a general lay reevaluation of the increasingly more radical members of the Boston party. The Court called for a general fast on April 12 to ask God's help in the present "weighty matters," smooth the way for prospective immigrants, and to "divert any evill plots which may bee intended."[34]

Because the Court was in session, Winthrop and Richard Bellingham, both Boston church members, were the only magistrates given leave to be present on the first day of Hutchinson's trial. The Boston meeting house, however, easily filled up without the others. Laypeople came to observe "from all the parts of the Countrey," while numerous ministers attended. Conspicuously absent were Hutchinson's chief male allies, negotiating for their future home in Narragansett Bay ("the good providence of God so disposed" it, wrote Winthrop; one might suspect human agency as well in the timing).[35] As with Hutchinson's civil trial, two accounts of the proceedings have survived, Robert Keayne's notes and Winthrop's description in *Short Story*. Both have their limitations. Keayne truncated and left out material, and it is not always possible to be sure exactly what his speakers meant to say. Winthrop's account is not sympathetic to Hutchinson and it is far shorter than Keayne's, but it appears to be basically accurate and complements Keayne in useful ways. At the trial's center, Cotton did his best, in the face of hostile and not unwarranted skepticism, to send Hutchinson into exile not as an excommunicant but as a visible saint in good standing in the Massachusetts communion of churches. He would fail, but that failure was by no means a foregone conclusion. Cotton was not helped by the fact that a number of persons present, most notably Shepard and Hutchinson herself, were at least as interested in fighting old battles as in working out a new coexistence.

The trial began after Cotton's morning lecture. Wilson reminded the audience of the solemnity of the event. Ruling lay elder Thomas Oliver told the congregation that Hutchinson had missed the lecture not out of contempt for the ordinance but because of weakness stemming from having been under long durance—besides having been confined to house arrest, she was pregnant. Elder Leverett asked the congregation to separate itself out from the rest of the audience so it could express its consent or dissent from the proceedings more easily. Leverett then read two lists of opinions attributed to Hutchinson. The first, submitted by Shepard and the ruling elder of his church, Edmund Frost, mostly concerned her familist-derived ideas about body, soul, and Christ. The second, from Weld and Eliot, focused mostly on her antinomianism. Leverett asked Hutchinson if these were her opinions.[36]

Hutchinson had prophesied divine vengeance on her last set of prosecutors, and time had not mellowed her. If the opinions were hers, she replied, they were errors; if they were Christ's, they were truth, whereupon she launched into an attack on Shepard. He came to her in private and claimed he did not intend to ensnare her. To then bring the matter to the church without "privately dealing" with her was a violation of scriptural rule. Shepard explained his visits and added that he did not know "wherein I could deale more lovingly with this your Sister than to bringe her thus before you." Hutchinson then argued that the positions on the soul's mortality and the spirit she raised with Shepard were only questions about the meaning of Scripture verses. Shepard responded that the "vilest Errors" were brought into churches by questions. Cotton agreed with him and requested that Hutchinson respond to each of the opinions on the lists.[37]

Hutchinson's first opinion concerned the mortality of the soul. Despite much back-and-forth with her, conducted by Cotton, Wilson, and Winthrop, Hutchinson held to her position. As she was being pressed, she again went on the offensive, raising the issue of her civil trial. She "grew into a passion" against Wilson for the speech he had made against her at the end of that trial, and Wilson "gave a full answer unto, shewing his zeale against her errors." Apparently he denounced Hutchinson's new opinions as "damnable" and "no lesse than Sadducisme and Atheisme." That prompted Hutchinson to demand to know for what errors she had been convicted, since "thear was no such Expression from me on this [at her civil trial]." Winthrop surmised, probably correctly, that she was trying to blame her errors on her imprisonment (and thus, indirectly, on her opponents). She was also probably protesting what she saw as the injustice of the conviction itself, since she had asked roughly the same question at the end of her trial. At this point, according to Keayne, "The most part of the Church . . . *by Lifting up of thear hands did show thear Dislike of [her opinion] and did condemn it as an Error.*"[38]

John Davenport, Cotton's house guest, now took over debating Hutchinson. He began ominously. Davenport, like the few historians who have paid attention to Hutchinson's new doctrines, associated them with the heresy of mortalism, despite there being little relationship. Mortalism, in all its many variations, posited that self-awareness was extinguished at death, and it was easily glossed by heresy hunters as "eat, drink, and be merry, for tomorrow you die" libertinism. Davenport warned Hutchinson that "Thay that speake for the Mortalitie of the soule speake most for Licentiousnesse and sinfull Liberty."[39]

Perhaps Davenport's warning softened Hutchinson up, for he soon achieved a breakthrough. He argued with her that the spirit was not an entity separate from the soul, as Hutchinson thought, but that it was the life of the soul or its bent and bias. After some exchange, Hutchinson exclaimed, "God by him hath given me Light." Hutchinson seemed genuinely relieved that she could abandon her new conception of the soul and merge it back with the spirit. That was not to say, however, that she had been wrong. She had erred, she said, only in terminology, for what Davenport called the life of the soul, she had called the spirit. She explained to the congregation that "I doe acknowledge my Expression to be Ironious but my Judgment was not Ironious." Some in the room, like John Eliot, were appalled, as he said shortly, that she would dismiss "so groce and so dayngerous an opinion" as only a mistake. Cotton, on the other hand, leapt at what he saw as an opening to eradicate her chief longstanding error about the unreality of sanctification and creature graces. Since Hutchinson now appeared to concede that the soul itself was immortal, he asked her if "the devine and gracious Qualeties" of the souls of believers went with them to heaven, and the evil qualities of the souls of the wicked went with them to hell. Cotton proceeded too fast, however. "I know not presently what to say to this," Hutchinson replied.[40]

Now that Hutchinson had recanted her first opinion, or, more precisely, claimed she never really held it, Cotton moved the discussion on to her next three, which collectively maintained that there was no resurrection of the body but a resurrection to union with Christ. Peter Bulkeley questioned Hutchinson bluntly about the familist implications of her opinion. If the resurrection was past for the saints, which familists held, then the institution of marriage was inevitably also past, as they were alleged to hold (Matt. 22:30: "In the resurrection they neither marry nor are given in marriage")—did Hutchinson maintain the "foule, groce, filthye and abominable opinion held by the Familists" of community of women? Women's good names, far more than men's, depended on their sexual propriety, and Hutchinson lashed back, comparing Bulkeley to a pharisee.

Davenport and Winthrop warned Hutchinson that she could not evade Bulkeley's conclusion. Elder Leverett came to Hutchinson's aid, remarking that Hutchinson did not deny that there was a resurrection of some sort of body, to which Hutchinson agreed.[41]

Other ministers, not impressed by Leverett's defense, showed increasing concern that so dangerous a heresy was being discussed at such length. In response to Hugh Peters, Hutchinson denied that Moses, Elijah, and Enoch were taken up to heaven in their natural bodies, and Davenport's patience came to an end: "These are opinions that cannot be borne." Wilson, in his disciplinary role as pastor, called for the congregation to hold up their hands if they were convinced that Hutchinson held "groce and damnable Heresies."[42]

A few laymen tried to defer Hutchinson's censure, to the displeasure of the ministers. Hutchinson was not yet convinced one way or the other, argued her son Edward, and she should not be condemned for opinions she was not settled in (the longstanding excuse made by/for the Boston radicals). He prompted Shepard to warn that if anyone agreed with Hutchinson, "the hand of the Lord will finde you out." Shepard repeated that he could not have shown more love to Hutchinson than by turning her over to her congregation and worried that she would "draw away many, Especially simple Weomen of her owne sex." Wilson suggested that the church move to admonition, but invited anyone else with objections to speak.[43] Hutchinson's son-in-law Thomas Savage found a relevant scriptural precedent in the apostolic church of Corinth's toleration of unsound opinions, while Edward Gibbons suggested they give Hutchinson more time to be convinced. Simmes pronounced himself "much greved" that members of the congregation would express unwillingness to proceed against Hutchinson on such a fundamental point as the resurrection of the body. He worried that if word of this got out to England "it will be one of the greatest Dishonors to Jesus Christ and of Reproch to thease Churches that hath bine done since we came heather."[44]

It was not only ministers who were growing displeased with the reluctant brethren. Ruling elder Thomas Oliver and his son John, both of whom had signed the petition in defense of Wheelwright, now spoke. Thomas asked the assembled ministers if the church needed unanimity to proceed to censure when not all the members consented, or whether the dissenting members themselves could be censured. Cotton replied that if the dissenters did so only out of natural affection, the church could proceed, and Davenport seconded him. John Oliver then proposed that Edward Hutchinson and Savage be admonished along with Hutchinson herself. The church by its silence agreed to the admonishments.[45]

In what must have been a highly charged moment, the elders conferred among themselves and requested that Cotton deliver the admonition, "as one whose Wordes by the Blessinge of God may be of more Respect." At least some of the elders certainly intended this request in part as a hard ball to Cotton, but he nimbly fielded it. He commenced by thanking them for the care they had shown for his church. Though acknowledging that he had been "slowe of proceeding" against church members, that was only for want of "sufficient Testimony." Now that they had "proceded in a way of God," it would be a "sine" not to act. Cotton thereupon admonished Hutchinson's relatives. For good measure he admonished the sisters of the congregation, "many of whom I fear have bine too much seduced and led aside by her." He was at pains, however, to let the congregation and the assembled ministers know that through Hutchinson, many of the women had "bine brought from Restinge upon any Duties or Workes of Righteousnes of your owne." Nonetheless, he warned the sisters to carefully discriminate between the good and bad they had received from Hutchinson and not to harden her by expressing sympathy for her. Then he addressed Hutchinson, again fulsomely and respectfully praising her many virtues and her evangelical successes. But the dishonor she brought upon herself was far greater than any previous honor. Turning to the hoary topic of familist anti-resurrectionist community of women, Cotton had the decency to first acknowledge that he had neither heard nor suspected that Hutchinson had been unfaithful to her husband. "Yet that will follow upon it," he warned. As he started to wax eloquent on Hutchinson's coming sexual degradation ("more dayngerous Evells and filthie Unclenes and other sines will followe than you doe now Imagine or conceave"), Hutchinson cut him off.[46]

She asked for permission to speak, afraid that because of her weakness she would forget to make the point when Cotton was finished. Cotton granted it. "All that I would say is this," Hutchinson said, reiterating the point she had made to Wilson, presumably for the same reasons, "that *I did not hould any of thease Thinges before my Imprisonment.*" Cotton acknowledged that he thought she was right. He warned her, however, that for a person of her spiritual reputation to entertain such opinions even as questions was as dangerous to others as holding them positively, an indication of the delicate dance that Hutchinson and Cotton had been doing around each other while they were perceiving each other as allies. He then finished with his admonition, emphasizing again, if less luridly, the moral collapse that would follow in the wake of Hutchinson's denials of natural immortality and physical resurrection and chastising her for the "Evell that you have done to many a poore soule" and the disgrace that she brought upon her congregation.[47]

Meanwhile, Shepard seethed at both Cotton's bestowing so much praise on Hutchinson and Hutchinson's presumptuous interruption during what was supposed to be entirely a sackcloth and ashes ritual—he would still be seething a year later. As soon as Cotton was finished, Shepherd voiced his displeasure. "Lest the Crowne should be set on her Hed in the day of her Humiliation," he wanted to get in a word "before the Assemblie break up." He was astonished that Hutchinson would dare to interrupt Cotton in the midst of a solemn admonition (and by implication, that Cotton would let her). He was further astonished that she dared claim not to have held any of these opinions before her imprisonment. She had told him when he visited her that if he had visited her earlier she could have told him much more about union with Christ, and that she could forget this statement made him fear greatly for the unsoundness of her heart. Eliot seconded him. Wilson ended the first day of Hutchinson's trial at this point, as it was eight o'clock. He called on her to reappear in a week's time.[48]

The final outcome of Hutchinson's trial was by no means clear at the end of the day. Hutchinson had hardly been willing to eat much crow. She challenged Shepard's right to bring charges, attacked Wilson for his earlier criticism of her, compared Bulkeley to a pharisee, confessed only to terminological confusion, not error, and interrupted Cotton's admonition. Yet it cannot be entirely a coincidence that while at least eight ministers were present, it was Shepard who protested the closure of the evening. Other persons, in contrast, expressed optimism, apparently because Hutchinson had yielded at all, which may give a glimpse of the community's assessment of her personality. Winthrop in his journal claimed that "all did acknowledge the special presence of God's spirit" at the trial. The General Court, he stated, "in regard that she had given hope of her repentance," licensed her to stay at Cotton's house for Cotton and Davenport to soften her up further.[49]

Winthrop's optimism appeared justified when the trial resumed a week later. Elder Leverett read out the remaining erroneous opinions, but Hutchinson's combative spirit had gone, apparently. She read a long retraction of all the errors she had been charged with, and she made no effort this time to excuse herself with a judgment/expression distinction. She had been wrong about the soul, and spirit, wrong about the resurrection of the body, wrong about Adam's righteousness, wrong that the Law given Moses might not be a rule of life, wrong that the command of faith was not part of the Gospel, wrong to have prophesied the destruction of the colony, wrong that she had shown irreverent carriage to the ministers, and sorry that she had drawn any away from hearing them. Sanctification could indeed be evidence of justification "as it flowes from Christ and is witnessed to us by the Spirit." Given the source, this was an extraordinary statement of contrition, even a vindication of her conviction. According to Cotton, it "far exceeded the expectation of the whole congregation, which then consisted of many churches, and strangers [persons not yet belonging to a church]." After hearing her recantation, "the Assembly," according to Winthrop, "conceived hope of her repentance."[50] Had the trial stopped at this point, Hutchinson would have left Massachusetts a member in good standing of the Boston church and, like some of the other exiles, might have found herself back in Boston eventually after a suitably apologetic and deferential petition to the General Court.

But, as Wilson immediately reminded Hutchinson, she still had to answer Shepard's accusation that she had held her errors before her imprisonment. She reiterated that it was her disrespect to the ministers and magistrates at her trial that led to her errors, and she was bluntly and recklessly dismissive of Shepard's charge: "If Mr. Shephard doth conceave that I had any of these Thinges in my Minde [before the trial], than he is deceaved." Elder Leverett asked that someone repeat what she said more clearly and Cotton obliged. He heard her very favorably, as had always been his wont. She had not fallen into gross and fundamental errors until she was imprisoned and the ground of it was the disrespect she showed the magistrates; she condemned herself and the root of it all was her pride. "She desires all that she hath offended to pray to God for her to give her a hart to be more truly humbled."[51]

When Cotton finished, Shepard immediately spoke up. He was appalled, he told the room, that at a time when Hutchinson should be showing nothing but abject humiliation, "she shall cast Shame upon others and say thay are mistaken." Moreover, the recantation that had made such a favorable impression on the assembly left him cold. What she had just said did not sound like "true Repentance," however Cotton might gloss it (both Shepard and Hooker thought that Cotton had engineered the trial to protect Hutchinson). "Any Hereticke may bringe a slye Interpretation upon any of thease Errors and yet hould them to thear Death." Specifically, when she claimed that sanctification flowed from Christ, had she really given up her old idea that Christ took up our creature graces and transacted them himself? Eliot shared Shepard's concerns.[52]

Cotton, perhaps suspecting that Shepard's concern about heresy was not only directed at Hutchinson, again ran interference for her, for the last time. "Sister was thear not a Time," he asked, "whan once you did hould that thear was no distinct graces inherent in us but all was in Christ Jesus?" All Hutchinson had to do was say, yes, she had once denied that God gave believers a holiness of their own, and she recognized her error. That, very likely would have been the end of the trial, let Shepard fume as he might.[53]

But saying yes would also mean acknowledging that she had held errors before her imprisonment. For whatever reason, that was a line of humiliation Hutchinson would not cross, and she fell back on her self-exculpatory tactics of the previous hearing. She had never really denied the reality of inherent graces, she insisted; she had only mistaken what the word "inherent" meant until Davenport cleared it up for her. Jaws dropped across the meetinghouse. A number of ministers and laity reminded her how adamantly she had denied inherent graces and Davenport himself expressed puzzlement. Hutchinson stuck to her position, however, using the same explanation she had the previous week: "My judgment is not altered though my expression alters." Zechariah Simmes exclaimed, "She lookes but to Spriges," meaning he doubted Hutchinson had truly repented of her errors. It is easy enough to share in the audience's amazement. To the extent that Hutchinson's rationale can be surmised, she may have meant that she never denied that the saints had a new holiness but had labeled it incorrectly because of what she was now claiming had been an erroneous conception of what "inherent" meant. In any case, Hutchinson was probably not a person to whom conceding serious error ever came easy, and she certainly would not have readily believed that ministers who had never experienced the seal of the Spirit could have known something significant about conversion that she did not. She may have been also playing by the rules of an earlier period where everyone maintained the pretense that they were all fundamentally saying the same thing since they were all godly.[54]

Hutchinson, however, faced an audience not entirely inclined to give her the benefit of the doubt about her godliness, and though her purchased immortalism and anti-resurrectionism were recent, inherent graces had been a heated topic for the last two years. Deputy Governor Dudley, present for this session, now focused the attack, just as he had done at Hutchinson's civil trial. Like Shepard, he must have been incensed by the leniency of Cotton's admonishment, and he opened with a heavy dose of sarcasm aimed as much at Cotton as at Hutchinson: "Mrs. Hutchinsons Repentance is only for Opinions held since her Imprisonment, but befor her Imprisonment she was in a good Condition, and held no Error, but did a great deale of Good to many." Dudley himself, he went on, knew of no harm she had done since her imprisonment, and he saw no repentance in her. He darkly wondered out loud if she had written her statement of repentance entirely herself, but that he would "not now Inquier to." He wanted the ministers to speak to the question of whether she held errors before her imprisonment. Weld cited an exchange with her about graces. Peters compared her to the still unidentified female prophet, the Woman of Elis, and said he thought she looked upon them as Jews in need of conversion. Wilson said although it was indeed a great sin that she had been disrespectful to the magistrates, and very likely God would have left her for it, he also would have left her for her pulling down of the ministers so that she could set herself up as a "greate Prophites." Shepard tried to bring down a summary judgment on her: "I thinke it is needles for any other now to speake and useless for the Case is playne, and hear is Witnesses enough."[55]

Other ministers, however, were not as ready as Shepard to bring the trial to closure. They pressed on, citing more incidents when Hutchinson had denied inherent graces before her imprisonment. It is very hard to read the mood in a room almost four hundred years distant through imperfect trial notes. But two things seem clear. The first is that all the speakers thought Hutchinson's answer to Cotton was objectively a lie. The second is that they still wanted to bring her around to admit and/or realize it herself. The last of the ministers in this round to speak was Hugh Peters. He asked Hutchinson to search her heart for further repentance and cautioned her that he feared she was not well grounded in her catechism! Peters had tried to put Vane down in his place fifteen months previously at the General Court, and in another decade back in England, he would be trying to put King Charles I down in his place and calling vociferously for his execution when he failed. Now, picking up Wilson's theme, but more gently, he asked Hutchinson to consider that she had stepped out of all the various subordinate identities she occupied—she had been a husband rather than a wife, a preacher rather than a hearer, and a magistrate rather than a subject—and she had not yet been humbled for this multiple subordination. It is unfortunate that by this point in the transcript Hutchinson's voice is heard no more.[56]

Winthrop followed Peters. He, too, seems to have been more interested in turning the trial into a teaching and healing experience than simply a punishment of Hutchinson, for he had a further request. Since diverse sisters of the congregation had "builded upon her Experience," he thought it would be "much to Gods Glory" for Hutchinson to explain what her good estate consisted of if it did not lie in ingrafting into Christ; after all, she had said once that a man could be ingrafted into Christ and still fall away.[57]

It might be expected that Winthrop would have been harsher with Hutchinson after all he had been through, but his concern points to one of the most interesting aspects of her church trial. It is hard to read Keayne's notes and not conclude that in spite all of the hostilities of the previous months, Winthrop and others in the building genuinely wanted Hutchinson back, and they were prepared to invest a great deal of time and care to get her back. They wanted her back because she had an unfathomably precious immortal soul that hung in the balance; because she had been a highly valued member of the community whose evangelical work "all the faithful imbraced" before she "set forth her owne stuffe," as Winthrop put it; and certainly because they were uncomfortable and uncertain about her influence on the women of the congregation. Moreover, this was no twentieth-century show trial; they wanted her to come back in a way that honored her integrity and freedom as a human being.[58]

Shepard, however, saw the time spent trying to get Hutchinson back as time to allow her to escape her just desserts. He now spoke up, all facade of restraint gone, and finally got the proceedings heading toward his desired end. They were not dealing with a visible saint, he told the assembly, one whose only fault was that she held incorrect opinions and could be dealt with by admonishment. He then delivered a dreadful charge, one that he had long implied in public but had managed, barely, to avoid saying directly—Hutchinson was in all likelihood a reprobate. They were dealing with "one that never had any trew Grace in her heart and that by her own Tenect." In other words, as he had been saying all along, the only way you could argue like Hutchinson against inherent graces was if you had never experienced them because God had not justified you. She was a "Notorious Imposter," and her judgment/expression distinction was "a Tricke of as notorious Subtiltie as ever was held in the Church." Now he "would have the Congregation judge whether ever thear was any Grace in her hart or no."[59]

Having proved that Hutchinson was not a saint by her theology, he demonstrated it again by a strikingly callous syllogism. Even granting her adamant claim that she held no errors until her imprisonment, if her cause had been good, then the spirit of glory and Christ would have rested on her in her imprisonment, as the apostle Peter said. But in her imprisonment, as she herself said, she fell into errors. Therefore the cause she suffered for was not Christ's cause. Where Winthrop had wanted Hutchinson to explain herself for the edification of those who had been led astray by her, Shepard suggested that the same purpose would be served by excommunication. Peters more cautiously agreed that Hutchinson's repentance only for errors after her imprisonment was not satisfactory.[60]

Whatever reservoir of patience with Hutchinson there was in the room was shallow, and the heat of Shepard's attack seems to have evaporated it among the ministers. Keayne's notes next record Wilson's accusing her of being an instrument of the devil, raised up to cause divisions among them. It was now clear, he claimed, with less than impeccable logic, that all the "wofull Opinions" in the colony came from her, since an unsound foundation had to be at the bottom of an unsound building. He asked the congregation to assent to excommunicating Hutchinson. All the ministers who now spoke, by Keayne's account, agreed, although for different reasons. For Cotton, Hutchinson's refusal to admit she had been in error accomplished what her attacks on the ministers, heterodox "inquiries," and prophecy of destruction to the General Court could not; they caused him to finally wash his hands of her. He was satisfied that Hutchinson was lying, he told the assembly, and should be excommunicated. He must have been appalled that Hutchinson could defile a divinely appointed ordinance by lying. He also presumably would have been highly irritated that she had thrown away the opportunity at rehabilitation he had worked so hard to provide her, with him sticking his neck out not a little for her in the process. She had also thrown away the last opportunity for him to demonstrate the basic soundness of his congregation and of his own judgment over the last few years. Davenport, more overtly compassionate, addressed Hutchinson directly, the only one of the speakers to do so, saying he feared that God would not let her see her falsehood until she had benefited from the ordinance of excommunication.[61]

Some laity, even those who had been forthright in moving against Hutchinson the previous week, expressed discomfort with this sudden turn of events. Thomas Oliver, instrumental in her admonishment, did not think the church would have moved with such speed. Someone else said she had confessed her sin and now the church should move with mercy. Her brother-in-law Richard Scott suggested they give her more time to be convinced of her lie. Cotton replied that doctrinal error should be dealt with patiently, but errors of practice could be moved against immediately.[62]

Shepard stepped in again to move the proceedings along: "I perceve it is the Desire of many of the Brethren to stay her Excommunication and to let a second Admonition lye upon her." He reiterated the heinousness of her lying, even in what was supposed to be a day of humiliation for her. Richard Mather cited Titus 3:10, to the same purpose, saying that a heretic after "once or twise Admonition" should be cut off like a gangrene. Elder Leverett shot back that the apostle said once and twice. Dudley replied that Hutchinson had been admonished on numerous occasions by private brethren and elders of other churches, and besides, to his mind that Scripture spoke of private admonition, not church admonition. A stranger said he consented to the church's moving against her for lying but not for her doctrine because she had repented of that. Wilson replied that she should be excommunicated for doctrine as well. He doubted that her repentance was sincere, and, a happy Scripture precedent coming to mind, he pointed out that God sent Joshua to destroy Achan even after he had repented. Cotton said that apostolic precedent demanded that they act immediately because she was being excommunicated for lying. Thereby, he later claimed, he "satisfyed the Scruples of some Brethren, who doubted it."[63]

In any case, Cotton's insistent signal that he was finished with Hutchinson seems to have settled the issue, for Keayne's notes next record Wilson's motion to excommunicate her. The church gave its consent by silence, the customary practice in early Massachusetts churches. The males of the Boston congregation thereby acquiesced to the most impressive public display of solidarity the ministers had managed in two years—a broad demonstration of lay/ministerial unity that would have been unimaginable had Hutchinson answered "yes" to Cotton's question. Given that the church's members included unrepentant signers of the Wheelwright petition and persons who had defied Charles I's pressure to contribute to his forced loan in England, that lay acquiescence cannot be explained simply in terms of laity being browbeaten by clergy.[64] Hutchinson had a bad case and the ministers a good one, by the ministerially nurtured theological and ethical standards of the colony. The laity might not have moved so fast to excommunicate her, perhaps in part because they did not share as strongly the anger of some ministers, articulated by Wilson and Peters, that Hutchinson had presumed to compete with them. Nonetheless, they did not see her punishment as unwarranted.

After a "convenient pause," Wilson pronounced the sentence of excommunication over Hutchinson and commanded her "as a leper" to leave the building. Wilson excommunicated her not only for lying but for doctrinal errors, which, given the conversation beforehand, was a bit of a fast one, not that anyone seems to have taken it too seriously. The church records have her excommunicated for lying, and Winthrop wrote as much in his journal and *Short Story*, as did Cotton in his reply to Robert Baillie.[65] An uneasy coalition of elders, magistrates, and ordinary male laity—some focusing on Hutchinson, some taking shots at Cotton, some wanting to move with haste, others more carefully, some wanting punishment, others rehabilitation, some wanting purging of the community, others healing, some irate about dogma, others more prepared to cut Hutchinson slack, pushed along by Shepard and massively assisted by Hutchinson herself—agreed that their communion of visible saints did not include Hutchinson, although, as Wilson's verbal sleight of hand at the end indicated, they might not have agreed as to why. It was a mirror of the complex politics that drove the entire controversy.

What Hutchinson was thinking while her trial moved to its conclusion is unrecorded, but any repentance she might have worked herself into feeling probably evaporated as the church refused to buy into her judgment/expression distinction. Winthrop noted that although some of her brethren suggested a respite in the proceedings to give Hutchinson time to reflect, she herself did not request one. As she left the meetinghouse, Mary Dyer rose up and accompanied her—Dyer was refining a piety of defiance that would get her hanged as a Quaker in the same town twenty-two years later. Winthrop recorded that a person standing by the door as Hutchinson left said to her, "The Lord sanctifie this unto you," and Hutchinson replied, "Better to be cast out of the Church than to deny Christ."[66] In a touch worthy of one of Hawthorne's allegories, the next day the snow that had covered the ground a foot and a half deep since the November trials began to melt. Why it did so, though, would have been open to providential debate. Was it because the American Jezebel would trouble the churches of Christ in Massachusetts no longer, or was it because the reincarnation of Elijah no longer had to rein herself in to accommodate the pharisees of Massachusetts? Winthrop claimed that "after [Hutchinson] was excommunicated, her spirits, which seemed before to be somewhat dejected, revived again, and she gloried in her sufferings, saying, that it was the greatest happiness, next to Christ, that ever befel her." "No story records the like of a woman, since that mentioned in the *Revelation*," he was to shortly write his brethren in England.[67]

The last story told of Hutchinson in Massachusetts is reliable in its details since it appears both in Winthrop's journal and in a manuscript written by her brother-in-law Edward Hutchinson, but that skeleton of reliable facts makes it all the more tantalizingly elusive to interpret. Ordered to leave the colony by the end of March, Hutchinson went to her farm at Mount Wollaston on March 28. She intended from there to go by boat to join Wheelwright in New Hampshire with her sister-in-law (Wheelwright's wife) and her mother-in-law. Why that destination would even cross her mind is hard to understand. Her husband had signed Coddington's compact and was presumably in Aquidneck at the time. Wheelwright made it plain that he opposed her chief doctrine of the denial of creature graces. He later showed himself concerned to set up his new church in a proper relationship to the churches of Massachusetts, which meant that he would not have let her participate in the Lord's Supper until she had the sentence of excommunication lifted by the Boston church. Perhaps she was still somewhat under the sway of Davenport and Cotton and open to (relatively) orthodox guidance, such as Wheelwright would provide. Perhaps she did not want to leave the comfort and services of an ordained minister, as would be the case in her new colony. Whatever her reasoning, when push came to shove, it did not persuade her. She changed her mind and went by land to Aquidneck. There would be no more compromises about her doctrines necessary and no more connection to a state-sponsored church; Hutchinson had burned all her bridges, assisted by her most bitter enemies, and the struggle with separatism that dated back at least to her memorable fast in England was over. Shortly thereafter, Plymouth governor William Bradford wrote to John Winthrop, saying he had heard that Hutchinson had retracted her confession of errors.[68]

ELEVEN

HOLDING FORTH DARKLY

MARCH 1638–FEBRUARY 1641

IN THE SPRING of 1638, the voluntary and involuntary exiles began departing in sizable numbers. Others probably wondered if they should be accompanying them, and still others probably watched them leave with a wide variety of feelings ranging from sorrow to relief to anger. For both those who stayed and those who left, it was time to start picking up the pieces after two years of violent quarrels and try to start to make sense of what they had just been through. Yet in 1638 the free grace controversy was far from over in Massachusetts. It continued on in complex and conflicting streams of reconciliation, suspicion, posturing, and sometimes open hostility and confrontation for at least another three years.

The departures of the spring put the Boston coalition under even more strain. The ties holding together what had only recently been the most glorious church in the world were stretched to and past the breaking point as church members openly pursued widely divergent ecclesiastical, theological, and geographical paths. The congregation may have agreed by its silence to excommunicate Hutchinson. But women had no official public voice, and a few subsequently made their dissatisfaction with the trial known loudly enough to provoke official reaction. Edward Hutchinson's maidservant, Judith Smith, was excommunicated within the month for public and private persistence in errors and for "sundry lyes then expressed by her and persisted in." Robert Harding and his wife, Philip, were so vocal in their criticisms that the General Court took notice of them the next year. Robert Harding made submission to Wilson, which satisfied the Court. But his wife did not, asserting in the Court that Hutchinson had deserved neither her civil nor church censure. The Court handed her over to the church, which excommunicated her "as a slaunderer and revyler both of the Church and commonwealth," whereupon she went off to Aquidneck on her own. Mary Dyer herself seems to have been excommunicated, although the church records make no mention of it.[1]

Dyer, Harding, and Smith give credence to the concerns about Hutchinson's appeal to her own sex, but how many women these vocal critics spoke for is unknown. Winthrop said that several women, appalled at

Hutchinson's trial by her insistence that she had never denied creature graces, wanted to offer their own testimony to the contrary, but their modesty prevented them. While Dyer at least was doctrinally committed to Hutchinson, some women who admired Hutchinson and continued to admire her even after the church trial may have simply not seen the doctrinal issues over which others got so worked up as all that important, a possibility suggested by a Hutchinson family story of convoluted lineage. Hutchinson's great-great-grandson, Massachusetts royal governor Thomas Hutchinson, was told by her great-granddaughter, Mrs. Winslow, that the grandmother of the minister Ebenezar Pemberton, a woman who crossed the Atlantic with the Hutchinsons as their servant, always spoke of Anne as "not only as a truly pious woman but as a kind benevolent woman forward in every good office."[2] Doctrine was not an issue one way or the other in this ancient memory of a visible saint.

Hutchinson's trial might have been more stormy had the preeminent male theological radicals not been purchasing their future home in Narragansett Bay. The very next Sunday, Mary Dyer's husband, William, having returned to Boston, was called before the church to explain his heterodoxy. Adam was not made in God's image, he argued before the congregation, there was no inherent righteousness, and the new creature was Christ and his church. Cotton disputed Scripture verses with Dyer, "according to his wonted meekness and moderation," but Dyer refused to back down. For refusing to retract his doctrines, the church admonished Dyer. It is a great loss that Dyer's admonition does not survive to be compared to Hutchinson's. Eventually two males did get excommunicated, John Underhill in 1640 and Anne Hutchinson's son Francis in 1641. Underhill mixed adultery with defiance about the Wheelwright petition; Francis Hutchinson was brazenly abusive on a visit back from Rhode Island, but he had been asking the church in vain to be released from his church covenant.[3] The striking gender differential between Boston and Roxbury in excommunications, three or four women and eventually two men against five or six men, perhaps reflects the more limited geographical range of women's social networks. It also may indicate that women were attracted to Hutchinson as much or more by her personal qualities as by any special appeal of her doctrines to women, as has sometimes been hypothesized, for various reasons.[4]

Those defiant Cottonians and theological radicals who chose exile in Aquidneck may not have been anticipating a long stay there. In the spring of 1638, Roger Williams argued with them against their hope and expectation that Vane would soon return as governor-general, even as Davenport and his party were giving their fear of a governor-general as one reason for leaving Massachusetts. The exiles' hope that Vane would come back to New England lingered at least until 1640.[5]

In the absence of their once and future governor, however, they quickly fell into quarreling. The Cottonians were soon writing Cotton, asking him what to do about the radicals in their midst. Well might they be concerned. In December 1638, Winthrop wrote with grim satisfaction about new errors being voiced by new would-be theologians there; Nicholas Easton, from Newbury, outdid Hutchinson in denigrating sanctification. One Herne, an obscure figure, taught that women had no souls. The Aquidneck community fell into complicated religious and political squabbles in 1639, which resulted in the formation of two towns, Portsmouth and Newport. That year Coddington, William Dyer, and John Coggeshall formed a church in Newport along with some excommunicated persons from Roxbury who publicly exercised.[6]

The relationship between Boston and Aquidneck was hopelessly tangled. Churches in principle could only excommunicate members or dismiss them to other churches, yet there was no proper church in Aquidneck. Ties of affinity and sympathy sometimes overrode the bonds imposed by the Boston church covenant as persons moved back and forth between the two communities and held widely divergent opinions on how to regard their erstwhile brethren and sisters. Cotton had to deny that he had said that members of Hutchinson's family who were members of the Boston church should not sit at table with her. In March 1639, Coddington, back in Boston, refused to acknowledge any sin in forming his church, and the Boston church admonished him. Under this kind of pressure, Coddington and others concluded that they had been de facto dismissed from the Boston church and were free to do as they pleased.[7]

At the end of February 1640, the Boston church sent a delegation to Aquidneck to check on its members.[8] The delegation refused to recognize the Newport church as a real church, and the Boston members in Newport refused to hear the delegation officially. The delegates apparently read eight doctrinal points informally to their brethren in the Newport church to probe their orthodoxy. Coddington affirmed all of them, but others "did professe thay durst not Answr possitively to them."[9] Anne Hutchinson was not a member of this church; she had already decided, perhaps through Roger Williams's influence, that there were no real churches among the Gentiles. According to Thomas Weld, the delegation made a game try to convince Hutchinson of her errors and restore her to the Boston church. Hutchinson, however, had no interest in repentance.[10] She was said to answer (not impossibly, given what we know elsewhere of her opinions), that the Boston church was a whore and strumpet, not a church of Christ. William Hutchinson said that he was "more nearly tied to his wife than to the church." The other excommunicated members, however, Mrs. Harding and Mrs. Dyer, desired communion with Boston. William Aspinwall, reported the Boston messengers, "being satisfied of the Righteous and just proseedings of the church in castinge out some of our members . . . refuseth to have any Communion with them in the thinges of God"—he would be back in Boston in two years.[11]

The Boston church heard the messengers' report on March 16. Most of the church wished to excommunicate those of its wandering sheep who acted recalcitrant. Wilson grimly announced that the sentence of Anathama Marinatha lay on Hutchinson's head, meaning that her excommunication, rather than being a vehicle for repentance, had formally cut her off forever from the Lord. A minority of members, however, refused to go through a ritual condemnatory severing of church ties that had already obviously broken. The church deferred action, with the reason given that the visit from Boston's delegation might have a belated good effect.[12]

On September 26, 1640, the Boston church again discussed the Aquidneck brethren. Coddington and others had written a defiant letter to the Boston church, explaining why they regarded themselves as freed from their ties to Boston—the failure of the church to take disciplinary measures against Winthrop for his behavior toward Wheelwright was one reason; Anne Hutchinson was not mentioned at all. (In Coddington's private correspondence with Winthrop in the early 1640s, he repeatedly brought up the injustice of Wheelwright's banishment without mentioning Hutchinson.)[13] A majority of the Boston church again wanted to move to excommunication, but a minority opposed. As a compromise gesture, Wilson read a reply by Cotton to Coddington's letter and said he would take the congregation's silence for approval to send it. But he did not get silence. John Button, a Wheelwright petition signer who had just come back from Aquidneck, said he thought it would be better to try to deal with the Aquidneck brethren in a private way, as they did not recognize the church. Wilson said that had already been tried unsuccessfully, and if this effort failed, it was time to think about excommunication. Edward Hutchinson said he refused to consent to the letter because it might be taken as a blanket endorsement of all the church and General Court had done. Wilson warned him that his objection would be looked upon with suspicion, but he refused to back down. We do not know if the letter was ever sent. Coddington, Coggeshall, and Dyer never returned to the church, and the Boston church records do not indicate that any further disciplinary action was ever carried out against them. Coddington's church suffered schism in 1641, when, according to Winthrop, the pantheistic teachings of Nicholas Easton alienated the more conservative Cottonians. One of these, Robert Harding, found himself back in Boston, where in 1644 he repentantly told the church that although he had strayed he had neither fallen into doctrinal error nor led anyone else into it.[14]

By contrast, Wheelwright's Exeter community started off smoothly. Perhaps twenty married males were there by the spring of 1638, around half of them with ties to Wheelwright going back to Lincolnshire. Presumably by 1638 it was clear that Wheelwright was not sympathetic to committed theological radicals—he refused offers from Aquidneck to minister to them, and he would shortly afterward acknowledge to Cotton that he had been unduly prejudiced in favor of the people who denied sanctification and unduly prejudiced against their opponents—and radicals went south.[15] The relationship between the Boston church and Exeter was straightforward: Exeter gathered a church, chose Wheelwright as its minister, and Boston dismissed members to this church.[16]

The only recorded conflict from the first years of Exeter did not involve theology but political allegiance. The town drew up a civil compact on July 4, 1639, that included extravagant professions of loyalty to the Crown. After some agitation the remarks were toned down, but shortly thereafter they were reinstated and one person even arrested for disloyal remarks about Charles I. On April 9, 1640, Exeter's assembly assigned the death penalty to anyone who would "practise Trechere, treson or rebellion, or shall revile his majestie the lords anoyted Contrarye to the Allegiance we professe and owe to our dread Souveraine."[17] The most radical puritan community in existence with any pretensions to orthodoxy, excepting possibly the Arnhem church in Holland, was also probably the most militantly royalist, a convoluted outcome of the days of threats about appealing to the king and perhaps also a prophylactic against the expansionist impulses of Massachusetts.

However much they had been engaged in the struggle against the "legalists," most of the Boston congregation was not prepared for exile or a protracted fight with their ministers and the rest of the church over Hutchinson, or over Wheelwright's sentence, or over unconventional theology in general. That reluctance was not simply pragmatism but part of a critical larger process of lay reassessment of and disengagement from Hutchinson and the radicals in the congregation. The process allowed the church to reestablish itself as a coherent community, and it helps explain the church's previous relative unity throughout the crisis.

All the evidence suggests that up until the winter of 1638, the "Hutchinsonians" (and the word is used here to mean the firm theological allies of Hutchinson, a group of indeterminate but small size) were as morally rigorous as Richard Rogers could have wanted, with Underhill the glaring exception. They were strict puritans, precisians, as these were called, albeit voluntary precisians rather than compulsive ones. As Weld acknowledged, they "would appear very humble, holy, and spirituall Christians, and full of Christ; they would deny themselves farre, speake excellently, pray with such soule-ravishing expression and affections." It was the fear-driven quality to the usual version of puritan precisianism that they objected to, not precisianism per se. If Hutchinson at her most extreme argued that the elect did not sin against the Law when they sinned, she also argued that nonetheless they sinned against Christ, a position not that different from Cotton's argument that the saints obeyed the Law not in itself but as it was in Christ. It was certainly not an invitation to moral laxity.[18]

But after Hutchinson's civil trial, this rigor slackened. Some in Hutchinson's circle (vagueness here is forced by the scantiness of the sources) grew lax in their family prayers, and some denied the lynchpin of puritan piety, the morality of the Sabbath. As their practice grew more unconventional, as they and Hutchinson grew more aggressive about their opinions, and as Hutchinson showed that she would rather lie than be humbled at her church trial, she and they ceased to be performatively puritan by the standards of their brethren and sisters. According to Weld, "these things exceedingly amazed their followers (especially such as were led after them in the simplicity of their hearts, as many were) and now they began to see that they were deluded by them." Or, as Winthrop put it, at this point Hutchinson "began evidently to decline, and the faithfull to bee freed from her forgeries."[19] Weld explained the impact of Hutchinson's church trial on her supporters at length:

> A great while they did not beleeve that Mistris *Hutchinson* and some others did hold such things as they were taxed for, but when themselves heard her defending her twenty nine cursed opinions in *Boston* Church, and there falling into fearfull lying, with an impudent fore-head in the open *Assembly*, then they belleved what before they could not, and were ashamed before God and men.[20]

Along with the alienating impact that the opinionists' behavior and militant heterodoxy had on the wider circle of the Boston church, Weld mentioned another factor that he regarded as crucial in lay disengagement. News of Mary Dyer's monster moved from female gossip circles to the attention of the magistrates after Hutchinson's church trial, and the following September, Hutchinson herself delivered a monstrous birth in Aquidneck. It was common in England for the laity to interpret monstrous births as divine punishments for the moral lapses of their parents, while the clergy drew broader and more public lessons from them.[21] For Dyer's and Hutchinson's births, both readings fused. The standard orthodox interpretation was that these monsters were not only divine punishment but a commentary on Hutchinson's monstrous opinions. According to Weld, the births, when added to the open heretical opinions and loosening of puritan strictness, had a specially strong effect on the opinionists' admirers, who "dared not sleight so manifest a signe from Heaven"—if you were beginning to wonder if Hutchinson and her circle were truly among the godly, the monsters seemed to speak decisively to the question.[22]

The monsters were capable of being given secular but no less hostile glosses as Massachusetts rumor networks set to work on them: "Sir Hen. Vane in 1637 went over as Governor to New England with two women, Mrs. Dier and Mrs Hutchenson," recorded the English undersecretary of state in 1667 from a traveler recently returned from Massachusetts, "where he debauched both, and both were delivered of monsters."[23] In this variant, the disorder of heresy was reduced to the primal disorder of unregulated sexuality, eerily suggesting a witches sabbath with Vane in the role of the devil, sowing the seeds of confusion, as Shepard had complained of him, but now literally. Whether given supernatural or secular explanations, the monstrous births confirmed the association of the theological radicals with disorder. Underhill's adultery became general knowledge at the same time as Hutchinson's monstrous birth, reinforcing the link between theological radicalism and immorality.[24]

Weld and Winthrop's analysis of the intrinsically provisional support of Hutchinson's wider circle of admirers was, in the last resort, the same as Cotton's. The majority of the Boston laity supported Hutchinson insofar as they perceived her as an eminent visible saint who basically supported Cotton. They began to withdraw their support of her not simply because the leadership of the church did so, but because they and the leadership were drawing the same negative conclusions about her and other radicals.[25] The parallel movement was opportune, for establishing a broad negative consensus about the radicals helped the process of reconciliation within the Boston church. The same intensified, unorthodox behavior and speech of the "erronists" that magnified their significance in the eyes of the Massachusetts establishment and its chroniclers as the hardened agitators of the disorder of the past two years—Hutchinson the American Jezebel— caused the support networks that gave them shelter and real influence to break apart.

Cotton himself had to engage in far more complex and delicate maneuvering than those of the laity who chose to remain in Boston. He was under deep suspicion by many men in Massachusetts's establishment, which gave him strong inducement to tone down the extravagance of some of his recent preaching and demonstrate his solidarity with his ministerial and magisterial brethren. Yet many of his previous supporters still regarded themselves, with some justice, as having only followed his lead. Not all of them could subsequently follow his wheel-about, and he had to explain himself to, and, when necessary, disentangle himself from these persons as well. And all the while he tried to keep the story he told to himself and others straight—he and his preaching had no responsibility for the recent troubles; he had been the abused "stalking horse" for a small group of heretics.

Already in June 1638 Cottonians in Aquidneck wrote him. They warned of Jane Hawkins's corrupt opinions, and they expressed their confidence that the real Cotton would return—he was like Sampson after his hair had been shorn, but he would soon arise again to smite the "opposite party." Cotton of course had no intention any more of smiting the opposite party. He wrote back, annoyed at their analogy, and explained that Hutchinson and her circle, "by blotting out the Law written in our hearts, and bringing in (instead thereof) the Increated life of the sonne of God . . . fundamentally opposed" the covenant of grace, while the "opposite party" merely "inverted" a "Branch or two . . . by setting the sight of works before the sight of Christ."[26]

Judging from his surviving sermons, Cotton seems to have avoided the themes of his recent preaching, and when he did touch on them, he retreated from his previous emphases. On March 30, 1640, he forcefully preached at Boston that one could find assurance from a conditional promise. "It is not impossible for justifyinge fayth to be wrought by a Conditionall promis . . . it is all one whether it be wrought by an absolute or conditionall promise . . . if ever yow herd or beleeved any other doctrine, I must professe, you never had it from me." Technically this was true, but he had not been given to expressing himself so emphatically. Thomas Marshall, one of the "chiefe stirring men" in the Wheelwright petition, spoke up, requesting clarification from his slippery teacher, "that nayther yow may be mistaken, nor my selfe mistake yow." He wanted to know if in this smoke screen of words Cotton was actually saying that one could deduce the righteousness of justification from observing a condition in oneself. Now pinned down, Cotton replied that he had been referring to a conditional promise absolutely applied. Cotton continued to preach that the Holy Ghost gave assurance by sending a word with power, but now he added firmly that you could only know if the word had been genuine by strict attention to the fruit of sanctification. And while he continued to call this experience of the Word a revelation, he immediately warned against "revelations without a word above it or beside it." On December 26 of that year, Cotton's sermon topic raised a question in the mind of Francis Lyle, a person who does not otherwise show up in the records of the free grace controversy: Lyle wanted to know if there could be people who recieved grace from Christ but who otherwise had no place in him. Cotton had been known to wax eloquent on how Christ and his benefits were bestowed in the covenant of works. But that was the past. Now he simply answered, "No Brother no man cane have sanctifying grace but such as have thear place in Christ." All others had only "common gifts and graces."[27]

Both Cotton and his listeners acknowledged that he had changed from the days of the free grace controversy. In 1642, Cotton told a correspondent writing about one of his manuscripts from that period to ignore it and read publications of his and other authors "where the naked Trueth of those Poynts is . . . more plainely and fully declared, and much more usefully unto edification." Cotton did not tell the correspondent what publications these would be.[28] Cotton Mather related an anecdote that almost certainly belongs to this period. A member of the church followed Cotton home after a sermon and "rudely told him that his ministry was become generally either dark or flat." Cotton replied, "Both, brother, it may be, both: let me have your prayers that it may be otherwise"—a mild and grave answer, as Mather termed it, but one that totally sidestepped Cotton's responsibility for the member's dissatisfaction.[29] Coddington wrote Cotton in early 1641, telling him that "it hath bene reported to us that Mr. Cotton now houlds forth things so darkly that if we had not knowne what he houlden forth before we knew not how to understand him," which is a fair summary of the contrast between his current and recent sermons. One can only imagine the pain and confusion of those who had been faithfully following the lead of Massachusetts's most prominent minister, defending what he defended and attacking what he attacked, and who now found themselves out on a limb alone. "So *eccentricke* in his motion," was the judgment of *Mercurius Americanus*.[30]

Cotton made gestures to his previous opponents more substantial than simply fudging his doctrine. On the occasion of a colony-wide fast on December 13, 1638, he finally engaged in a dramatic display of public breast-beating. According to Winthrop, he did "confess and bewail, as the churches', so his own security, sloth, and credulity," and he acknowledged that some persons "such as had been seducers of others" had been justly banished—was this for the first time in public? Another account of the fast has him weeping, explaining that God had left him for a time, which caused him to fall into spiritual slumber, and thanking his brethren for their watchfulness over him. According to the minister Nathaniel Ward, Cotton's performance "greatly gladdened the hearts of his hearers." Cotton's 1640 letter to Aquidneck that Wilson submitted for the congregation's approval said forthrightly that Wheelwright had been justly punished for his errors and sermon.[31]

Yet Cotton's pride, conscience, and convictions limited the degree to which he could accommodate his opponents. Another listener to Cotton's fast sermon remembered chiefly not that Cotton had shown contrition but that he "vindicated himself." Cotton declared "what good seed he had sown, and its dissimilitude from that which the Enemy had sown," and he proved by "*Jerome* and Authentick Authors . . . how similar the Tares in *Judea* were to the wheat." Cotton may have justified Wheelwright's sentence in public at least once, but he and his church conspicuously continued to accept the unrepentant Wheelwright as a legitimate orthodox minister. By contrast, as late as 1642, Weld and Eliot regarded Wheelwright's doctrine as heretical. It is doubtful that either Wilson or Cotton pursued erroneous opinions in their congregation very aggressively, since we know of only one person besides Hutchinson who was admonished for them. The Mount Wollaston community, with no resident preacher until late 1639, was a place in particular where errors were said to continue to thrive. But distant from Boston, and with no prominent members of the ministerial/magisterial elite to raise those errors to great heights, Mount Wollaston could be left alone. Although Cotton did not pursue erroneous doctrine too vigorously, he worked hard to come up with verbal fudging formulae whereby Wheelwright and others could come to terms with their opponents without ostensibly meaning anything different than they had all along.[32] He was indeed weaving in eccentric motion.

Nonconfrontation had ever been Cotton's preference, and until Winthrop and Wilson got sucked into taking sides, theirs as well. In terms of the Boston congregation itself, this strategy, along with the laity's readjustment, worked. At the end of 1639 Winthrop congratulated himself and Wilson in his journal for "carrying themselves lovingly and helpfully upon all occasions" and "not withdrawing themselves, (as they were strongly solicited to have done)." As a result, "the Lord brought about the hearts of all the people to love and esteem them more than ever before, and all breaches were made up, and the church was saved from ruin beyond all expectation; which could hardly have been, (in human reason,) if those two had not been guided by the Lord to that moderation." All breaches were certainly not made up, as Winthrop claimed, and he himself could still receive some pointed jabs over a year later.[33] Nonetheless, Boston had successfully managed an intricate tacking maneuver, perhaps accomplished by some persons with more pragmatism than principle, that would have capsized a less skillfully handled congregation. The early Massachusetts historians, however, recorded no more assertions about its being the most glorious church in the world.

What the reverberations of the controversy were on relations between ministers and laity in other churches is hard to determine. It has been claimed that the controversy "served to erode the confidence of the ministers in the brethren."[34] Perhaps, but demonstrating that claim would not be simple. Ministers had ample other reasons to be disillusioned with the brethren by the end of the 1630s, grudging financial support and the eagerness of the laity to assert their prerogatives perhaps chief among them. Moreover, we only know of two churches where the free grace controversy created serious disturbance, Roxbury and Boston. It is likely that without ongoing personal connections and ease of access to Cotton's lectures, if then, Bostonian doctrine might have seemed impossibly and frighteningly rarified—no assurance allowed until the Spirit had applied an absolute promise. Peter Bulkeley later said that "some" in his Concord congregation were "wavering" during the controversy, which prompted him to preach a sermon cycle on the covenant of grace. The congregation received Bulkeley's doctrine, he claimed, with "unanimous approbation and consent, as the truth of God" and pressed him to publish it.[35]

For all we know, the laity in most other churches similarly pulled ranks around their ministers fairly quickly. Even from the limited evidence that survives, it is clear that the opponents of Boston did not come only from the colony's ministerial/magisterial elite. Town deputies on the General Court monitored Wheelwright's sermons and initiated the charges against him, and it was deputies who took the lead in trying to bar the Boston deputies in the spring of 1637, while the colony's electorate cleansed the magistracy of "Mr. Vane's party" in the election that year. The "Newtowne brethren" seem to have been as aggressive as their minister, while the clergymen writing to Cotton at the end of 1636 claimed that laity had been offended by their silence. As in England, the laity were at least as willing to militantly defend orthodoxy as to rebel against it. In the wake of the controversy, laity and ministers alike showed appreciation for the usefulness of conversion narratives in keeping out heretics. Probably the controversy generally heightened lay and ministerial vigilance to the danger of doctrinal deviancy.[36]

But that vigilance did not necessarily translate into increased repression.[37] The General Court, like Cotton, became eccentric in its motions as it discovered that there were limits on its ability to impose uniformity on the church life of the colony. Complaining that those who had been excommunicated were taking the sentence too lightly and presenting themselves overboldly in other assemblies, the Court in September 1638 gave excommunicants a six-month limit to get back in the good graces of their churches or face presentation before the Court. This order, confusing the disciplinary realm of the magistrate with the disciplinary realm of the church and conflicting with the ministerial "Model" of 1635, evidently proved unworkable and was repealed within a year. Cotton himself opposed it.[38] The most visible and aggressive manifestations of radical Protestantism had been repressed to a point where there was no longer a consensus for mobilizing against them.

Thomas Shepard, however, remained in attack mode. He had what seemed to him good reasons: excommunicants insufficiently repentant; the General Court at the limits of its disciplinary powers; Cotton and the Boston church sending out very mixed messages about their own contrition; and erroneous opinions still circulating among the laity. One would scarcely guess from Shepard's surviving writings of 1638 and 1639 that he and his allies had succeeded in driving substantial numbers of people out of the colony and had firm control of the government. In one of his lectures probably shortly after Hutchinson's excommunication, Shepard attacked absolute promises as leading to the forsaking of the Scriptures, cautioned against seeming shows of repentance by evil persons, and made a not very veiled warning against accepting Vane as governor-general: "if ever any shall come under an appearance of piety, and promise of protection, safety, liberty, only your Government must be a little altered; slumber here and you shall sleep in your enemies arms." An earthquake struck New England on June 1, 1638, a few weeks after Shepard's "Abimelech" election sermon. Shepard told his congregation that the earthquake, the harsh winter, and a disastrously cold and wet spring were God's way of letting the whole world know that the godly went to New England "for ordinances, but they have forsaken the Lord, and not sought after a god in ordinances." God would be likely to follow up with a pestilence, he warned. On another occasion he explained to his congregation that the free grace controversy itself was God's punishment on the colony for neglecting the ordinances. Shepard turned again to millenarian themes in his Thursday lectures, telling his audience that the glory of the renewed Jewish church would "consist not in immediate Revelations, but in Sanctification" while Malachi's spirit of burning would be one "not which burns up all holiness, but filthiness." As for Massachusetts, Shepard's opponents had worshiped a "new Calf," and "never shall our glory be recovered till these evils are confessed and lamented, and the sin of the heart, which begat them."[39]

Cotton's show of repentance in December 1638 may have impressed Nathaniel Ward, but Ward had been willing two years earlier to say conciliatory things to Anne Hutchinson. It was not sufficient for Shepard. "Mr. Cotton repents not, but is hid," Shepard wrote grimly to himself in early 1639. Cotton continued to preach his old doctrine, however toned down, Shepard complained, and he had attempted to exonerate Hutchinson in her church trial, even after she had exposed the depths of her heresy.[40] Yet Cotton and his ministerial brethren had lapsed into a convenient mutual look-the-other-way mode; no synod was ever going to assemble again to grill him further.

Shepard continued to fight out the issues of the free grace controversy in his pulpit throughout 1639. Near the end of that year he voiced resentment over how ministers like him had been "trampled upon by some." And why this anti-ministerial hostility? It was, Shepard explained to his audience, only "for preaching the Gospel of Christ" (which is of course how Wheelwright explained his own troubles). There might not have been many outward signs of trouble and dissent left in Massachusetts, but that did not fool Shepard. His opponents were too cowed to defend their doctrines openly, but they had not reformed: "Though they keep it in, yet how many are there whose hearts go after these detestable things!" Up almost to the very end of the lecture cycle in September 1640, Shepard continued his attacks on Boston doctrine. He also brooded about leaving the colony, in part because of the blandishments of his father-in-law, Hooker, to move to Connecticut, but also because, as he noted to himself, "Mr. Vane will be upon our skirts"—the Commission for Plantations sent a stiff order demanding the charter in 1638 and a more conciliatory one in 1639.[41]

This festering ill will and suspicion, in which Shepard was surely not alone, provoked open conflict shortly after Shepard finished the cycle. The conflict is particularly interesting, because it does not seem to have involved Boston directly. Rather it pitted people against each other who had been united against Boston. As Winthrop's journal tells the story, Richard Mather's Dorchester church was much taken with a newly arrived minister, Jonathan Burr, and offered him the position of the church's teacher. But around the end of the summer of 1640, Richard Mather decided that Burr "delivered some points savoring of familism." No source explains what that savor of familism was, but there must be a connection with a document surviving in the Winthrop papers dated September 23, 1640. The document laid out the boundaries of a legitimate experience of the immediate witness of the Spirit. That experience was uncommon, the document stated, but if Christians were sure that they were sanctified, they might "have the Testimony of Gods love by the Spirit, without cleeringe up in some measure of the truth of his Graces allso, either precedent or concomittant together with the witness of Gods love." Nevertheless that testimony was always agreeable to the Scripture's word and "sence" (that is, a communally agreed upon interpretation). Moreover the testimony of the Spirit, even if agreeable to the word and sense of the Scriptures, had to always be further tried by the Bible to make sure it was not a delusion. Eight ministers signed the document, including Burr, Mather, Shepard, and Wilson, but not Cotton (a tacit understanding?).[42]

Burr demonstrated in this document that he was neither familist nor even Cottonian in his conception of the witness of the Spirit—this was straightforward Sibbesian doctrine, such as would have a long life in Massachusetts.[43] Yet evidently for Mather it was insufficient, and he kept up his agitation. Winthrop related that the Dorchester church requested that Mather confer with Burr and the church be informed where the difference between them lay. Burr wrote down his positions. He expressed himself in some propositions in a way that clearly indicated he was erroneous, according to Winthrop, "but this was again so qualified in other parts as might admit of a charitable construction." Mather, however, put the worst possible spin on the entire document when reporting his conclusions to the church, and he did not inform Burr in advance of his dissatisfaction. Moreover, he insisted Burr held false doctrines even when Burr specifically disclaimed them. Members of the church proceeded to take sides and the conflict "grew to some heat and alienation."[44]

Thomas Hooker commented on the fast-growing controversy in a letter from Hartford to Thomas Shepard dated November 2, 1640, probably in response to an account by Shepard. It is the only contemporary commentary on the controversy besides Winthrop's, and it gives some insight into the still panicky frame of mind of some of the ministers. Hooker fully shared Shepard's discontent with the way the free grace controversy had resolved itself and with Cotton himself. Now he was not exactly surprised at the Burr controversy: "That the ould carnall opinions are formented and take with carnall hearts I do not wonder but I did ever feare and expect." Nevertheless he found it strange that Burr, a newcomer, would "gather up scattered forces to make a fresh onset," and that "after a cause hath been sentenced in open view." The only explanation could be that he was "heartened under hand to it" and apt to "keep a party." He was the visible tip of a bigger conspiracy; it was 1636 all over again. Hooker heard that there were several persons in Connecticut who "look that way." The exile Aspinwall had just visited Hartford. After Hooker, probably in response to his presence, preached a sermon arguing that the Gospel was the only rule or revelation of a man's good estate, Aspinwall had the nerve while dining with the governor to cite the sermon as evidence that all parties now agreed that sanctification itself could not be a first evidence. Hooker and Samuel Stone now feared "a suddayne alarm." They wanted the proceedings of the Synod of 1637 published.[45]

It took a four-day meeting in early February 1641 to end the Burr controversy. Governor Dudley, Deputy Governor John Winthrop, and about ten ministers examined the case and the way it had been handled. While the debates of this conference have been lost, Winthrop presents the panel as evenhandedly rebuking both sides, Burr for his "unsafe" expressions and Mather for his precipitous response—conference members probably disagreed about which one more needed rebuking. Burr and Mather both acceded to the rebuke and Burr "did again fully renounce those erroneous opinions of which he had been accused, confessing that he was in the dark about these points, till God, by occasion of this agitation, had cleared them to him, which he did with much meekness and many tears."[46] Christ was no longer divided.

I read Winthrop's account of Burr's apology to mean that Burr confessed that although he had never held the doctrines he was accused of, he was unaware of the complicated Massachusetts theological context into which he had launched his sermons. That apology provides a handle by which we can get hold of how Burr could trigger such a strong hostile reaction. For what is truly odd about the controversy is that Burr seems to have been a widely admired minister, who very possibly never said anything remotely heterodox. Edward Johnson, militant defender of New England orthodoxy and admirer of Thomas Shepard, was so taken with Burr that he wanted him as minister at his own church. He waxed enthusiastic over Burr's preaching in his verses: "Exhorting all their faith on [Christ] to center / Soules ravisht are by him in thy sweet speech." Even Thomas Hooker, according to Cotton Mather, when he finally heard Burr preach, exclaimed, "Surely this man wont be long out of heaven, for he preaches as if he were there already." Burr died on August 9, 1641, leaving behind him not a savor of familism but a fragrance of self-denying saintliness so strong that Mather a half century later devoted pages of the *Magnalia* to describing it. "The most experienced Christians in the country," Mather claimed, "found still in his *ministry*, as well as in his whole *behaviour*, the breathing of such a *spirit* as was very greatly to their satisfaction."[47]

Clearly Burr was no Wheelwright. His preaching was not intentionally divisive; militant foes of Boston admired it highly. William Hubbard, who may have heard him, suggested that the conflict possibly arose because Burr's phrases were excessively "wire-drawn." That is not much to go on, but my guess is that Burr preached on the wonder of God's love and the raptures of the Spirit's witness of that love. He perhaps did not linger overlong on the terrors of God's law, a conjecture given some support by a sermon of his that Shepard recorded. Nothing unsound about that in itself, but in his Christocentric focus he perhaps failed to sufficiently emphasize self-scrutiny and self-questioning. That failure, in the still tender atmosphere of 1640 New England, could rub some people the wrong way, just as it would shortly in England.[48] In Burr's case it caused some ministers to precipitously conclude that behind his phrases lurked a hidden but all-too-familiar mystery. Yet others who had been persuaded that heresy was afoot in Boston refused to buy into this reading. The coalition that had attacked Boston was not willing to be reassembled for an assault on Dorchester. How the controversy might have escalated had Burr been more of a Wheelwright and not so willing to repeatedly turn the other cheek is anyone's guess. Some scholars argue that the free grace controversy was more about tone and affect than specific doctrines.[49] Contemporaries would have been puzzled and even insulted by that claim, but in the case of the Burr incident those scholars might be correct—and the result was sound and fury and, in the end, a damp squib.

The Burr incident had a curious afternote. Shortly after Burr died, his widow, Frances, married ex-magistrate and Wheelwright petition signer Richard Dummer. Dummer's first wife had been a strong supporter of radical Boston doctrine and had drawn her husband in.[50] Perhaps Dummer and Burr recognized in each other kindred spirits. They could practice their piety together not in an anxious effort to reassure themselves of their salvation but as a continuing praise of the God whom they knew had already manifested his rare and infinitely precious love to them and spared them from eternal flames. If they translated that praise into novel theological propositions or succumbed to the temptation to reflect on the spiritual status of those they disagreed with, their thoughts have escaped the historical archives.

The Burr incident is the last direct recorded tremor of the free grace controversy. From Shepard's letter to Cotton in 1636 to the Dorchester conference in 1641 stretches an unbroken documentation of suspicion and pulpit agitation. What at its height ballooned into the worst internal political crisis of colonial Massachusetts ended, as far as the documentation is concerned, in the way it had begun five years previously—a spat between ministers and their lay admirers with intimations of heterodoxy lingering in the background. The final episode had different leading actors and different alliances than the bulk of the controversy. But that variation is appropriate enough, for the free grace controversy had a multiplicity of agents, loyalties, and flash points. It was an irreducibly pluralistic conflict.

Historians, however, tend to invoke either John Cotton or Anne Hutchinson to explain it. Some argue, with David D. Hall, that John Cotton's "differences of opinion with the other ministers in Massachusetts were at the heart of the Controversy." Cotton's doctrines, of course, made it possible for him to get sucked into controversy, and he played a central role as both an actor and a trophy for both sides. Yet he and Wilson had worked out a satisfactory modus vivendi before the controversy erupted and did so again after it subsided. Given Cotton's status and his disinterest in seeking confrontation, those differences of opinion in themselves scarcely get to the controversy's heart. They do not explain why some ministers chose to blow Cotton's doctrine up into familism while others did not, or why Cotton developed such a violent antipathy to certain ministers' doctrinal stances, or why he was prepared for so long to turn a blind eye to the theological radicals within his congregation—"slow to believe these things of them, and slower to bear witness," John Norton reluctantly acknowledged.[51] Those are the issues that lie at the heart of his involvement in the controversy itself.

Other historians, generally less interested in theology, see Hutchinson, either in herself or in the reactions she provoked, at the center of unrest. Hutchinson, too, was critical to the controversy. Highly censorious, gifted at evangelism, and endowed with a sense of prophetic mission, Hutchinson reinforced her influence by her high social status and her excellent connections with men like Vane and Cotton. She was a focal point for lay theological radicalism, yet her gender's low public profile and her visible piety made her a difficult target for opponents. The wide admiration Hutchinson enjoyed among the women of Boston helped ensure that large numbers of them felt a personal stake in the controversy, while the homosocial nature of the gatherings in which she worked most openly probably heightened the sense of men like Shepard that the "mysteries" of Boston were "hidden."

But those mysteries might have remained hidden, even embryonic, if Henry Vane had not arrived. It was Vane who institutionalized and, for all we know, began the strange Bostonian hybrid of Cottonianism and English radical doctrines and encouraged its spread under the mantle of his status and authority. That status and authority, inserted into the flimsy political structure of the colony, allowed for the play of extravagant hopes and lurid fears around him, both of which greatly magnified the conflict's importance and made it far more intractable than it might have otherwise been.

Other individuals made decisive contributions to the generation and sustaining of the controversy. Wheelwright consistently alienated his ministerial brethren by his borderline, divisive preaching, and he weakened Cotton's own credibility by Cotton's defense of him. It was the ongoing struggle between Wheelwright and other ministers that thrust the conflict into the political arena in a particularly destabilizing way, beginning the arc that ended with the trials of Hutchinson and others seven months later. As Cotton reminded Wheelwright in 1640 while trying to nudge him into apologizing for his part in the conflict, a number of people suffered simply because of their "inordinate zeale to your Innocency."[52]

Nor could conflict have taken on the virulent form it did without the relentless heresy-hunting of men like Shepard, casting the mantle of deviance as widely as they could and seeking constantly to convince their brethren that there could be no neutrals in this conflict. Shepard's proactive role cannot be neglected. Historians have concluded from the controversy, for example, that "the greatest internal danger to puritanism on both sides of the Atlantic came from its own left wing" and that for puritans, the free grace controversy's "irrepressible dynamic provided an object lesson about the dangers inherent in an emphasis on justification by faith alone." Yet that argument is correct only up to a point. It was not simply puritanism's "left wing" or "an emphasis on justification by faith alone" that caused the free grace controversy or threatened puritanism's stability. As English historians are only starting to explore, puritanism generated not only its own destabilizing radical wing but its own destabilizing "radical" Lauds, eminently respectable figures who attempted to impose a uniformity on the diversity and tolerance of their movement, regardless of the costs. Radical orthodoxy could be just as divisive as radical heterodoxy, and even feed the latter. Shepard and his allies, in defining the Boston coalition in order to mobilize against it, helped that coalition define itself, helped perpetuate it, and certainly helped ensure that its breakup would be hard and divisive; *Mercurius Americanus* claimed that the theological deviancies of the Boston radicals "would never have advanced so much, had not the *Antiperistasis* of your vehement prosecution forced them into a habit."[53] Anne Hutchinson in her final form was in part Shepard's creation. Disorder was a systemic issue in puritanism.

John Winthrop has been generally recognized as the leading lay figure in the Massachusetts establishment's attack on the "antinomians," while historians leave the attack itself largely undifferentiated. A few scholars, though, portray him roughly as he liked to portray himself, walking a "fine line of moderation" between extremes, in this case, the antinomians and those who were out to crush them.[54] Winthrop's willingness to act highhandedly in defense, as he saw it, of the Gospel and the commonwealth helped to aggravate the crisis, and he did not have the support of a majority of the magistrates for his activism until the end of Wheelwright's trial. Still, he was a moderate in the sense that he also grasped that keeping hot Protestantism functionally coherent required containment, flexibility, and patience, not single-minded repression. Allies like Shepard and Dudley, had they been given free rein, very likely would have driven Cotton and the bulk of the Boston congregation out of Massachusetts and possibly gone after Vane himself; even if Cotton had remained to attend the synod, it would have collapsed in failure. In those cases, the long- and short-term prospects for the survival of the colony would have been very much in doubt. If any one of those with a share in fanning the flames of controversy can be given credit for keeping Massachusetts intact during it, Winthrop can.

As for what the free grace controversy was about, that cannot be reduced to a single issue. With its framework of familists, antinomians, bishops, papists, Arminians, Antichrist, Jesuits, Spanish designs, and the devastation of Germany, it was clearly about the religious tensions tearing Europe apart and fraying the English godly community itself. All sides in the free grace controversy could easily picture themselves as frontline troops in the apocalyptic struggle between a militant Protestantism and its enemies, a struggle in which assurance of salvation was a key but elusive weapon and enemies capable of endless disguises. "In our strife, we had forgotten wee were brethren," William Coddington later wrote to John Winthrop.[55]

Doctrinally the core energizing question of the controversy was whether or not you had to know that God loved you before you could trust the signs that you loved him. Although scholars sometimes rush in to take sides in that dispute—transcendental mysticism against toughminded realism—they probably should hold back unless they are prepared to play for the participants' stakes. Both sides agreed that God condemned the foolish virgins who got the answer wrong to an eternity of unimaginable torments. Both sides also agreed that genuine conversion took place only after sinners had fully grasped that otherwise inevitable fate. The saints, by whatever yardstick they used to measure it, struggled to comprehend the dizzying heights of God's unmerited, redeeming love through the incomprehensibly awful and vast shadow of damnation those heights cast over the overwhelming majority of humanity. The vista is not one that later, more liberal belief systems can easily replicate.

Besides that core dispute, there were other common threads in the free grace controversy. For many people the controversy must have been about the bewildering sight of brethren tearing into each other and about finding themselves being pushed unwillingly into taking sides. For those who did aggressively take sides, whichever side they took, laity and clergy alike, it was about heresy and about the endangering of immortal souls, about abuse and even persecution of beloved ministers, and about the problems attendant on recreating a minority style of religiosity in a land crowded with saints. It was about the Last Days and the Church being always under the Cross, and this affliction being especially pertinent in the 1630s.

For both sides, it was about rooting out unconscious hypocrisy, shows of false holiness, and the human pride that would substitute its own inventions for the will of God. It was about whose preaching obstructed or promoted the "clear revelation of Gods free grace."[56] It was about antinomianism in the very loose sense that it was a dispute about the place of duties and holiness in the life of believers, while a few radicals were literally antinomian in that they denied that the moral law had a commanding power over them. It was critically about familism in that the horrific specter of familism is what the Massachusetts authorities believed they were combating, with some justification. Had it simply been and "antinomian" and not a "familist" controversy, it never would have reached such a level of intensity.

Nonetheless, there was no single controversy, free grace, antinomian, familist, or otherwise; the issues varied from time to time and from individual to individual. Within the anti-Boston party, some ministers dismissed absolute promises altogether, some did not; some denied an immediate witness of the Spirit, some did not; some argued for gracious preparation, some did not; as Hubbard said, some worried about the tendency of Boston doctrines, while others found the doctrines themselves already a danger. For some people the controversy was about the countenancing of sin, about the denial of the power of the Gospel, and about God's punishments on a people who turned away from him and his ordinances. For some it was about John Cotton's obscure preaching of familism. It was about fantasies of social and moral engulfment: "Hells Cataracts . . . of Errors . . . broached to the hazard of the ruine of the Churches," boatloads of Grindletonians descending upon the colony, the destruction of the Bible, massacres by Münsterian fanatics, and a massive satanic design to destroy the liberties and churches of New England. Perhaps it was even a plot by the Jesuits to advance Roman tyranny and universal monarchy.[57]

For Boston the free grace controversy cannot be reduced to a single issue or a single perspective. It was about interference with the revelation of greater depths to the Gospel and with a prophetess of God raised up for some great purpose, or it was about the harassment of brethren and sisters who were basically sound, if holding some absurd points; it was about the fact that the children of the bondwoman would always persecute the children of the free and about the need to preach the Gospel even if it led to a combustion in the commonwealth. It was about the need to oppose papist doctrines, about the need to burn Antichrist before the Jews could be converted and the Millennium take place. It was about ministers who kept Christians chained to the Law when they should have been experiencing Gospel liberty. It was about unjust actions by a barely legitimate government. For John Underhill, it was about head, heart, and groin being united in predatory harmony. Given that Lincolnshire immigrants were represented among Boston activists in numbers far beyond their proportion of the population of Boston, the controversy for many participants was clearly about personal loyalties that predated immigration.[58]

Both lay and ministerial opponents of Boston occasionally articulated the controversy to be about envy of the ministers and about persons who, in Hugh Peters's words, forgot that they were supposed to be subjects, not magistrates, hearers, not preachers, and wives, not husbands. By definition, however, the representatives of the local ministerial/magisterial elite and their supporters would be prone to interpret and portray attacks on them in terms of patriarchal insubordination, and it is not surprising that they occasionally employed this rhetoric. And it is not surprising if attacks on those representatives did carry undertones of resentment of their authority, or if part of the satisfaction of doing radical theology was the freedom from ministerial constraints. However, the rhetoric of insubordination was not employed very often. That infrequency is also not surprising; for, as everyone at the time knew well, "Mr. Cotton's party" was a coalition movement publicly led by magistrates, preachers, and husbands (with a gentlewoman behind the scenes), and it was strong only in the locality of those persons' domiciles; geographic location, not class or gender, was the main social factor in determining the broad divisions of the controversy. As *Mercurius Americanus* demonstrates, the coalition was perfectly prepared to turn the language of deference and subordination, both secular and religious, against their opponents—a despicable, illegitimate government had overthrown the noble Governor Vane and dared to lay hands on Wheelwright, one of the Lord's anointed. The magistrates and ministers of Massachusetts, a shaky group of patriarchs, were attacked under the mantle of a more impressive patriarchal pair, Cotton and Vane. In terms of Calvinist political theory, such a movement would scarcely register as legitimate resistance, let alone sinful rebellion against the divinely ordained powers that be.[59] On top of everything else, the free grace controversy was about the common colonial problem of reproducing hierarchical English lines of political authority in situations where those lines were confused.

However great the mélange of issues and the heat they engendered, Massachusetts emerged from the free grace controversy in 1641 intact with its ministerial and magisterial elite more or less cohesive. Ironically, that happened just as English puritans were about to take control of the English government with very different results. As Charles I's power ebbed away to a parliament increasingly dominated by its puritan wing, antinomian/familist and millenarian preaching openly appeared on puritanism's "left" wing; sects started to emerge; disagreements over church polity loomed increasingly large; and, above all, disputes among alleged brethren were managed with self-defeating vituperativeness. As in Massachusetts, heresy hunters complained bitterly of the slowness of the godly public to recognize that heretics were not godly. Puritan empowerment produced not consensus, but, as a preface writer to one of Cotton's books said, "unparalleled times of universal contention, totally polemical."[60] Puritans proved unable to establish a viable alternative to the Laudian system they had overthrown. The English people gratefully welcomed the return of Charles II in 1660, and puritans would never again be in a position to implement a godly commonwealth. The contrast between Old and New England is worth exploring. Both in its ill-tempered cacophony and in its demonstration of how widely divergent paths to salvation among the godly had become, the free grace controversy foreshadowed English puritanism's oncoming internal struggles. Yet the outcome did not. What was it about puritanism in England and New England that accounts for this?

In England puritanism throve in the early seventeenth century because many prominent persons in and out of the Church of England hierarchy could not agree on how punitive an attitude, if any, to take to nonconformists. Their lack of consensus both encouraged and restrained hot Protestantism. Passionate evangelical ministers and zealous laypeople prepared to exercise a certain amount of discretion could practice their piety with a considerable amount of freedom. At the same time, the most radical doctrines necessarily usually remained subterranean; intra-puritan heresy hunters had little access to mechanisms of repression; arguments over the fine points of what a properly reformed church should look like were pointless; and the godly clergy in general had a vested interest in restraining their disagreements in the face of common enemies in the English church and government. How long this precarious and continually renegotiated balance could have lasted, absent Charles I and Laud, is anyone's guess.

It took the specific circumstance of puritans finally getting what they wanted that brought the tension between puritanism's drives to diversity and unity to the fore. Massachusetts was the first polity that the godly controlled, and, as it would in England, that control had two conflicting results. The first was a sudden outbreak of radical and lay creativity, a heady sense of bonds being broken, of religious empowerment. The millennial fervor and divisive doctrinal speculation in the Boston church was at least in part a result—*Mercurius Americanus* suggested that some radicals' anticipation of the glories of New England before emigrating "scrued their meditations in way of preparation for your society, to a sublimination in doctrine." The second result was the polar opposite of the first. Puritan empowerment invited the clarification of issues that had previously been beyond resolution—what was the proper form of church polity; what were the genuine boundaries of orthodoxy—and it held out the chimeric possibility of resolving these unresolvable issues through state power. Diversity became amplified at the heart of Massachusetts's ministerial and magisterial elite precisely when it appeared that diversity among the godly could finally be squashed. The result was the most spectacular puritan dispute before the Civil War. Puritanism may have represented, as Patrick Collinson has recently written, "the mainstream, ongoing thrust of the Protestant Reformation." The free grace controversy demonstrates how little it took to make the currents of that stream extremely turbulent.[61]

Those currents swamped puritans in England once they came to power in the 1640s, yet Puritans in Massachusetts managed to ride them. They succeeded in instituting a recognizable, relatively coherent version of godly, state-supported Christianity. Apart from the vastly more complex religious and political challenges English puritans faced, recent historians account for that achievement in different ways. It has been suggested that it was due to a successfully negotiated complex give and take among laity, ministers, and magistrates, or that it came about because of the absence of large numbers of the ungodly and the presence of an "extremely cohesive and class-conscious" "thinking class." Perhaps, but in the free grace controversy Massachusetts very nearly did not succeed. In that case, historians would be analyzing how the tensions of the free grace controversy inevitably caused the brittle negotiating mechanisms of puritanism to break down, or be referring to the implosion caused by the absence of large numbers of the ungodly and the presence of too many professional intellectuals.[62]

As it was, the resolution of the free grace controversy and the survival of Massachusetts were ultimately made possible not because of any special quality of American puritanism but because of a special circumstance of New England. On neither side of the Atlantic were evangelical English Protestants able to develop a consensus that whipping, imprisoning, and executing persons many perceived as godly was an acceptable way of negotiating hot Protestantism's conflict between theoretical unity and practical diversity. America offered the alternative of mobility.[63] Hutchinson's prophetic powers could be shuffled off to a dark corner of the region. Whatever his ultimate intentions, Vane by leaving gave the Massachusetts establishment a chance to reconstitute and reassert itself, while others seriously unhappy with the turn of events in the colony did not need to stay around to defend a lost cause. The General Court had viable alternatives to Wheelwright's suggestion that they execute him.

As with many other disputes of the founding years of New England, mobility ultimately resolved the free grace controversy. That suggests that the single most important underlying factor in the successful institutionalization of Reformed Christianity in seventeenth-century New England was not English resourcefulness or adaptability but the initial decimation of the Indians through epidemics and war. A reduced native population greatly facilitated the process of visible saints moving away from each other. The hot Protestantism that flared up so dangerously in the free grace controversy thereby repeatedly bought time to cool down into something less flammable and leave America with its legacy of high intellectual endeavor, communitarianism, visionary zeal, and coercive, moralistic evangelism.

Indeed, it is striking just how deeply the free grace controversy was implicated in the migrations that were to define the cultural geography of New England. The three most important ministers to come to America, Cotton, Hooker, and Davenport, each saw fit to end up in a separate colony, a luxury English puritans could not afford. It has long been surmised that one of the reasons Hooker set up Connecticut was his desire to put distance between himself and Cotton. Ego and differing ideas on church government have been advanced as possible sources of tension. We now know that Hooker departed warning about Cotton's teaching on assurance. Some historians have assumed that Davenport left Massachusetts around the same time as Anne Hutchinson out of disgust for the spiritual repression he saw taking place in the free grace controversy. The evidence for this is tenuous, if it exists at all. One might more plausibly look for connections in Davenport and his associates' desire to put distance between themselves and any possible governor-general and in the fact that in New Haven they set up a famously severe church and state order that would have whipped a Hutchinson, Wheelwright, or Vane into line or out in very short order. In any case, the free grace controversy did nothing to present Massachusetts in a favorable light to them: "Wee were not worthy of Mr. D[avenport] and his People here," wrote Cotton upon their leaving.[64] Wheelwright and his followers pushed puritanism into New Hampshire and then into Maine, territory previously associated with godless fishermen and conformist ministers. Heterodox, semi-anarchic, and religiously tolerant Rhode Island managed to survive among its land-hungry and none too scrupulous neighbors due in no small measure to the accumulation of ability and population it acquired as fallout from the free grace controversy. The differences that might have finished Massachusetts played a significant role in giving New England its eventual shape.

TWELVE

GODLY ENDINGS

THE BURR incident ended the free grace controversy as a controversy, as a sustained series of interlocked public events. But the incident hardly ended the controversy's impact on the lives of the individuals who had generated and sustained it. In some cases it followed them to their graves, in others, it drove them to them. It was carried across the Atlantic into the religious and political tumult of mid-century England, with important consequences.

Some historians have presented the free grace controversy as ultimately a triumph of sorts for Shepard. Shepard and Hooker's moralistic and "legal" style of preaching established domination over a more charismatic and mystical variety represented by Cotton.[1] Unfortunately, we simply do not know enough about the preaching of most Massachusetts ministers to be able to say whether the controversy had any effect one way or another on their preaching, and the little we do know does not suggest the establishment of a Shepardian-Hookerian hegemony.[2] Shepard and Hooker, gauging from their reactions after the Synod of 1637 and beyond, would have been very surprised to have learned that in the judgment of some historians they had won.

What does seem clear is that Shepard came out of the free grace controversy with permanent psychic scars. His early preaching was a mixture of calls for a strictness and self-vigilance so impossibly severe as to pass into ineffability and vivid evocations of union with Christ as a process of near ecstatic emotional release—God's fist versus Christ's embrace. Shepard's experience of the free grace controversy—immorality, astonishing heresy, the possible imminent demise of the churches and even of their representatives—seems to have tipped the scale decisively on the former side. His already highly developed suspiciousness of human spontaneity led him easily to conclude that subjugation to a severe and easily angered God through a relentless round of duties was the only check on the wicked anarchy of the human heart. Perhaps it was in the immediate aftermath of the free grace controversy that he had his congregation organize private meetings to examine one another for growth in grace and report back to him—with the possibility of excommunication for those who failed the examination, according to one account.[3]

Shepard's suspicions were only reinforced by the antinomian/familist horrors emerging out of England in the early days of the English Revolution. When Giles Firmin wrote to Shepard from England in the 1640s gently suggesting that his severe preaching caused unnecessary worry and suffering to sound Christians, Shepard unrepentantly replied that "Axes and Wedges" were needed "to hew and break this rough, unhewn, bold, yet professing Age."[4] He continued to attack any reliance on visions, dreams, and absolute promises for assurance (all equally delusive) and warned those practicing such techniques that the Lord would "burn you to ashes."[5]

Yet Shepard's sermons, like his painful journal, suggest that he lashed out at what he lacked. Sermon notes taken two years before his death record him trying to explain, as he had so many times before, "why many Christians lived in doubts." Christians had to learn to live without feeling, he said, to trust in their own love to God even if they did not experience it reciprocated. "An immeddiat manifestation of god the fathers love is not the clearest nor the sweetest," he insisted. But the notes record old familiar protesting voices emerging in response, "you will say is not the spirits testimony most clear?" Shepard replied that it did not witness to itself but only to a condition in us. Another voice would not trust that answer: "You will say a man may deceive himself." Shepard could only insist in reply that a Christian in principle could know for certain that he loved Christ. Why then so many Christians lived in doubts Shepard could not answer any more than he had ever been able to.[6]

Around the time that Shepard preached these sermons, he wrote down his spiritual autobiography for the benefit of his son, which included his last brief account of the free grace controversy. Shepard still firmly placed the blame on Cotton, Vane, and Hutchinson and their promulgation of "familism," while Wheelwright, justly convicted, was "a man of a bold and stiff conceit of his own worth and light." It is unlikely that Shepard ever reflected that he himself might have displayed an excessively bold and stiff conceit of his own worth and light in that dispute; his only comment on his role was self-pitying: "[I]t was an uncomfortable time to live in contention."[7] Shepard, of all the participants, left the most enduring monument from the controversy: *The Parable of the Ten Virgins* has been reprinted intermittently down to the 1990s, a compelling analysis over the centuries for at least some Christians of genuine assurance and of the countless ways that hypocrites can delude themselves into thinking they possess it.[8]

Shepard's vocation of anxiously, angrily, and imploringly reconciling the elect with their offended deity ended in 1649. A description of his death suggests that he may have experienced some final comfort. As ever with Shepard, however, that comfort was carefully confined and cautiously expressed: "To those that were about him, he bade them love Jesus Christ dearly, that little part that I have in him, is no small comfort to me now."[9] Hooker, by contrast, died two years previously after enjoying thirty years of peace and closed his eyelids with his own hands before expiring.[10]

Winthrop continued for the rest of his life on the course he had followed during the free grace controversy, harsh to committed religious dissenters while more willing than many of his colleagues to put energy and patience into reclaiming them. The voters of Massachusetts showed their appreciation of him by returning him as governor seven more times before his death in 1649, although he suffered an occasional demotion to deputy governor or even assistant largely as a rebuke to his continued dislike of restraints on rulers and legal niceties.[11]

Winthrop died a death worthy of a saint; according to Cotton Mather, "he enjoyed in his holy soul the great consolations of God!" But before he reached those enjoyments, Mather reported, Satan buffeted him, and God, he felt, abandoned him. Perhaps it was at this stage of despair that a story circulating in more than one form after his death can be inserted. Dudley pressed Winthrop on his deathbed to sign a banishment order, but Winthrop refused, saying "he had done too much of that work already." In another version, Winthrop was "trobled on his death bed" for the banishments of Hutchinson and others during the free grace controversy.[12] Whatever basis in fact the stories have, their circulation testifies to an undoubtedly accurate popular perception of Winthrop as a moderating influence in the colony.

Cotton returned to his former preeminence after the free grace controversy. "His latter days were like the clear shining of the sun after rain," as Hubbard tactfully put it. He became a major spokesman for New England Congregationalism and an authority on the contemporary meaning of the prophetic books of the Bible who kept the London presses very busy. He resumed his role, spectacularly disrupted in the free grace controversy, as a sought-after transatlantic spiritual counselor. John Wilson praised him after his death as "a most skillful compounder of all differences in doctrine or practise according to God" (did Wilson pause at all before he wrote those lines?).[13]

Cotton's long-term attitudes toward the free grace controversy seem to have been complex. In print, he carried on his quarrel with Hooker and Shepard's doctrine of preparation, but discreetly, one cause he passed down to his friend John Norton.[14] On the other hand, Cotton denied emphatically that it was "legal" to receive assurance "by all the former works of the Word and Spirit," an unqualified statement it would be impossible to imagine him making at the height of the free grace controversy.[15] In the same vein, he told auditors how to examine themselves to "let you see whether you are given to Christ by God or no." Yet the mystical Cotton had not disappeared. He could preach passionately on believers' experiences of the life of Christ, insisting that these experiences were real and not "but sudden flashes and pangs"—Shepard had warned a few years previously, "Its not Glorious (brethren) to have a flash or vision: but to love the word aright that is truly Glorious."[16] One could leap from the mystical, mild, and doctrinally restrained John Cotton of the English sermons to the mystical, mild, and doctrinally restrained John Cotton of the scanty remains from the later 1640s without a hint that extraordinary things had happened in his preaching in between.

Yet Cotton's own account of the free grace controversy, also written in this period, scarcely shows the accommodating, flexible, and repentant minister that he elsewhere seems to have been. Robert Baillie, for example, reacted indignantly when he read Cotton's reply to him, for he saw in it little genuine contrition. He pointed out that when Cotton explained the sources of his grief over the free grace controversy, he spent as much ink lamenting the vigor with which the opponents of Boston had pursued the church as he did over the heretics in his congregation or his own laxness. Baillie also noticed that Cotton nowhere gave any indication that he found anything wrong with Wheelwright's fast-day sermon or anything right with the sentence Wheelwright received. Worst of all, according to Baillie, Cotton printed the five doctrinal points on which he disagreed with the elders going into the Synod of 1637 along with his reasons for them, but he nowhere printed the elders' response nor explained how the disagreements were resolved.[17]

Enigmas of attitude and intention envelop the posthumous publishing of Cotton's sermons from the free grace controversy. Shortly before Cotton's death, two people came to him with copies of their notes of his sermons from 1637 on the covenant of grace, asking him to go over them. It was no secret to Cotton that such notes often found their way into print and that these would be in effect his doctrinal last will and testament. William Hubbard certainly regarded them as such.[18] The sermon notes did to Reformed orthodoxy roughly what John Coltrane did to "My Favorite Things," yet Cotton went carefully over them, clearing up any inaccuracies and, judging from the printed results, doing nothing to tone them down. One can only wonder what sort of signal he meant to give out to his brethren. Was this a final assertion that the Cotton of 1637 was doctrinally sound? Perhaps there is a connection with his final published piece, a preface to John Norton's *Orthodox Evangelist*. There Cotton called on Protestants who "excell in holiness and knowledg, and yet seem (and but seem) to vary (though Logically, yet not Theologically) in some doctrines of Grace . . . mildly to bear with differences of judgment." Cotton, it is said, died a richly comfortable death in 1652, already tasting the joys he would experience in heaven. It seemed appropriate to his memorializers that God should have a comet blaze in the sky at the time.[19]

Wheelwright's troubles continued to affect him for at least two decades. After much coaching from Cotton and a trip to the Bay in 1643 to consult with the elders, he wrote two very carefully worded letters to John Winthrop. He wanted his banishment lifted. Toward this end, he profusely apologized to Winthrop for his "sins" during the free grace controversy. Acknowledging that the doctrinal controversy between him and the elders was not as serious as he thought at the time, Wheelwright professed to repent of the role he played in stirring up the dispute. He had made excessively "censorious speeches"; his adherence to "persons of corrupt judgment" might have encouraged them; and he used "unsafe and obscure expressions" at the synod. Wheelwright, however, took back with the left hand what he gave with the right, making it plain that it was not his sins but false accusations of "dangerous revelations and gross errors" that had brought about his banishment. Wheelwright had sinned, in other words, but he had not committed any legal offenses. Winthrop, giving Wheelwright's letters an optimistic reading, asked him to come in person to the Court and confess his guilt, which Wheelwright had no intention of doing. In May 1644 the Court lifted Wheelwright's sentence of banishment anyway, claiming that he had made "particular, solemn and serious acknowledgment, and confession by letter, of his evil carriages and of the Courts justice upon him for them." If Wheelwright ever wrote such a letter, it has not survived; the Court was probably making a very liberal interpretation of his previous correspondence, prompting Hubbard to comment sardonically that "if they had overdone in passing his sentence, it might in part help to balance it, that they were so ready to grant him a release." Charles Francis Adams suggested that the Court might have hastily granted Wheelwright a pardon with wording that made it look like he confessed to lend credibility to the recently appeared *Short Story*.[20]

Certainly they would not have gotten even Wheelwright's limited apology if he had first read that account. Wheelwright was furious at discovering that his name was being dragged through the mud in English publications—he would sooner turn Catholic, he indignantly claimed, than antinomian or familist. *Mercurius Americanus* was the first family response, although Wheelwright's role in it is unclear. Wheelwright left for England in 1655, shortly after he had skirted another trial for his recent appearance in a Boston pulpit. He apparently intended only a short visit to England, perhaps to clear his name, since he did not sever his ties with Hampton, New Hampshire, where he was currently ministering.[21] In any event, the trip turned out to be protracted. In England, he published a defense of himself that showed no trace of the slender apology he wrote to Winthrop; stayed with Henry Vane; and managed an audience with Oliver Cromwell, who gave him moral support for what he had gone through. Cromwell, in Wheelwright's judgment, seemed "very orthodox and gracious, no way favoring sectaries," which was just how Wheelwright always viewed himself.[22]

The seventy-year-old Wheelwright returned to New England in 1662, after things had turned very bad for puritans in England, in time to assist in the persecution of Quakers. He ministered at Salisbury, New Hampshire, and felt reconciled enough to the Massachusetts establishment to preach for funds for Harvard College in 1673. In the 1670s, Wheelwright, irascible to the end, poured a great deal of energy into a bitter personal feud with the leading Salisbury layman, Robert Pike. Their intense mutual hostility may have developed from Pike's greater tolerance for Quakers or it may have gone back to the 1630s, for Pike was one of the Newberry residents in 1637 who traveled thirty miles to be made freemen and vote Vane out of office. The feud, with highhanded behavior on the part of both men, split the Salisbury congregation into factions who pursued each other in the church and courts. In 1677, a Massachusetts General Court commission reported that it had managed to reconcile the eighty-five-year-old Wheelwright with the sixty-one-year-old Pike, "though with some difficulty." Wheelwright died two years later, remembered by Cotton Mather as "a valued servant of the church in his generation."[23]

Many members of the Hutchinson clan stayed in or eventually returned to Boston. Their place in the social and religious order of Massachusetts, high to begin with, was such that Hubbard regretted even having to bring up their family name in his history ("noted for eminent piety, great integrity of judgment, and faithful service in the church of God," he said of them). How they interpreted their recent history is unknown. There was an intriguing moment at the Boston church trial of Richard Wayte for theft in 1640. Wayte had just apologized for not revealing to the church adulterous revelations that Underhill had shared with him during the 1637 Pequot expedition. Anne Hutchinson's son-in-law Thomas Savage pressed him hard. Since God had shown him the "wickednes of Revelations," did Wayte feel repentant about a revelation of his salvation that he had received after his previous excommunication? Savage reminded him that Savage and Hutchinson's son Edward had privately dealt with him about it. Wilson, of all people, reminded Savage that God could genuinely send Wayte "some support to kepe him from sinkinge." One might read the exchange as meaning that Hutchinson and Savage had drastically changed their opinions, but it more likely means that they had never been uncritical supporters of the radical fringe of their church (and that Wilson should not be pigeonholed too quickly either). Edward, however, did forthrightly tell the church in 1640 that he could not condone all that church or commonwealth had done during the free grace controversy, and he later fought for tolerance of Quakers and Baptists. Savage, on the other hand, is recorded as reporting a "tumultuous" Quaker meeting to the

Boston magistrates in 1662. Samuel Hutchinson, banned temporarily in 1637, published a small treatise defending the concept of the Millennium in 1667, but it gives no hint of his attitude toward Anne Hutchinson or Wheelwright's theology.[24] The only thing that is safe to say about Anne Hutchinson's relatives and others from her circle who stayed in Boston is that whatever their private convictions, those convictions did not seem pressing enough to leave traces in the historical archives.

The exiles in Rhode Island fell beyond the domination of a state-supported church structure and learned clergy. They were free to follow whatever spiritual paths seemed appropriate to them.[25] For a few in the early 1640s, the path led to Samuel Gorton, far more aggressive and far more theologically reliant on familism than Hutchinson—Cotton, Wilson, and most of Massachusetts's magistrates wanted to kill him when they got their hands on him in 1643.[26] In 1656 Quaker missionaries arrived in Rhode Island. Although the Quakers rejected predestination—no assurance through an absolute promise—in their talk of an indwelling Christ and the guidance of the Spirit and the danger of the letter of the Scriptures, the Massachusetts exiles would have heard much that was familiar to them from the days of the most glorious church in the world. The more esoteric doctrines of the Quakers, denials that physical bodies were resurrected and the claim that Christ's physical body was not in heaven but was the church, would have seemed a vindication of Hutchinson in her most familist-tinged phase—by the 1680s, familists in England summed themselves up as "refined Quakers," which was an apt description, even if it reversed the lineage.[27] William Coddington turned Quaker and wrote to his former Massachusetts brethren protesting Wheelwright's conviction again and calling on them to "turn to the Light within you. . . . Even Christ in you the Hope of Glory, which was declared to you by the Servant of the Lord *John Cotton.*" He was not the last Quaker to claim Cotton's mantle.[28] At least ten exiles, including Hutchinson's close followers, Mary Dyer and Jane Hawkins, identified with the Quakers. The martyr Dyer was remembered by her Quaker associates as "so fit for great affairs that she wanted nothing that was Manly, except only the Name and the sex."[29]

For Anne Hutchinson the result of the free grace controversy was to accelerate her drive toward complete separatism. She may not have been consciously revolting against patriarchal hierarchies in Massachusetts, but now in Aquidneck with no learned clergy to defer to, acknowledging them did not seem so critical—she "ordinarily prated every Sabbath day," according to Edward Johnson, "publically" Winthrop added, which is to say that she taught openly before meetings of both sexes.[30] Hutchinson and her three or four families of followers became Seekers, perhaps under the influence of Roger Williams, denying that there was any true magistracy in the world or any true church. They may have also begun to question traditional understandings of the Trinity itself (or become more open in expressing what would have been the most hidden and dangerous element in Boston lay theology).[31] Hutchinson engaged in what amounted to a guerrilla holy war against the Boston church, sending it admonitions and engaging in mutually bitter correspondence with its members. The teachers of Massachusetts, with no exceptions now, Hutchinson wrote in a sharp exchange of letters with Thomas Leverett, spoke with the voice of Balaam, the false prophet of Revelation, and Massachusetts's churches, Boston included, were not to be the preparatory vehicles for the Millennium; they would suffer Babylon's doom, as part of "those Cities of the Nations, which the Lord hath said should fall, Rev. 16.19."[32]

In 1641, Hutchinson's family clashed head-on with the Massachusetts authorities. Winthrop had registered dismay a year previously when a godly young preacher coming from the West Indies, William Collins, chose to settle with Hutchinson. Witchcraft was an attractive explanation to the Massachusetts elite, just as it would soon be to account for the otherwise inexplicable appeal of Quakers.[33] Now, Collins and Hutchinson's son Francis, whose request the previous year to be dismissed from the Boston church had been denied, traveled to Massachusetts to confront the Boston church with its iniquities. The magistrates brought them in for questioning. They interrogated Collins about a letter he had written in which he had called the Massachusetts churches and government antichristian and called Charles I the king of Babylon. Francis Hutchinson, according to Winthrop, did not agree with Collins "resolutely in all," but he had called the Boston church a "strumpet."[34]

The magistrates laid heavy fines on Collins and Hutchinson in part, according to Winthrop, to keep them prisoners and in part to try to squeeze the Hutchinson family for the expenses of the Synod of 1637. As winter approached, however, and the prisoners refused to pay, their fines were lowered to get rid of them. The two still chose to sit in jail, and the magistrates finally expelled them from the colony on their own security. According to Samuel Gorton, the authorities spoke "some threatening words afterward, as though they would fetch them again."[35]

In the meantime, Massachusetts began attempting to annex land near Aquidneck and indictated designs on the entire Narragansett Bay region. The colony's resolve led Thomas Weld, now in England, to cobble together a spurious legal document, the "Narragansett Patent," to validate its claim, and it led the Massachusetts government itself to eventually sponsor the murder of Vane's admirer Miantonomi, who had sold Aquidneck to its English settlers. Roger Williams's alarm was such that he returned to England to seek a proper patent for Rhode Island, and it is unsurprising that Hutchinson and her family anticipated risking either their lives or their consciences in the entirely plausible event of Massachusetts taking over the colony. Hutchinson's last recorded new scriptural revelation, after her husband died in 1642, was that the Lord had prepared a city of refuge for her in present-day Westchester County, New York, then claimed by New Netherland.[36]

Hutchinson's city of refuge lay in the midst of the Wecqueasgeek band of Indians who were intermittent participants in the bloody Indian clashes with the Dutch known as Governor Kieft's War (1640–45). Edward Johnson wrote that they warned Hutchinson not to settle among them. But she remembered the verses that had assured her of salvation back in England and asserted that "though all nations and people were cut off round them, yet should not they." "They were become all one Indian," she claimed. She was wrong, possibly because a corrupt Dutch official never passed on her payment for her land to the Wecqueasgeeks. In August or September 1643 the Indians killed her and most members of the three families with her, drove their cattle into their houses, and burned the houses down. Sixteen people died, according to Winthrop; a few women and children escaped by boat. Hutchinson's opponents had no difficulty picturing her in hell.[37]

Henry Vane usually drops out of the story of the free grace controversy with his departure to England in 1637. When scholars reinsert the controversy into the ongoing history of English puritanism, they see its actual impact as exemplary, rather than causal, and ignore Vane altogether. Certainly the controversy did play a heavy symbolic role in English religious disputes. It was widely broadcast with the publication of *Short Story* in 1644, and thereafter. Presbyterians seized upon it as demonstrating the pitfalls of Congregationalism. Throughout the century, opponents of radical theology alluded to its catalog of errors with horrified fascination.[38]

Yet through Vane, the free grace controversy had direct and considerable impact on England. Vane might have attempted to get an appointment as Massachusetts governor-general on his return to England. The effort has left no trace, but neither have most of his activities before 1640. It is at least possible, since we know he intended to leave the country, one way or another. Cotton's friend Thomas Goodwin organized an English Congregationalist church in the mid-1630s, under Cotton's influence, dominated by persons who had been involved in the Warwick patent. Goodwin's church and Boston had a direct link—Vane. In the summer of 1638 he planned to accompany the church to Arnhem, Holland. In Arnhem the church became known for its pietistic experiments and for a millenarianism that discovered congregationalism in prophetic Scripture texts, as at least some Massachusetts Congregationalists had already done, and located the seal of the Spirit as the climax of the Gospel. The Arnhem church's apocalyptic fervor helped set the Congregationalist ecclesiastical agenda in the Civil War.[39]

Vane and Boston were certainly not the only source of millenarian congregational zeal in Holland in the late 1630s, and how much they directly influenced the Arnhem church is impossible to determine. But Vane demonstrably generated controversy in England as soon as he returned. Among the Warwick patentees, Lord Say and Sele wrote indignantly to Cotton in 1638, Vane, together with unnamed friends (possibly Underhill) disseminated his radical Boston doctrine successfully and controversially, covering it with Cotton's mantle. Say and Sele's fellow patentee, Lord Brooke, in all likelihood picked up from Vane his own approving misunderstanding of Cotton's theology; only Brooke's death in 1643, Richard Baxter later claimed, kept him from coming completely under Vane's sway.[40]

Vane rose rapidly in power in England. Charles I appointed him secretary of the navy in 1639, and he was knighted and took a seat in Parliament in 1640 at the age of twenty-seven. When the Civil War broke out in 1642, Vane switched sides and emerged as a political and ecclesiastical radical, working closely with Lord Brooke in the militant wing of parliament. He became a major player in both domestic and foreign affairs for the duration of the Long and Rump Parliaments. Next to Cromwell himself, Vane may have been most responsible for the eventual dominance of the radical Independent faction over parliament. Vane broke with Cromwell when Cromwell dissolved the Rump Parliament in 1653 and retired from active politics until Cromwell's death in 1658. He returned as a major radical political figure when the Rump was reinstated upon Cromwell's death, and he threw in his lot with the army in the last desperate attempt, opposed by many moderate puritans, to block the return of Charles II in 1660. Charles promised indemnity to all except those who were involved in the execution of his father. Vane should have been covered by the indemnity, but he was deemed too dangerous to leave free and became the single exception. After two years in prison, Vane was put on trial, accused of intending the death of Charles II (because of his commonwealth government posts) and of "trying to overturn the ancient government of England." On trial, Vane proved militantly unapologetic about his past and about the necessity for kings to be subordinate to parliament. Charles, like Thomas Shepard, found Vane's political principles beyond bearing and ordered him beheaded on Tower Hill on June 14, 1662.[41]

Even as Vane assumed an English leadership role, his New England connections remained strong. His favors to Massachusetts prompted Winthrop to make an appreciative comment in his journal in 1645. He even-handedly concerned himself with Rhode Island affairs, however, and tried to prod the Massachusetts authorities toward religious tolerance. Anne

Hutchinson's brother-in-law Richard, wealthy London merchant and militant parliamentarian, became Vane's deputy as treasurer of the navy and eventually succeeded him in the post.[42]

Theologically, Vane remained grounded in radical Massachusetts doctrine, while expanding it with Socinian-inspired speculation on the nature of the Trinity. He retained his admiration for Anne Hutchinson, and there are perhaps traces of Vane's Boston days in the writings of his close friend, the Platonist Peter Sterry. It may not be entirely coincidental that when Edward Hutchinson returned to England, he regularly attended Sterry's sermons. While Vane gathered around him a circle of admiring "Vanists," to whom he delivered sermons in the great hall of his Lincolnshire mansion, orthodox ministers, as in Massachusetts, found his speculation mystifying and offensive. Vane in turn passionately and bitterly kept his conviction, learned in Massachusetts, that most puritan ministers lived in and preached a damnable covenant of works and would inevitably persecute those in the covenant of grace. "None are more confident of their being within the covenant of Grace, freed from any danger of the covenant of Works," Vane wrote, "than ['Orthodox' ministers], who . . . hug in their bosoms, the principles and life of the covenant of Works. . . . None being more ready than these, to lay Heresie, Blasphemy, and high Notions at the wrong door of others, in hopes to make themselves appear the sound and good Physicians." Orthodox ministers, according to Vane, were the second beast of Revelation 13:11, "set out and adorned with the purity and perfection of the first *adam* (renewed upon him by the blood of Christ,) *to make warre with the true Saints of the most high, and to weare them out with his cruelty and rage*, pretending to visible Saintship."[43]

This conviction underlay Vane's new learned militant commitment to religious liberty and drove much of his radical politics—if Vane could help it, England was not to repeat the outcome of the free grace controversy. He fought hard in parliament to minimize the power of the clergy. His most important diplomatic coup came in late August 1643 when he negotiated the Solemn League and Covenant with the Scots, giving parliament the vital aid it needed to continue resisting Charles I. The Scots wanted a commitment in return from the English to an intolerant Presbyterian national church, but Vane inserted wording in the treaty that upon close reading committed the English to nothing. Even as Anne Hutchinson was meeting her bloody end, Vane was protecting the saints from antichristian ministers and magistrates. In the 1650s, Vane supported the politically radical millenarian Fifth Monarchy Men, a number of whose leading members had been in Boston at the time of the free grace controversy.[44] As a highly visible promoter of radicalism, Vane encountered much the same kind of hostile, hysterical response in England that he had in Massachusetts. Besides accusations of being a Jesuit tool, a 1659 London broadside charged that he and the Fifth Monarchists were plotting to massacre all the city's citizens—shades of 1637. There were rumors in that politically unstable year that the Quakers, hated by much of the English nation, had annointed Vane king.[45]

While in prison after the Restoration, Vane offered his impending beheading as proof that the "Reformed part of the Church" was "fiercer enemies [to the godly] than any others whatsoever." On the scaffold, Vane may have recalled Wheelwright's fast-day exhortation: "Sampson slew more at his death, then in his life, and so we may prevaile more by our deathes, then by our lives." By all accounts, he met the ax of the Reformed part of the Church with exemplary courage. Vane called the crowd to witness in his manner of dying proof that he would shortly be in heaven and took the executioner's blow "with so much composedness, that it was generally thought, the government had lost more than it had gained by his death"—a stirring final scene to the most influential personal script written in the free grace controversy.[46]

There must have been grim, knowing looks in Massachusetts when news of Vane's death arrived. His execution fulfilled a bloody prophecy a minister made slightly before his departure; perhaps Shepard had reminded his brethren that Abimelech died by a millstone dropped on his head.[47] The establishment seemingly had the last word in revelations; Massachusetts still existed; Vane and Hutchinson were dead.

But Massachusetts only had twenty-two more years of autonomy left in which to chase the theocratic dream of Elizabethan puritans like William Perkins and Richard Rogers of a religiously and morally cleansed Reformed Christian polity—one state, one church, one godly path to heaven. Its charter was finally voided for good in 1684 during Charles II's general assault on corporate charters. Charles conducted his assault under the shield of a widespread fear that the disorder of two decades of failed puritan rule in England might return.[48] Vane had contributed no small share to that disorder, and the free grace controversy exemplified why and how it arose. Thus, Hutchinson had been right in 1637 when she predicted destruction on the Massachusetts magistrates for trying to export their problems, right in ways both broader and more symbolic than she had intended, but right nonetheless—their inability to work out a way to live with their hotter brethren and sisters prophesied puritanism's doom.

NOTES

INTRODUCTION

1. George Bancroft may have been the first to use the label "Antinomian Controversy," or at least popularize it, in his *History of the United States, from the Discovery of the American Continent* (Boston, 1834). It seems to have become standard thereafter.

2. The impact of the free grace controversy in England is discussed in chapter 12.

3. Miller, "Preparation"; Miller, *Colony*, 59–67. Pettit, *Heart*; John S. Coolidge, *The Pauline Renaissance in England: Puritanism and the Bible* (Oxford, 1970); R. T. Kendall, *Calvin and English Calvinism to 1649* (Oxford, 1979); Delbanco, *Puritan*, 211–12; and Knight, *Orthodoxies* are the major studies that, in a variety of ways, represent Cotton (and Hutchinson, whom they do not sharply distinguish from Cotton) as advocating a purer and more profound Reformed piety than his opponents.

4. Stoever, *Faire*.

5. Gura, *Glimpse*; Knight, *Orthodoxies*.

6. Battis, *SS*; Staloff, *Making*, chaps. 3, 4. For pioneering and/or prominent examples of an extensive and diverse literature on gender and the free grace controversy, see Ben Barker-Benfield, "Anne Hutchinson and the Puritan Attitude to Women," *Feminist Studies* 1 (1973): 65–96; Lyle Koehler, "The Case of the American Jezebels: Anne Hutchinson and Female Agitation during the Years of the Antinomian Turmoil, 1636–1640," *William and Mary Quarterly*, 3d ser., 31 (1974): 55–78; Elaine Huber, *Women and the Authority of Inspiration* (Lantham, MD, 1987); Lang, *Prophetic*; Marilyn J. Westerkamp, "Anne Hutchinson, Sectarian Mysticism, and the Puritan Order," *Church History* 59 (1990): 482–96; Porterfield, *Female*; Kamensky, *Governing*; Norton, *Founding*. See also Selma R. Williams, *Divine Rebel: The Life of Anne Marbury Hutchinson* (New York, 1981), decidedly unscholarly in its relative indifference to factual accuracy and adequate documentation but still insightful.

7. Going hand in hand with the neglect of narrative, logically enough, is a widespread tendency to be careless with facts. I have generally not noted my factual disagreements with authors.

8. Battis, *SS*, is the last monographic narrative. Battis's prosopographical work remains valuable, but his central argument that the free grace controversy was driven by Anne Hutchinson's twin curses of a menopausal crisis and a weak husband has been ignored, except to be held up for indignation or ridicule. Other Battis interpretations will be dealt with in the course of this book. Westerkamp, "Anne Hutchinson, Sectarian Mysticism, and the Puritan Order," 485.

9. There have been three synthetic accounts of the free grace controversy since the 1960s: David S. Lovejoy, *Religious Enthusiasm in the New World: Heresy to Revolution* (Cambridge, 1985); Gura, *Glimpse*; and Staloff, *Making*, chaps. 3, 4. The exception to this rule about archival avoidance is Rutman, *Winthrop's Boston*, which systematically used the Cotton Papers at the Boston Public Library, as did

Battis, *SS*, to a lesser extent. With the publication of Sargent Bush, Jr.'s edition of John Cotton's correspondence, *JC*, most of the important archival material is now available in print.

10. For a discussion, see Richard Cust and Ann Hughes, "Introduction: After Revisionism," *Conflict in Early Stuart England: Studies in Religion and Politics, 1603–1642*, ed. Richard Cust and Ann Hughes (London, 1989), 1–46.

11. Robert Sanderson, *XXXIV Sermons* (London, 1689), 15; John Cotton in Williams, *Complete Writings*, 2:198.

12. "The hotter sort of protestants are called puritans," claimed Elizabethan presbyterian Percival Wilburn, as cited in Patrick Collinson, *The Elizabethan Puritan Movement* (1967; reprint, Oxford, 1990), 27.

13. Ann Hughes, "Anglo-American Puritanisms," *Journal of British Studies* 39 (2000): 1–7. The pluralism of American puritanism in general has been a stock emphasis in American puritan studies since the 1960s, as a reaction to Perry Miller's evocation of a monolithic "New England mind," although it has not yet been adequately applied to the free grace controversy. For the use of the term "puritanism" to mean an ongoing and inherently pluralistic set of negotiations around shared religious motifs, see David D. Hall, "Narrating Puritanism," in *New Directions in American Religious History*, ed. Harry S. Stout and D. G. Hart (New York, 1997), 51–83.

14. Morton, *Memorial*, 91.

15. Collinson, *Elizabethan Puritan Movement*, 334.

16. Knight, *Orthodoxies*, raises this issue, although the details of her arguments leave a great deal to be desired.

17. Stoever, *Faire*.

18. T. D. Bozeman, "'The Glory of the Third Time': John Eaton as Contra-Puritan," *Journal of Ecclesiastical History* 47 (1996): 638–54.

19. Conrad Russell, *The Fall of the British Monarchies, 1637–1642* (Oxford, 1991).

CHAPTER ONE
ASSURANCE OF SALVATION
IN THE EARLY SEVENTEENTH CENTURY

1. The description of Shepard is based on *WWP*, 136.

2. Shepard, *Works*, 1:61, 29, 85, 70, 57, 89.

3. *Sincere Convert* was deliberately intended to be terrifying, since its theme was the wide variety of ways in which people could deceive themselves into thinking they were saved when they were not. Shepard intended to follow it with sermons describing what true converts were like, and he eventually published a treatise on that subject, *The Sound Believer*, which was often reprinted but not as frequently as *Sincere Convert*. *Sincere Convert* has had at least thirty-two editions over the the centuries, including five in German and one in Algonquin.

4. *God's Plot*, 49; Webster, *Godly*, 169–70.

5. Notes on Sermons Delivered by Thomas Shepard, 1637–1638, p. 253, MHS.

6. Perry Miller, *The New England Mind: The Seventeenth Century* (Cambridge, 1939), 49–50.

7. The following arguments about sixteenth-century puritanism are developed at greater length in my "Weak Christians, Backsliders, and Carnal Gospelers: Assurance of Salvation and the Pastoral Origins of Puritan Practical Divinity in the 1580s," *Church History* 70 (2001), 462–81. There were scholastic ways to argue for both a powerful sense of assurance and its fragility at the same time, which early Reformed divines did. This ambidextrousness has made it possible for some scholars to dismiss the importance of the change in ministerial attitude outlined below. See Joel R. Beeke, *Assurance of Faith: Calvin, English Puritanism, and the Dutch Second Reformation* (New York, 1991), chap. 4. But since those ministers making the change perceived themselves as engaged in something new (see below), it seems safest to assume that they knew what they were about.

8. Edward Dering, *XXVII Lectures, or Readings, upon Part of the Epistle Written to the Hebrues*, in *M. Derings Workes* (London, 1614), n.p. (the passage is found in "The fourteenth Lecture, upon the residue of the 6. verse [of the 3rd chap.]"; John Moore, *A Bryefe and Necessary Catechisme* (London, 1577), sig. Biir. On this very influential catechism, see Patrick Collinson, *Godly People: Essays on English Protestantism and Puritanism* (London, 1983), 298. Eusebius Paget used the phrase in his catechism, *Short Questions and Amsweres, Conteyning the Summe of Christian Religion* (London, 1579), sig. C4v; John Foxe, *A Sermon of Christ Crucified, Preached at Paules Crosse the Friday before Easter, Commonly Called Goodfryday* (London, 1570), sig. Siiiv. See also Laurence Chaderton, *An Excellent and Godly Sermon Most Needefull for This Time, Wherein We Live in All Securityie and Sinne, to the Great Dishonour of God, and Contempt of His Holy Word* (London, 1578?), sig. Diiv, Ciii 3r; John Knewstub, *Lectures of John Knewstub upon The Twentieth Chapter of Exodues, and Certeine Other Places of Scripture* (London, 1577), 39; Richard Greenham, *The Workes* (London, 1605), 53. See also Ian Green, *The Christian's ABC: Catechisms and Catechizing in England c. 1530–1740* (Oxford, 1996), 388–90.

9. Richard Rogers, *Seven Treatises* (London, 1603), 54.

10. William Perkins, *The Workes of That Famous and Worthy Minister of Christ in the University of Cambridge, Mr. William Perkins* (London, 1613–18), 1:599. For introductions to Perkins and his theology, see H. C. Porter, *Reformation and Reaction in Tudor Cambridge* (Cambridge, 1958), 288–313; Ian Breward, ed., *The Works of William Perkins* (Abingdon, 1970), 80–99; Richard A. Muller, "Perkins' *A Golden Chaine*: Predestinarian System or Schematized *Ordo Salutis*?" *Sixteenth Century Journal* 9 (1978): 69–81; R. T. Kendall, *Calvin and English Calvinism to 1649* (Oxford, 1979), 51–76; Richard A. Muller, *Christ and the Decrees: Christology and Predestination in Reformed Theology from Calvin to Perkins* (Durham, 1986), chap. 6; Michael McGiffert, "The Perkinsian Moment of Federal Theology," *Calvin Theological Journal* 29 (1994): 117–48.

11. For Rogers's life, see M. M. Knappen, *Two Elizabethan Puritan Diaries* (1933; reprint, Gloucester, 1966), 17–35. For the chronology of writing *Seven Treatises*, see ibid., 69, 71, and Rogers, *Seven Treatises*, sig. B3v. Irvonwy Morgan discusses Rogers at length throughout *The Godly Preachers of the Elizabethan Church* (London, 1965).

12. Rogers, *Seven Treatises*, 573; *God's Plot*, 43; Robert C. Winthrop, *The Life and Letters of John Winthrop*, 2d ed. (Boston, 1869), 1:102. Counting abridgments and extensive extracts, *Seven Treatises* went into over forty editions.

13. Rogers, *Seven Treatises*, sigs. A3r–Arv.

14. Perkins, *Workes*, 1:286.

15. See, for example, Lewis Baylie, *The Practice of Pietie* (London, 1613), 237; Paul Baynes, *Briefe Directions unto a Godly Life* (London, 1618), 33; Robert Bolton, *Some Generall Directions for a Comfortable Walking with God*, 2d ed. (London, 1626), 326; John Brinsely, *The True Watch, and Rule of Life*, 6th ed. (London 1614), 163; Richard Stock, *The Doctrine and Use of Repentance* (London, 1610), 122.

16. *WP*, 3:339, 340. I am drawing on an account of Winthrop's conversion that he wrote in 1637, more than twenty years after the events he described took place. He kept a diary during those events that agrees with his later account in its evolving affective tone, although not in its specific descriptions. Cohen, *God's Caress*, chap. 8, compares the two.

17. *WP*, 3:341.

18. Ibid.

19. *God's Plot*, 101.

20. Perkins, *Workes*, 1:369; Sibbes, *Works*, 1:49, 70, 124.

21. Culverwell, *A Treatise of Faith* (London, 1623), 41, 45. See also Matthew Storey, ed., *Two East Anglian Diaries, 1641–1729*, Suffolk Records Society, no. 36 (Woodbridge, 1994), and the second sermon in John Archer, *Instructions about Right Beleeving* (London, 1645), "Christ Is the Bread of Life." John Rogers, *Obel or Beth-shemesh* (London, 1653), 411.

22. Cf., *God's Plot*, 110, 111, 162, 167, 168, 189.

23. *God's Plot*, 162, 154; *WP*, 3:342.

24. Perkins, *Workes*, 1:241.

25. *God's Plot*, 94, 149, 157, 196.

26. John Downe, *A Treatise of the True Nature and Definition of Justifying Faith* (Oxford, 1633), 25–26; Firmin, *Real Christian*, sig. Cv; John Rogers, *A Treatise of Faith*, 3d ed. (London, 1629), "Preface"; Kendall, *Calvin and English Calvinism*, 91–92; Stoever, *Faire*, 132–37; John Von Rohr, *The Covenant of Grace in Puritan Thought* (Atlanta, 1986), 156–57. Cf. Westminster Confession of Faith, chap. 8, par. iii.

27. *God's Plot*, 161, 205.

28. Cohen, *God's Caress* takes John Winthrop's account of his successful search for assurance as normative, even while noting that the bulk of accounts on which he primarily relies, church relations from Thomas Shepard's congregation, do not really fit this model. They "dwell more on preparation than on the life of faith" and "not many people openly exalted in profound joy or sublime peace" (212–13). Cohen suggests that the Scripture texts these narratives employ might be an encoded way of communicating emotions such as Winthrop recorded. I find it more straightforward and in line with ministerial laments to assume that the surface affective tone in these narratives is also the deep one.

29. *PTV*, 1:44.

30. Arthur Hildersham, *Lectures upon the Fourth of John* (London, 1629), 46; Culverwell, *Treatise*, 3; Brinsley, *True Watch*, 172; Bolton, *Gernerall Directions*, 354; Richard Rogers, *Certaine Sermons Preached and Penned by Richard Rogers* (London, 1612), 203.

31. Some historians seek explanations for this evangelical moroseness in evangelism's alleged appeal to certain character types and by allegedly uniquely evangelical severe childrearing habits. For a highly partisan introduction to this approach and to its critics, see Philip Greven, "The Self Shaped and Misshaped: *The Protestant Temperament* Reconsidered," in *Through a Glass Darkly: Reflections on Personal Identity in Early America*, ed. Ronald Hoffman, Mechal Sobel, and Fredrika Teute (Chapel Hill, 1997), 348–65.

32. *God's Plot*, 9; Solomon Stoddard, *An Appeal to the Learned* (Boston, 1709), 16.

33. Cf. Stoever, *Faire*, 148.

34. Bolton, *Generall Directions*, 334; Hildersham, *Lectures*, 312; Perkins, *Workes*, 1:sig. Hhr.

35. Jean Delumeau, *Sin and Fear: The Emergence of a Western Guilt Culture, 13th–18th Centuries*, trans. Eric Nicholson (New York, 1990).

36. Rogers, *Seven Treatises*, 25, 575.

37. Bartimeus Andrews, *Certaine Verie Worthie, Godly and Profitable Sermons, upon the fifth Chapter of the Songs of Solomon* (London, 1583), 52–53; Rogers, *Seven Treatises*, 99; Perkins, *Workes*, 1:425.

38. Rosemary O'Day, "The Reformation of the Ministry, 1558–1642," in *Continuity and Change: Personnel and Administration of the Church in England, 1500–1642*, ed. O'Day and Felicity Heal (Leicester, 1976), 55–75; Peter Lake, "Robert Some and the Ambiguities of Moderation," *Archiv fur Reformationsgeschicte* 71 (1980): 259–60. On the changing role of ministers in the Reformation, see, E. Cameron, *The European Reformation* (Oxford, 1991), 148–50, 390–96, Andrew Pettegree, "The Clergy and the Reformation: From 'Devilish Priesthood' to New Professional Elite," in *The Reformation of the Parishes: The Ministry and the Reformation in Town and Country*, ed. A. Pettegree (Manchester, 1993), 1–21.

39. Perkins, *Workes*, 1:284.

40. Ibid., 1:115.

41. Greenham, *Workes*, 266; Arthur Dent, *The Plaine Mans Path-way to Heaven* (London, 1601), 259; Thomas Hooker, *The Saints Dignitie, and Dutie* (London, 1651), 74.

42. Paul S. Seaver, *Wallington's World: A Puritan Artisan in Seventeenth-Century London* (Palo Alto, 1985), 43. For an extended, positive interpretation of this mode of piety, see Michael McGiffert, "The People Speak: Confessions of Lay Men and Women," in *God's Plot: Puritan Spirituality in Thomas Shepard's Cambridge* (Amherst, 1994), 141–45.

43. Sibbes, *Works*, 1:138. That Sibbes was here identifying settled knowledge with the seal of the Spirit is apparent from the Scripture he cited, Ephesians 1:13.

44. Sibbes, *Works*, 1:138.

45. See, for example, Paul Baynes, *A Commentarie upon the First Chapter of the Epistle of Saint Paul, Written to the Ephesians* (London, 1618), 297; John Forbes, *A Letter Resolving This Question: How a Christian Man May Discern the Testimonie*

of Gods Spirit (Middelburgh, 1616), 69–70, 80–81; Elnathan Parr, *The Workes of that Faithfull and Painfull Preacher, Mr. Elnathan Parr* (1622; reprint, London, 1651), 64–65; Perkins, *Workes,* 1: 284, 369; Timothy Rogers, *The Righteous Mans Evidences for Heaven* (London, 1617), 17, 141–50; Robert Whittell, *The Way to the Celestial Paradise* (London, 1620), 89–90; Thomas Wilcox, *A Discourse Touching the Doctrine of Doubting* (London, 1598), 153–54; Thomas Wilson, *The Christian Dictionary* (London, 1612), 146; Wilson, *A Commentary on the Most Divine Epistle of St. Paul to the Romans,* 3d ed. (London, 1653), 278. Determining in experiential terms the difference between the human emotions of joy and peace that divines agreed were induced by the conventional witness of the Spirit and their supernatural counterparts induced by the extraordinary witness falls outside of the province of the historian. The difference may have been as much in how to define experience as in the experiences themselves.

46. For discussions of the seal, or witness, of the Spirit, see Bolton, *Generall Directions,* 326–27; Edward Elton, *Three Excellent and Pious Treatises* (1623; reprint, London, 1653), 192–93; Andrew Willet, *Hexapla* (Cambridge, 1611), 359–60; Sibbes, *Works,* 3:457, 5:440–43, 7:377; John Preston, *The New Covenant, or, The Saints Portion* (London, 1634), 400ff. For secondary discussions, see Joel R. Beeke, "Personal Assurance of Faith: The Puritans and Chapter 18.2 of the *Westminster Confession*," *Westminster Theological Journal* 55 (1993): 1–30; Beeker, *Assurance of Faith,* 253–59; Michael A. Eaton, *Baptism with the Spirit: The Teaching of Dr. Martyn Lloyd-Jones* (Leicester, 1989), chap. 3; Sinclair B. Ferguson, *John Owen on the Christian Life* (Edinburgh, 1987), 116–21; Stoever, *Faire,* 120–22.

47. Sibbes, *Works,* 3:440, 5:541; Preston, *New Covenant,* 401; Bolton, *Generall Directions,* 326–27.

48. William Erbery *The Testimony of William Erbery* (London, 1658), 67–68.

49. Geoffrey F. Nuttall, *The Holy Spirit in Puritan Faith and Experience,* 2d ed. (Chicago, 1992), 58–59. Cohen, *God's Caress,* 100, treats Preston's discussion of the assurance the witness of the Spirit gave as a commentary on assurance in general, which it is not. Stoever, *Faire,* 120–23, is keen to set up a sharp division between orthodox piety and "antinomianism." While his discussion of Sibbes's conception of the "intuitive" seal is in itself careful and lucid, he proceeds to minimize the extent to which Sibbes emphasized the superiority of this form of assurance over the conventional modes. By the end of his discussion, there is scarcely any difference.

50. Alastair Hamilton, *The Family of Love* (Cambridge, 1981); J. Dietz Moss, *"Godded with God": Hendrik Niclaes and His Family of Love* (Philadelphia, 1981); Christopher W. Marsh, *The Family of Love in English Society, 1550–1630* (Cambridge, 1994).

51. Richard A. Muller, *Post-Reformation Reformed Dogmatics,* vol. 2, *Holy Scripture: The Cognitive Foundation of Theology* (Grand Rapids, 1993).

52. Bolton, *Generall Directions,* 328, 334; Preston, *New Covenant,* 396–402; Sibbes, *Works,* 1:22, 5:441; Thomas Goodwin, *The Returne of Prayers* (London, 1636), 40.

53. *WP,* 3:340, 342.

54. Romans 8:15, 16 is the key text for understanding how Winthrop conceptualized his experience. *WP,* 3:342–43. Cohen, *God's Caress,* chap. 8, has the best

analysis of Winthrop's protracted search for assurance, but he misses the theological specificity of Winthrop's experience of the witness of the Spirit, as do other interpreters of Winthrop. See Morgan, *Visible*, 71–72; Daniel Shea, *Spiritual Autobiography in Early America* (Princeton, 1968), 101. Morgan and Cohen both read the period up to this climactic experience as a textbook example of preparation for justification (see chapter 13). But it is important to note that Winthrop never indicated that he perceived his struggles in this way. In fact, he claimed that the evidence of his sanctification—"my hunger after the word of God, and my love to the saints"—had been "as great (if not more)" before he had experienced the seal of the Spirit (*WP*, 3:343). He had been seeking confirmation that his earlier experiences of assurance had been genuine, which is not the same as starting from scratch.

55. *WP*, 3:344.

56. *God's Plot*, 42–43; Shepard, *Works*, 1: 276. On Robert Brearley and Grindletonianism, see D. B. Foss, "Grindletonianism," *Yorkshire Archeological Journal* 67 (1995): 147–54. Shepard might have been referring to Hendrik Niclaes, *Dicta H.N.* (N.p., 1574?), fol. 26r–v.

57. *God's Plot*, 157, 159, 101, 137–38, 170, 212, 161, 149.

58. Ibid., 84, 85, 93, 172, 181, 206, 199.

59. *WWP*, 50.

60. For the purposes of this book, "familist" refers to motifs taken from familism proper and from its anabaptist and medieval mystical sources, which is roughly the limits that contemporaries place on the term. See, for example, *PTV*, 2:92–94. For discussions of the soteriological underground, see Como, "Puritans," and Lake, *Boxmaker's Revenge*, chap. 7.

61. John Crandon, *Mr. Baxters Aphorisms Exorized and Anthorized* (London, 1654), sig. C2r–v; Como, "Puritans," 301.

62. Sibbes, *Works*, 5:452.

63. *WJ*, 664.

CHAPTER TWO

LIVELY STONES

1. Roger Clap, *Memoirs of Capt. Roger Clap* (Boston, 1731), 25.

2. John S. Coolidge, *The Pauline Renaissance in England: Puritanism and the Bible* (Oxford, 1970).

3. Giles Firmin, *Weighty Questions Discussed* (London, 1691), 22.

4. *GH*, 604; *MCA*, 1:302–21; Morton, *New-England's Memorial*, 188; Robert Keayne Sermon Notes, 1: May 4, 1627, and August 20, 1628; 2: Month 2, 20, 1645, MHS; Notes of Ipswich Preachers, February 12, 1646, MHS; Hutchinson, *History*, 1:222.

5. *WJ*, 98.

6. Unless otherwise indicated, biographical details are taken from Ziff, *Career*.

7. Norton, *Abel*, 33; Percentor Venables, "The Primary Visitation of the Diocese of Lincoln by Bishop Neile, A.D. 1614," *Associated Architectural Societies, Reports and Papers* 16 (1881): 50.

8. For discussions of Cotton's preaching style, see Edward H. Davidson, "John Cotton's Biblical Exegesis: Method and Purpose," *Early American Literature* 17 (1982): 119–37; Alfred Habegger, "Preparing the Soul for Christ: The Contrasting Sermon Forms of John Cotton and Thomas Hooker," *American Literature* 41 (1969): 342–54; Norman Grabo, "John Cotton's Aesthetic: A Sketch," *Early American Literature Newsletter* 3 (Spring 1968): 4–10; Teresa Toulouse, "'The Art of Prophesying': John Cotton and the Rhetoric of Election," *Early American Literature* 19 (1985): 279–99; Everett Emerson, *John Cotton, Revised Edition* (Boston, 1990), chap. 3; Jesper Rosenmeier, "'Clearing the Medium': A Reevaluation of the Puritan Plain Style in Light of John Cotton's *A Practicall Commentary upon the First Epistle Generall of John*," *William and Mary Quarterly*, 3d ser., 37 (1980): 577–91.

9. In these ways Cotton resembled Richard Sibbes, whom he greatly admired, thus if "Sibbesianism" is described in terms of affective choices, Knight, *Orthodoxies*, is justified in calling the English Cotton Sibbesian. But while Knight is good at showing how different divines could occupy considerably different affective spaces in the same universe of orthodoxy, her description of Sibbes is at best one-sided and often wrong. In critical ways, it resembles no one so much as Tobias Crisp, the notorious "antinomian" minister active around 1640. Knight acknowledges that in her interpretation of Sibbes she is at variance with most scholars, and she should be read as a supplement to rather than replacement for them. She asserts rather than demonstrates the existence of a large party of Sibbesians; the party, with the characteristics she assigns it, did not exist. In any case, as will be seen below, Cotton in Massachusetts was not a Sibbesian; he was a ministerial party of one (or two, counting Wheelwright).

10. Cotton, *Christ the Fountain of Life* (London, 1641), 72.

11. Baillie, *Dissuasive Vindicated*, 22–24. For a discussion of Cotton's deployment of the Holy Spirit in his last published English sermon cycle, and how Anne Hutchinson might have heard such preaching, see Michael G. Ditmore, "A Prophetess in Her Own Country: An Exegesis of Anne Hutchinson's 'Immediate Revelations'," *William and Mary Quarterly*, 3d ser., 57 (2000): 364–65.

12. Cotton's last surviving English sermon cycle, John Cotton, *A Practical Commentary, or an Exposition with Observations, Reasons, and Uses upon the First Epistle Generall of John* (London, 1658), from 1629 or later, was an extended discussion of how love of the brethren proved that one had been saved. The difference between these sermons and those Cotton gave in Massachusetts in the 1630s is so striking that Delbanco, *Puritan*, 120, 277n. 5, considers them to have been delivered early in Cotton's ministry, based on "my own sense of Cotton's stylistic and intellectual development." But Cotton, *Practical*, 154, refers to John Preston as deceased. Preston died in 1629.

13. *AC*, 33. The theology of Hutchinson and Wheelwright supports Cotton's claim. Scottow, *Narrative*, 301.

14. Cotton, *Cotton*, 215–16. Cotton, here explaining in the mid-1640s the origins of a treatise he wrote on reprobation (see below), traced it to "answers" clearing reprobation from Baron's objections, which a fellow minister wanted elaborated. In 1626, he gave a complementary explanation to James Ussher, saying

that the questions and answers at the beginning of his treatise came from a catechism written "long ago." See David Como, "Puritans, Predestination, and the Construction of Orthodoxy in Early Seventeenth-Century England," in *Conformity and Orthodoxy in the English Church, c. 1560–1660*, ed. Peter Lake and Michael Questier (Woodbridge, 2000), 75.

15. For a lucid exposition of the various conceptions of predestination then current in England, see Sean F. Hughes, "The Problem of 'Calvinism': English Theologies of Predestination c. 1580–1630," in *Belief and Practice in Reformation England: A Tribute to Patrick Collinson from his Students*, ed. Susan Wabuda and Caroline Litzenberger (Aldershot, 1998), 229–49.

16. For a recent discussion and bibliography of the extensive scholarly literature on covenant theology, see John Coffey, *Politics, Theology and the British Revolutions: The Mind of Samuel Rutherford* (Cambridge, 1997), 117–22.

17. Cotton, 216.

18. Venables "Primary Visitation," 50; William Twisse, *A Treatise of Mr Cottons, Clearing Certaine Doubts Concerning Predestination* (London, 1646), 45–46.

19. For a detailed analysis of Cotton's treatise, his exchange with Twisse, and their contexts, see Como, "Puritans, Predestination," 64–87. For the troubles of other godly ministers, see Como, "Puritans," 68–74; Michael P. Winship, "Contesting Control of Orthodoxy among the Godly: William Pynchon Reconsidered," *William and Mary Quarterly*, 3d ser., 54 (1997): 801–2; Lake, Boxmaker's Revenge, chap. 8.

20. Twisse, *Treatise*, 82; Cotton, *Treatise*, 29–34.

21. *JC*, 273.

22. Ibid. Wheelwright cited the same passage from Zanchius in *Brief*, 21, and referred to Zanchius elsewhere in the book, 3, 19. Zanchius's position is explained in Robert W. A. Letham, "Saving Faith and Assurance in Reformed Theology: Zwingli to the Synod of Dort" (Ph.D. diss., University of Aberdeen, 1979), 1:210–12. Zanchius was the only theologian Cotton referred to in his reply to Robert Baillie in the 1640s when defending his belief that the Holy Spirit dwelt in believers. See Cotton, *Cotton*, 222.

23. Michael P. Winship, " 'The Most Glorious Church in the World': The Unity of the Godly in Boston, Massachusetts in the 1630s," *Journal of British Studies* 39 (2000): 82; Thomas Gataker, *An Answer to Mr. George Walker* (London, 1642), 34; Edward Norris, *The New Gospel Not the True Gospel* (London, 1638), 19; Robert Towne, *A Reassertion of Grace* (London, 1654), sig. A2r; Shepard, *Works*, 1:317–23. The Bible was capable of very different readings on this issue. See Michael McGiffert, "The Problem of the Covenant in Puritan Thought: Peter Bulkeley's *Gospel-Covenant*," *NEHGR* 130 (1976): 115.

24. Twisse, *Treatise*, 63.

25. There are enough similarities between Cotton's arguments about faith and union with Christ and those in William Pemble, *Vindiciae Gratiae* (London, 1629), 10–15, to suggest that Pemble might have influenced Cotton. Robert Lord Brooke, *The Nature of Truth* (London, 1641), 152–53, drew his conception of faith from Cotton, probably through his friend Henry Vane, and he cited Pemble

to justify this interpretation of faith. Cotton later also cited Daniel Chamier and William Twisse, along with Pemble, in support of his claim about faith's passivity (*AC*, 401). For Cotton's earlier insistence on the active "work" faith had to do before and during justification see John Cotton, *The Way of Life* (London, 1641), 308–11. Knight, *Orthodoxies*, 112, asserts that Sibbes, like Cotton, treated faith as a consequence of justification, giving no citation. But see Sibbes, *Works*, 1:222, where Sibbes describes faith as active in the application of justification.

26. Cotton never gave a succint definition of what he meant by a conditional promise applied absolutely. But he seems to have envisioned someone hearing, say, that Christ died for sinners and finding assurance in the very hearing of the promise. Believers would then apply the promise to themselves on the basis of their assurance. See *WP*, 3:351.

27. *AC*, 94, 189.

28. John Foxe, *Actes and Monuments* (London, 1837), 4:635.

29. Paul Baynes, *A Commentarie upon the First Chapter of the Epistle of Saint Paul, Written to the Ephesians* (London, 1618), 325, 329; Sibbes, *Works*, 1:95, 5:444; Samuel Rutherford, *A Survey of the Spirituall Antichrist* (London, 1648), 40–41.

30. Fiske, *Notebook*, 146. Olive Farwell is an obscure figure, but her husband, Henry, was made a freeman in 1639. See James Savage, *A Genealogical Dictionary of the First Settlers of New England* (Boston, 1860–62), 2:147.

31. *AC*, 24–25.

32. Ibid., 26, 29.

33. Ibid., 32, 33. Bracketed text words "as" and "of grace" from *JC*, 233.

34. For brief synopses, see *AC*, 80, 183, 115, and Cotton, *Cotton*, 63–65. For a full-length exposition, see Cotton, *Treatise*, 124–217. One hesitates to make sweeping generalizations about seventeenth-century Reformed theology, given how vast it was and how little explored by scholars it still is, but I believe that this is where Cotton was most original, and part of my reason for believing that is because this is where his fellow ministers seemed most often to have no idea what he was talking about.

35. Cotton, *Treatise*, 163, 191, 204–5.

36. Miller, *Colony*, 56; Delbanco, *Puritan*, 123, Knight, *Orthodoxies*, 116–7, 153; Lang, *Prophetic*, 7; Pettit, *Heart*, 139; Gura, *Glimpse*, 169, 239; Jesper Rosenmeier, "New England's Perfection: The Image of Adam and the Image of Christ in the Antinomian Crisis, 1634 to 1638," *William and Mary Quarterly*, 3d ser., 27 (1970): 450; R. T. Kendall, *Calvin and English Calvinism to 1649* (Oxford, 1979), 182–83. But see Michael Schuldiner, *Gifts and Works: The Post-Conversion Paradigm and Spiritual Controversy in Seventeenth-Century Massachusetts* (Macon, GA, 1991), 72–80.

37. Cotton, *Treatise*, 107. Cotton, *AC*, 96, distinguished between the "first assurance" that "grace and mercy is wholly and absolutely laid up in Christ," at which time believers might receive Christ "in truth (although not in sense)" and the "first assurance of Comfort." Henry Vane made the same distinction which suggests that it was widely accepted in the Boston congregation. See Vane, *Retired*, 213, 224.

38. *AC*, 57; Cotton, *Cotton*, 63.

39. Cotton, *Treatise*, 126–27, 82–85; Theodore Dwight Bozeman, *To Live Ancient Lives: The Primitivist Dimension in Puritanism* (Chapel Hill, 1988), 250; Stoever, *Faire*, 177.

40. Webster, *Godly*, 157–58.

41. Patrick Collinson, *The Elizabethan Puritan Movement* (1967; reprint, Oxford, 1990), 433; Francis Marbury, *A Fruitful Sermon Necessary for the Time* (London, 1602); Selma R. Williams, *Divine Rebel: The Life of Anne Marbury Hutchinson* (New York, 1981), 12–23.

42. J. T. Cliffe, *The Puritan Gentry: The Great Puritan Families of Early Stuart England* (London, 1984), 179.

43. Jonathan Barry, "Literacy and Literature in Popular Culture: Reading and Writing in Historical Perspective," in *Popular Culture in England, c. 1500–1850*, ed. Tim Harris (New York, 1995), 76–77. One would expect from Hutchinson's background that she could write, but there is more positive evidence—a transcript of a part of a letter that, although misdated, has Hutchinson's distinctive theological voice and references to her writing and delivering a signed retraction and disowning authorship of a manuscript—see *AC*, 305, 379; *WJ*, 249–50; S. G., *Glass*, 9. *Glass* is conventionally attributed to Samuel Groome, but Leon Howard, "The New England Glass: Some New Reflections Seen in an Old Mirror," *Journal of Unconventional History* 7 (1996): 8–28, argues that Samuel Gorton is the probable author. A letter from Hutchinson's sister, Katherine Scott, to John Winthrop, Jr., survives; presumably the sisters were given a similar education. See MHS *Collections*, 5th ser., 1 (1871): 96–97. The letter itself, in the Winthrop Papers, MHS, is written in an adequate but not particularly fluent hand.

44. Kenneth Charlton, *Women, Religion and Education in Early Modern England* (London, 1999), 103 passim.

45. Samuel Hutchinson, *A Declaration of a Future Glorious Estate of a Church to Be Here upon Earth, at Christs Personal Appearance for the Restitution of All Things, a Thousand Years before the Ultimate Day of the General Judgement* (London, 1667). Edward Hutchinson, *A Treatise Concerning the Covenant and Baptism* (London, 1676). I am assuming, for the lack of evidence to the contrary, that Edward Hutchinson, who, after a period in Massachusetts, returned to Alford and became a governor of its grammar school is identical with this author. While the author's soteriology is generally conservative, compare Hutchinson, *Treatise*, 94, with *AC*, 264. Reginald G. Pudding, *History of the Parish and Manors of Alford with Rigsby and Ailby with Some Account of Well in the County of Lincoln* (Horncastle, 1930), 149. *WWP*, 143.

46. Robert Brenner, *Merchants and Revolutionaries: Commercial Change, Political Conflict, and London's Overseas Traders, 1550–1653* (Princeton, 1993), 365; Keith Lindley, *Popular Politics and Religion in Civil War London* (Aldershot, 1997), 145. Richard is sometimes confused with Anne's son of the same name, who did come to New England.

47. Battis, *SS*, 36, claims that Cotton noted that she attended his services occasionally in Lincolnshire, but the source he gives makes no mention of this. Other historians sometimes repeat Battis's claim.

48. The best account of Hutchinson as a religious figure remains James Fulton Maclear, "'The Heart of New England Rent': The Mystical Element in Early Puritan History," *Mississippi Valley Historical Review* 42 (1956): 641–43.

49. *AC*, 337. I assign Hutchinson's experiences to the early 1630s because they are framed by Cotton's new theology and because the state of the Church of England at the time would invite a fast like hers. The Court never actually got around to proceeding on the heresy charge since Hutchinson had already provided ample grounds for a conviction by that time (see chapter 9). What I am reading as an account of finding assurance has not been recognized by historians for, I think, two reasons. The first is that Winthrop badly and misleadingly garbled it in his paraphrase in *Short Story*, *AC*, 271–72. Hutchinson, in her trial transcript, was clear that this event preceded a fast she had over the state of the Church of England, even though she discussed it after discussing the fast. After explaining how she found assurance she said, "Being thus, he did show me this (a twelvemonth after) which I told you of before [referring to the fast]" (*AC*, 337). But Winthrop, when providing his rough and tendentious paraphrase, put the fast first chronologically, and historians tend to follow him. The second reason is that in the fuller transcript a critical concept is clothed in mildly recondite scriptural terminology (see n.52 below).

50. The transcript gives only the Scripture reference. Winthrop in *Short Story* quoted only the above lines. See *AC*, 272. Ditmore, "Anne Hutchinson's," 377 n.50, sees this citation as probably simply referring to New England's destruction. He is reluctant to connect it with what Hutchinson immediately afterward said in the trial transcript about turning to a covenant of works (see n.52), claiming that there is not a clear logical transition. While the verse from Jeremiah clearly carried the meaning for Hutchinson that Ditmore reads in it (see 243 above), deliverance from captivity was also commonly used as a conversion metaphor, and the sequence of conversion and subsequent turning aside to a covenant of works that Hutchinson by my reading proceeded to outline was a lively one in the Boston congregation. Ditmore suggests that an editorial dash in the middle of this passage means that an inderminate but potentially large amount of material was omitted at that point, but single editorial dashes in themselves elsewhere in the trial transcript do not seem to indicate a break in continuity of meaning, and there is no reason to think that this passage is the only exception.

51. *AC*, 338. See chapter 12 for a later use of the verse.

52. *AC*, 337. She told the Court, "After he was pleased to reveal himself to me I did presently like Abraham run to Hagar." The reference, derived from Galatians 24: 22–31, would have been instantly recognizable to a seventeenth-century audience. In *Short Story*, the official Massachusetts version of the crisis, written by John Winthrop and Thomas Weld, Winthrop straightforwardly substitutes "covenant of works" for "run to Hagar" (*AC*, 272). For Cotton's comments on the dangers of converts running to Hagar, see *AC*, 55–56.

53. The nearest documented separatists lived a little over ten miles away from her home in England. See Helena Hajzyk, "The Church in Lincolnshire c. 1595–c.1640" (Ph.D. diss., Cambridge University: 1980), 374. For an example of another future New England woman fasting for the same reason, see Fiske, *Notebook*, 43.

54. Thomas Taylor, *Christs Victory over the Dragon* (London, 1633), 706–8. Bryan W. Ball, *A Great Expectation: Eschatological Thought in English Protestantism to 1660* (Leiden, 1975), 141–46; Paul Christianson, *Reformers in Babylon: English Apocalyptic Visions from the Reformation to the Eve of the Civil War* (Toronto, 1978), passim; Christopher Hill, *Antichrist in Seventeenth-Century England* (London, 1971); Peter Lake, "William Bradshaw, Antichrist, and the Community of the Godly," *Journal of Ecclesiastical History* 36 (1985): 570–89.

55. For a close analysis of this passage, see Ditmore, "Anne Hutchinson's," 365–71.

56. John Bunyan's classic autobiography, *Grace Abounding to the Chief of Sinners* (London, 1666), has many examples of this visceral experience of Scripture texts.

57. *AC*, 336–37. After unsatisfactory efforts to learn who Antichrist was, Hutchinson told the Court, "the Lord was pleased to bring this scripture out of the Hebrews. He that denies the testament denies the testator." In this critical passage, Hutchinson fused 1 John 4:3 with the King James Hebrews 9:16, 17, which uses the word "testatour." Hutchinson used at least one other King James citation, Isaiah 30:20, at her trial. See Ditmore, "Anne Hutchinson's," 391n. 10. See also Henry Vane's use of 1 John 4:1, 2, 3 in *HC*, 1:95, discussed in chapter 5, note 18. In John Cotton's sermons on 1 John, *Practical Commentary*, 285, he warned the laity to be on guard against false teachers, referring to papists, Arminians, separatists, an antinomians. Harry Stout, "Word and Order in Colonial New England," in *The Bible in America: Essays in Cultural History*, ed. Mark A. Noll (New York, 1982), 32, argues that Hutchinson used the Geneva Bible exclusively at her trial, as did John Wheelwright in his fast-day sermon, whereas their opponents favored the King James version. Stout draws large conclusions from this alleged scriptural apartheid. He is wrong, however, about Wheelwright as well as Hutchinson. The text for Wheelwright's fast-day sermon, Matthew 9:15, comes from the King James version. Stout does not discuss Cotton, who, while making his own translations, leaned toward the King James version. See Larzer Ziff, in Cotton, *Cotton*, 44 n. 3. Ministers in general freely drew on both translations or made their own. See Elizabeth Dale, "Debating—and Creating—Authority: A Legal History of the Trial of Anne Hutchinson, November, 1637" (Ph.D. diss., University of Chicago, 1995), 203–6.

58. John Calvin, *Institutes of the Christian Religion*, ed. John T. McNeil, trans. Fred Lewis Battles (Philadelphia, 1960), book 2, chap. 9, sec. 5. Cf. Cotton, *Way of Life*, 99–100. Stoever, *Faire*, 167, suggests a sectarian source for Hutchinson, but this does not seem necessary to posit. See also Como, "Puritans," 206.

59. *AC*, 337, 339.

60. Cf. Ditmore, "Anne Hutchinson's," 354–55.

61. Charles Edwards Banks, *The Planters of the Commonwealth* (Baltimore, 1967), 113; *PTV*, 1: 111.

62. *BCR*, 16–18; *WJ*, 106; Rutman, *Winthrop's Boston*, 37.

63. *AC*, 382, 322.

64. *AC*, 323, 325; *BCR*, 19.

65. William Wardwell, Alford's tavern keeper, Gamaliel Wait, and perhaps already his brothers, Richard and Thomas, and Anne Hutchinson's brother-in-law

Edward and his wife Sarah, along with Anne's son Edward preceded her to Boston, as did her Alford neighbors Philemon and Susan Pormort. A few at least probably arrived before Cotton. *BCR*, 17, 18. Robert Charles Anderson, *The Great Migration Begins: Immigrants to New England, 1620–1633* (Boston, 1995), 3:1922. Victor Channing Sanborn, "The Lincolnshire Origin of Some Exeter Settlers," *NEHGR* 68 (1914): 64–80; Roger Thompson, *Mobility and Migration: East Anglian Foundations of New England, 1629–1640* (Amherst, MA, 1994), 197.

66. Alice Morse Earl, *Margaret Winthrop* (New York, 1895), 173; Rutman, *Winthrop's Boston*, 74; *BCR*, 10; *MR*, 1:145, 175; Bernard Bailyn, *The New England Merchants in the Seventeenth Century* (1955; reprint, New York, 1964), 35, 40–41.

67. *AC*, 308. On the dynamics of women's childbirth communities, see Norton, *Founding*, 222–39.

68. For the dynamics of lay puritan piety, see Paul S. Seaver, *Wallington's World: A Puritan Artisan in Seventeenth-Century London* (Palo Alto, 1985); and Diane Willen, "'Communion of the Saints': Spiritual Reciprocity and the Godly Community in Early Modern England," *Albion* 27 (1995): 19–41. On conventicles' legal and cultural place in English society, see Patrick Collinson, "The English Conventicle," *Studies in Church History* 23 (1986): 223–59.

69. *WP*, 1:297; *MCA*, 1:418–19; Foster, "New England," 629.

70. *AC*, 412, 309.

71. Ibid., *AC*, 412, 268, 308, 309, 413.

72. Sara Mendelson and Patricia Crawford, *Women in Early Modern England, 1550–1720* (Oxford, 1998). There is still a tendency among some historians to conflate prescription with practice and portray pre–Civil War puritan women as confining their piety to household and domestic ends. See Phyllis Mack, *Visionary Women: Ecstatic Prophecy in Seventeenth-Century England* (Berkeley, 1992): 105–8; Patricia Crawford, *Women and Religion in England, 1500–1720* (London, 1993), chap. 4; Jacqueline Eales, "Samuel Clarke and the 'Lives' of Godly Women in Seventeenth-Century England," *Studies in Church History* 27 (1990): 365–76. For an effort to read a standard male source against its grain, see Peter Lake, "Feminine Piety and Personal Potency: The Emancipation of Mrs. Jane Ratcliffe," *The Seventeenth Century* 2 (1987): 143–65. See also Thomas Freeman, "'The Good Ministrye of Godlye and Vertuouse Women': The Elizabethan Martyrologists and the Female Supporters of the Marian Martyrs," *Journal of British Studies* 39 (2000): 8–33. For a broader perspective on the opportunities provided for women by puritan piety, see Diane Willen, "Godly Women in Early Modern England: Puritanism and Gender," *Journal of Ecclesiastical History* 43 (1992): 561–80.

73. Michael P. Winship, "Briget Cooke and the Art of Godly Female Self-Advancement," *Sixteenth-Century Journal* (forthcoming); Lake, "Feminine Piety," 143–65; Willen, "Godly Women," 561–80; David R. Como, "Women, Prophecy, and Authority in Early Stuart Puritanism," *Huntington Library Quarterly* 61 (2000): 203–22; Thomas Clendon, *Justification Justified* (London, 1653), "To the Reader"; Samuel Ainsworth, *A Sermon Preached at the Funerall of That Religious Gentle-woman Mrs Dorothy Hanbury, Wife to Edward Hanbury Esq. Living at Kelmarch in Northampton-shire* (London, 1645).

74. For a general discussion of women and puritanism in New England, see Marilyn J. Westerkamp, *Women and Religion in Early America, 1600–1850: The Puritan and Evangelical Traditions* (New York, 1999), chap. 2.

75. *AC*, 412. Winthrop should not be taken at face value when he claimed that Hutchinson "had more resort to her for counsell about matter of conscience, and clearing up mens spirituall estates, then any Minister (I might say all the Elders) in the Country" (*AC*, 308). That claim came in an account he wrote after Hutchinson's excommunication, when he was at pains to magnify the gulf between the height of her acceptance and her subsequent fall. If it were true, it would be hard to understand why Boston had so little support outside its immediate environs once controversy broke out.

76. *AC*, 263, 381. But magistrate and sometimes governor Thomas Dudley three years later said that Hutchinson started making parties within six months of her arrival (*AC*, 318). Dudley, however, did not like her from the beginning, was not a Boston resident, and was haranguing her impromptu at her trial to get some mileage out of a charge that was otherwise about to collapse.

CHAPTER THREE
THE MOST GLORIOUS CHURCH IN THE WORLD

1. *BCR*, 21.

2. The best account of Wheelwright's life is Charles H. Bell, "Memoir of the Reverend John Wheelwright," in *John Wheelwright*, ed., Charles H. Bell, Prince Society Publications no. 9 (Boston, 1876): 1–78. See also Edmund M. Wheelwright, "A Frontier Family," *Colonial Society of Massachusetts Publications* 1 (1895): 271–303.

3. Samuel A. Green, "Rev. John Wheelwright," *MHS Proceedings*, 2d ser., 8 (1894): 505–17.

4. The analogy would be with William Leverich, founding minister of Sandwich in 1636, for whom see *Extracts from the Itineraries and Other Miscellanies of Ezra Stiles, D.D., LL.D. 1755–1794 with a Selection from His Correspondence*, ed. Franklin Bowditch Dexter (New Haven, 1916), 161. *MCA*, 1:243; R. A. Lovell, Jr., *Sandwich: A Cape Cod Town* (Sandwich, 1984), 36; *MHS Collections*, 3d ser., 4 (1834):180.

5. George Bishop, *New-England Judged, by the Spirit of the Lord* (London, 1703), 368.

6. Hanserd Knollys, The Life and Death of that Old Disciple of *Jesus Christ* and Eminent Minister of the Gospel, Mr. Hanserd Knollys, Who Dyed in the Ninety Third Year of His Age (London, 1692), 9.

7. Ibid., 11, 12.

8. Ibid., 13–14.

9. Ibid., 15.

10. William Perkins, *The Workes* (London, 1613–18), 1:203; Richard Greenham, *The Workes* (London, 1605): 10. See also *WP*, 1:166–67; John Rogers, *Obel or Beth-shemesh* (London, 1653), 397; Thomas Shepard, *A Trial of Regeneration* (N.p., 1641), 9. *PTV*, 2:92–93; Como, "Puritans," 341–45.

11. *MR*, 3:344.

12. Jonathan Mitchel Sermons, MHS, Boston, (second sermon in manuscript).

13. Ibid.

14. Ibid.

15. *GH*, 350; Wheelwright, *Brief,* 28. Wheelwright says that this sermon was preached at the Court of Election, but it is hard to picture Wheelwright being asked to give an election-day sermon by magistrates who drove him out of Massachusetts in the not too distant past and who were about to heavily qualify the endorsement of his orthodoxy that he had requested of them. Yet it is hard to see how a printer's error could have produced this phrase.

16. Wheelwright, *Brief,* "To the Christian Reader."

17. For Vane and his career, see James K. Hosmer, *The Life of Young Sir Henry Vane* (Boston, 1889); Violet A. Rowe, *Sir Henry Vane the Younger: A Study in Political and Administrative History* (London, 1970); T. B. Howell, *A Complete Collection of State Trials* (London, 1809–26), 6:194; George Sikes, *The Life and Death of Sir Henry Vane, Kt.* (N.p., 1662), 8.

18. Hutchinson, *History,* 1:57.

19. Will of John Cotton, *NEHGR* 5 (1851):240; Karen Ordahl Kupperman, *Providence Island, 1630–1641: The Other Puritan Colony* (New York, 1993), 325–28; Hutchinson, *History,* 1:58, 65; Edward Hyde Clarendon, *The History of the Rebellion and Civil Wars in England* (Oxford, 1843), 75; *BCR,* 19; *WJ,* 219; *Second Report of the Record Commissioners of the City of Boston; Containing the Boston Records, 1634–1660, and the Book of Possessions* (Boston, 1881), 5; *WJ,* 165–68; *WP,* 3:276; *WWP,* 102.

20. Baillie, *Dissuasive,* 57, was the first to identify in print Winthrop as the author of the narrative sections in *Short Story.* Samuel Rutherford, *A Survey of the Spirituall Antichrist* (London, 1648), 171, repeated the attribution. I know of no scholar who questions it. *WP,* 4:183; Cotton Mather's limited abilities as a synthetic historian broke down completely when dealing with the free grace controversy in the *Magnalia Christi Americana.* He never discussed Vane in the context of the controversy, only when he was discussing Massachusetts governors, and there all he did was quote two starkly contrasting opinions about Vane and retreat into a flurry of word play. See *MCA,* 1:136–37. His preferred explanation of the free grace controversy throughout the *Magnalia* was that it was caused by a small group of heretics centering on Hutchinson. Elsewhere, however, he recognized the importance of the ministerial dividing line that most people at the time acknowledged: the issue of whether sanctification was a first evidence of justification. This acknowledgment was especially awkward for his filiopietism, since he was Cotton's grandchild and drawn himself to the immediate witness of the Spirit. See *MCA,* 1:431–32, 2:508.

21. *AC,* 264; Vane, *Retired,* 97; *GH,* 298; Firmin, *[Panourgia],* "To the Reader"; Shepard, *God's Plot,* 65; *WP,* 3:415.

22. David Como and Peter Lake, "Puritans, Antinomians, and Laudians in Caroline London: The Strange Case of Peter Shaw and Its Contexts," *Journal of Ecclesiastical History* 50 (1999): 685, 686, 707; John Traske, *The True Gospel Vindicated from the Reproach of a New Gospel* (N.p., 1636), 23; Edward Norris, *The New Gospel Not the True Gospel* (London, 1638), 2, 18, 25, 29. For the probable familist influences on Traske, see Como, "Puritans," 151–58.

23. Gerard Croese, *The General History of the Quakers* (London, 1696), 148; *AC*, 280, 281; William Allan Dyer, "William Dyer," *Rhode Island Historical Society Collections* 30 (1937): 25; Como and Lake, "Puritans, Antinomians," 685. Gura, *Glimpse*, 36, 60, 239–40, draws attention to the parallels between the Boston radicals and Traske and emphasizes that Hutchinson was probably not the only source of radical opinions in Massachusetts. Thomas Weld, Edward Johnson, and *Mercurius Americanus* all speak of persons (in the plural) bringing erroneous doctrines with them from England. *AC*, 201; *WWP*, 124; *MA* 190. Robert Towne, the radical minister most likely because of his proximity to have had any influence on Lincolnshire puritans, denied in *Monomachia* (London, 1654), 32, knowing anything about the New England dissidents or their ideas beyond what he read in *Short Story*. But see 276 n.18.

24. *AC*, 219, 220, 223, 225, 382. Scholars not infrequently claim that there is no way of knowing what Hutchinson really taught, but as will be shown in later chapters, there are numerous well-documented sources for her teaching, all consistent with each other. Hutchinson herself acknowledged holding the errors of which she was accused at her church trial, and the Boston church, in a much better position to know than modern scholars, excommunicated her for denying that she held her chief tenet, the absence of created graces in believers. *Mercurius Americanus*, another Boston insider source, states that Hutchinson held most of the errors condemned at the Synod of 1637 (197). Where we have to guess is the timing of the development of her theology and the extent to which she developed it on her own or in give and take with others in the Boston congregation. But there are hints on these issues as well.

25. Porterfield, *Female*, 98.

26. *AC*, 264; Pettit, *Heart*, 142; Cooper, *Tenacious*, 51; Staloff, *Making*, 43; Battis, *SS*, 258; Marilyn J. Westerkamp, "Anne Hutchinson, Sectarian Mysticism, and the Puritan Order," *Church History* 59 (1990): 486; Morgan, *Puritan*, 140–41. But see Foster, "New England." Historians who focus on Cotton tend to ignore the issue of lay radicalism. Knight, *Orthodoxies*, even turns the standard story on its head by arguing that "Cotton's party was not at all unorthodox," and that Henry Vane himself did not maintain a "sectarian variation of what we call 'orthodoxy' . . . but a vibrant alternative within the mainstream of Puritan religious culture" (22, 3). It would take formidable muscle power to squeeze what we know of Vane into any mainstream framework of orthodoxy, even Cotton's, and, apart from asserting that it could be done, Knight does not make the attempt. Historians following Battis, *SS*, use a petition supporting Wheelwright to demonstrate a large group of Hutchinsonians, but support for Wheelwright does not automatically demonstrate "Hutchinsonianism." For the petition and its context, see chapter 7.

27. *AC*, 264, 216, 276.

28. *GH*, 281; *AC*, 264, 419, 433. Much of Hubbard's *History* for this period consists of long verbatim passages from Winthrop's *Journal*, thus the rare occasions when he takes the trouble to modify Winthrop are especially important. Winthrop wrote, "All the congregation of Boston, except four or five, closed with these opinions, or the most of them." Hubbard inserted the qualifying clause "in a manner" after "Boston." *WJ*, 207; *GH*, 293.

29. Firmin, [Panourgia], "To the Reader"; MA, 199, 192. On Hutchinson's relatives, see 240–41 above. I incline toward the son's authorship because that is the name on the title page and because the wittiness of the style is out of keeping with Wheelwright's other works. For a discussion of the authorship, see Sargent Bush, Jr., "John Wheelwright's Forgotten Apology: The Last Word in the Antinomian Controversy," New England Quarterly 64 (1991): 42–44.

30. Both Shepard, PTV, 1:81, and Johnson, WWP, 126, recorded "opinionists" saying that God sees no sin in his elect. That claim was a rallying cry of John Eaton, most prominent of the English "antinomians," and his followers. It did not flow naturally out of Cottonianism because it stemmed from theological emphases that were not at all central to either Cotton or to Hutchinson's divinity. God saw no sin in his elect, the argument went, because that sin was cloaked with Christ's imputed righteousness. See John Eaton, The Honey-Combe of Free Justification (London, 1642), 362–65; Tobias Crisp, Christ Alone Exalted (London, 1690), 286–88, 405–6 passim. See also T. D. Bozeman, "The Glory of the 'Third Time': John Eaton as Contra-Puritan," Journal of Ecclesiastical History 47 (1996): 638–54. The emphasis of some in the Boston congregation that assurance was always full and without doubt was characteristic of some English radicals but it was not Cotton's doctrine, nor was the claim that the moral law was abrogated for believers, a doctrine that Hutchinson herself seems to have been slow to pick up on. What is odd about the free grace controversy is not that snippets of Eatonism should have shown up, but that so few did. The insults that the Eatonites hurled against their ministerial opponents, "dead faith," "anabaptist," and "justiciaries," were not recorded in Massachusetts, while, except for one reference to Robert Towne (AC, 32), I have found no other Massachusetts allusions to Eaton or the stormy controversies with puritan ministers he and his allies were involved in. At least as regards the opponents of Boston, this might be explained in terms of the heavy polemical focus on familism, which was much less pronounced in the London controversy.

31. Vane, Retired, 351; Baillie, Dissuasive, 64.

32. Thomas Hutchinson, "Hutchinson in America," Egerton MS 2664, p. 13, British Library, gives credit to Vane directly. Winthrop in Short Story, AC, 264, states that Hutchinson set up her conventicles after she had the support of "some of eminent place and parts"—Vane is not mentioned openly in Short Story. AC, 264. The Synod of 1637 gives the attendance figure as sixty or more (WJ, 234). The figure of 600 adults is extrapolated from the roughly 360 men resident in Boston in 1637. See Battis, SS, 330–44. Rutman, Winthrop's Boston, 179, estimates the total 1637 Boston population as 1,000. AC, 215, 413, 286, 207–8.

33. AC, 413.

34. MA, 198; JC, 280n. 15; AC, 314.

35. AC, 434, 399. Staloff, Making, 42, states that Cotton failed to crack down on the deviants in his congregation because he intended them to "delegitimize all or most of the other members of the thinking class while confirming Cotton's supreme charismatic authority." He "attempted to use the Antinomians in the same fashion that Mao Tse-tung used the Red Guards in his struggle for absolute preeminence against the other members of the inner party elite." The only evidence that Staloff offers for this argument is a quotation from Norman Pettit stat-

ing that up until the Synod of 1637 Cotton believed the "Bostonians"' cause to be his own, which seems like a slender reed to bear such a weighty assertion.

36. *AC*, 413.

37. *MCA*, 1:276; Hall, *Faithful Shepherd*, 102–3, 148; Baillie, *Dissuasive Vindicated*, 29; *AC*, 207; Firmin, [*Panourgia*], "To the Reader"; *AC*, 381, 420.

38. Como, "Puritans," "Prologue."

39. See Lyle Koehler, "The Case of the American Jezebels: Anne Hutchinson and Female Agitation during the Years of Antinomian Turmoil," *William and Mary Quarterly*, 3d ser., 31 (1974): 55–78, for the starkest presentation of this perspective.

40. William Pynchon, *The Meritorious Price of Our Redemption* (London, 1650), sig. A2r.

41. *AC*, 420; Scottow, *Narrative*, 301. It was standard in this period to define heresy as maintaining an erroneous opinion for an article of faith. See Anthony Milton, *Catholic and Reformed: The Roman and Protestant Churches in English Protestant Thought, 1600–1640* (Cambridge, 1995), 164n. 52. That definition allowed for flexibility in practice; errors could be tolerated as long as they did not impinge upon articles of faith, which were variously defined. Two fragmentary bits of evidence suggest that radicals were calculated in their expressions. Winthrop, writing in the winter of 1637–38, cited radicals telling inquirers that they would learn more of their doctrines later on, and said that one of the radicals "reproved the rest, telling them that they had spoyled their cause, by being over hasty and too open" (*AC*, 278). Cotton later cited a letter, probably by Vane, to a leading "opinionist," advising the person, Cotton claimed, to hold forth in public, or before witnesses, "noe more than [Cotton] might goe along with" (*JC*, 303). Without a date and more details, and with only unfriendly interpreters speaking of it, it is difficult to do too much with the letter. I do think that Hutchinson and perhaps others were playing a delicate game with themselves and others, and I think that the opponents of the radicals, who eventually included Cotton and Wheelwright, were tempted to retrospectively read their heterodoxy as more long settled than it was.

42. *AC*, 232, 319; Cotton, *Treatise*, 74, 112, 199; Patrick Collinson, "The English Conventicle," *Studies in Church History* 23 (1986): 241.

43. *AC*, 205. Technically this was orthopraxy, not orthodoxy.

44. John Crook, *A Short History of the Life of John Crook* (London, 1706), 9; Laurence Clarkson, *The Lost Sheep Found* (London, 1660), 5–6; Robert J. Naeher, "Prayerful Voice: Self-Shaping, Intimacy, and the Puritan Practice and Experience of Prayer" (Ph.D. diss., University of Connecticut, 1999). Extemporaneous prayer was a powerful advertising tool for sect-masters and would-be prophets looking for followers among the godly. See Alexandra Walsham, "'Frantick Hacket': Prophecy, Sorcery, Insanity, and the Elizabethan Puritan Movement," *Historical Journal* 41 (1998): 37; Como, "Puritans," 126.

45. *JC*, 309; *AC*, 363.

46. *AC*, 209.

47. Scottow, *Narrative*, 301; *WJ*, 106; *GH*, 280. See also Rutman, *Winthrop's Boston*, 110–11.

48. Not all the sources cited below refer to the Millennium, and it is possible that not all of the persons cited below held that the glorious church would last a thousand years. What is important is not the precise duration of the church but the evidence for the expectation circulating within the Boston church that they were preparing the way for this church.

49. Perry Miller, *Errand into the Wilderness* (New York, 1956); Theodore Dwight Bozeman, *To Live Ancient Lives: The Primitivist Dimension in Puritanism* (Chapel Hill, 1988), chap. 3; Michael P. Winship, "Contesting Control of Orthodoxy among the Godly: William Pynchon Reconsidered," *William and Mary Quarterly*, 3d ser., 54 (1997): 804–5.

50. J. T. Cliffe, *The Puritan Gentry: The Great Puritan Families of Early Stuart England* (London, 1984), 210–11; Shepard, *Works*, 1:40; John Cotton, *A Brief Exposition of the Whole Book of Canticles* (London, 1642), 193–98, chap. 7, 239–40, 257–58. Robert Sanderson, *XXXIV Sermons* (London, 1689), 18.

51. Shepard, *PTV*, 1:9, 10; *AC*, 155, 165, 166. Bozeman, *To Live Ancient Lives*, 229, claims that millenarianism was not influential in New England until 1639. He points out that Shepard drew on a number of themes about the Last Days besides millenarianism in *PTV*. But at a minimum, Shepard's statements demonstrate that in 1636 people in Massachusetts were associating their church order with millenarian themes and that Shepard did not dismiss their claims out of hand. Bozeman does not discuss Wheelwright's sermon. For other evidence for millenarian expectations in Boston in the mid-1630s, see J. F. Maclear, "New England and the Fifth Monarchy: The Quest for the Millennium in Early American Puritanism," *William and Mary Quarterly*, 3d ser., 32 (1975): 238–42. Bryan W. Ball, *A Great Expectation: Eschatological Thought in English Protestantism to 1660* (Leiden, 1975), 128; Henoch Clapham, *Antidoton or a Sovereign Remedy against Heresy and Schism* (London, 1600), 33; Keith Thomas, *Religion and the Decline of Magic: Studies in Popular Beliefs in Sixteenth- and Seventeenth-Century England* (London, 1971), 135; Walsham, " 'Frantick Hacket'," 46. *AC*, 308, 380; S. G., *Glass*, 9.

52. *JC*, 303.

53. *AC*, 420. Wilson left on a trip to England at the end of 1634 and returned at the same time as Vane and Shepard arrived.

54. Stephen Denison, *The White Wolf* (London, 1637), "To The Reader."

55. *GH*, 280; *AC*, 207, 381, 168; Firmin, *[Panourgia]*, "To the Reader."

56. "By 1636 the revival [brought on by Cotton's arrival] was over. . . . The collapse of the revival engendered a mood of acute religious anxiety" (*AC*, 14–15). Cf. Hall, *Faithful Shepherd*, 159. See also Gura, *Glimpse*, 246; David S. Lovejoy, *Religious Enthusiasm in the New World: Heresy to Revolution* (Cambridge, 1985), 66–67. Hall's argument had two bases. The first was that new church membership in Boston peaked in the months immediately after Cotton's arrival, the second that in June 1636, Cotton, presumably responding to this spiritual decline, preached a sermon at Salem in which, according to Hall, he bewailed a false sense of general security in the colony. See *A Sermon Preached by the Reverend, Mr. John Cotton* (Boston, 1713), 30–33. But new memberships had reached their low point in the first half of 1635 and had improved significantly in the months preceding his sermon. See *BCR*, 16–21. The sermon does reflect Cotton's concerns about

practicing puritan piety in Massachusetts (see chapter 4), but it is primarily a denunciation of the pharisaic censoriousness that led to separation and indicated that its practitioners were still under a covenant of works—an apt enough topic in a town where separatist tendencies were still strong half a year after Roger Williams had been banished. For a discussion of the anti-separatist thrust of this sermon, see Morgan, *Visible*, 102–3. In any case, there is no real indication that Cotton's arrival initiated a colony-wide revival, as Hall, *Faithful Shepherd*, 157, claims; his one piece of evidence, an account of what sounds like a revival in the early days of the colony, is not datable with any precision, but its heavy emphasis on conversation narratives would almost certainly not put it in the period shortly after Cotton's arrival. See Roger Clap, *Memoirs of Capt. Roger Clap* (Boston, 1731), 4–5. The only other church whose records from this period survive, Charlestown (and thus the only other means of assessing Hall's claim), had a roughly one-third drop in new members in the year after Cotton came. See "Records of the Charlestown Church," *NEHGR* 23 (1869): 191.

57. Scottow, *Narrative*, 307; *GH*, 280.

CHAPTER FOUR
PRACTICING PURITANISM IN A STRANGE LAND

1. *God's Plot*, 55; *AC*, 28–29.

2. Ibid., 27, 29.

3. Ibid., 26.

4. Ibid., 25

5. Ibid., 29, 31, 33, 32.

6. Cotton, *Cotton*, 63–65. This depiction of the process of assurance is from a sermon that is largely an attack on what Cotton deemed the "legal" righteousness of Salem's separatists, but the depiction itself is buttressed by a heavy and unqualified emphasis on the necessary observable holiness that both precedes and follows assurance. For the contrast with Cotton's later preaching, see 117–19 above.

7. William Ames, *The Marrow of Theology*, trans. and ed. John Eusden (Boston, 1968), 188. For a good discussion of puritan exegetical techniques and the ways in which divines negotiated scriptural contradictions, see Lisa Michelle Gordis, " 'Mighty in the Scriptures': Art and Unsettlement in Puritan Quotation" (Ph.D. diss., University of California, Los Angeles, 1993), 43–84. On the puritan conception of the church and the importance of orthodoxy to it, see Anthony Milton, *Catholic and Reformed: The Roman and Protestant Churches in English Protestant Thought, 1600–1640* (Cambridge, 1995), 129; Peter Lake, *Puritans and Anglicans? Presbyterianism and English Conformist Thought from Whitgift to Hooker* (London, 1988), 127 passim; and John Coolidge, *The Pauline Renaissance in England: Puritanism and the Bible* (Oxford, 1970), passim.

8. Edward Elton, *An Exposition of the Epistle of Saint Paul to the Colossians*, 2d ed. (London, 1620), 8–9; *AC*, 77; Arthur Hildersham, *Lectures upon the Fourth of John* (London, 1629), 289–90; John Norton, *A Discussion of that Great Point in Divinity, the Sufferings of Christ* (London, 1653), "Epistle Dedicatory."

9. Michael P. Winship, "'The Most Glorious Church in the World': The Unity of the Godly in Boston, Massachusetts in the 1630s," *Journal of British Studies* 39 (2000): 82; Como, "Puritans," 61.

10. Thomas Taylor, *Regula Vitae, The Rule of the Law under the Gospel* (London, 1631), 158; George Selement and Bruce C. Woolley, eds., *Thomas Shepard's Confessions, Colonial Society of Massachusetts Collections*, no. 58 (Boston, 1981): 131; Peter Lake and David Como, "'Orthodoxy' and Its Discontents: Dispute Settlement and the Production of 'Consensus' in the London (Puritan) Underground," *Journal of British Studies* 39 (2000): 65; Ronald A. Marchant, *The Puritans and the Church Courts in the Diocese of York, 1650–1642* (London, 1960), 5–8.

11. Norton, *A Discussion*; Norton, *The Heart of N-England Rent* (Cambridge, 1659); Norton, *Abel*, 35, 41–42.

12. *AC*, 425.

13. It may be relevant that Shepard portrayed his childhood as one of deprivation and frustrated love. See *God's Plot*, 37–39.

14. Cotton, *Cotton*, 60. Perry Miller laid out his argument in "Preparation," 253–86, and *Colony*, 59–67. "Preparation for Salvation" must be one of the most unconstructively influential articles written on American history, setting highly misleading parameters for scholars working over a half century later. What was truly unfortunate about Miller's article was that it represented a U-turn from his brief, brilliant, and far more accurate sketch of Hutchinson and her opponents' quarrel in *The New England Mind: The Seventeenth Century* (Cambridge, 1939), 390. Pettit, *Heart*, built on Miller's argument, but his thesis was disputed by Lynn Baird Tipson, Jr., "The Development of a Puritan Understanding of Conversion" (Ph.D. diss., Yale University, 1972), 327–30; Stoever, *Faire*, 192–99; and Cohen, *God's Caress*, 80n. 14, 84n. 25. See also David D. Hall's preface to Pettit, *Heart*. Thomas Hooker acknowledged that Cotton taught preparationism. Wheelwright went through a seven-year period of preparatory bondage before he received assurance. Henry Vane in the 1650s preached preparationism to his "Vanists" in the great hall of his Lincolnshire mansion. Thomas Hooker, *The Application of Redemption . . . the First Eight Books* (London, 1656), 29; Firmin, *Real Christian*, 7; Wheelwright, *Brief*, 27; Forster, MS 48.D.41, p. 63, Victoria and Albert Museum.

15. Weld (*AC*, 202) and Johnson (*WWP*, 125), both claimed that opinionists denied the use of preparation. But Shepard made no mention of such a denial, nor did Winthrop or Hubbard, nor did the errors condemned at the Synod of 1637, which suggests the marginality of the issue. Como, "Puritans," 300; William Kiffin, *Remarkable Passages in the Life of William Kiffin* (London, 1823), 10–11.

16. Cotton was expressing his preparationism at the time of the free grace controversy with idiosyncratic terminology, but it does not seem to have disturbed his opponents. Books and articles continue to repeat that the free grace controversy revolved around Cotton's denial of preparation. See, for example, R. T. Kendall, *Calvin and English Calvinism to 1649* (Oxford, 1979), 171; David S. Lovejoy, *Religious Enthusiasm in the New World: Heresy to Revolution* (Cambridge, 1985), 65; Raymond D. Irwin, "Cast Out from the 'City upon a Hill'; Antinomian Exiles in Rhode Island, 1638–1650," *Rhode Island History* 52 (1994): 3–19; Jean Cameron, *Anne Hutchinson, Guilty or Not? A Closer Look at Her Trials* (New York,

1994), chap. 1; Staloff, *Making*, chap. 3. Cooper, *Tenacious*, 47; Sandra M. Gustafson, *Eloquence Is Power: Oratory and Performance in Early America* (Chapel Hill, 2000), 21–25. Knight, *Orthodoxies*, 20. Knight links Cotton's alleged anti-preparationism to Sibbes, claiming that Sibbes only urged zeal after justification (118–19). But see Sibbes, *Works*, 1:47, where Sibbes in his most popular treatise describes the zeal needed before justification.

17. The early Reformers disagreed on whether true repentance preceded or followed justification, Bullinger, for example, argued that repentance came first, while Calvin argued that it did not. Early English nonconformists like Arthur Dent and Richard Greenham followed Bullinger, as did the Marian martyr John Rogers. Perkins self-consciously disagreed with Dent and Rogers, while acknowledging that they were godly divines. See William Perkins, *The Workes of that Famous and Worthy Minister of Christ in the University of Cambridge, Mr. William Perkins* (London, 1613–18); Richard Greenham, *The Workes* (London, 1605), 92; Robert W. A. Letham, "*Saving Faith and Assurance in Reformed Theology: Zwingli to the Synod of Dort*" (Ph.D. diss., University of Aberdeen, 1979), 1:51. This earlier godly conception of repentance would have stayed in circulation if only because of the extraordinary popularity Arthur Dent's sermon on the topic enjoyed. *Of Repentance* was first published in London in 1582 and went through at least thirty-seven printings by 1637. It was translated into Welsh.

18. For a discussion of Hooker's teaching on preparation, see Cohen, *God's Caress*, 81–84. Cohen's claim that Shepard did not agree with Hooker but was normative in his preparationism needs clarification (87n. 35). Hooker followed his mentor John Rogers, as he explained in his preface to Rogers's *Treatise of Faith*, 3d ed. (London, 1629), in arguing that the final stages of preparation were in themselves saving. As Cohen notes, Shepard did not call these stages saving, but he did insist that the soul had to be severed from sin before justification by a work of the Spirit unique to the elect. He was fully aware that in making this claim, he differed from "many holy and learned" divines. See Shepard, *Works*, 1:162–171. Shepard's terminology was less provocative than Hooker's, but the conception was virtually identical. For a contemporary recognition of Shepard's and Hooker's departure from the puritan mainstream, see Firmin, *Real Christian*, 88. Daniel Rogers, one of John Rogers's sons, placed a period of "hope" between "the horrours of the law, and the grace of the Gospell." See *Practicall Catechisme* (London, 1632), 101. Puritans on both sides of the Atlantic, if they even raised the issue of preparation's having a middle stage between faith and unregenerate nature, generally rejected that argument. See William Pemble *The Workes of the Late Learned Minister of God's Holy Word, Mr. William Pemble* (Oxford, 1659), 78, 81–84; John Ball, *A Treatise of the Covenant of Grace* (London, 1645), 339; Anthony Burgess, *Vindiciae Legis* (London, 1647), 89; John Owen, *The Doctrine of Justification by Faith* (London, 1677), 97–105; John Norton, *The Orthodox Evangelist* (London, 1658), 166–93; James Allen et al., *The Principles of the Protestant Religion Maintained* (Boston, 1690); 110; Samuel Willard, *A Compleat Body of Divinity* (Boston, 1727), 436, 441–42.

19. Sargent Bush, Jr., *The Writings of Thomas Hooker: Spiritual Adventure in Two Worlds* (Madison, WI, 1980), 252; Hooker, *Application*, 27–54. Much of what Knight, *Orthodoxies*, calls "Amesian" divinity boils down to the Hooker-Rogers

conception of preparation, and much of the specifics of what she has to say about Shepard and Hooker is helpful in understanding the dynamics of the free grace controversy.

20. *WP*, 3:200, 390; *GH*, 173; State Papers, Colonial, PRO, London, C/O 1/9, fol. 159. According to Hooker in early 1636, God did not witness to something "which was not wrought before, but makes it manifest and more clear." Notes of Newtowne Sermons, 1636, p. 42, Shepard Family Papers, American Antiquarian Society, Worcester, Massachusetts. No author of the sermons is given, but the possibilities would be Hooker, Shepard, or Samuel Stone. The style clearly seems to me Hooker's. Moreover, the sermons are on Revelation 2, and one of Shepard's converts mentioned hearing Hooker preach on that chapter of Revelation around this time. See Mary Rhinelander McCarl, "Thomas Shepard's Record of Relations of Religious Experiences, 1648–1649," *William and Mary Quarterly*, 3d ser., 48 (1991): 461. Other passages in these sermons may allude to Boston doctrines, but the motifs they deploy are too common to be certain.

21. Besides all the contemporary evidence for the limited geographical range of the controversy, see Scottow, *Narrative*, 301.

22. Wheelwright, *Brief*, 7; Webster, *Godly*, 33, 194–96; *MA*, 224; *MCA*, 1:418; *WWP*, 120.

23. Cotton himself may have flirted with the doctrine in England, and in a convoluted way, that flirtation perhaps pushed him to the opposite extreme. At any rate he did not then regard it as a serious issue. John Rogers himself did not see his differences with other ministers as very serious. See John Cotton, *A Practical Commentary, or an Exposition with Observations, Reasons, and Uses upon the First Epistle Generall of John* (London, 1656), 39; Rogers, *A Treatise of Faith*, 128.

24. Lake, *Boxmaker's Revenge*, chap. 8; Michael P. Winship, "Contesting Control of Orthodoxy among the Godly: William Pynchon Reconsidered," *William and Mary Quarterly*, 3d ser., 54 (1997): 801–2.

25. Hartlib Papers, 29/2/55b–56a; Firmin, *Real Christian*, 19. Hooker, often mistaken as representative of New England orthodoxy, explored preparation at extraordinary length and in extraordinary detail in his preaching. There is no evidence that anyone else, including Shepard, preached preparation with anything like Hooker's convoluted detail. Shepard shared roughly the same Rogerian emphasis, however, and he cared about it strongly—failure to grasp that sin had to be severed before justification could occur, he claimed, was the "cause of all that counterfeit coin and hypocrisy in this professing age." See Shepard, *Works*, 1:165.

26. Cotton, *Treatise*, 40, 150; Thomas Shepard Sermons, 1637–38, p. 78, MHS (cf. Shepard, *Works*, 1:164); *JC*, 367; *AC*, 175–77.

27. Sibbes, *Works*, 1:97; Patrick Collinson, "The English Conventicle," *Studies in Church History* 23 (1986): 252; Collinson, "The Cohabitation of the Faithful with the Unfaithful," in *From Persecution to Toleration: The Glorious Revolution and Religion in England*, ed. Ole Peter Grell, Jonathan I. Israel, and Nicholas Tyacke (Oxford, 1991), 51–76. Peter Lake, "William Bradshaw, Antichrist, and the Community of the Godly," *Journal of Ecclesiastical History* 36 (1985): 570–89; Lake, "'A Charitable Christian Hatred': The Godly and Their Enemies in the 1630s," in *The Culture of English Puritanism, 1560–1700*, ed. Christopher Durston and Jacqueline Eales (Basingstoke, 1996), 145–83. Delbanco, *Puritan*, occa-

sionally alludes to but leaves unelaborated the challenge the lack of opposition in New England presented to puritan religiosity. Delbanco, "Looking Homeward, Going Home: The Lure of England for the Founders of New England," *New England Quarterly* 59 (1986): 382, claims that the writings of New Englanders who repatriated testify "more than anything else" to the "need for a visible enemy."

28. *PTV*, 1:104.

29. Ibid., 1:104, 37, 105.

30. Patricia Caldwell, *The Puritan Conversion Narrative: The Beginnings of American Expression* (Cambridge, 1983), chap. 3; Notes of Newtowne Sermons, 1636, pp. 134–37.

31. *PTV*, 1:104–5.

32. Harry S. Stout, *The New England Soul: Preaching and Religious Culture in Colonial New England* (New York, 1986), 24–25. Stout gives no citations, primary or otherwise, for his argument, but it stems from Perry Miller. Miller laid out his argument in "Preparation," 253–86, and *Colony*, 59–67. Gura, *Glimpse*, 178, while repeating this argument, does try to document Boston's antisocial tendencies. He claims that a later reference by Cotton to the value of hypocrites to the church demonstrates that in the aftermath of the free grace controversy, Cotton "saw fit to emphasize, as he had not done before, the social obligations of all members of a Puritan commonwealth." But Cotton had made the exact same point at the height of the controversy, so repeating it later hardly demonstrates a change of heart. See Cotton, *Treatise*, 176.

33. Bernard Bailyn, *The New England Merchants in the Seventeenth Century* (1955; reprint, New York, 1964), 40–41, points out that merchants were heavily represented among the "antinomians" and sees this as one of a number of quarrels they had with the magistracy. Battis, *SS*, 263, richly elaborates on Bailyn's original argument. He suggests that the proto-capitalist merchants' and craftsmen's economic values clashed with the "organic social philosophy" of the rest of the colonists. "Antinomianism" with its predestined guarantee of salvation regardless of behavior allegedly allowed them to divorce their assurance of salvation from the pull of guilt that their business practices might otherwise have induced in them. Staloff, *Making*, chaps. 3 and 4, restates the argument, buttressing it by a highly selective citation of Massachusetts economic legislation, while Breen, *Transgressing*, 50–55, considerably reworks it. The argument was not felicitous to begin with, as it rested on nothing more than post hoc, ergo propter hoc reasoning. With Boston as the chief mercantile town in the colony, it had many merchants and craftsmen. One would expect therefore that many of them were caught up in the free grace controversy. But that connection is serendipity, not evidence that these groups were especially susceptible to "antinomianism." Proponents of the merchant/antinomian theory have not attempted to demonstrate that merchants in general, either in Massachusetts or England, were disproportionately represented among antinomians, the only way to meaningfully ground this thesis. Many militant Bostonians were from Lincolnshire, but no one suggests that there was something peculiar about Lincolnshire—apart from the fact that Cotton, Wheelwright, and Hutchinson lived there—that produced antinomians. A number of Boston merchants and tradesmen who went to Rhode Island eventually became

Quakers, a result that turns the merchant/antinomianism thesis on its head, given that Quakers rejected predestination, and thus absolute promises, and stressed the relationship between salvation and holiness. For the improbability that Boston's chief magisterial pursuer, Thomas Dudley, had an "organic social philosophy," see 292 n.15 below. There is no relationship between the antinomian/entrepreneurial argument and the argument that in later periods of American history evangelical, conversionist piety and entrepreneurial spirit went hand in hand. Both parties in the free grace controversy practiced evangelical, conversionist piety.

34. *AC*, 169; Lang, *Prophetic*, 50. For a more cautious and more accurate expression of this line of argument, see Sydney V. James, *John Clarke and His Legacies: Religion and Law in Colonial Rhode Island, 1638–1750* (University Park, PA, 1999), 7. There is a related tendency among scholars to cast the religious dispute between Boston and its opponents in dichotomized terms such as individualistic and subjective (Boston) versus communal and objective. See, for example, Lang, *Prophetic;* Stoever, *Faire;* Breen, *Transgressing.* These divisions have some validity, but since they are anachronistic, they can also oversimplify and distort. Each side, for example, regarded the other's approach to assurance as subjective and individualistic, insofar as it substituted human judgment for the revealed truth of God; each side described the other as proud. It was precisely because Cotton found the usual ways of seeking assurance hopelessly subjective that he sought the objectivity of revelations to anchor them, while the fear that those conventional ways were indeed only subjective haunted their promulgators. The opponents of Boston worried that its doctrines would lead to sin and the abandonment of the Bible, both of which, by definition, were bad for society, yet simple obedience to external communal norms was not what they were looking for either; in itself, such obedience, or what Shepard would call the "gilded rottenness" of a "moral performance," was a refined path to Hell (*PTV*, 1:178). Both sides assumed that sainthood was capable of external, communal evaluation. Cf. Michael W. Kaufmann, *Institutional Individualism: Conversion, Exile, and Nostalgia in Puritan New England* (Hanover, NH, 1998), chap. 4.

35. Hall, *Faithful Shepherd*, 163. Hall states that it was the "legal" preachers, like Hooker, Shepard, and Bulkeley, and, by implication, not Cotton, or for that matter, what he calls the "Antinomian style of ministry," who preached for conversion (161). But why a conversion would be more likely to take place under, say, Bulkeley's preaching than Cotton's Hall does not explain. As has been shown, the other preacher with an "Antinomian style of ministry," John Wheelwright, gained a reputation in Lincolnshire as being especially good at conversions. Knight, *Orthodoxies*, 112, 146, also argues that Cotton, along with "Sibbesians" in general, directed his sermons to those already converted. She cites as evidence Cotton's saying that the written word could not bring about a conversion. But Knight lifted that quotation out of context from a passage in which Cotton was demonstrating the importance of a preaching ministry for conversion. Cf. John Cotton, *Christ the Fountain of Life* (London, 1641), 181: "[A]ll the work that reading could reach unto, could not reach to beget and wake saving faith, which is the principall scope of preaching." Gustafson, *Eloquence Is Power*, 21–25, repeats the Hall-Knight argument. Cotton himself vigorously rejected the claim that ministers of

gathered churches were not to preach for conversion. See Cotton in Williams, *Complete Writings*, 2:211–14.

36. Alfred A. Cave, *The Pequot War* (Amherst, MA, 1996), 19. See also Ronald Dale Karr, "'Why Should You Be So Furious?': The Violence of the Pequot War," *Journal of American History* 85 (1998): 876–909. For a discussion of the relationship between the violent rhetoric of the free grace controversy and the violence of the Pequot War, see Ann Kibbey, *The Interpretation of Material Shapes in Puritanism: A Study of Rhetoric, Prejudice, and Violence* (New York, 1986), chap. 5.

37. See Baird Tipson, "Invisible Saints: The 'Judgment of Charity' in the Early New England Churches," *Church History* 44 (1975): 460–71, for the best description of what was radical about this requirement. Morgan, *Visible*, 98–99, suggests that the conversion narratives originated in the enthusiasm generated by Cotton's preaching. But see Michael G. Ditmore, "Preparation and Confession: Reconsidering Edmund S. Morgan's *Visible Saints*," *New England Quarterly* 67 (1994): 298–319. For conflicting interpretations of the impetus behind the conversion narratives, see Stephen Foster, "English Puritanism and the Progress of New England Institutions, 1630–1660," in *Saints and Revolutionaries: Essays in Early American History*, ed. David D. Hall, John M. Murrin, and Thad W. Tate (New York, 1984), 3–37; Foster, *Long Argument*, 156, 161–63; and Susan Hardman Moore, "Popery, Purity, and Providence: Deciphering the New England Experiment," in *Religion, Culture, and Society in Early Modern Britain*, ed. Anthony Fletcher and Peter Roberts (Cambridge, 1994), 257–89.

38. *PTV*, 2:54, 164; Hall, *Faithful Shepherd*, 99–100. Alison Games, *Migration and the Origins of the English Atlantic World* (Cambridge, 1999), 140–41, in a careful study of adult immigrants from the year 1635, concludes that perhaps 65 percent were not church members three years after arrival, although half or more of these eventually would be.

39. *PTV*, 1:37.

40. Ibid., 1:8.

41. Cotton, *Treatise*, 100–101; *AC*, 32.

42. *AC*, 326.

43. *GH*, 281, 302; *JC*, 303; John Underhill, *Newes from America* (London, 1638), in *MHS Collections*, 3d ser., 6 (1837): 22.

44. T. H. Breen, *The Character of the Godly Ruler: A Study of Puritan Political Ideas in New England, 1630–1730* (New Haven, 1970).

45. Charles M. Andrews, *The Colonial Period of American History*, 2d ed. (New Haven, 1964), 1:365–68; Frances Rose-Troup, *The Massachusetts Bay Company and Its Predecessors* (New York, 1930), chap. 6.

46. Scottow, *Narrative*, 300; *WJ*, 123, 124, 129, 142; *WP*, 3:397–98; William Bradford, *Of Plymouth Plantation, 1620–1647*, ed. Samuel Eliot Morison (New York, 1953), 273; *MR*, 1:117–18.

47. Samuel Maverick, "A Briefe Description of New England," *MHS Proceedings*, 2d ser., 1 (1885): 240.

48. *WJ*, 142, 144–45; Maverick, "Briefe," 246; Francis J. Bremer, "Endicott and the Red Cross: Puritan Iconoclasm in the New World," *Journal of American Studies* 24 (1990): 5–22; *WJ*, 176–77.

49. John Cotton in Williams, *Complete Writings*, 2:46–48.

50. *WJ*, 136–37; *MR*, 1:142–43. Excerpts from the model are spread throughout Roger Williams, *The Bloudy Tenent of Persecution, for Cause of Conscience* (1644) in Williams, *Complete Writings*, 3:221ff. Specific examples are from pp. 390, 248, 292. Cf. *WJ*, 150. See Robert F. Scholz, "Clerical Consociation in Massachusetts Bay: Reassessing the New England Way and Its Origins," *William and Mary Quarterly*, 3d ser., 29 (1972): 391–414.

51. Morton, *Memorial*, 100; *WJ*, 149–51, 158; *JC*, 204–8.

52. *WJ*, 158, 163–68, 746; *MR*, 1:156, 157, 158, 160–61; Morgan, *Dilemma*, 131. The creation of the council of permanent magistrates in April 1636 perhaps came out of the same impulse to increase the majesty and authority of the government. See *WJ*, 174.

53. *WJ*, 165–68; *MR*, 1:168; Morgan, *Visible*, 101; Michael McGiffert, "The People Speak: Confessions of Lay Men and Women," in *God's Plot: Puritan Spirituality in Thomas Shepard's Cambridge* (Amherst, MA, 1994), 138; Rutman, *Winthrop's Boston*, 179.

54. *WJ*, 169, 173–74; Shepard, *Works*, 1:cxxix, cxxxi, cxxxii; Rathband, *Briefe Narration*, 8. Foster, "English," 19, explains Shepard at Dorchester as in effect outbidding Boston radicals by setting the standard of a gracious, as opposed to legal, conversion very high. But he notes only Shepard's attack on the "legal" narratives, not his attack on those that recounted "fits and dreams." In any event, Shepard had already demonstrated in his English preaching that his standards of genuine conversion could be dizzyingly high. Gura, *Glimpse*, 162, remarks on the tendencies toward antinomianism and Arminianism.

55. *GH*, 274. B. R. Burg, *Richard Mather of Dorchester* (Lexington, KY, 1976), 30–37. Rathband, *Briefe Narration*, 8.

56. Giles Firmin, *Weighty Questions Discussed* (London, 1692), 22.

CHAPTER FIVE
SECRET QUARRELS TURN PUBLIC

1. *WWP*, 68, 102, 197, 125.

2. Ibid., 127, 134.

3. Ibid., 133–35.

4. *AC*, 413; *WWP*, 135. Delbanco, *Puritan*, 140–41, has an interesting description of the effect of such language, but he is wrong to ascribe it to the challenge of evangelism in Massachusetts. Shepard had preached like this in England

5. I used an imprecise technique to date the passages from *PTV*. There is a passage, *PTV*, 1:163, that seems to be directed to the General Court in its May 1637 sitting, and I assumed that Shepard went through the material up to this point at a relatively even rate, although I did not presume to date specific passages within more than a couple of months. The results seem to fit. In November and December, as conflict clearly became more open, Shepard's attacks became more overt and pointed (see 95–96 above). Shepard later said that after discussions between Cotton and the other ministers broke down, he started openly attacking Boston doctrine, which would have been in January and February. *WJ*, 208, also note that pulpit rhetoric heated up at this time. At the appropriate place in *PTV*, Shepard's rhetoric makes a pronounced leap in virulence (see 108–11 above). Cot-

ton in sermons of his that were subsequently published and which no scholar has suggested were later than 1637 made an allusion to a remark by Shepard in *PTV* that also provides a chronological reference; see 117 above. A caution against trying to date too precisely is provided by a sermon notebook in the MHS long mislabeled simply as "Sermons on the Keys to the Kingdom." On examination it proved to be a listener's notes on this lecture series. The notebook covers the first fifty pages or so of *PTV*, starting on page 4 of the 1695 edition, but it may contain about twice as much material, which gives an indication of how much Shepard expanded his sermons from his written notes. Unfortunately, most of the ink in the notebook is badly faded. The notebook has been recataloged as Thomas Shepard, Sermons on the Parable of the Ten Virgins, [1636–40]. This system of dating *PTV* breaks down after Shepard's sermon to the General Court, with an absence of external markers and increasingly brief written notes.

6. *PTV*, 1:72, 31.

7. Ibid., 1:44, 45.

8. Patrick Collinson, *The Religion of Protestants: The Church in English Society, 1559–1625* (Oxford, 1982), 132–40, 258; Collinson, "Lectures by Combination: Structures and Characteristics of Church Life in 17th-Century England," *Bulletin of the Institute of Historical Research* 48 (1975): 182–213; *MCA*, 1:313; *WJ*, 130, 138, 316–18; Samuel Clarke, *The Lives of Thirty-Two English Divines* (London, 1677), 191.

9. *WWP*, 136.

10. *WS*, 194; *AC*, 320. Battis, *SS*, 129, and Charles Francis Adams, *Three Episodes in New England History* (Boston, 1891), 1:171n. 3, state that the critical meeting with Hutchinson that I am identifying with the one discussed by Winthrop took place on December 12. But there is no positive evidence for that date. Battis, *SS*, 121, claims the October discussion recorded by Winthrop occurred at the General Court on October 25, citing *MR*, 1:181. But that source says nothing about such a discussion, and *WJ*, 194, says that the October meeting was private, which rules the Court out. We know from internal evidence that the meeting with Hutchinson that later got her convicted took place while the General Court was sitting (*AC*, 320). It had to occur before some ministers gathered to write Cotton a set of questions "a little before" an indeterminate time in the middle of December (*WJ*, 203) since that set of questions refers back to the meeting (see below). Thus the meeting took place either in October or December. Ministers, when they committed their recollections of the meeting to writing in December, had sharply conflicting memories about one exchange, which gives credence to the October date (see 90), and since Winthrop mentions no meeting in December, there is no reason to create one. The only problem with the October date is that Winthrop does not mention the critical exchanges with Hutchinson and Wheelwright, although he says both were present at the meeting. But Hugh Peters said that the ministers desired Cotton "to tell us wherein the difference lay between him and us" before they called Hutchinson, which accounts for what Winthrop did describe (*AC*, 320). Winthrop seems to have had his report of the meeting secondhand, and some participants did not regard the discussion with Hutchinson as very serious at the time, although others clearly did (*AC*, 334). If Winthrop's failure to record the exchange with Hutchinson seems so serious as to call into

question the October date for it, the same objection becomes even greater for a December date. Not only did Winthrop fail to record Hutchinson's remarks at this alleged December meeting, he failed to record the meeting at all, even though it was attended by at least half of Massachusetts's ministers and most of the leading figures of the Boston congregation.

11. *AC*, 332, 344.

12. *AC*, 324, 322; *PTV*, 1:110. Even the friendly witnesses Thomas Leverett and John Cotton acknowledged that Hutchinson had compared the ministers to the apostles before they had received the full measure of the Spirit (*AC*, 333, 334). When testifying for the second time under oath the ministers were reluctant to assert that Hutchinson directly said at the conference that they preached a cove-nant of works (*AC*, 346–47). They were firm, though, that she had said they were not able ministers of the New Testament. Hutchinson claimed that if she had done so, it had only been in a one-on-one conversation (*AC*, 333). She acknowledged at her trial that she considered the ministers to preach a covenant of works like the apostles (*AC*, 325).

13. Vane, *Retired*.

14. *WJ*, 206, gives a description of the covenant of works that reads like a synop-sis of Vane's. See also *AC*, 264–65.

15. Vane, *Retired*, 113–14; *AC*, 25. The argument implied that Christ was mu-table and therefore lesser than God the Father. For the only other reference to anti-Trinitarianism among Hutchinson's circle that I have located, see chapter 12.

16. Vane, *Retired*, 172, 119, 117, 191, 197.

17. Ibid., 322. See errors 12 and 13 condemned at the Synod of 1637, *AC* 222.

18. Vane wrote to Winthrop, after Wheelwright had been convicted and before Hutchinson had publicly disclosed her revelations, that the magistrates and minis-ters who had persecuted him walked in the "way of workes and antichristianisme." Although by this time Wheelwright was saying as much and Cotton at least found the argument plausible, Vane demonstrated it by citing the same verses Hutchin-son had received in her fast, 1 John 4: 1–3, to prove his point—Winthrop, not yet knowing of Hutchinson's revelation, understandably found Vane's exegesis nonsensical. *HC*, 95, 110. For Hutchinson's association of Christ coming in the flesh with Matt. 1:18, and both with justification and assurance, see S. G., *Glass*, 9. John Cotton, *A Practical Commentary, or an Exposition with Observations, Rea-sons, and Uses upon the First Epistle Generall of John* (London, 1658), 285, associ-ated the antichristian denial of Christ coming in the flesh with a denial of his "humane simplicity." It seems probable that Hutchinson's linking of 1 John 4:3 and Matt. 1:18 within a soteriological context was original and one that a minister aware of the early Christian disputes over the nature of Christ's incarnation would not have been likely to make. Christ coming into the flesh of believers has a familist resonance to it, but I think this is coincidental.

19. *AC*, 63.

20. Ibid., 334, 336, 326, 319, 376.

21. Ibid., 355, 64.

22. Ibid., 334; *WJ*, 194–95. See Cotton's exegesis of Ephesians 1:17 in Cotton, *Treatise*, 185–87.

23. Samuel Rutherford, *A Survey of the Spirituall Antichrist* (London, 1648), 41.

24. Thomas Wilson, *A Christian Dictionary* (London, 1612), 402. Cf. Stoever, *Faire*, 68; *WJ*, 195. For Cotton's position on the indwelling of the Spirit, see Cotton, *Cotton*, 218–22; *PTV*, 1:170. Como, "Puritans," 151–52. See also Goeffrey F. Nuttall, *The Holy Spirit in Puritan Faith and Experience*, 2d ed. (Chicago, 1992), 49–50.

25. Wheelwright, *Brief*, 23; Thomas Shepard, *A Trial of Regeneration* (N.p., 1641), 36; John Knewstub, *A Confutation of Monstrous and Horrible Heresies, Taught by H.N.* (London, 1579), sig. 4r; *WJ*, 197; *AC*, 278; *GH*, 303.

26. Winthrop left a large space at the end of the October 21 entry, probably intending to leave room for a preface to the next entry, which described the meeting of ministers. At an unknown date, he partially filled in that space with intemperate descriptions of Hutchinson and Wheelwright that shed heat but little light. James Savage, the last person to see this portion of the journal, recorded that there was a "large blank" after the section on Hutchinson and another "large blank" after the Wheelwright entry. See John Winthrop, *The History of New England from 1630–1649*, ed. James Savage (Boston, 1853), 200–201. Of Hutchinson, Winthrop wrote,

One Mrs. Hutchinson, a member of the church of Boston, a woman of a ready wit and bold spirit, brought over with her two dangerous errors: 1. That the person of the Holy Ghost dwells in a justified person. 2. That no sanctification can help to evidence to us our justification.—From these two grew many branches; as, 1, Our union with the Holy Ghost, so as a Christian remains dead to every spiritual action, and hath no gifts nor graces. Other than such as are in hypocrites, nor any other sanctification but the Holy Ghost himself. (*WJ*, 193)

The two "errors" are worded too inconclusively to be sure of what Winthrop meant. Both errors can be read as identical with Cotton's teachings. (Cotton's claim that sanctification could not be a first evidence was sometimes expressed as Winthrop phrased it.) The branches cannot, however, but Winthrop did not claim that she brought these from England. On Wheelwright, Winthrop wrote, "There joined with her in these opinions a brother of hers, one Mr. Wheelwright, a silenced minister sometimes in England" (*WJ*, 194). This simple conflation of Wheelwright with Hutchinson was flagrantly inaccurate. Hubbard, usually content to copy Winthrop verbatim in his own history, modified the line to read, "those opinions, or in some other very near them," a construction ambiguous enough to be defensible (*GH*, 286). Winthrop's relatively benign description of Wheelwright in the October 25 entry contradicts this one, and the large areas of blank page, along with the sweeping intemperateness of the entries themselves, suggests that Winthrop may have written some or all of the passage much later. This would not have been uncommon for him—the entry for December 10, 1636 (*WJ*, 204), has a passage referring to the March 1637 sitting of the General Court.

27. Francis J. Bremer, "The Heritage of John Winthrop: Religion along the Stour Valley, 1548–1630," *New England Quarterly* 70 (1997): 515–47. For Knewstub's attacks on the Family of Love, and the way they possibly exacerbated the

problem Knewstub intended to eliminate, see Christopher Marsh, "Piety and Persuasion in Elizabethan England: The Church of England Meets the Family of Love," in *England's Long Reformation, 1500–1800*, ed. Nicholas Tyacke (London, 1998), 141–66. Winthrop's anxieties may have also stemmed in part from the alarming knack of his son, John Winthrop, Jr., for finding familist-tinged acquaintances. See Como, "Puritans," 322–84.

28. My reconstruction of the contents of the Mount Wollaston petition is based on interpreting *WJ*, 195–6, in the context of *WJ*, 305, and *BCR*, 10. The standard explanation of the following incident is that Winthrop blocked an effort by the "Hutchinsonians" to humiliate Wilson, who did not preach Cotton's doctrine, by installing a minister more to their taste. See, for example, Battis, 121; *AC*, 6; Ziff, *Career*, 118; Stoever, *Faire*, 26; Gura, *Glimpse*, 247; Cohen, *God's Caress*, 265; William G. Mcloughlin, "Anne Hutchinson Reconsidered," *Rhode Island History* 49 (1991): 18; Staloff, *Making*, 47; and Lang, *Prophetic*, 24. There is no evidence to support this interpretation, nor is there any evidence that Wilson had yet fallen out with much of the congregation. Moreover, this interpretation ignores the Mount Wollaston petition. If the impetus for the petition had any connection with Wilson at all, it would have been in a desire to get some distance from him.

29. *WJ*, 187. See also *JC*, 303, where John Cotton seems to be giving a conspiratorial interpretation of this attempt. Winthrop elsewhere (*WJ*, 187, 305) ascribed the motivation for setting up a new church simply to distance. There were perhaps a variety of intentions behind it.

30. Hubbard, more cautious than Winthrop and, I think, more accurate, changed Winthrop's claim that the petitioners were "of the opinion of Mrs. Hutchinson" to "being of the forementioned opinion," which, in context, referred to the position Wheelwright had just defended in his conference with the ministers that the Holy Spirit dwelt in believers but not in a personal union, an opinion that other ministers at the conference also defended. *GH*, 286; *WJ*, 195.

31. *WJ*, 195–96.

32. Ibid., 197.

33. *WJ*, 197.

34. Rathband, *Briefe Narration*, 24. Rathband exploited any opportunity he had to make New England Congregationalism look bad, so it is virtually certain that if he had been told that one intention behind electing Wheelwright was to humiliate or displace Wilson, he would have said as much. *Second Report of the Record Commissioners of the City of Boston; Containing the Boston Records, 1634–1660, and the Book of Possessions* (Boston, 1881), 14, 15; Marion Sophia Arnold, *A Brief History of the Town of Braintree in Massachusetts* (Boston, 1940), 8; *MR*, 1:217; Thomas Lechford, *Plain Dealing: Or, Newes from New-England*, ed. J. Hammond Trumbull (1642; reprint, Boston, 1868), 41.

35. *WJ*, 197, 200–201.

36. *PTV*, 1:81.

37. Ibid., 2:15, 1:86. The proximity of this passage to the October conference is further suggested by the absence of a discussion of the earnest of the Spirit as its seal anywhere else in *PTV*.

38. *WJ*, 201; *MR*, 1:185. Historians from Thomas Hutchinson to Edmund S. Morgan have interpreted Vane as meaning that he wanted to bail out as he felt

his popularity slipping away outside Boston. See Hutchinson, *History*, 1:48; Peter Oliver, *The Puritan Commonwealth* (Boston, 1856), 174; Morgan, *Dilemma*, 143.

39. *WJ*, 201–2; *MR*, 1:185.

40. *WJ*, 202.

41. Ibid.; *GH*, 290.

42. *JC*, 302; *AC*, 204; *MR*, 1:187.

43. Morton, *New-England's Memorial*, 91.

44. *AC*, 46, 62, 338–39; *WJ*, 203.

45. *AC*, 48, 50; *WJ*, 206.

46. *AC*, 61–62, cf. 63, 64.

47. *AC*, 65–68, 73, 72.

48. Ibid., 88–89, 123.

49. Ibid., 109, 113, 122, 130.

50. *AC*, 97, 102, 103, 134, 94, 84.

51. John Allin and Thomas Shepard, *A Defence of the Answer Made unto the Nine Questions or Positions Sent from New-England* (London, 1645), 14.

52. The first Boston proposition dismissed the Hooker-Shepard conception of preparation. The second said that faith was passive in justification. The third said that if you had become convinced of your justification only by reasoning (which was the usual method), then to doubt it was no sin, since you had never genuinely known it. The fourth said that people had to first perceive the truth of their justification before they could perceive the truth of their sanctification. The fifth said that the Spirit did not use sanctification to persuade a believer that its witness was true—in other words, sanctification might confirm one's assurance, but it did not tell people more than they knew already. *WP*, 3:326.

53. When the Bostonians argued that Christ apprehended a believer first in order of nature before faith, the Newtowne brethren translated this into the far more radical proposition that justification occurred without faith. Where the Bostonians had argued in line with Cotton's emphasis that the word of the Bible "doth worke Faith . . . because God doth use it as an ordinance," the Newtownians had written, "It is the only use of the word to worke Faith"—one did not need Scriptures at all presumably after one had faith. The Bostonians had made the knife-edge Cottonian argument that after justification the soul fetched strength from Christ—in other words, graces were active, which was the orthodox position—but it only did so because the Holy Spirit enabled it to. Newtowne heard this as an argument that faith was passive after justification as well as during it. When the Bostonians argued that one could not build one's justification on a conditional promise, the Newtownians wrote down the far more radical claim that the Bostonians denied that the Lord commanded the soul to believe conditional promises. The Newtowne brethren took the Boston argument about absolute promises and assurance to mean that one did not have to try the Spirit by the word of the Bible. *WP*, 3:327, 326.

54. *WP*, 3:326.

55. The entry includes a reference to the March 1637 meeting of the General Court, and the final line of the journal paragraph, "in conclusion, the ground of all was found to be assurance by immediate revelation," suggests that the paragraph was written after Hutchinson's civil trial in November 1637 (*WJ*, 206).

56. *WJ*, 206.

57. *JC*, 356; John Cotton, *The True Constitution of a Particular Visible Church, Proved by Scripture* (London, 1642), 6.

58. *WJ*, 230, 204.

59. Ibid., 205, 230.

60. Robert C. Winthrop, *The Life and Letters of John Winthrop*, 2d ed. (Boston, 1869), 2:151; *WP*, 3:338–44, 327; Foster, *Long Argument*, 332n. 17.

61. *WP*, 3:328.

62. Winthrop argued that it was intrinsic to God's justice that a sinner close with Christ in order to be justified. Not so, replied Shepard. To make any behavior of God's compulsory for him stinted his freedom of action and autonomy, both characteristics that Reformed theology emphasized. What Winthrop should have said, Shepard argued, was that the requirement was intrinsic to God's revealed will, not his secret nature. *WP*, 3:328.

63. Morgan, *Dilemma*, 142; Gura, *Glimpse*, 249; Dewey D. Wallace, Jr., *Puritans and Predestination: Grace in English Protestant Theology, 1525–1695* (Chapel Hill, 1982), 152; *AC*, 410.

64. David D. Hall, *Worlds of Wonder, Days of Judgment: Popular Religious Belief in Early New England* (New York, 1990), 22–28.

65. *WP*, 3:338. Shepard might have been referring to a treatise on faith someone in Hutchinson's circle gave Winthrop. See *AC*, 379.

66. *WP*, 3:338.

CHAPTER SIX
CONVICTING JOHN WHEELWRIGHT

1. Catherine Davies, "'Poor Persecuted Little Flock' or 'Commonwealth of Christians': Edwardian Protestant Conceptions of the Church," and Jane Facey, "John Foxe and the Defence of the English Church," in *Protestantism and the National Church*, ed. Peter Lake and Maria Dowling (London, 1987), 78–102, 162–92.

2. Stuart Clarke, *Thinking with Demons: The Idea of Witchcraft in Early Modern Europe* (Oxford, 1997), chap. 22; Conrad Russell, *Parliaments and English Politics: 1621–1629* (Oxford, 1979), 407–8.

3. *WP*, 3:5–7, 61–62, 78–79. For an example of the general concern of persons deeply involved in the colonization of Massachusetts for Germany, see J. T. Peacey, "Seasonable Treatises: A Godly Project of the 1630s," *English Historical Review* 113 (1998): 666–79. This was a project of c. 1632 to write and send religious treatises to Germany. Almost all of its twenty-five subscribers had close connections with Massachusetts, some being officers of the Massachusetts Bay Company and some past or future immigrants. Peacey suggests that the intended destination for the religious treatises was Massachusetts itself. But the intended recipients were identified as "reformed Churches" currently engaged in literally bloody and devastating warfare. Bodo Nischan, "Confessionalism and Absolutism: The Case of Brandenburg," in *Calvinism in Europe, 1540–1620*, ed. Andrew Pettegree, Alastair Duke, and Billian Lewis (Cambridge, 1994), 181–204.

4. *WJ*, 207–8.

5. *God's Plot*, 65; *WJ*, 208.

6. *PTV*, 1:114, 122. Caroline M. Hibbart, *Charles I and the Popish Plot* (Chapel Hill, 1983), 15.

7. *PTV*, 1:114, 119, 120. For the terrifying, if latent, potential in Calvin's scattered remarks on unconscious hypocrites, see David Foxgrover, "'Temporary Faith' and the Certainty of Salvation," *Calvin Theological Journal* 15 (1980): 220–32.

8. *PTV*, 1:121, 122.

9. Ibid., 1:117–18.

10. Ibid., 1:126.

11. Ibid., 1:127; *AC*, 64, 84.

12. Ibid., 1:127.

13. Ibid., 1:128–29.

14. Ibid., 1:119.

15. *AC*, 265.

16. Webster, *Godly*, chap. 3, p. 66; Alexandra Walsham, *Providence in Early Modern England* (Oxford, 1999), 142–50; Foster, *Long Argument*, 97–98. *WP*, 3:306.

17. *AC*, 291. For a sampling of puritan prescriptions for fasting, see Arthur Hildersham, *The Doctrine of Fasting and Praier, and Humiliation for Sinne* (London, 1635), 53–57; Henry Holland, *The Christian Exercise of Fasting, Private and Publicke* (London, 1596), 9–13; Nicholas Bownde, *The Holy Exercise of Fasting* (London, 1604), 26–57, quotation from p. 37.

18. Wheelwright, *Brief*, 9; *MA*, 216.

19. *AC*, 156–58.

20. Ibid., 159, 161, 158, 163, 166.

21. Ibid., 164.

22. Ibid., 165, 162.

23. Ibid., 168–69.

24. Ibid., 169, 171, 172.

25. *WJ*, 208.

26. Ibid., 162.

27. Ibid., 208.

28. Battis, *SS*, 144; Gura, *Glimpse*, 172.

29. William Coddington, *A Demonstration of True Love unto You the Rulers of the Colony of the Massachusetts in New-England* (N.p., 1674), 17; Battis, *SS*, 144; Ziff, *Career*, 122–23.

30. *WJ*, 208; *MCA*, 1:275, 280.

31. *WJ*, 208; *JC*, 303. For a general discussion of after-sermon questions, see Richard Mather, *Church-Government and Church-Covenant Discussed* (London, 1643), 78–79.

32. *AC*, 209–10.

33. *JC*, 302–6; *MA*, 220; Giles Firmin, *Weighty Questions Discussed* (London, 1692), 21. Firmin gives the only surviving example of what that questioning was like.

34. *MA*, 224; *MCA*, 1:312. S. G., *Glass*, 24–28, preserves a list of ministerial statements that some lay person or persons found offensive. Some sound as if they

came from Hooker's circle while others are more moderate. The overlapping issue of church covenants is mixed in, foreshadowing debates over the Half-way Covenant.

35. *PTV*, 1:132; Cotton, *Treatise*, 37. "It hath been handled in another congregation" is how Cotton introduced Shepard's comment about angels. See Cotton, *Treatise*, 44; *PTV*, 1:138.

36. Cotton, *Treatise*, 39–40, 100.

37. Ibid., 43.

38. Ibid., 91, 98–99, 199.

39. Ibid., 102, 141; *MA*, 222.

40. *JC*, 308.

41. Ibid., 255; Wheelwright, *Brief*, 8, 14, 16.

42. My definition of sedition is drawn from *AC*, 249, 292–99. Battis, *SS*, 214–15, discusses the English law of sedition and its applicability to Wheelwright's case. Crime at the time was considered sinful as well as illegal, and legal codes were not the only sources for defining crimes. The legal struggles of the free grace controversy appear to mostly, but not entirely, run on a separate track from the simultaneous efforts to give Massachusetts a written legal code.

43. Hartlib Papers, 40 1/7a; Wheelwright, *Brief*, 7; *JC*, 318.

44. Wheelwright, *Brief*, 7.

45. Hartlib Papers 40 1/7a. The Hartlib Papers document the charges, note that Wheelwright denied them all when he discovered them, and claim that he was correct, except about sanctification evidencing justification (which, because of the wording, could be argued either way). The Hartlib list includes two more charges, one a variation on the sanctification charge, the other "That absence of Christ is the onely cause of fasting."

46. The Court secretary did not list those present for this session, but William Spencer of Cambridge attended the one in April. The tally of those present is from S.G., *Glass*, 6. John M. Murrin, "Magistrates, Sinners, and a Precarious Liberty: Trial by Jury in Seventeenth-Century New England," in *Saints and Revolutionaries: Essays in Early American History*, ed. David D. Hall, John M. Murrin, and Thad W. Tate (New York, 1984), 156; Joseph B. Felt, *The Ecclesiastical History of New England* (Boston, 1855–62), 2:611; Richard S. Dunn, *Puritans and Yankees: The Winthrop Dynasty of New England, 1630–1717* (Princeton, 1962), 106–7; Robert Brenner, *Merchants and Revolution: Commercial Policy, Political Conflict, and London's Overseas Traders, 1550–1653* (Princeton, 1993), 523–28; *WJ*, 666; S. G., *Glass*, 6–7; *AC*, 283.

47. *MR*, 1:189; *WJ*, 209.

48. *WJ*, 209.

49. Ibid., 209–10; Williams, *Complete Writings*, 3:271, 407.

50. *AC*, 283, 284.

51. Williams, *Complete Writings*, 3:383; *AC*, 285. On the High Commission and the ex officio oath, see Roland G. Usher, *The Rise and Fall of the High Commission* (Oxford, 1913).

52. *AC*, 288.

53. Wheelwright, *Brief*, 8, 14.

54. *JC*, 254. Peter Bulkeley would later spend many pages of a treatise he wrote on the covenant of grace refuting the claim that faith was a consequent condition of the covenant of grace. Bulkeley collapsed Wheelwright's argument into the antinomian argument that justification occurred before faith. In spite of Wheelwright's insistence that sanctification was a secondary evidence of justification, "the end of [his] opinion" was that a believer must "never look at this or that in your selves." Bulkeley's conclusion was not fair to Wheelwright, but Wheelwright did nothing to put his opponents at ease. Bulkeley, *The Gospel-Covenant; or The Covenant of Grace Opened*, 2d ed. (London, 1651), 357.

55. *AC*, 288.

56. S. G., *Glass*, 6–7.

57. Two accounts of the trial record Cotton's critical intervention: Wheelwright, *Brief*, 14; S. G., *Glass*, 6–7.

58. S. G., *Glass*, 7.

59. *AC*, 288–89, 421.

60. *AC*, 290–91.

61. Murrin, "Magistrates," 164; Felt, *Ecclesiastical History*, 2:611; Coddington, *Demonstration*, 13. *MR*, 1:185. Wheelwright's contempt of the Court lay in his preaching this incendiary sermon on a day that the Court intended for reconciliation.

CHAPTER SEVEN
ABIMELECH'S FACTION

1. *AC*, 289.

2. Ibid., 290. I am assuming here that the Protestation is the same, at least in terms of its contents, as a Remonstrance that Winthrop and Shepard both mention. Neither of the documents survives. The reasons for assuming they are the same is that their arguments appear to have been at least broadly similar and that four persons whom we know signed the Remonstrance—Vane, Colburn, Coddington, and Coggeshall—were all members of this Court. Coggeshall seems to have indicated that these were one and the same document. This document, if it is only one document, is not the same as the petition signed immediately after the trial, sometimes called the "remonstrance and Petition" for the latter contains different arguments. *WJ*, 211; *AC*, 251, 255, 290; *WP*, 3:416; 4:8–9.

3. *AC*, 277; David Zaret, *Origins of Democratic Culture: Printing, Petitions, and the Public Sphere in Early Modern England* (Princeton, 2000), 86–99.

4. *AC*, 261, 249, 250.

5. *WWP*, 174; *AC*, 261; *WP*, 3:513–14; *MR*, 1:209. Battis, *SS*, 150, says that seventy-four men signed, but the list that number is based on, *MR*, 1:211–12, is a slightly more inclusive list of people who either signed or defended the petition, or were otherwise considered unreliable. Battis's breakdown of signatures to the petition by towns is unreliable because it is based on the same list.

6. Battis, *SS*, 258–61; *JC*, 302, 309; *AC*, 282. Battis, *SS*, built his analyses of the "Hutchinsonians" around the assumption that signing the petition demonstrated that one was part of the "Hutchinsonian movement," and his assumption has been widely picked up by subsequent scholars. Stephen Foster has suggested

that Boston's increasing radicalism reflected the growing "embittered extremism" of English puritan immigrants under Laudian persecution. See Foster, "English Puritanism and the Progress of New England Institutions, 1630–1660," in *Saints and Revolutionaries: Essays in Early American History,* ed. David D. Hall, John M. Murrin, and Thad W. Tate (New York, 1984), 3–37; Foster, *Long Argument,* 156, 161–63. His interpretation in conjunction with the immigrants of 1635 is elaborated by Alison Games, *Migration and the Origins of the English Atlantic World* (Cambridge, MA, 1999), 147. However, later immigrants are, if anything, heavily underrepresented among Boston activists when total yearly immigration figures are factored in. Massachusetts's population at the beginning of 1634 was perhaps 3,000, with somewhat under 1,000 coming in 1630. Another 1,000 came in 1634, 2,000 in 1635, something over 500 in 1636 (with an outmigration to Connecticut), 1,500 in 1637, and 3,000 in 1638. (Figures from Rutman, *Winthrop's Boston,* 179. Games's "contemporary estimate" (138) for 1635, 3,000, is a misreading of William Hubbard's estimate for 1638.) Battis's "core" and "periphery" groups of "Hutchinsonians," his most reliable list of activists, which include the petition signers, have 64 people emigrating before 1634 and 33 thereafter. This makes the earlier immigrants significantly overrepresented among the activists. The best represented year is 1630, with 33 men. The second largest cohort among the activists, 1635, has 10, which makes it, proportionate to the number of immigrants that year, one of the most underrepresented years. If one adds Battis's "peripheral" group through 1638 (which is something of a stretch), the figures become 83 and 104, which approaches but does not reach a proportionate distribution. See Battis, *SS,* 295.

7. *WJ,* 211.

8. *JC,* 309; Wheelwright, *Brief,* 7, 14–15; *WJ,* 216, 293, 255.

9. *AC,* 283, 291–99; Wheelwright, *Brief,* 24.

10. Ibid., 295; *WP,* 3:416. John M. Murrin, "Magistrates, Sinners, and a Precarious Liberty: Trial by Jury in Seventeenth-Century New England," in *Saints and Revolutionaries: Essays in Early American History,* ed. David D. Hall, John M. Murrin, Thad W. Tate (New York, 1984), 161–63.

11. Wheelwright, *Brief,* 13; *AC,* 298; Sargent Bush, Jr., "John Wheelwright's Forgotten *Apology:* The Last Word in the Antinomian Controversy," *New England Quarterly* 64 (1991): 32.

12. I suspect this is chiefly because Miller, *Colony,* 57, called Bulkeley, Shepard, and Hooker the three most "vindictive prosecutors" of Hutchinson, but he offered no explanation as to why he lumped all three together. Hall printed a manuscript doctrinal discussion between Bulkeley and Cotton (*AC,* 34–42). Acknowledging that there was no internal evidence to date the manuscript, he speculatively assigned it to 1636. That date was sheer guesswork, and Hall presented it as such (if I were to guess, I would put it around the time of the letter discussed on 131–32 above), but later historians reproduced Hall's speculation as a statement of fact, which made Bulkeley appear out in front in his opposition to Cotton. There is no evidence, as far as I am aware, of Bulkeley's having the deep, personal suspicion of Cotton and his motives that both Hooker and Shepard displayed.

13. Peter Bulkeley, *The Gospel-Covenant; or The Covenant of Grace Opened,* 2d ed. (London, 1651), 325. Cf. the comments of then Boston church member Giles

Firmin, *[Panourgia]*, 24: "Many Christians meet with such comforts of the Spirit
. . . which much refresh for the time and may be afterwards remembred: but these
comforts go off; but the *Evidence* which arise from the sound work of *Faith* and
Regeneration, that is abiding as to the Foundation of it." Firmin argued that if a
person did not see evidence of transformation, it would be a "lye" to take comfort
from an absolute promise.

14. *JC*, 254.

15. Ibid., 255–6.

16. Ibid., 256.

17. *WJ*, 212.

18. Ibid., 216. The manuscript in the Hartlib Papers, 40/1/10A, has the title
"A Briefe of Mr Cottons 3d Answere to the Elders in the Baye May the 13. daye.
1637."

19. *God's Plot*, 65.

20. Thomas Hutchinson, "Hutchinson in America," Egerton MS 2664, p. 17,
British Library; *MHS Collections*, 6th ser. 1 (1886): 295; *MCA*, 1:484.

21. *WJ*, 216.

22. Hutchinson, *History*, 1:56; *MR*, 1:188; *WJ*, 214; *WWP*, 139; *MCA* 1:124;
MHS Collections, 6th ser. 1 (1886): 295.

23. Hutchinson, *History*, 1:56; *WJ*, 1:215; *AC*, 258.

24. *WJ*, 215; *MR*, 1:195.

25. *WJ*, 217. Cotton claimed that he, the elders, and various laypeople concluded a synod was necessary, whereupon they approached the magistrates. He
also claimed that Wheelwright's fast-day sermon followed this agreement. See *AC*,
399–400. *WJ*, 206, seems to indicate that the ministers decided on a synod in
March. The earliest date associated with the planning of the synod is a letter from
Hooker to Shepard dated April 8, 1637, in which Hooker was not enthusiastic
about it. See Hutchinson, *History*, 1:60.

26. .*WP*, 3:415.

27. *WJ*, 219; *WWP*, 113.

28. See chapter 10, note 7.

29. *PTV*, 1:1:163.

30. *MR*, 1:196.

31. Will of Thomas Dudley, *NEHGR* 5 (1851): 295; *GH*, 552, 553; *MCA*,
1:217; "Life of Thomas Dudley," *MHS Proceedings* 11 (1871): 219; "Autobiography of Major-General Daniel Denison," *NEHGR* 46 (1892): 128. The date of
Dudley's removal to Roxbury is my reconciliation of these last two sources.

32. *WJ*, 217.

33. Ibid., 225; Firmin, *[Panourgia]*, "To the Reader."

34. *AC*, 418; *WJ*, 215, 253.

35. Alfred A. Cave, *The Pequot War* (Amherst, MA, 1996), chapter 4; *God's
Plot*, 67; *AC*, 253–54.

36. *AC*, 253–54; *MA*, 219, 227; Perry Miller, *Orthodoxy in Massachusetts,
1630–1650* (Cambridge, 1933), 164; Battis, *SS*, 156; Gura, *Glimpse*, 252; Marilyn
J. Westerkamp, "Anne Hutchinson, Sectarian Mysticism, and the Puritan Order,"
Church History 59 (1990): 485; David S. Lovejoy, *Religious Enthusiasm in the New
World: Heresy to Revolution* (Cambridge, 1985), 71; Frank Shuffelton, *Thomas*

Hooker, 1586–1647 (Princeton, 1977), 245; Knight, *Orthodoxies,* 18. Peter Linebaugh and Marcus Rediker, *The Many-Headed Hydra: Sailors, Slaves, Commoners, and the Hidden History of the Revolutionary Atlantic* (Boston, 2000), 90–92, seize on this reading and leap into factual, chronological, and interpretive free fall with it. There is no other account of this incident, even in Winthrop's journal. Alfred Cave has recently suggested that Bostonian reluctance to serve (at least in a way of which Winthrop approved) might also have had another source. The previous December the Court had created military commanders for the various counties. It gave the Middlesex command to Winthrop, a person with no military experience, who had no intention of actually leading his recruits, over Boston's John Underhill, a professional soldier. Underhill resented being passed by, and so might have others (Cave, *The Pequot War,* 140). The issue would not have arisen for the muster in April because Vane as governor was chief general of the forces. *MR,* 1:186–87.

37. *HC,* 1:94; John Underhill, *Newes from America* (1638), in *MHS Collections,* 3d ser., 6 (1837): 21; *AC,* 253; Firmin, *Real Christian,* 284; *WJ,* 230; Edward Calamy, *A Continuation of the Account of the Ministers, Lecturers, Masters and Fellows of Colleges and Schoolmasters, Who Were Ejected or Silenced after the Restoration in 1660* (London, 1727), 2:297; Fiske, *Notebook,* 7; Roger Clap, *Memoirs of Capt. Roger Clap* (Boston, 1731), 15; Wheelwright, *Brief,* 3.

38. *AC,* 275.

39. Fiske, *Notebook,* 7; *WJ,* 226; *HC,* 1:93, 94. The only people known by name to have been excluded by this order were Hutchinson and Hanserd Knollys. Knollys arrived in the summer of 1638 and quickly went to Dover, Hew Hampshire, for a short-lived, not very happy pastorate, perhaps at the instigation of John Underhill. For a brief summary, see Charles E. Clark, *The Eastern Frontier: The Settlement of Northern New England, 1610–1763* (Hanover, NH, 1983), 40–41. For other Lincolnshire emigrants to whom this order may have applied, see Charles H. Bell, *History of the Town of Exeter, New Hampshire* (Exeter, 1888), 21–40.

40. *HC,* 1:79–81.

41. Ibid., 1:83, 82.

42. For a secular interpretation of this debate, see Miller, *Orthodoxy,* 234–41.

43. *HC,* 1:95, 88.

44. Ibid., 1:95, 90–91, 93. Vane also argued that persons with erroneous doctrine should not be rejected but "pitied and reformed," which has been read generously by some historians as meaning that Vane already had reached his later support of religious toleration. James K. Hosmer, *The Life of Young Sir Henry Vane* (Boston, 1889), 65; Violet A. Rowe, *Sir Henry Vane the Younger: A Study in Political and Administrative History* (London, 1970), 6. But Vane spoke of reforming, not tolerating, and elsewhere in this document (*HC,* 91) agreed that persons who did not bring true doctrine into the commonwealth did not need to be accepted.

45. *HC,* 1:90; Charles M. Andrews, *The Colonial Period of American History,* 2d ed. (New Haven, 1964), 1:420–21.

46. *WJ,* 226.

47. *JC,* 310; *AC,* 414.

48. Baillie, *Dissuasive*, 63; Baillie, *Dissuasive Vindicated*, 30; John Callender, *An Historical Discourse on the Civil and Religion Affairs of the Colony of Rhode Island*, Rhode Island Historical Society *Collections*, no. 4 (Providence, 1838), 85.

49. Cotton claimed to Baillie that the intended removal happened in 1638, and historians tend to take him at face value. He acknowledged that the removal was in response to the immigration order but claimed that the order had been passed after Hutchinson had been banished. He also asserted that he planned on emigrating only because of his desire for peace, and he claimed that Williams had been in exile for many years when these events happened. The net effect of his fabrications was to chronologically distance himself from the controversy, soften his oppositional stance, and undermine the credibility of Williams's testimony. *AC*, 414, 416. Previously when writing in a less-exposed context, Cotton was explicit that the planning for the removal took place before the synod, which also makes a great deal more sense. See Cotton in Williams, *Complete Writings*, 2:80–84. See also *JC*, 302, where Cotton places a critical meeting with Winthrop and Dudley after Wilson's August 1637 speech, not in 1638, as he does in *AC*, 415. Cotton once wrote that it was legitimate to "conceale our mindes, and put our adversaries upon proofe" if those adversaries were acting as "captious questioners" (*HC*, 1:64).

50. Isabel MacBeath Calder, *The New Haven Colony* (New Haven, 1934), 46–49.

51. Firmin, *[Panourgia]*, "To the Reader"; *WJ*, 225.

52. Franklin Bowditch Dexter, ed., *Extracts from the Itineraries and Other Miscellanies of Ezra Stiles, D.D., LL.D. 1755–1794 with a Selection from His Correspondence* (New Haven, 1916), 370; *WP*, 4:23.

53. *WJ*, 229; George Sikes, *The Life and Death of Sir Henry Vane, Kt.* (N.p., 1662), 8; Hutchinson, *History*, 58; *GH*, 236.

54. *AC*, 251; *HC*, 1:86, 103.

55. *HC*, 1:107.

56. Ibid., 1:112.

57. Ibid.

58. "Thomas Shepard's Election Sermon in 1638," *NEGHR* 24 (1870): 361–66.

59. Ibid., 365.

60. Ibid., 364–65, 366. Cf. Carl Bangs, *Arminius: A Study in the Dutch Reformation* (Nashville, 1971), 303.

61. *A Report of the Record Commissioners, Containing the Roxbury Land and Church Records* (Boston, 1881), 189; William M. Lamont, *Marginal Prynne, 1600–1669* (London, 1963), 141, 187; Carla Gardina Pestana, "City on a Hill under Siege: The Puritan Perception of the Quaker Threat to Massachusetts Bay, 1656–1661," *New England Quarterly* 56 (1983): 338–40; Richard Baxter, *A Holy Commonwealth* (1659), ed. William Lamont (Cambridge, 1994), 31–32; T. B. Howell, *A Complete Collection of State Trials* (London, 1809–26), 6:197.

62. "Shepard's Election Sermon," 366; *WJ*, 229; *MR*, 1:200; *GH*, 294; *WP*, 3:461; Firmin, *[Panourgia]*, "To the Reader."

CHAPTER EIGHT
RECLAIMING COTTON

1. The literary conceit of weaving in Jenny Geddes and the Cotton quotation was taken from Charles Francis Adams's discussion of Ferndinando Gorges in *Three Episodes in New England History* (Boston, 1891), 1:300.

2. *WP*, 3:460–63.

3. *WJ*, 230; *JC*, 302–3; *AC*, 415. Battis, *SS*, 164, dates Cotton's acceptance of Wilson's explanation as mid-July, but his source, *WJ*, 230, indicates that it occurred between August 5 and 17. Cotton's explanation (*JC*, 306), of why he accepted the reasons for Wheelwright's banishment, even if accurate, refers to incidents that took place in the interval between his sentence and his banishment.

4. *WJ*, 223; *MCA*, 1:325. Knight, *Orthodoxies*, 16, 24, claims that Davenport encouraged dissenters and stood steadfastly by Cotton at the synod. I know of no evidence that would support either claim and Knight offers none.

5. "Life of Thomas Dudley," *MHS Proceedings* 11 (1871): 216.

6. *JC*, 289.

7. *AC*, 400. Cotton's comment on Hooker and others was recorded by John Higginson in Cotton Mather, *The Everlasting Gospel* (Boston, 1700), sig. B2iiiv. Although the comment is undated, the context in which Higginson presented it seems to put it in the period before the synod, which Higginson attended. When the final list of issues between Cotton and the other ministers was drawn up for discussion at the synod, Hooker's preparationism was not among them. A list, *AC*, 44–45, titled "New England 1637 Questions agreed upon by all the Elders of the Bay to be conferred upon at a Meetinge," presumably dates from these conferences; the questions concern Cotton's and Wheelwright's doctrines, sometimes put in extreme form, as well as more radical doctrines.

8. *AC*, 400–6; *GH*, 299–301.

9. Foster, "New England," 647–48.

10. The eighty-one errors are listed in order numerically in *AC*, 219–43.

11. Subsequent references are to the "errors" themselves, not the pages they are found on. Errors 17, 20, 23, 25, 29, 30, 38, 46, 44, 47, 48, 45, 58, 60, 62, 63, 67, 69, 72, 75, 77, 78.

12. Errors 7, 22, 43, 49, 59, 70.

13. Errors 1, 14, 15, 18, 35.

14. Errors 8, 21, 26, 27, 55, 68.

15. Errors 16, 23, 25, 32, 73.

16. Errors 32, 42, 56.

17. Error 13.

18. Cf. Wheelwright's comment from his fast-day sermon, "Therefore ought no works of sanctification be urged upon the servants of God, so as if they had a power to do them" (*AC*, 162).

19. *MA*, 210. Cf. Cotton, *Treatise*, 41.

20. *MA*, 205.

21. *MCA*, 2:512.

22. *WP*, 3:460. Foster, "New England," 652, claims that Underhill probably picked up his opinions in Holland before he had ever met Anne Hutchinson. Foster reached his conclusion on the assumption that Jane Holmes's encounter with

Underhill (see below) took place in 1635. But *WJ*, 262–63, clearly identifies the encounter with Underhill's return voyage to Massachusetts in 1638.

23. James F. Cooper, Jr., "The Confession and Trial of Richard Wayte, Boston, 1640," *William and Mary Quarterly*, 3d ser., 44 (1987):322.

24. *WJ*, 263.

25. George Selement and Bruce C. Woolley, eds., *Thomas Shepard's* Confessions, Colonial Society of Massachusetts *Collections*, no. 58 (Boston, 1981): 78–79; Firmin, *[Panourgia]*, 14. Cf. Thomas Shepard, Hebrews 10:23, June 16, 1644, Sermons by Thomas Shepard and Thomas Allen, Shepard Family Papers, American Antiquarian Society, Worcester, Massachusetts: "Yea somtyms [assurance comes] after a pipe, or a pot or after some secreat whoredomes committed, and now hee sees grace is hereby mightily magnified and heeres all the ground of his peace."

26. *MA*, 192.

27. *WWP*, 171; *WJ*, 232.

28. *MA*, 208; *GH*, 299; *AC*, 427; *WJ*, 232.

29. *WWP*, 157, 171; *AC*, 213.

30. *AC*, 408; *JC*, 303; William Aspinwall, *Thunder from Heaven* (London, 1657), 38.

31. *JC*, 303; *AC*, 408.

32. *WJ*, 232.

33. *WJ*, 233; *BCR*, 282.

34. *AC*, 422; *WWP*, 173.

35. Error 40.

36. Errors 20, 37, 43, 45, 61, 66, 73.

37. Errors 48, 49.

38. Error 37, "we are compleatly united to Christ, before, or without any faith wrought in us by the Spirit" is almost identical to a "query" Cotton brought to the synod. It is intriguing that the "confutation" of this error is the most carefully qualified of any of them. I suspect that Cotton wrote it. Error 38 claims there can be no true closing with Christ in a conditional promise; this is very close to Cotton, but he did acknowledge closing with Christ in a conditional promise applied absolutely. Error 41 is Cotton's doctrine that each member of the Trinity plays a predominant role in conversion at different times.

39. Errors 38, 60, 69.

40. Error 75. See also the "confutation" of "unsavoury speech" no. 2, *AC*, 244–45, which also suggests Cotton's hand.

41. *WJ*, 232; *AC*, 408; *MCA* 1:310, 2:514; Charles Chauncy, *Seasonable Thoughts on the State of Religion in New-England* (Boston, 1743), vii.

42. *AC*, 213. Wheelwright's four theses were: justification goes in order before believing; assurance of justification from works of sanctification is not our assurance of faith; the Faith of God's elect, whereby they believe on Christ, is grounded upon a free, simple, absolute promise of Grace; all promises proper and peculiar to the Gospel, are absolute (Wheelwright, *Brief*, 15–21). Winthrop said five points were debated (*WJ*, 233). His five points were a conflation of some of the above, together with the question of the nature of the new creature, which became an issue in the course of the synod.

43. *AC*, 213.

44. *WJ*, 234.

45. *AC*, 213; *WJ*, 234.

46. *GH*, 303; Wheelwright, *Brief*, 23; *AC*, 422; *WJ*, 505, 233.

47. *AC*, 411.

48. *AC*, 410; Wheelwright, *Brief*, 21.

49. *MCA*, 2:514; Norton, *Abel*, 34; Baillie, *Dissuasive*, 37. I find problematic the claim in Kamensky, *Governing*, 76, that the synod's debates had "a practiced, incantory, and, above all, controlled quality" and that the tenor of all disagreements was "controlled" and "respectful." She cites neither Mather, Baillie, nor Wheelwright.

50. *JC*, 273.

51. "Abraham believed God, and it was counted unto him for righteousness. Now to him that worketh is the reward not reckoned of grace, but of debt. But to him that worketh not, but believeth on him that justifieth the ungodly, his faith is counted for righteousness."

52. *MCA*, 2:514; *AC*, 411.

53. *WJ*, 233; *JC*, 309; *MCA*, 2:514.

54. *WJ*, 233.

55. *MCA*, 2:514–15; *GH*, 300. Harry S. Stout, *The New England Soul: Preaching and Religious Culture in Colonial New England* (New York, 1986), 25, says of the synod's deliberations, "After protracted debate Cotton was led to see how obedience to New England's biblically deduced institutions constituted a form of 'sanctification.'" He cites no sources from the synod in making this claim and it is, at least for me, extremely hard to extrapolate from the debates themselves to his conclusion.

56. Wheelwright, *Brief*, 6.

57. *WJ*, 234–35. See Cooper, *Tenacious*, 54–55, for a commentary on these resolutions.

58. Phillip H. Round, *By Nature and Custom Cursed: Transatlantic Civil Discourse and New England Cultural Production, 1620–1660* (Hanover, NH, 1999), 131; Kamensky, *Governing*, 76; Staloff, *Making*, 57. Cf. David D. Hall, *Worlds of Wonder, Days of Judgment: Popular Religious Belief in Early New England* (New York, 1990), 64–67.

59. *WWP*, 172, 174; *AC*, 213; "Scituate and Barnstaple Church Records," *NEHGR* 10 (1853): 39.

60. *AC*, 213; Hutchinson, *History*, 1:61; *WJ*, 235; *GH*, 304; John Cotton, *The Way of the Churches of Christ in New-England* (London, 1645), 107.

61. Hutchinson, *History*, 1:61.

62. Thomas Hooker, *The Application of Redemption . . . the First Eight Books* (London, 1656), 40. For the dates of Hooker's sermons, see Douglas Shepard, "The Wolcott Shorthand Notebook Transcribed" (Ph.D. diss., State University of Iowa, 1957). Sargent Bush, Jr., *The Writings of Thomas Hooker: Spiritual Adventure in Two Worlds* (Madison, WI, 1980), suggests that at least some of the sermons published in *The Saints Dignitie and Dutie* (London, 1651) were preached in Boston and that they all made reference to the free grace controversy. But the evidence Bush adduces is not very persuasive. Bush sees as a "clear reference to the doctrines of the Wheelwrights, the Cottons, and the Hutchinsons" (88) a passage in which

Hooke talks of the need for people to try themselves by signs (68). Though the passage does attack "antinomianism," there is no mention in it of Cotton or Hutchinson's distinctive doctrines; these are generic, English doctrines. Bush further argues that this sermon was probably preached in Boston because Hooker twice alluded to "this city" in it. Boston did not become a city until 1822; it was routinely and correctly referred to as a town throughout the colonial period. Hooker certainly would not have been likely to have used the word "city" in connection with it on the basis of its physical appearance alone—a traveler to Boston in 1638 remarked that the settlement looked more like a village than a town. See *MHS Collections*, 3d ser., 3 (1833): 225. It seems far more likely that the sermon was preached in London at the height of the antinomian stirs there. In other sermons, Hooker made at least two references to parishes, which would rule out an American origin for them (211, 227). Throughout *The Saints Dignitie*, the social situation Hooker addresses reads to me like an English one. Bush acknowledges that the evidence for a Massachusetts origin for these sermons is "far from conclusive" (94). I could not find positive evidence for a Massachusetts origin in any of the sermons and in a number of sermons positive evidence for an English origin. The social complexity alluded to throughout the sermons further suggests that they are all English in origin.

63. *WJ*, 235.

CHAPTER NINE
THE NOVEMBER TRIALS

1. *AC*, 248, 422–23; *WP*, 3:499; *God's Plot*, 66. Hutchinson, *History*, 1:63, has an odd passage that he places at this time: "At length [Hutchinson] forsook the public assemblies, and set up what she called a purer worship in her own family. It is not improbable that she was encouraged herein by Mr. Vane." I do not know what Hutchinson's source for this claim would be. He had already discussed her conventicles, so he was not confusing those with this. Vane was already gone.

2. *WJ*, 253–55.

3. Battis, *SS*, 174–75; *WJ*, 239; *AC*, 248.

4. *MR*, 1:205; *AC*, 258, 251–52.

5. *WJ*, 240; *MR*, 1:206; *AC*, 252.

6. *AC*, 252–54; *JC*, 306.

7. *AC*, 256–57, *MR*, 1:207.

8. *AC*, 257–61.

9. *MCA*, 1:129. See Norton, *Founding*, 374–88, for an analysis of the trial that systematically discusses the differences between the two versions.

10. *AC*, 312.

11. Ibid., 313–14. Including rulers within the compass of the Fifth Commandment was standard at this time. See Ian Green, *The Christian's ABC: Catechisms and Catechizing in England c. 1530–1740* (Oxford, 1996), 452–53.

12. *AC*, 314.

13. Ibid., 269; Porterfield, *Female*, 95; Norton, *Founding*, 378–82.

14. Ibid., 316–17.

15. Dudley clerked for the distinguished godly jurist Sir Augustine Nicolls in the early 1590s. The grandfather of Theophilus, earl of Lincoln, had left the estate with extensive debts, which Dudley's management, according to Cotton Mather, removed. Theophilus himself, besides being a militant puritan, was an encloser and fen drainer, both disruptive and controversial activities, often considered at variance with traditional agrarian paternalism. *MCA*, 1:132–33; John Langton Sanford, *The Great Governing Families of England* (Edinburgh, 1865), 1:207–8; Laurence Stone, *The Crisis of the Aristocracy, 1558–1641* (Oxford, 1965), 330, 356. For the sometimes dubious techniques the gentry used to increase the incomes of their estates, see Felicity Heal and Clive Holmes, *The Gentry in England and Wales, 1500–1700* (Stanford, 1994), 104–16. In Massachusetts, Winthrop once accused Dudley of usury. See *WJ*, 66. The earl of Lincoln owned numerous manors, whose courts Dudley as steward would have supervised.

16. J. S. Cockburn, *A History of English Assizes, 1558–1714* (Cambridge, 1972), 109; *AC*, 318.

17. *AC*, 318, 326.

18. Ibid., 321, 326, 333.

19. Ibid., 326.

20. Ibid., 330. Cf. Michael Dalton, *Country Justice* (London, 1647), 273.

21. *AC*, 327.

22. Ibid., 328–29. Breen, *Transgressing*, chap. 1, portrays the clash between Stoughton and Winthrop as broadly reflective of antinominan/orthodox tensions in New England. Yet her portrayal of both individuals is problematic. Stoughton, while concerned that basic English legal norms be followed, did not show as "disinclination to censure" Hutchinson, as Breen claims; he made it continually clear that he though that Hutchinson was guilty. There is no evidence at all for Breen's claim that "Stoughton's interest in legal niceties [at Hutchinson's trial] seemed elitist and ungodly" to the Massachusetts colonists. Moreover, contrary to Breen, Winthrop's initial reluctance to require oaths does not appear from the trial transcript to have had "the compelling ring of plain common sense" to a significant portion of the General Court, just as the bulk of colonists distrusted his general disregard for legal niceties and eventually managed to get a code of written laws over his objections. Certainly, the word "antinomian" is being stretched well past the breaking point when Breen claims that Stoughton spoke in "antinomian accents" by requesting the oaths (27, 28, 37).

23. *AC*, 329–30.

24. Ibid., 325, 330–32.

25. Ibid., 332.

26. Cockburn, *History*, 121.

27. *AC*, 333.

28. Ibid., 334.

29. Ibid., 334–36.

30. Kai T. Erikson, *Wayward Puritans: A Study in the Sociology of Deviance* (New York, 1996), 93, 94; Ann Fairfax Withington and Jack Schwartz, "The Political Trial of Anne Hutchinson," *New England Quarterly* 51 (1978): 226–40, quote from 230; Staloff, *Making*, 62.

31. Charles Francis Adams, *Three Episodes of Massachusetts History* (Boston, 1892), 1:499; Edmund S. Morgan, "The Case against Anne Hutchinson," *New England Quarterly* 10 (1937): 635–49; Samuel Eliot Morison, *Builders of the Bay Colony* (Boston, 1958), 123; Battis, *SS*, 202; Norton, *Founding*, 386; Philip Ranlet, *Enemies of the Bay Colony* (New York, 1995), 40; Jean Cameron, *Anne Hutchinson, Guilty or Not? A Closer Look at Her Trials* (New York, 1994), 160; Ziff, *Career*, 139.

32. Staloff, *Making*, 65–66, draws a similar conclusion, as does Gura, *Glimpse*, 259, and Michael G. Ditmore, "A Prophetess in Her Own Country: An Exegesis of Anne Hutchinson's 'Immediate Revelations'," *William and Mary Quarterly*, 3d ser., 57 (2000):359.

33. *WJ*, 241.

34. Battis, *SS*, 202; Morgan, *Dilemma*, 151; Staloff, *Making*, 66; Ziff, *Career*, 139; Erikson, *Wayward Puritans*, 97; Gura, *Glimpse*, 259.

35. *WWP*, 128; Norton, *Founding*, 387. Cf. Ditmore, "Prophetess," 359–61, noting the studied nature of this part of her testimony.

36. Withington and Schwartz, "Political Trial," 237.

37. *AC*, 336–37.

38. Ibid., 337.

39. Ibid., 338. See Ditmore, "Anne Hutchinson's," 378–84, for a close analysis of Hutchinson's prophecy.

40. Selma R. Williams, *Divine Rebel: The Life of Anne Marbury Hutchinson* (New York, 1981), 22.

41. *AC*, 338.

42. *MCA*, 1:314.

43. Michael P. Winship, *Seers of God: Puritan Providentialism in the Restoration and Early Enlightenment* (Baltimore, 1996), 19–20; Phyllis Mack, *Visionary Women: Ecstatic Prophecy in Seventeenth-Century England* (Berkeley, 1992), 75–79; Alexandra Walsham, "'Frantick Hacket': Prophecy, Sorcery, Insanity, and the Elizabethan Puritan Movement," *Historical Journal* 41 (1998): 49–50; Samuel Rutherford, *A Survey of the Spirituall Antichrist* (London, 1648), chap. 7.

44. *AC*, 339; Thomas Hooker, *The Danger of Desertion* (London, 1641), 14.

45. Cotton, *Treatise*, 214–15; Jonathan Mitchel Sermons, MHS, Boston (second sermon in manuscript).

46. Cotton, *Treatise*, 214; *AC*, 274.

47. *AC*, 274.

48. Ibid., 338–40, 273; *WP*, 4:23.

49. *AC*, 339–40.

50. Ibid., 342.

51. Ibid., 342–43.

52. Ibid., 343.

53. Ibid., 344.

54. Ibid., 345–46.

55. Ibid., 347.

56. Ibid., 347–48.

57. Erikson, *Wayward Puritans*, 101; Delbanco, *Puritan*, 137; *AC*, 303.

58. *MR*, 1:207.

59. Morgan, "Case," though not originating this argument, established the currently dominant variant when he argued that it was Hutchinson's revelations in themselves, not their content, that got her convicted. See, for example, Withington and Schwartz, "Political Trial"; Ziff, *Career*, 140–41; Marilyn J. Westerkamp, "Anne Hutchinson, Sectarian Mysticism, and the Puritan Order," *Church History* 59 (1990): 482–96; Staloff, *Making*, 66–72; Cameron, *Hutchinson*, chap. 9; Sandra M. Gustafson, *Eloquence Is Power: Oratory and Performance in Early America* (Chapel Hill, 2000), 32. But it is safe to say that had Hutchinson disseminated a revelation that bishops were antichristian, she would have never appeared as a defendant in a New England court. Conversely, had she threatened God's vengeance on the Court without invoking revelations, she would have been convicted. The evidence for the slander charge was strong, and Greensmith had already been convicted on a similar charge. This is not to dispute that Hutchinson's claiming revelations as her source of authority made her appear even more of a menace to public order.

60. Cynthia B. Herrup, *The Common Peace: Participation and the Criminal Law in Seventeenth-Century England* (Cambridge, 1987), 144.

61. Withington and Schwartz, "Political Trial"; 230. Battis, *SS*, 217–19, makes the case for the legal plausibility of Hutchinson's conviction well, although he does not discuss her contempt of court. Battis does claim that the Court's acting as judges, jurors, and prosecutors had no English precedent and "overthrew any semblance of justice the proceedings might have offered" (220). But this is to strain at a gnat after swallowing a camel. The freemen of Massachusetts accepted that the Court could take on those roles, so Massachusetts standards of justice were not violated, and, for what it is worth, there was English precedent in the procedures of the House of Lords when trying a peer for a felony or treason. See David L. Smith, *The Stuart Parliaments, 1603–1689* (London, 1999), 35.

62. Mary Beth Norton, "'The Ablest Midwife That We Knowe in the Land': Mistress Alice Tilly and the Women of Boston and Dorchester, 1649–1650," *William and Mary Quarterly*, 3d ser., 55 (1998): 105–34.

63. *WJ*, 242. This section of *Short Story* ends with an "amen" on *AC*, 280, and it was clearly written in the winter for an audience unfamiliar with New England.

64. *AC*, 265.

65. Bryce Twister, "Anne Hutchinson's 'Monstrous Birth' and the Feminization of Antinomianism," *Canadian Review of American Studies* 27 (1997):139. The scholarly literature that locates gender issues as central to the free grace controversy is extremely varied, and some of it is very skillful and insightful (see introduction, note 6). But it is inadequate for an understanding of the overall controversy because it tends to simply assume that Hutchinson was the central figure, which licenses it to not to analyze anyone else independently: Vane and Wheelwright are side players, labeled "supporters" and "followers" of Hutchinson and then mostly ignored; Cotton's role goes largely unexamined; and the multifaceted and multidirectional indignation of Shepard is omitted altogether.

66. *MR*, 1:207; *AC*, 262.

67. *MR*, 1:209; *AC*, 277–78.

68. *MCA*, 1:386; *MR*, 1:208; *WWP*, 200–201; Samuel Eliot Morison, *The Founding of Harvard College* (Cambridge, 1935), 182–83.

69. *WP,* 3:510. For interesting speculation on Margaret Winthrop and Anne Hutchinson, see Williams, *Divine Rebel,* 138.

70. *AC,* 244, 280; *WP,* 3:510.

CHAPTER TEN
AN AMERICAN JEZEBEL

1. Notes on Sermons delivered by Thomas Shepard, 1637–38, p. 259, MHS; *AC,* 310.

2. *MA,* 191; *AC,* 278–79, 422; Wheelwright, *Brief,* 24–25. But see 297 n.36 below for a possible connection with Hutchinson.

3. *AC,* 278–79; *MA,* 191; Wheelwright, *Brief,* 24–25.

4. *AC,* 278–29; *WWP,* 129.

5. *AC,* 279; *MR,* 1:209, 211; *WJ,* 241. Scholars, with a few exceptions, tend to see the authorities' crackdown in November as overreaction. But Staloff, *Making,* 59, suggests that it was mild and reflected the influence of Winthrop. Ronald D. Cohen, "Church and State in Seventeenth-Century Massachusetts: Another Look at the Antinomian Controversy," *Journal of Church and State* 12 (1970): 475–94, strongly defends it.

6. Battis, *SS,* 258–61, 272–74.

7. *WJ,* 242. Winthrop's lists have the recantations of two people not on the Court's original list. Nor was Henry Flint, who recanted in 1639, on this list. *WP,* 3:513–16. Rutman, *Winthrop's Boston,* 179, gives 8,000 as the total population of the colony. I extrapolated the number adult males from the roughly 360 in Boston (Battis, *SS,* 330–44) out of a town population of roughly 1,000.

8. *WJ,* 242. Boston has the most comprehensive surviving lists of recantations. There is no evidence that twenty-three of the Boston fifty-eight ever recanted, and ten of the twenty three stayed in Boston after the controversy or returned after a short period in exile. Nor do we know how many recanted with the reservations expressed by John Underhill, Samuel Wilbore, and Thomas Savage—they apologized that the manner gave offense, but not for the cause. See *WP,* 3:515–16, 4:121–22; *WJ,* 263. Ralph Mousall of Charlestown, though he came in voluntarily to recant, was dismissed as a deputy from the Court the next year because of speeches he had made in support of Wheelwright. See *MR,* 1:236. A good portion of those singled out for disarmament may have obeyed relatively quickly, but almost exactly two years later the General Court passed an order "that all that were disarmed, remaining amongst us, carrying themselves peaceably, shall have their arms restored to them" (*MR,* 1:278). Six months after that, the Court records report Henry Flint's acknowledging his fault in signing the petition, which may have been the minimum concession on his part necessary to become the first minister of the new official town of Mount Wollaston (*MR,* 1:289). A year and a half thereafter, in October 1641, ex-magistrate Richard Dummer gave satisfaction to the Court, perhaps a limited and argumentative satisfaction, since the Court referred him to John Wilson and John Eliot for his opinions. See *MR,* 1:339.

9. *MR,* 1:213, 217; *MCA,* 1:386; Roland L. Warren, *Loyal Dissenter: The Life and Times of Robert Pike* (Lantham, MD, 1992), 49–55.

10. *AC*, 27–28, 32, 51, 67, 100–104; *PTV*, 1:171; for Dyer, see 212 above; Vane, *Retired*, chaps. 6, 7. Some historians have claimed that one index of the dramatic gulf between the sensibility of the Bostonian theologians and their opponents was that the latter were restorationists, looking back to the Garden of Eden, while the Bostonians were eschatological, looking to the perfection of the Last Days, but as Vane's example as well as Hutchinson's (191–92 above) suggest, that difference may be not too much more than an effect of the serving documentation. See Jesper Rosenmeier, "New England's Perfection: The Image of Adam and the Image of Christ in the Antinomian Crisis, 1634 to 1638," *William and Mary Quarterly*, 3d ser., 27 (1970): 435–59. Knight, *Orthodoxies*, 20. Rosenmeier is more reliable than Knight, but he still exaggerates the differences between the Bostonians and their opponents. Shepard, for example, did believe in the millennial kingdom (61, 222 above), and Hutchinson did not think that the history of redemption was over (see 191). See also Theodore Dwight Bozeman, *To Live Ancient Lives: The Primitivist Dimension in Puritanism* (Chapel Hill, 1988), chap. 7.

11. *AC*, 304, 354, 355, 362, 361, 358. Jean Cameron, *Anne Hutchinson, Guilty Or Not? A Closer Look at Her Trials* (New York, 1994), 175–79. On the relationship to familist doctrine, see 200 above, 296 n.12, 297 n.30 below.

12. Caroline Walker Bynum, *The Resurrection of the Body in Western Christianity, 200–1336* (New York, 1995); *AC*, 301, 302, 352, 363; Hendrik Niclaes, *Evangelium Regni* (N.p., 1575?), fols. 51r–v, 83v–84r. For the association of Christ's non-physical resurrection with anabaptism and enthusiasm in Shropshire in the early 1630s, see Peter Studley, *The Looking-Glasse of Schisme* (London, 1633), 158, 160–61. I thank David Como for this reference. I am interpreting the fragments that are all that survive of Hutchinson's mature speculation in the light of Vane's comments on Adam and Christ's active and passive obedience in *Retired*. Although Vane was not nearly as radical as Hutchinson, their ideas easily relate as different branches from a shared speculative trunk. It was conventional to argue that the church was Christ's mystical body, but certainly not his human nature. Peter Shaw was also accused of arguing that the soul was mortal. See David Como and Peter Lake, "Puritans, Antinomians and Laudians in Caroline London: The Strange Case of Peter Shaw and Its Contexts," *Journal of Ecclesiastical History* 50 (1999): 707.

13. S. G., *Glass*, 9.

14. *AC*, 352, 300, 376. Hutchinson acknowledged that she had said all these things.

15. *AC*, 304, 216.

16. *WJ*, 245.

17. Shepard Sermons, 136; "Scituate and Barnstaple Church Records," *NEHGR* 10 (1853): 37; *AC*, 301.

18. John Callender, *An Historical Discourse on the Civil and Religion Affairs of the Colony of Rhode Island*, Rhode Island Historical Society *Collections*, no. 4 (Providence, 1838), 85; *WP* 4:41; John Russell Bartlett, ed., *Records of the Colony of Rhode Island and Providence Plantations, in New England* (Providence, 1856), 1:52; Battis, *SS*, 304–7, 312–16, 322–28. The "marginal men" are from Battis's "peripheral" group. This is a more problematic list than Battis's "core" and "sup-

port" groups. An unknown number were certainly leaving the colony over the government's disputes with Roger Williams and Robert Lenthall, while some may have simply been attracted to the better climate in Narragansett Bay. There were undoubtedly other emigrants whom the surviving records have missed.

19. John Clarke, *Ill Newes from New-England* (London, 1652), sig. Bir.

20. William Coddington, *A Demonstration of True Love unto You the Rulers of the Colony of the Massachusetts in New-England* (N.p., 1674), 13.

21. *WP*, 4:245, 278.

22. Ibid., 3:22, 34, 4:14; Robert Keayne Sermon Notes, 2: September 27, 1640, MHS.

23. *WJ*, 244; *AC*, 212.

24. *AC*, 217.

25. Ibid., 216; cf. *WJ*, 244. The lying may have had to do with claiming Cotton's support. See *AC*, 385.

26. *WP*, 3:513–16, 4:353–54. Roxbury church members Henry Bull, Nicholas Parker, and John Walker are listed as Boston residents in the Court disarmament order. *MR*, 1:212; Battis, *SS*, 306–7.

27. *A Report of the Record Commissioners, Containing the Roxbury Land and Church Records* (Boston, 1881), 79, 81; *AC*, 280, 219. Six people were excommunicated from Boston over the course of three years in connection with the controversy. See 211–12.

28. Ms. Am 1506, pt. 2, no. 25, Boston Public Library.

29. For Weld's career upon his return to England, see Roger Howell, "Thomas Weld of Gateshead: The Return of a New England Puritan," *Archaeologia Aeliana*, 4th ser., 48 (1970): 303–32.

30. *A Report*, 81; Ms. Am 1506, pt. 2, no. 25.

31. *WJ*, 245. Cotton's tract, "A Doctrinal Conclusion," arguing forcefully for inherent righteousness, in John Cotton, *The Covenant of Gods Free Grace . . . from That Text of 2 Sam. 23. Ver. 5.* (London, 1645), 27–33, also published in John Cotton, *A Treatise* (Boston, 1713), probably comes from this period.

32. *AC*, 301; *WJ*, 245; *JC*, 51–52.

33. *AC*, 301, 351–54.

34. *MR*, 1:233, 266; *AC*, 248.

35. *AC*, 301; *WJ*, 250.

36. *AC*, 351. Keayne seems to have omitted a significant number of Hutchinson's opinions in recording these lists. Winthrop gave a much greater number in *Short Story*, *AC*, 301–3. When Hutchinson retracted her errors, some of those she retracted were mentioned by Winthrop but were not on Keayne's lists (*AC*, 374–76). The only errors listed by Winthrop that cannot be traced anywhere in Keayne's notes of the trial are 12, 28, and 29. Of those, only 12, denying the evidence of absolute as well as conditional promises, is major, and if Winthrop recorded it correctly, Keayne's silence on it is puzzling.

37. *AC*, 303, 353–54.

38. Ibid., 358, 303.

39. Ibid., 358. For an overview of English mortalism, which was heavily identified with familism, see Norman T. Burns, *English Mortalism from Tyndale to Milton* (Cambridge, 1972). Burns notes that Hutchinson's purchased immortality has

no significant relationship to his topic (70). Nonetheless, exposure to mortalist Scripture exegeses could have started Hutchinson off, and Niclae's writings easily allow for other interpretations besides straightforward mortalism. J. F. Maclear, "Anne Hutchinson and the Mortalist Heresy," *New England Quarterly* 54 (1981): 74–103, is the starting point for subsequent scholarly discussions of Hutchinson's new theology. Porterfield, *Female*, 97–98; Gura, *Glimpse*, 90–91. Maclear sees Hutchinson's "mortalism" as "singly Puritan" in origin, an organic evolution from previous positions (103). But the parallels with familism, including the denial of Christ's bodily resurrection, which Maclear does not discuss, are too extensive to be coincidental.

40. *AC*, 361, 360, 363.

41. Ibid., 362, 305. Hutchinson referred to John 8:53. On the stereotypical association of familism with sexual license, see Kristin Poole, *Radical Religion from Shakespeare to Milton: Figures of Nonconformity in Early Modern England* (Cambridge, 2000), chap. 3; Norton, *Founding*, 232.

42. *AC*, 364.

43. Ibid., 367.

44. Ibid., 364–67.

45. Ibid., 367–68. Coercive majoritarian pressure on dissenters was a normal part of Massachusetts church procedures. See Richard Mather, *Church-Government and Church-Covenant Discussed* (London, 1643), 60; John Cotton, *The Way of the Churches of Christ in New-England* (London, 1645), 95.

46. *AC*, 368–72. Lang, *Prophetic*, 46, argues that Cotton's denial of suspecting Hutchinson indicates that he really did. It therefore demonstrates for Lang that "loathing [toward Hutchinson] arose, in part at least, from the imputation of sexual crimes." I would damn Cotton for pastoral insensitivity had he not put in that disclaimer; Lang damns him because he did.

47. *AC*, 372.

48. *AC*, 372–73; *God's Plot*, 78; *WJ*, 247.

49. *WJ*, 249. Winthrop explained the Court's decision very differently after Hutchinson had been excommunicated. See *AC*, 305.

50. *AC*, 376, 431, 306.

51. Ibid., 306, 377.

52. Hutchinson, *History*, 1:63; *AC*, 377.

53. *AC*, 378.

54. John Cotton, *A Censure of That Reverend and Learned Man of God Mr. John Cotton* (London, 1656), 54, uses what sounds like a proverb, "To cut off some sprigs [shoots] when others lye hid," to the same effect as Simmes. I could not find the proverb, however, in the reference sources I consulted. Historians have sometimes scrambled very inventively to interpret Simmes's words. See *AC*, xx, 378. Patricia Caldwell, "The Antinomian Language Controversy," *Harvard Theological Review* 69 (1976): 345–67, has suggested that Hutchinson was a victim of a heightened sensitivity to the ambiguity of language. Perhaps, but only if it is noted that this was a strongly self-willed sensitivity, as her audience did not find the terminological distinction between graces in us and graces in Christ that hard to grasp. See Cameron, *Anne Hutchinson*, chap. 10, for a portrayal of Hutchison simply as a legitimately confused Bible reader.

55. *AC*, 379–81. For suggestions on the identity of the Woman of Elis, see Gura, *Glimpse*, 242.

56. *AC*, 383.

57. Ibid.

58. A common scholarly reading of this day is that the ministers did not have any intention of allowing Hutchinson the space to repent, given the seriousness of her crimes; they were simply acting out their roles as good shepherds, and when she did repent they had to abruptly reverse course and deny that her repentance was sincere. But this reading squeezes together very different ministerial and lay agendas, all of which seem overt in Keayne's notes, into a single purpose and leaves unexamined Hutchinson's own performance. See Kai T. Erikson, *Wayward Puritans: A Study in the Sociology of Deviance* (New York, 1966), 105; Cameron, *Anne Hutchinson*, 201; Staloff, *Making*, 71–72. Phillip H. Round, *By Nature and Custom Cursed: Transatlantic Civil Discourse and New England Cultural Production, 1620–1660* (Hanover, NH, 1999), 142.

59. *AC*, 383.

60. Ibid., 384.

61. Ibid., 384–85.

62. Ibid., 385–86.

63. Ibid., 386–87, 432.

64. Cooper, *Tenacious*, 39; Richard Cust, *The Forced Loan in English Politics: 1626–1628* (Oxford, 1987), 298–99.

65. *AC*, 388, 307; *BCR*, 22; *WJ*, 250; *AC*, 425.

66. *AC*, 281, 307.

67. *WJ*, 250, 256; *AC*, 308.

68. Thomas Hutchinson, "Hutchinson in America," Egerton MS 2664, p. 19, British Library; *WJ*, 25; *WP*, 4:23.

CHAPTER ELEVEN
HOLDING FORTH DARKLY

1. *BCR*, 22, 25; *MR* 1:259, 262; Robert Keayne Sermon Notes, 2: June 14, 1640, MHS; *AC*, 395. For Dyer's excommunication, see *AC*, 393. The Boston church records did not always record excommunications. The only reason we know that Robert Parker had been excommunicated on July 24, 1636, a day for which the records only list new memberships, is that the records give that date for his excommunication when they record his being reaccepted on December 6, 1635. See *BCR*, 20. I thank James F. Cooper, Jr., for his assistance.

2. *AC*, 307; Thomas Hutchinson, "Hutchinson in America," Egerton MS 2664, p. 20, British Library.

3. *AC*, 282; *GH*, 303; Firmin, *[Panourgia]*, "To the Reader"; *WJ*, 255; *BCR*, 28, 34; Keayne Notebook, July 20, 1640.

4. See, for example, Lad Tobin, "A Radically Different Voice: Gender and Language in the Trials of Anne Hutchinson," *Early American Literature* 25 (1990): 253–70; Norton, *Founding*, 398; Marilyn J. Westerkamp, "Anne Hutchinson, Sectarian Mysticism, and the Puritan Order," *Church History* 59 (1990): 482–96.

5. *WP*, 4:2, 25; *WJ*, 251; Franklin Bowditch Dexter, ed., *Extracts from the Itineraries and Other Miscellanies of Ezra Stiles, D.D., LL.D. 1755–1794 with a Selection from His Correspondence* (New Haven, 1916), 370.

6. *JC*, 277–79; *WJ*, 274; Sydney V. James, *John Clarke and His Legacies: Religion and Law in Colonial Rhode Island, 1638–1730* (University Park, PA, 1999), 26. On the early years of Aquidneck, see Dennis Allen O'Toole, "Exiles, Refugees, and Rogues: The Quest for Civil Power in the Towns and Colony of Providence Plantations, 1636–1654" (Ph.D. diss., Brown University, 1973), 138–264. David D. Lovejoy, *Religious Enthusiasm in the New World: Heresy to Revolution* (Cambridge, 1985), 87, perhaps alone of the numerous historians who assume a large contingent of "Hutchinsonians," puzzles over Hutchinson's "almost studied inability to get along with her supporters" in Aquidneck, but there is no reason to think that the exiles, for the most part, defined themselves primarily as her supporters.

7. *JC*, 320–22; *WP*, 4:245.

8. Hall, *AC*, 389, gives the date as 1639, but Robert Keayne's Notebook, the source of this excerpt, was using old-style dating. The difference in dating is important for understanding the opinions of various people mentioned in the document.

9. Keayne Notes, 2:June 14, 1640.

10. There is a tendency to portray Hutchinson as a passive victim rather than an active participant in shaping her destiny. In an extreme expression of this tendency, Kamensky, *Governing*, 92, states that male "antinomians" could "revisit, rethink, and restate what they had said amiss. Hutchinson's words in contrast, could not be retracted or reframed. Her prophecy would have no other public outlet in the New England establishment: not from the pulpit, not in an exchange of letters, not though the London press. Her sentence of silence was irrevocable, her exile absolute." But Hutchinson certainly could have retracted her words had she any interest in doing so, and had she been prepared to make the right kind of apology, there is no reason to think that her sentence of banishment could not have been eventually lifted—the General Court had made concessions during her church trial when it thought there was hope she would repent, and the church was trying to get her to repent in 1640. Though the pulpit was barred her, the rest of Kamensky's claims about her lack of outlets is wrong. She did exchange letters (see 242 above). London press censorship broke down in early 1641; female religious readicals started to publish; Vane was a rising power in Parliament, and Hutchinson's brother-in-law Richard was a wealthy and radical London merchant. Had Hutchinson written something for publication, there is a good chance it would have been published.

11. *AC*, 215. Robert Keayne, *AC*, 392, recorded the church messengers giving an account of their meeting with Hutchinson to the Boston church that carried roughly the same sense as Weld's version. *AC*, 386–87; *MR*, 1:338.

12. *AC*, 393. The term is from 1 Corinthians 16:12. See also John Cotton, *The True Constitution of a Particular Visible Church, Proved by Scripture* (London, 1642), 12. *AC*, 392, 393, 395; *WJ*, 321.

13. *WP*, 4:278, 490.

14. Keayne Notes, 2: September 26, 1640; *JC*, 332–34; *WJ*, 364. The conflict was probably not as purely theological as Winthrop indicated. See James, *John Clarke*, 27. Keayne Notes, 2: June 2, 1644. For a commentary on Harding, see Lazar Ziff, "The Social Bonds of Church Covenant," *American Quarterly* 10 (1958): 454–62.

15. Charles H. Bell, *History of the Town of Exeter, New Hampshire* (Exeter, 1888), 11; *AC*, 423; *JC*, 305.

16. *BCR*, 23.

17. Bell, *History*, 15–19.

18. *AC*, 205, 303.

19. Ibid., 216, 310.

20. Ibid., 216.

21. Alexandra Walsham, *Providence in Early Modern England* (Oxford, 1999), 194–203.

22. *WP*, 4:25. Lang, *Prophetic*, 45, claims that the interest of Winthrop and others in Hutchinson's and Dyer's monstrous births was "inordinate" and therefore proof of a sexual and misogynist persecutory zeal. She does not reveal, however, the yardstick by which she measures "inordinate." The births were extraordinary coincidences, given the crimes Dyer and Hutchinson were suspected of and the providential framework within which everyone functioned. In the 1660s, a distinguished Cambridge University academic wrote a book to prove that monstrous births and other "wonders" were natural phenomena and thus unsusceptible to providential interpretation. Even he, however, did not try to find a natural explanation for Hutchinson and Dyer's babies, "monstrous beyond the possibilities of nature." See John Spencer, *A Discourse Concerning Prodigies*, 2d ed. (London, 1665), 364. Winthrop's descriptions of the births was accurate enough for one scholar to medically diagnose them. See Anne Jacobson Schutt, " 'Such Monstrous Births': A Neglected Aspect of the Antinomian Controversy," *Renaissance Quarterly* 38 (1985): 85–106. See also Valerie Pearl and Morris Pearl, eds., "Governor John Winthrop on the Birth of the Antinomians' 'Monster': The Earliest Reports to Reach England and the Making of a Myth," *MHS Proceedings* 102 (1990): 21–37. See *AC*, 215, for a "Hutchinsonian" interpretation of Dyer's fetus.

23. *MHS Proceedings*, 1st ser., 13 (1873–74): 132.

24. *WJ*, 264.

25. Cooper, *Tenacious*, 52–53 presents this lay disengagement as a result of the ministers' demonstrating their united opposition to Hutchinson and her errors. It seems to me that contemporary evidence suggests the laity's disengagement was more complex, conflicted, and independent.

26. *JC*, 277–79.

27. Keayne Notes, 2: August 3, 1640, October 4, 1640, March 30, 1640. Lyle arrived in Boston in 1637 and joined the church in 1639. James Savage, *A Genealogical Dictionary of the First Settlers of New England* (Boston, 1860–62), 3:133; Charles Henry Pope, *The Pioneers of Massachusetts, a Descriptive List* (Boston, 1900), 288. See also George Selement, "John Cotton's Hidden Antinomianism," *NEHGR* 129 (1975): 283–94.

28. *JC*, 368.

29. *MCA*, 1:216–17. Mather says the member was later excommunicated for his heresies and that he "afterwards died of those damnable heresies," which may allude to Francis Hutchinson's leaving the communion of churches and so being killed by the Indians.

30. *JC*, 347; *MA*, 196.

31. Edward Winslow, *The Danger of Tolerating Levellers in a Civill State* (London, 1649), 76–77. Ward presented this as the accurate version of a story told of Cotton in Samuel Gorton, *Simplicities Defence* (London, 1646), Rhode Island Historical Society *Collections*, no. 2 (Providence, 1835), 122. *WJ*, 336. Cf., *JC*, 302–6.

32. Scottow, *Narrative*, 301; *WP*, 4:353–54; *WWP*, 199; *JC*, 307–8.

33. *WJ*, 315, 363.

34. Hall, *Faithful Shepherd*, 110–11.

35. Peter Bulkeley, *The Gospel Covenant* (London, 1646), sigs. A4v, A4iiiir. The inaccessibility of the Bostonian path to salvation is stressed by Breen, *Transgressing*, chap. 1. Breen speculates that the ordinary colonists' rejection of "antinomianism" was due to their being provincial and of "middling status." By contrast, she claims that antinomianism was "broadly popular among Massachusetts elite" and "people who felt equally at home in a transatlantic and provincial environment" (55). But "antinomianism" was only broadly popular among Boston's elite, not Massachusetts's, while the main actors on each side of the controversy had a transatlantic orientation. In England, antinomianism was never broadly popular among any group anywhere, which makes it unlikely that provinciality played a major role in accepting or rejecting it in Massachusetts. Whether middling status in the transatlantic English world made one more or less drawn to radical religion than elite status would require a broader study than Breen attempts. Breen seems to be using the word "antinomian" to mean tolerationist, although toleration was not broadly popular among Massachusetts's elite, and "transatlantic" to refer to the new merchants of Robert Brenner, *Merchants and Revolution: Commercial Change, Political Conflict, and London's Overseas Traders, 1550–1653* (Princeton, 1993).

36. Peter Lake and David Como, "'Orthodoxy' and Its Discontents: Dispute Settlement and the Production of 'Concensus' in the London (Puritan) Underground," *Journal of British Studies* 39 (2000): 52, 59; Como, "Puritans," 62–64; *WP*, 4:11; *Early Records of the Town of Dedham* (Dedham, 1886–1936), 1:2; Richard Mather, *Church-Government and Church-Covenant Discussed* (London, 1643), 23; Fiske, *Notebook*, 7; Cooper, *Tenacious*, 55–57, argues that this heightened vigilance (and the institutionalizing of means for it) was the only significant result of the free grace controversy.

37. Gura, *Glimpse*, 250, has argued that the free grace controversy convinced Massachusetts's leaders of the dangers of openness and toleration of dissent. "From this point on, they began to define . . . their notion of how, precisely, the civil and religious spheres intersected." But Massachusetts's leadership had started to move forcibly against openness and dissent before the free grace controversy broke out, as its actions against Roger Williams and Salem demonstrated. The free grace controversy at most accelerated that process. Dudley and Winthrop had clashed over the issue of repression versus leniency before the free grace controversy, and in all

likelihood they clashed during it. That, too, needs to be kept in mind when assessing the effects of the controversy itself. Dudley, *WP*, 4:86, for example, wrote to Winthrop at the end of 1638, recommending vigorous action against Thomas Lechford, who was arguing for the validity of bishops. Confidently smelling heresy in Lechford's arguments, he reminded Winthrop that "wee sawe our error in suffering Mrs. Hutchinson too long." Dudley's comment can be taken as an example of a new intolerance on the part of the Massachusetts establishment, but it was more likely intended as a personal prod to, and dig at, Winthrop—who, after all, was responsible for their suffering Hutchinson so long?

38. For discussion of this order and its repeal, see Hall, *Faithful Shepherd*, 134. Williams, *Complete Writings*, 3:381; John Cotton, *An Expostion upon the Thirteenth Chapter of the Revelation* (London, 1655), 19.

39. *PTV*, 2:15–16; Shepard Sermons, 259; MS AM 1671 (2), by permission of the Houghton Library, Harvard University. This is an unpaginated collection of occasional sermons in Shepard's hand delivered from early 1638 to 1640. The analysis is from the first sermon. *PTV*, 2:56.

40. *God's Plot*, 74.

41. *PTV* 2:94–5 (*PTV* 2:110 has the date of December 10, 1639), 177; *WP*, 4:99; Lucius R. Paige, *History of Cambridge, Massachusetts* (Boston, 1877), 46–51. The comment about Vane, from the flyleaf of his collection of conversion narratives, is undated. *WJ*, 262, 290–91. Winthrop, *WJ*, 258, seems to express confidence already at the beginning of June 1638, that the king's troubles in Scotland precluded attention to New England. But this is a later entry, since it refers to the large number of ships that arrived that year in the past tense.

42. *WP*, 4:286–87.

43. The Massachusetts Reforming Synod of 1679 adopted the English Congregationalists' Savoy Declaration, which modified chapter 18 of the Westminster Confession of Faith on assurance to include an explicit reference to the immediate witness of the Spirit. The immediate witness of the Spirit continued to be cultivated by an unknown number of laypeople as well as by at least a small group of ministers, passing down to Cotton Mather and Solomon Stoddard. Jonathan Edwards fiercely rejected it altogether from his own pastoral experience during the Great Awakening. See Cotton Mather, *Signatus* (Boston, 1727); Jonathan Edwards, *The Religious Affections*, ed. John E. Smith (New Haven, 1959), 229–39 passim. Edwards said that after an early attraction Stoddard rejected the "notion of the witness of the Spirit, by way of immediate suggestion" (230n. 1). Cotton Mather's attraction to the immediate witness of the Spirit caused a certain amount of tension in his effort to cast a uniform blanket of fileo-piety over the founding generation, when he was well aware that they disagreed over this issue. See *MCA*, 1:431–32, 2:508.

44. *WJ*, 343.

45. Vol. 240, no. 38–39, Massachusetts State Archives. I am assuming that the initials "B.M." in Hooker's letter mean "Brother Mather."

46. *WJ*, 344.

47. *WWP*, 192; *MCA*, 1:373 (*GH*, 279, gives same anecdote without identifying Hooker).

48. *GH*, 277; Thomas Shepard, *The Confessions of Diverse Propounded to Be Received & Were Entertained As Members*, New England Historic Genealogical Society, Boston. Burr's sermon is the final one in the book. It is on afflictions and stresses that God afflicts out of love, rather than anger, and will eventually comfort his saints. It also stresses the importance of ministers and ordinances. Cf. Paul S. Seaver, *Wallington's World: A Puritan Artisan in Seventeenth-Century London* (Palo Alto, 1985), 107.

49. That is my understanding of at least one line of argument in Delbanco, *Puritan*, and Knight, *Orthodoxies*.

50. *A Report of the Record Commissioners, Containing the Roxbury Land and Church Records* (Boston, 1881), 77; *MCA*, 1:374.

51. *AC*, 4; Norton, *Abel*, 36.

52. *JC*, 308.

53. Foster, "New England," 660; Gura, *Glimpse*, 274; *MA*, 190.

54. John Lee Schweninger, *John Winthrop's World: History as Story; the Story as History* (Madison, WI, 1992), 82; Staloff, *Making*, 59. On Winthrop's self-presentation, see Richard D. Dunn, "Introduction," *WJ*, xxviii.

55. *WP* 4:278.

56. Wheelwright, Brief, 1.

57. Scottow, *Narrative*, 301.

58. Battis, *SS*, 295, with "Boston activists" being substituted for "Hutchinsonian movement."

59. James F. Cooper, Jr., "Anne Hutchinson and the 'Lay Rebellion' against the Clergy," *New England Quarterly* 61 (1988): 381–97; Quentin Skinner, *The Foundations of Modern Political Thought* (New York, 1978), 2:191–348.

60. Thomas Edwards, *Gangraena: Or a Catalogue and Discovery of Many of the Errours, Heresies, Blasphemies and Pernicious Practices of the Sectaries of This Time, Vented and Acted in England in These Last Four Years* (London, 1646), 148; Nathaniel Holmes in Cotton, *Cotton*, 170.

61. *MA*, 190; Patrick Collinson, "Comment on Eamon Duffy's Neale Lecture and the Colloquium," in *England's Long Reformation, 1500–1800*, ed. Nicholas Tyacke (London, 1998), 73.

62. Foster, "New England," 658–60. Staloff, *Making*, xiv; Timothy H. Breen and Stephen Foster, "The Puritans' Greatest Achievement: A Study of Social Cohesion in Seventeenth-Century Massachusetts," *Journal of American History* 60 (1973): 5–22. This is not to dispute whether the mechanisms the various authors discuss worked in the ways that they present them, only that they were not perhaps the most important factors in accounting for stability.

63. William L. Sachse, "The Migration of New Englanders to New England, 1640–1660," *American Historical Review* 53 (1947): 251–78, discusses repatriation as a pressure valve for dissent. For discussions of the extent to which coercion could be used in orthodox New England and how it worked, see Foster, "New England," 659; Foster, *Long Argument*, 289–90.

64. *JC*, 274. Delbanco, *Puritan*, 155–59, may have been the first to advance the claim that Davenport was strongly sympathetic to the causes of Cotton and Hutchinson. He based it partially on very free interpretations of carefully selected lines from Davenport's small body of publications and partially on the fact that

Davenport was more pastorally sensitive to Anne Hutchinson at her church trial than some of the other ministers and admonished a New Haven congregant instead of moving directly to excommunicate her. Knight, *Orthodoxies*, takes Davenport's opposition to Massachusetts as a given, even claiming that he "preached a doctrine of salvation opposed to that of most of the ministers of the Bay, including Wilson, Hooker, Shepard, Bulkeley, and Hugh Peters" (19). If so, there is no evidence that anyone in Massachusetts noticed. Like Delbanco, Knight interprets isolated phrases from Davenport loosely. But his conception of the witness of the Spirit was Sibbesian, not Cottonian, as was Shepard's, Wilson's, Bulkeley's, and, for all we know, Peters's. From what remains of his writings, Davenport's way of preaching assurance would not have raised an eyebrow among the other ministers. See John Davenport, *The Saints Anchor-Hold in All Storms and Tempests* (London, 1661), 35–41.

CHAPTER TWELVE
GODLY ENDINGS

1. Miller, "Preparation," 253–86; Miller, *Colony,* 57–67; Delbanco, *Puritan*; Knight, *Orthodoxies*, are the main proponents of this line of argument. Miller, "Preparation," among other arguments, advanced critiques Giles Firmin made of Hooker and Shepard in *Real Christian* to support his case about New England, and this argument has been picked up by other scholars. See Hall, *Faithful Shepherd*, 166; Delbanco, *Puritan*, 211–12; Delbanco, "Looking Homeward, Going Home: The Lure of England for the Founders of New England," *New England Quarterly* 59 (1986): 383–84; and Knight, *Orthodoxies*, 164–65. Firmin, however, criticized three, not two, ministers. The third was Daniel Rogers, who never came to America, and what Firmin was criticizing all three for was a style of preaching they had developed together in Essex, England, and for books of theirs that had been published from English sermons. There was nothing referring back to the New England environment in Firmin's critique. Other authors have assumed that Firmin's critique represented the more allegedly liberal theological attitude of the 1670s. See James W. Jones, *The Shattered Synthesis: New England Puritanism before the Great Awakening* (New Haven, 1973), chap. 2. But Hooker and Shepard's contemporaries also expressed concern about the severity of their preaching.

2. Peter Bulkeley did not share Shepard and Hooker's distended obsession with the dark deceits of the depraved human heart, extreme, at least in my impression, even for puritans, which made Bulkeley far more confident than they about relying on the evidence of sanctification for assurance and probably contributed to his being more flexible about absolute promises. Against Shepard (and Ezekiel Culverwell), he argued that sanctification was easier to discern than faith. See Peter Bulkeley, *The Gospel-Covenant; or The Covenant of Grace Opened*, 2d ed. (London, 1651), 264, 325 passim. Charles Chauncy, in what could have been a response to Hooker, Shepard, and Bulkeley, warned against preachers' placing excessive emphasis on preparation before justification and on believers' placing excessive reliance on sanctification afterward. See Charles Chauncy, *[Yhovah tsidekanu] Or the Plain Doctrin of the Justification of a Sinner in the Sight of God* (London, 1659), 127, 150, 151. Very little survives from Dedham's "sweet-tempered" minister

James Allen. But those scanty remains include notes from a sermon preached in 1648 in which Allen stressed to his auditors that God wanted them to experience fullness of joy; that they were to "neglect not any measure of joy you can attaine unto"; and that the reason so few saints experienced fullness of joy was that "they look much at there owne corruption and little at Christ." See *MCA*, 1:462; Seaborn Cotton's notes on Sermons of John Cotton, BV Cotton, New York Historical Society, New York, 2d pag., 17, 15. For John Norton on Hooker and Shepard's preparationism, see 237 above. The Burr case indicates that some ministers were trigger-happy after the free grace controversy, but Richard Mather was compelled to eat humble pie just as much as Burr. Any career-savvy young ministerial candidate noting the way churches chased Burr to be their minister would be unlikely to conclude that soul-ravishing preaching (like the Allen example) no longer paid in Massachusetts.

3. Rathband, *Briefe Narration*, 39. Thomas Weld, *An Answer to W.R. His Narration of the Opinions and Practices of the Churches Lately Erected in New-England* (London, 1644), 53, did not deny the existence of the meetings but rhetorically asked if anyone had ever been excommunicated "meerely for non-proficiency."

4. Firmin, *Real Christian*, 55.

5. Thomas Shepard, Hebrews 10:23, June 16, 1644, Sermons by Thomas Shepard and Thomas Allen, Shepard Family Papers, American Antiquarian Society, Worcester, Massachusetts.

6. Notes of Sermons by Thomas Shepard, 1647, MS, Philips Academy, Andover, Massachusetts. I thank Douglas Winiarski for telling me of this source.

7. *God's Plot*, 65.

8. *The Parable of the Ten Virgins* was reprinted at roughly fifty-year intervals in England and Scotland up to the 1850s, with one Dutch edition in 1743. After editions in the 1850s in the United States and Scotland, it lay dormant for over a hundred years until taken up again by American evangelical publishers. The Tyndale Bible Society published an edition in the early 1970s and Soli Deo Gloria Publications of Ligonier, Pennsylvania published an edition in 1990.

9. Shepard, *Works* 1:277.

10. *MCA*, 1:350.

11. Morgan, *Dilemma*, 165–66, 201; *WJ*, 212; Hartlib Papers, 40/5/3A.

12. *MCA*, 1:130; Hutchinson, *History*, 1:151; *MHS Collections*, 5th ser., 1 (1871): 96.

13. *GH*, 302; *JC*, 20.

14. Cotton, *Cotton*, 271. John Cotton, *A Brief Exposition with Practical Observations upon the Whole Book of Canticles* (London, 1655), 56, 57–58, 132–33. John Norton, *The Orthodox Evangelist* (London, 1657), chap. 8. Norton agreed with Cotton that faith was passive in union with Christ (260–61), but argued that it was active in justification (315), denied that the Holy Spirit dwelt in believers (250), claimed assurance came through syllogisms (175), and argued that sanctification represented a restoration of the image of God in Adam in a way that met Cotton's objections that sanctification had to be something more (203–4). Knight, *Orthodoxies*, 126, in line with her assumption that Hooker won the free grace controversy, sees a complex political strategy in *Orthodox Evangelist*; Norton "deftly appeased the regnant orthodoxy . . . while still covertly disseminating the

core of Sibbesian piety." Knight offers no evidence that Norton felt the need to appease anyone or covertly disseminate anything, nor is there any reason why he should have. Norton's thorough attack on Hooker and Shepard's conception of preparation, which placed them in the company of papists, Pelegians, and Arminians, is not a notable example of deft appeasement.

15. Cotton, *Brief,* 58.

16. Seaborn Cotton's notes, sermon on 17 John 2; 1:65. Thomas Shepard, Hebrews 10:23, June 16, 1644.

17. Baillie, *Dissuasive Vindicated,* 32–33, 28, 36–37.

18. *GH,* 302. The first set of notes was published as John Cotton, *The Covenant of Grace, Discovering the Great Work of a Sinners Reconciliation to God* (London, 1655). Ann Kibbey, *The Interpretation of Material Shapes in Puritanism: A Study of Rhetoric, Prejudice, and Violence* (New York, 1986), 155, suggests a significant difference in tone between the two sets of notes. I was not able to find that significant difference, either from my own reading or from her examples.

19. John Cotton, in Norton, *Orthodox Evangelist,* "To the Reader." *MCA,* 1:272.

20. *WJ,* 505–7; *MR,* 2:50, 67; *GH,* 368; Charles Francis Adams, *Three Episodes of Massachusetts History* (Boston, 1892), 2:541.

21. *MR,* 3:344; Wheelwright, *Brief,* 15. As Exeter filled up with immigrants who had not moved out of loyalty to Wheelwright, pressure grew in the town to unite with Massachusetts. It did so in 1643. Wheelwright, still under banishment, founded the town of Wells, Maine, along with some of his original followers before taking up the Hampton ministry in 1647. See Charles E. Clark, *The Eastern Frontier: The Settlement of Northern New England, 1610–1763* (Hanover, NH, 1983), 46–47. On the date of Wheelwright's departure, see Sargent Bush, Jr., "John Wheelwright's Forgotten *Apology:* The Last Word in the Antinomian Controversy," *New England Quarterly* 64 (1991): 39.

22. Hutchinson, *History,* 1:165.

23. Charles H. Bell, *History of the Town of Exeter, New Hampshire* (Exeter, 1888), 39; Roland R. Warren, *Loyal Dissenter: The Life and Times of Robert Pike* (Lantham, MD, 1992), chap. 8, quotation from 125; *MCA,* 2:511.

24. *GH,* 283; James F. Cooper, Jr., "The Confession and Trial of Richard Wayte, Boston, 1640," *William and Mary Quarterly,* 3d ser., 44 (1987): 322–23; Alison Games, *Migration and the Origins of the English Atlantic World* (Cambridge, 1999), 150; *MR,* 1:338; Samuel Hutchinson, *A Declaration of a Future Glorious Estate of a Church to Be Here upon Earth, at Christs Personal Appearance for the Restitution of All Things, a Thousand Years befor the Ultimate Day of the General Judgement* (London, 1667).

25. Battis, *SS,* 304–28, forms the basis of the following identifications.

26. *WJ,* 487; Samuel Gorton, *Simplicities Defence* (1646), Rhode Island Historical Society *Collections,* no. 2 (Providence, 1835): 123, 133–34. 138. Gorton was not one to shy away from bombastic excess, which does not produce complete confidence in his descriptions of Wilson and Cotton, but see Cotton's comment on Gorton in *Cotton,* 223. For Gorton, see Gura, *Glimpse,* chap. 10. Richard Carder, Sampson Shotten, Robert Potter, and William Wardall are Gortonists from Battis's lists of participants in the free grace controversy. The other Gortonists on that

list may have had nothing to do with the free grace controversy. Randell Holden is not on any of Battis's lists, although he clearly should be, since he was one of the original signers of the Aquidneck compact.

27. Morton, *Memorial*, 165; Rufus M. Jones, *Studies in Mystical Religion* (London, 1909), 447. Jones in chapter 18 lays out some of the parallels between the Quakers and the Family of Love, which are far too extensive to be merely coincidental. For discussions of Quaker doctrines, see Ralph Paul Bohn, "The Controversy between Puritans and Quakers to 1660" (Ph.D. diss., University of Edinburgh, 1955), chap. 4; T. L. Underwood, *Primitivism, Radicalism, and the Lamb's War: The Baptist-Quaker Conflict in Seventeenth-Century England* (New York, 1997). There is little evidence for direct familist influence on the Quakers, nor, given the diffusion of familist ideas, is it necessary. One link might be Grindletonianism, as suggested by Geoffrey F. Nuttall, *The Holy Spirit in Puritan Faith and Experience*, 2d ed. (Chicago, 1992), 178–79. Nuttall's suggestion of a link between Anne Hutchinson and the early Quakers through the ex–New England minister Christopher Marshall instead reinforces the typologies of this book (179). Marshall went to Exeter with Wheelwright, and rather than supporting the Quakers, as Nuttall indicates, attacked them. See A. G. Matthews, *Calamy Revised: Being a Revision of Edmund Calamy's Account of the Ministers and Others Ejected and Silenced, 1660–2* (Oxford, 1998), 340. For the direct familist influences on an important early Quaker, see Geoffrey Nuttall, *James Naylor: A Fresh Approach* (London, 1954).

28. William Coddington, *A Demonstration of True Love unto You the Rulers of the Colony of the Massachusetts in New-England* (N.p., 1674), 17; George Keith, *A Refutation of Three Opposers of Truth* (Philadelphia, 1690), 68. Ironically, Keith, who had heard of the free grace controversy from "divers yet alive," focused on an issue that had not been a major one in the controversy, the Holy Spirit's personal dwelling in the souls of the saints (as opposed to a personal union, which was a major issue). Perhaps Keith's mistake reflects the vagaries of memory of his informants.

29. Henry Bull, Richard Burden, Jeremy Clarke, William Coddington, Thomas Cornell, Richard and Mary Dyer, and William Freeborn are from Battis's lists. To them can be added Richard and Katherine Scott (Anne Hutchinson's sister), Nicholas Easton, and Jane Hawkins. Gerard Croese, *The General History of the Quakers* (London, 1696), 148.

30. *WJ*, 287; *WWP*, 186.

31. *WJ*, 287, 362; Thomas Lechford, *Note-Book*, American Antiquarian Society *Transactions and Collections*, no. 7 (Worcester, 1885), 435–37. In this draft of a letter to William Collins and Francis Hutchinson, Lechford asked Hutchinson if he still denied the eternal Sonship of Christ.

32. *WJ*, 287; S. G., *Glass*, 9; *AC*, 392.

33. *WJ*, 329–33. Hubbard, *GH*, 341, unlike Winthrop, presented Collins as heterodox in the West Indies and claimed that he had imbibed "familist" principles from a woman in Gloucestershire. If there is anything to Hubbard's story, the source of it may have been Edward Norris, a Gloucestershire minister arriving in Massachusetts in 1638, who had himself battled "familists."

34. Winthrop's description of Collins and Hutchinson's opinions about Massachusetts and its churches is in accord with Anne Hutchinson's letter, so it is likely to be reasonably accurate. *WJ*, 362–63; *JC*, 320–22; Gorton, *Simplicities*, 58; William Bradford, *Of Plymouth Plantation, 1620–1647*, ed. Samuel Eliot Morison (New York, 1953), 318.

35. *BCR*, 34; *WJ*, 362–63, *MR*, 1:336, 340, 344; Lechford, *Note-Book*, 435–37; Gorton, *Simplicities*, 58.

36. Thomas Aspinwall, "The Narragansett Patent," *MHS Proceedings* 4 (1862): 41–47; Neal Salisbury, *Manitou and Providence: Indians, Europeans, and the Making of New England, 1500–1643* (New York, 1982), 225–35; Gorton, *Simplicities*, 59; *Records of the Colony of Rhode Island and Providence Plantations, in New England*, ed. John Russell Bartlett (Providence, 1856), 1:125; Rhode Island Historical Society, *Collections* 2 (1835): 270.

37. Allen W. Trelease, *Indian Affairs in Colonial New York: The Seventeenth Century* (Ithaca, 1960), 67–71, 77; *WWP*, 186–87; *WJ*, 475; Robert Bolton, *The History of the Several Towns, Manors, and Patents of the County of Westchester, from Its First Settlement to the Present Time* (New York, 1881), 2:30–31, 30n. "c." Bolton made the common nineteenth-century mistake of conflating the Mohicans of New York with the Mohegans of Connecticut, which prompted Mary Jane Lewis, "A Sweet Sacrifice: Civil War in New England" (Ph.D. diss., State University of New York, Binghamton, 1986), 328–29, to have Hutchinson killed by a Massachusetts-directed Indian hit squad led by Edward Johnson. I thank Neal Salisbury for his assistance. Bulkeley, *Gospel-Covenant*, 327.

38. Thomas Edwards, *Antapologia* (London, 1644), 40, 83, 165–66; Baillie, *Dissuasive*, chap. 3; Thomas Hill, *The Good Old Way, Gods Way, to Soule-Refreshing Rest* (London, 1644), "The Epistle Dedicatory"; Samuel Rutherford, *A Survey of the Spirituall Antichrist* (London, 1648), chap. 15; Thomas Underhill, *Hell Broke Loose: or An History of the Quakers Both Old and New* (London, 1660), 11–12; *The Whole Works of the Rev. Mr. John Flavel* (London, 1820), 3:557; Daniel Williams, *Gospel-Truth Stated and Vindicated* (London, 1692), passim. See also John Shaw, "The Life of Master John Shaw," *Surtees Society Publications* 65 (1875): 65.

39. *JC*, 283; Keith L. Sprunger, *Dutch Puritanism: A History of English and Scottish Churches of the Netherlands in the Sixteenth and Seventeenth Centuries* (Leiden, 1982), 226–32; Foster, *Long Argument*, 30, 163. Edwards, *Antapologia*: 32; David Walker, "Thomas Goodwin and the Debate on Church Government," *Journal of Ecclesiastical History* 34 (1983): 85–97; Stanley P. Fienberg, "Thomas Goodwin's Scriptural Hermeneutics and the Dissolution of Puritan Unity," *The Journal of Religious History* 10 (1978): 32–49. For the debate over the Arnhem authorship of a key millenarian tract, see Mark R. Bell, *Apocalypse How? Baptist Movements during the English Revolution* (Macon, 2000), 69n. 22.

40. George Sikes, *The Life and Death of Sir Henry Vane, Kt.* (N.p., 1662), 8; *JC*, 283; Robert Lord Brooke, *The Nature of Truth* (London, 1641), 153–54; Richard Baxter, *Reliquae Baxteriana* (London, 1696), 75.

41. James K. Hosmer, *The Life of Young Sir Henry Vane* (Boston, 1889), 510; Corinne Comstock Weston and Janelle Renfrow Greenberg, *Subjects and Sovereigns: The Grand Controversy over Legal Sovereignty in Stuart England* (Cambridge, 1981), 145–47.

42. *WJ*, 608; *HC*, 1:152–53; *Records of the Colony of Rhode Island and Providence Plantations*, 1:285; John Endicott, "The Copy of a Letter to Sir Henry Vane," *MHS Collections* 21 (1825): 36. In the 1650s Richard was a member of William Greenhill's gathered congregation in Stepney. Greenhill published many of Thomas Shepard's works. See G. E. Aylmer, *The State's Servants: The Civil Service of the English Republic, 1649–1660* (London, 1972), 247–50; Bernard Capp, *Cromwell's Navy: The Fleet and the English Revolution, 1648–1660* (Oxford, 1989), 303. Cf. Bernard Bailyn, *The New England Merchants in the Seventeenth Century* (1955; reprint, New York, 1964), 88–89.

43. Baillie, *Dissuasive*, 64. Thomas Hutchinson, "Hutchinson in America," Egerton 2664, p. 22, British Library; Forster Ms 48.D.41, Victoria and Albert Museum; Vane, *Retired*, 201, 369. For an introduction to Vane's religious thought, see David Parnham, *Sir Henry Vane, Theologian: A Study in Seventeenth-Century Religious and Political Discourse* (Madison, WI, 1997). Parnham draws attention to Vane's similarities with John Cotton in chapter 7 but does not discuss lay Bostonian opinions. For negative judgments on Vane's theology, see Baxter, *Reliquae*, 75; Gilbert Burnet, *Bishop Burnet's History of His Own Times* (London, 1724), 1:164; Martin Finch, *Animadversions upon Sir Henry Vanes Book* (London, 1656). For Vane's followers, see Baxter, *Reliquae*, 75. In *Richard Baxters Catholick Theologie* (London, 1675), 2d pag.: 107, Baxter identifies Sterry's equating of the Law and the letter of the Scriptures with Vane. See Peter Sterry, *A Discourse of the Freedom of the Will* (London, 1675), 173ff. Sterry's interpretation there of 2 Corinthians 3:6, "the letter killeth, but the Spirit giveth life," was the same as Hutchinson's. See "Examination," *AC*, 325–26. Sterry also stressed the witness of the Spirit, the unreliability of relying on sanctification for assurance, and the unconditionality of the covenant of grace. See Peter Sterry, *The Rise, Race, and Royalty of the Kingdom of God in the Soul of Man* (London, 1683), 63, 78–79, 129, 135–46, 351–52. None of this need have been picked up from Vane, but the fact that Sterry became Lord Brooke's chaplain in 1639 while Vane was actively proselytizing in Brooke's circle makes a Bostonian influence possible. Baxter, *Reliquae*, 75, called Joshua Sprigge Vane's "chief" among his "more open Disciples." Thomas Hutchinson, "Hutchinson in America," Egerton MS 2664, British Library, p. 22.

44. Anthony Fletcher, *The Outbreak of the English Civil War* (New York, 1981), 103–4; Samuel R. Gardiner, *The History of the Great Civil War, 1642–1649* (London, 1897), 1:229–31; Edward J. Cowan, "The Solemn League and Covenant," in *Scotland and England, 1286–1815*, ed. Roger A. Mason (Edinburgh, 1987), 189–91; B. S. Capp, *The Fifth Monarchy Men: A Study in Seventeenth-Century English Millenarianism* (London, 1972), 121–23, 240, 246, 267.

45. Ronald Hutton, *The Restoration: A Political and Religious History of England and Wales, 1658–1667* (Oxford, 1985), 53; Barry Reay, *The Quakers and the English Revolution* (New York, 1985), 84. Vane protected the Quakers but he disapproved of their behavior and considered them spiritually deluded, for they mistook the light of natural conscience for Christ within them. See Hutton, *Restoration*, 122; Vane, *Retired*, 184.

46. Vane, *Retired*, 199–201, 321–22; Baxter, *Reliquae*, 75; Burnet, *History*, 1:164; Finch, *Animadversions*; Henry Vane, *Two Treatises* (N.p., 1662), 55; *AC*, 166; T. B. Howell, *A Complete Collection of State Trials* (London, 1809–26),

6:197; Hutton, *Restoration*, 163; Burnet, *History*, 1:164. For Vane's impact on an important Restoration radical, see Jonathan Scott *Algernon Sidney and the English Republic, 1623–1677* (Cambridge, 1988), passim.

47. *GH*, 236.

48. For the revocation of the Massachusetts charter, see J. M. Sosin, *English America and the Restoration Monarchy of Charles II: Transatlantic Politics, Commerce, and Kinship* (Lincoln, 1980), chap. 14. It had been ruled that the original revocation of 1637 had been voided by the Act of Oblivion because it was never carried out. For the English context, see Paul D. Halliday, *Dismembering the Body Politic: Partisan Politics in English Towns, 1650–1730* (Cambridge, 1998), chaps. 5, 6. Agitation for the revocation of Massachusetts's charter began long before Charles's crackdown, but it cannot be a coincidence that it was only during that crackdown that it was finally driven to a conclusion.

INDEX

Abimelech, Henry Vane compared to, 146, 246

Achan, and Anne Hutchinson, 208

Adam, 88, 245; Fall of, 4, 30, 31, 191; image of God in, 99, 191

Adams, Charles Francis, 238

Alford (Lincolnshire), 37, 45, 196

Ames, William, 66

anabaptists, 22, 97, 179, 296n.12

Antichrist, 8, 39, 88–89, 107, 112–13

antinomian controversy, London, 67–68, 90

antinomian controversy, Massachusetts. *See* free grace controversy

antinomianism, 25, 27, 81, 104, 115, 154, 193, 302n.35; and capitalism, 74, 271n.33

apostles, 35, 40, 87, 89, 182, 193

Aquidneck (Rhode Island), 210, 211, 215; founding of, 194–95; religious disputes in, 213

Arminianism, 30–31, 71, 81, 100, 104, 107, 147

Arnhem (Netherlands) church, 215; and Boston church, 243

Aspinwall, William, 128, 213–14, 224; banished, 169; dismissed from Court, 167; drafts "remonstrance and Petition," 128; as messenger at Synod of 1637, 156–57

assistants. *See* General Court, assistants to

assurance of salvation, 4, 99; and faith, 13, 14, 17–18; puritan clergy and, 13–21, 67; rareness of, 18–19, 250n.28; Reformed theology of, 14; Roman Catholicism and, 13; and sanctification, 14–17, 90, 100, 112–13, 117; soteriological underground and, 26; weak Christians and, 14–15, 17, 18–19, 20, 21. *see also* Cotton, John; Farwell, Olive; Hutchinson, Anne; Knollys, Hanserd; promises, absolute and conditional; Shepard, Thomas; Underhill, John; Winthrop, John

backsliders, 20

Baillie, Robert, 30, 56, 57, 144, 160, 238

Balston, William, 194; punished by General Court, 186

baptism, radical interpretation of at Mount Wollaston, 188

Baptists, 194, 196, 240

Baron, Peter, 30, 31

Baxter, Richard, 5; on Henry Vane, 147, 244

Bellingham, Richard, 121

Bible, 23, 28, 30, 100, 105, 188–89; letter of, 110, 196; presumed unity of, 66

Bilney, Thomas, 33

Bolton, Robert: and assurance, 19; on witness of the Spirit, 22

Boston (Lincolnshire), 29, 30

Boston (Massachusetts) church, 41, 50, 77, 194, 212, 220, 242, 243; admonishes Salem church, 80; agrees to try Anne Hutchinson, 197; and Aquidneck, 213–14; attempt to make John Wheelwright minister at, 92–94, 278n.28; beginnings of, 28–29; and civil order, 74, 272n.34; debates Holy Spirit, 95; discipline of, 60; excommunications at, 208–9, 211–12; and Exeter church, 215; growing intolerance of, 140; and Newtowne church, 101–2; reassesses Hutchinsonians, 215–17; responses to Anne Hutchinson's excommunication by women of, 211–12; revival at, 40, 266n.56; and Roxbury church, 86; tolerance of, 62–63. *See also* Cotton, John; Hutchinson, Anne; Hutchinsonians; Wheelwright, John; Wilson, John; Winthrop, John

Boston (Massachusetts), town of, 28; and Mount Wollaston, 93; population of, 40, 55; town meeting, 50

Bradford, William, 210

Bradstreet, Simon, 121, 173

Brearley, Robert, 24, 68

Brinsley, John, on assurance, 19

Brooke, Robert Greville, Lord, and Henry Vane, 50, 244

Brown, Richard, 174, 181

Buckingham, George Villiers, duke of, 107

Bulkeley, Peter, 156; and Concord church, 221; on John Wheelwright, 131–32; letter to John Cotton of, 131–32; modera-

CPSIA information can be obtained at www.ICGtesting.com
Printed in the USA
BVOW11*1239070814

361802BV00003B/9/P

9 780691 089430